Copyright for Schools

Copyright for Schools
A Practical Guide
Fifth Edition

Carol Simpson

 LINWORTH

AN IMPRINT OF ABC-CLIO, LLC
Santa Barbara, California • Denver, Colorado • Oxford, England

Copyright 2010 by ABC-CLIO, LLC

Library of Congress Cataloging-in-Publication Data

Simpson, Carol, 1949–
   Copyright for schools : a practical guide / Carol Simpson. — 5th ed.
     p. cm.
   Includes bibliographical references and index.
   ISBN 978-1-58683-393-0 (alk. paper)
1. Fair use (Copyright)—United States—Popular works.   2. Copyright—United States—
Popular works.   I. Title.
   KF3020.S575   2010
   346.7304'82—dc22   2010031901

ISBN: 978-1-58683-393-0

14 13 12 11 10   1 2 3 4 5

This book is also available on the World Wide Web as an eBook.
Visit www.abc-clio.com for details.

Linworth
An Imprint of ABC-CLIO, LLC

ABC-CLIO, LLC
130 Cremona Drive, P.O. Box 1911
Santa Barbara, California 93116-1911

This book is printed on acid-free paper ∞

Manufactured in the United States of America

Table of Contents

Table of Figures xv
About the Author xvii
Acknowledgments xix
Introduction to the 5th Edition xxi

Chapter 1: The Law 1
   History. 1
     Origin in the United States 1
   What it is now 1
     Rights of a copyright holder. 2
       Reproduction. 3
       Adaptation. 3
       Distribution. 4
         Limitation on right of distribution: First sale doctrine 4
       Public performance 5
         What is "public" 5
       Public display. 6
       Digital transmission of sound recordings 6
     Moral rights 7
   How does one get a copyright? 7
   What can't be protected by copyright? 8
     Work for hire 10
     Ideas. 11
   Duration of copyright. 12
   Protected or not? 13
   Registering a work 13
   Recent laws. 14
     No Electronic Theft Act. 14
     Visual Artists Rights Act. 14
     Digital Millennium Copyright Act. 15
     Sonny Bono Copyright Term Extension Act. 16
     Digital Performance Right in Sound Recordings Act 16
     TEACH Act. 16
     Family Entertainment and Copyright Act 17
   Penalties for infringement. 17
   Liability 19
     State copyright laws 20
   Related laws 20
     Contract law 20
     Privacy statutes. 21
     Trademark law 21

Trade secret law 21

Why is any of this significant for schools? 22

How is a school prosecuted? 24

What if there is no trial? 24

Why worry? Why bother? 25

Works cited 25

Chapter 2: Public Domain 27

What is it? 27

How does something get into the public domain? 27

How long does public domain last? 28

What can you do with public domain materials? 29

How do you find public domain materials? 29

Related cases 30

Chapter 3: Licensed and Royalty-Free Materials 31

How do "copyright-free," "royalty-free," "license," and "lease" differ? 31

How can I use royalty-free materials? 31

Sources of royalty-free materials 32

Chapter 4: Fair Use 35

What is it? 36

Difference between statutory fair use and guidelines 36

Examples of fair use analysis 37

Factor 1: Purpose and character of use 38

Factor 1, part 1: Nonprofit educational use 38

Factor 1, part 2: Criticism, commentary, news reporting 38

Factor 2: Nature of copyrighted work 39

Factor 2, part 1: Factual or creative? .39

Factor 2, part 2: Published or not published? 39

Factor 3: Amount of work used? 40

Essence of work 40

Factor 4: Effect of use on market for or value of work 41

Commercial use 42

Misrepresentation 42

What would happen if everyone were to 43

Various types of guidelines 43

To whom does it apply? 44

Schools versus libraries 45

Works cited 46

Chapter 5: Print Materials in Schools 47

What typical activities are covered? 48

Photocopying—issues 49

Phonorecords—issues 50

Graphics—issues 50

Murals—issues 50

Scanning—issues 51

What rights are affected? 51

Reproduction 51

Distribution 51

Adaptation 52

Display 52

What guidelines affect print materials? 52

Kastenmeier report 52

Details of report 52

Single copies for teachers 52

Multiple copies for classroom use 54

Brevity 55

Spontaneity 56

Cumulative effect 56

Examples of acceptable multiple copying 58

Examples of unacceptable multiple copying 58

Copies for handicapped students 59

Print permission issues 60

Consumable materials 60

Periodicals 61

Graphics 63

Student work 65

Scanners 66

Resources for understanding 67

Fair use of print materials glossary 67

Related cases 67

American Geophysical Union v. Texaco Inc., 37 F.3d 881
(2d Cir. 1994) 67

Princeton University Press v. Michigan Document Services, Inc.,
99 F.3d 1381 (6th Cir. 1996) 67

Bridgeman Art Library Ltd. v. Corel Corp., 36 F. Supp. 2d 191
(S.D.N.Y. 1999) 67

Basic Books, Inc. v. Kinko's Graphics Corp., 758 F. Supp. 1522
(S.D.N.Y. 1991) 68

Blackwell Publishing Group v. Excel Research Group, LLC, No. 07-12731,
2009 WL 3287403 (E.D. Mich. Oct. 14, 2009) 68

Hotaling v. Church of Jesus Christ of Latter-Day Saints, 118 F.3d 199
(4th Cir. 1997) 68

Works cited 68

Chapter 6: Audiovisual Materials in Schools 71

What typical activities are covered? 72

Movies—issues 73

TV/cable/satellite—issues 73

Web—issues 74

Sound recordings—issues 74
What rights are affected? 74
    Reproduction 75
    Distribution 75
    Adaptation 75
    Public performance 75
    Public display 76
    Digital transmission 76
What guidelines affect AV materials? 76
    5 yes/no questions 77
        Nonprofit educational 77
        Classroom or similar place 77
        Instructors and pupils in the course of face-to-face teaching activities 77
        Legally acquired copy 77
            Library 77
            Student or teacher 77
            Borrowed from library 77
            Rented from video store 79
            Caveat: digital downloads 79
            Recorded off-air 79
        Face-to-face teaching activities 80
    Umbrella licenses 81
    Home use only 82
    Movie cautions 82
    Examples of analysis 83
    Off-air recording guidelines 84
        "Air" versus cable versus satellite 84
        Recording in anticipation 89
Public performance rights 90
Examples of acceptable performances 91
Examples of unacceptable performances 91
Archiving audiovisual works 92
Closed captioning 93
Video distribution 94
Digital video servers/video streaming servers 95
Sound recordings 95
    Non-instructional performances of sound recordings 97
    Copying sound recordings 98
Sampling 99
The MP3 dilemma 101
Related cases 102
    A&M Records, Inc. v. Napster, Inc., 239 F.3d 1004 (9th Cir. 2001) 102
    Clean Flicks of Colo. v. Soderbergh, 433 F. Supp. 2d 1236 (D. Colo. 2006) 102
    Columbia Pictures Industries v. Redd Horne, 749 F.2d 154
    (3d Cir. 1984) 102

Encyclopaedia Britannica Educational Corp. v. Crooks, 542 F. Supp. 1156
(W.D.N.Y. 1982) 103

Gilliam v. American Broadcasting Companies, Inc., 538 F.2d 14
(2d Cir. 1976) 103

Works cited 103

Chapter 7: Music Materials in Schools (Print and Recorded) 105

What typical activities are covered? 105

Reproduction of sheet music—issues 105

Performances of sheet music—issues 106

Reproduction of recorded music—issues .106

Performances of recorded music—issues 106

Adaptation of sheet music—issues 107

What guidelines affect music? 107

Print music 108

Recorded music 108

What rules/laws are different about recordings? 109

Music in performance 109

Broadcasting music 110

Performance rights organizations 111

Permissions and licenses 111

Resources for understanding 114

Related cases 114

A&M Records, Inc. v. Napster, Inc., 239 F.3d 1004 (9th Cir. 2001) 114

Works cited 114

Chapter 8: Multimedia in Schools 115

What typical activities are covered? 115

Student multimedia projects—issues 115

Teacher multimedia projects—issues 115

What rights are affected? 116

Reproduction 116

Adaptation 116

Distribution 116

Public performance 116

Public display 116

Digital transmission 116

What guidelines affect multimedia? 116

Multimedia guidelines 117

Special definitions for multimedia 118

Multimedia—covered or not? 118

Retention and access 119

Secure network 119

Insecure network 119

Quantity limits 120

How many copies? 121

Other restrictions 122
Attribution 122
Multimedia tips 123
Resources for understanding 124
Works cited 124

Chapter 9: Distance Learning in Schools 125
History of distance learning and copyright 125
TEACH Act guidelines 126
Policy makers 127
Information technology staff 127
Instructors/developers 128
Digitizing for online learning 129
Resources for understanding 129
Work cited 129

Chapter 10: Internet in Schools 131
What typical activities are covered? 131
Printing pages—issues 131
Bookmarks—issues 132
Links—issues 132
Copying pages to local servers—issues 132
Redistributing pages—issues 133
E-mail—issues 133
Chat and IM—issues 133
What rights are affected? 134
Reproduction 134
Adaptation 134
Distribution 134
Public performance 134
Public display 134
Digital transmission 135
The difference between an AUP and copyright 135
Special rules for Internet 135
Registered agent 136
Why is this important? 136
What guidelines affect the Internet? 136
Special considerations for different Internet services 140
E-mail 140
Newsgroup and discussion list information .141
Web page information 141
Chat 141
Copying Internet code 142
Web 2.0 applications 142
Social networking 143
Podcasting 143

YouTube, Teacher Tube, and similar sites 144

Flickr, Picasa, Snapfish, and similar photo-sharing sites 145

Delicious, Digg, Technorati, and other social bookmarking sites 146

Wikis and other user-contributed online databases. 146

Kindle and other e-books. 147

Blogs and other self-publishing. 148

Twitter and other microblogging tools 149

Second Life, MUDs, MOOs, and other virtual worlds. 149

Resources for understanding. 149

Works cited 149

Chapter 11: Computer Software in Schools. 151

What typical activities are covered? 151

Multiple installs—issues. 152

Networking—issues 152

Checking out software—issues. 153

Clip art—issues 153

Types of infringement. 153

Direct infringement 153

Indirect infringement. 154

Contributory infringement 154

Vicarious liability for infringement by another person 154

What rights are affected?. 154

Reproduction. 155

Adaptation. 155

Distribution. 155

Public performance 155

Public display. 155

Special rules that affect computer software 155

License versus copyright 155

Legitimate copying versus piracy. 156

Software for free? 157

Lending software 158

Single-user programs 158

Networking 159

The software police. 159

Copyright infringement versus plagiarism. 160

Software management tips 161

Resources for understanding. 161

Works cited 162

Chapter 12: School Library Exemptions 163

Preservation 164

Interlibrary loan 165

ILL copying 165

Rule of five. 167

    Periodicals 167

    Other print materials 168

    Examples and caveats. 168

    What to do when you can't meet CONTU requirements. 169

Facsimile 170

Scanning 170

Cautions about ILL 171

Photocopying. 171

    Unattended copiers 172

    Copying orders. 173

    Copies for vertical file or item repair 173

    Reserves 174

    Electronic reserves 174

Works cited 175

Chapter 13: Permissions. 177

Copyright versus contract. 177

Permissions. 179

    Writing permission letters 179

Student and parent permissions 184

Works cited 185

Chapter 14: Managing Copyright in Schools. 187

Issues of managing copyright 187

Managing things. 188

Managing people 190

Important recommendations in copyright management 191

Chapter 15: Copyright and Administrators 193

Suggestions for administrators 195

Work cited 196

Chapter 16: Copyright Policies 197

Why have one?. 197

What should a policy contain? 198

Works cited 199

Chapter 17: Appendices 201

Appendix A—Copyright compliance agreement. 201

Appendix B—Copyright dos and don'ts for schools 202

Appendix C—Copyright for kids 204

Appendix D—Useful sources of information 205

Appendix E—Copyright warning notices 211

Appendix F—Sample copyright policy 213

Appendix G—Release form 214

Appendix H—Copyright and plagiarism guidelines for students 215
Appendix I—How much material may I use in my PowerPoint presentation?. 216
Appendix J—Significant copyright law section references. 217
Appendix K—Bibliography of selected works on copyright 218
Appendix L—Important Internet links for copyright information 223
Appendix M—Sources of audiovisual works with public performance rights 225
Appendix N—Database of copyright actions against schools 237
Appendix O—Copyright questions and answers: A reproducible brochure. 237
Appendix P—Copyright infringement reporting form .240

Index. 241

Table of Figures

1.1	Sample copyright registration	9
1.2	Example cease and desist letter	23
4.1	Example of fair use test in action	38
6.1	Audiovisual performance worksheet	78
6.2	Copyright verification form	80
6.3	Off-air video log sample	87
6.4	Off-air video log	87
6.5	Off-air recording verification	88
6.6	Off-air recording label	89
6.7	Sample purchase order	90
6.8	Sample duplication log	99
6.9	Audio-recording duplication log	100
8.1	Sample documentation	123
10.1	Rainforest Maths screenshot	139
12.1	Sample CONTU card system	167
13.1	Request for permission	182
13.2	Sample request for permission	183
17.1	Copyright responsibilities for educators	238

About the Author

CAROL SIMPSON joined the University of North Texas School of Library and Information Sciences faculty in August 1998 after serving in the public schools for 25 years as a high school teacher, school librarian, district library director, and library technology director. At the university, Dr. Simpson taught courses in an online environment. She specialized in preparing courses for the Web and received the university's Distributed Learning Pioneer Award.

Dr. Simpson received a BS degree in art education from Southwestern University. She also holds an MA degree in instructional media and an MLS degree, both from the University of Texas at Austin. Her doctoral studies were completed at Texas A&M University in Commerce, with a major in curriculum and instruction and a concentration in educational technology. She received her law degree from Southern Methodist University Dedman School of Law, where she was associate case note/comment editor for the *SMU Science and Technology Law Review*. She now practices school law with a firm in Plano, Texas.

She is the author of *Copyright for Administrators, Copyright Catechism,* and four previous editions of *Copyright for Schools,* and she edited *Ethics for School Librarians: A Reader.* She also writes a copyright column for *Library Media Connection* magazine. She is in demand as a presenter and trainer and has traveled from coast to coast presenting at conferences and staff development sessions.

2010

Acknowledgments

Any time an author undertakes to write a book, she must rely on the charity of others to accommodate the multitude of questions and unfulfilled promises that occur during the writing process. Doing an extensive revision is no different. This revision began literally the day after I submitted the manuscript for the fourth edition, when I received a question that I knew immediately would generate a new section in this edition of the book. So my first acknowledgment is to all the school personnel who send me copyright questions that spark my creative juices and force me to think in new channels. Second, I give my utmost thanks to my Linworth (now ABC-CLIO) colleagues Marlene Woo-Lun, Cyndee Anderson, Gail Dickinson, Judi Repman, Shelley Glantz, Kate Vande Brake, and Wendy Medvetz, who gently keep me on track and good-naturedly accept my excuses that "the manuscript is not done yet." I also thank Dr. Sara Wolf of Auburn University for her remarkable ability to review sections of the manuscript-in-progress and provide excellent feedback and suggestions for new topics at the same time she is participating in physical activities that would shut down lesser minds. Thanks are due also to my law firm colleagues at Schwartz & Eichelbaum, Wardell Mehl and Hansen, P.C., who daily practice preventive school law: it is easier and less expensive to prevent a lawsuit than to fight one.

My deepest thanks go to my husband, who daily asked, "What page are you on now?" This one is for him.

C. S.

Introduction to the 5th Edition

Welcome to that frightening yet oddly fascinating world of copyright. As educators, you deal with copyright protected materials daily, and you create a fair share of those materials yourselves. Copyright law puts educators smack in the middle of the issue—as creators they want to uphold copyright in their own creations, but as educators they want to use as much copyrighted materials as will enhance their teaching and their students' learning. Invariably, both sides suffer in the exchange. Each side has valid arguments to support its position, which makes knowing what is "right" a difficult proposition.

Copyright is a freeway. Just as going above the speed limit can net you a ticket, so can going too slow. Generally, a driver must maintain a reasonable speed. Despite what some would tell you, even if "everyone" is going over the speed limit, a police officer can still pick you out among the pack and give you a ticket. It makes no difference that many others got away with their violation of the limit. You still broke the law and can be held responsible. Going too slow on the freeway can get you into hot water as well—mostly with other drivers. To extend the analogy to copyright law, failure to take advantage of maximum limits hurts students, teachers, and administrators. And even if copyright anarchists insist otherwise, exceeding the limit by more than a little bit certainly brings your transgression to light, much as the higher you exceed the speed limit, the greater your chances of getting a ticket.

This edition of *Copyright for Schools* updates aspects of the law that affect schools. "Copyright catechism"—questions and answers about common copyright problems in schools—remains. The questions are hypothetical. These aren't answers to specific, real-life quandaries, and the answers certainly don't substitute for competent legal advice, but they can guide you as you wrestle with your own copyright conundrums.

Not every possible combination of facts can be included in these sample questions. I routinely get questions from folks who say something such as, "I read your book, but the book I want to copy from is 100 pages, and the book in your example is 150 pages, so I'm not sure if my use is okay." Chances are that the examples you see here will not match your situation exactly. This book isn't intended to be a "flip-to-the-answer-in-25-words-or-less" book. If you have never read a copyright book from cover to cover, now is the time. A "big picture" viewpoint is essential when you are considering alternatives. For example, when someone wants to use video in a staff development session, permission is typically required because the showing to adult employees doesn't fit under the educational exemptions. But a portion of the same video may be perfectly appropriate under the multimedia guidelines. So a simple change of presentation style avoids a tricky assessment and lengthy and possibly frustrating permission request.

In previous editions of this book, I stated that I was not an attorney. I can say that no longer. Since publication of the last edition of the book, I've completed law school and passed the bar exam, and I now practice school law. I continue to do staff development workshops between other legal tasks. But one thing has not changed: this book should not be relied on for legal advice. A book such as this lays out the copyright landscape so that you can see where you are in general. But for specific advice, you should consult with an attorney who has a comprehensive understanding of copyright law and understands the unique environment of K–12 education. In many instances, just a small variation of the facts can turn an arguable fair use into a clear violation.

This monograph presents the safest position—that level of practice considered to be within legal limits by the most conservative application of the law. Certainly you might choose to stretch the recommendations, and you might never be challenged. In some instances, the recommended practices might even be considered ultraconservative. The National Commission on New Technological Uses of Copyrighted Works aka CONTU) Guidelines, for instance, if followed to the letter, might deny some user an arguably legitimate interlibrary loan. Some interpretations must necessarily be a judgment call, and they are so noted.

Nevertheless, as I have said in multiple editions of this book, don't feel so frightened of copyright that you fail to employ every available opportunity to provide resources to your students, teachers, and colleagues. But the further afield you go from conservative interpretation, the stronger your rationale and your documentation should be. You will need both, if challenged.

> *The further afield you go from conservative interpretation, the stronger your rationale and your documentation should be.*

Infringers frequently rationalize their acts in regard to copyright, but such explanations will not stand up to legal scrutiny. In fact, recently some educators and university faculty have encouraged teachers to press the fair use envelope far beyond what their district legal counsel might advise and beyond what their district policy might allow. The idea that if everyone does it, it must be okay (or copyright owners cannot object) is reckless. Although these advisors may be well-intentioned, they won't have to pay the legal bill if your district happens to be the one the copyright owner decides to sue. You always want to check district policy before striding off into the brave new world of forced "fair" use. Your district will not thank you if your courageous political statement results in legal fees or fines.

Above all, stand fast. The easiest road is not always the right and proper way. For many reasons, our government and the governments of dozens of countries around the world have protected authors and enabled educators to utilize intellectual property for research and teaching. The interests of one group influence and restrict the rights of the other. The balance is fragile. As educators and librarians, we want to provide whatever our patrons desire. As teachers and citizens, we have an obligation to model ethical and lawful behavior for our students. Make no excuses.

The information presented in this volume is intended not as a substitute for qualified legal advice, but rather as a way to help you determine whether you need to consult an attorney for detailed guidance on a given situation. If you have any doubt that your activities are within the law, first read the law itself. It is readily available online (see Appendix J). The suggestions and guidelines contained within this book can help you decide whether you are erring too far on the side of conservatism, or whether you might be straying to the hazardous side of the street. If in doubt, consult an attorney—preferably one who specializes in intellectual property (commonly listed as copyrights, trademarks, and patents or some combination of those terms). Because copyright and intellectual property are not required courses in law school, often specialists in educational law are unaware of the multitude of layers of copyright protection. I know of several instances in which school districts' attorneys have given advice that was inaccurate based on even the most liberal interpretation of copyright law. Many copyright attorneys will consult with you for an hour, providing authoritative legal advice, for the sum of a couple of hundred dollars. When dealing with your professional livelihood, two or three hundred dollars is a small sum to pay for a good night's sleep and can provide enough dependable backup for a firm stand against those who would have you participate in questionable activities.

All these rules and regulations may seem too complicated to be worth the trouble. After all, you haven't been caught so far, right? In difficult economic times, businesses are less likely to let things pass. Cease and desist letters are on the rise, and copyright watchdog agencies are even coercing educational entities to give up information about students so that students (and faculty members) can be sued individually. More than ever before, you must inform yourself of the rules and closely gauge your practice to provide the maximum resources to your school community. Walking that fairly narrow line between too much and not enough requires both study and practice. This book should start you off on the former, and you can refer to it in the future for the latter. I wish you the best in your journey.

Carol Simpson
May 2010

Chapter 1

The Law

It has a name: Title 17, United States Code, Public Law 94-553, 90 Stat. 2541, as amended. Kind of dry-sounding, isn't it? Who would guess that this could be one of the most obtuse and complex laws and arguably the most hated law affecting schools today? But that it is: US copyright law.

If you are reading this book, you have somehow been affected by the law. Perhaps you want to use someone else's material, and you were stopped or cautioned by a colleague or superior; or you are reading about it for a class you are taking; or you have been assigned duties dealing with copyright-protected materials, and you want to protect yourself and your institution. Regardless of the reason, you need to know something about copyright law, and you need to know it quickly. "Quickly" may be more than you can expect, but getting to know the law is a matter of a few key concepts. Once you have those in mind, they apply fairly regularly to just about any situation you might encounter.

History

Copyright dates back several centuries, to English common law. Tradition holds that the British Statute of Anne (enacted in 1710) is the first true copyright "law," though there had been attempts prior to that date to control copying of materials (Feather, 1980). Even chaining books to shelves and restricting the copying to trained monks in monasteries was a form of copyright enforcement.

Origin in the United States

As early as the beginning of the 18th century, publishers and authors in England had a legal right to control reproduction of their works. The United States based its original copyright law on the English version as well as providing protection through wording in the U.S. Constitution: "securing for limited times to authors . . . the exclusive right to their . . . writings" (Article I, Section 8). Although many school people may be surprised, George Washington signed the first U.S. copyright law in 1790. Most people believe that copyright is a much more recent invention. The U.S. law has been rewritten several times over the ensuing years. The last major revision occurred in 1976, with minor modifications in the years since.

What it is now

Copyright has changed over the years. From the first U.S. copyright law signed by George Washington in 1790 to the current iteration passed in 1976 and tweaked almost annually since, copyright has had a significant impact on the United States. But knowing what happened before is useful only in obtuse cases dealing with old material. Most school employees will find that 99.99 percent of their copyright questions can be addressed by the current law. So what you need to know is this: what does a copyright owner own, and what must I exercise caution in using?

Rights of a copyright holder

The six rights owned by a copyright holder are the rights of

1. *reproduction,*
2. *adaptation,*
3. *distribution,*
4. *public performance,*
5. *public display, and*
6. *digital transmission of sound recordings.*

Knowing what a copyright owner owns is key to understanding how to interpret most copyright situations. Starting initially as simply a right to copy (hence the term "copyright") or print, the rights of the copyright holder in the United States have gradually expanded to the six aforementioned rights accorded to the original creator. You don't have to violate all six rights to infringe a copyright. An infringement may violate all six rights at the same time, but you violate copyright if you abridge even one of the six exclusive rights.

What the creator does with the rights given in a copyright is his own business. Rights are similar to property rights in that the owner may rent, lease, lend, or sell outright any or all of the rights in the work. The rights may be sold as a bundle or can be meted out, on either an exclusive or a nonexclusive basis. For example, if you purchase a video program with public performance rights, it is unlikely that you would be the only person who has purchased those performance rights. It would be likely that the copyright owner has offered a public performance license to many people besides you.

It is also possible that the rights sold or licensed are not for an infinite period of time. It is not unusual for an author to sell the rights to a book to a publishing company. However, in the contract of sale, there may be a clause that states the rights to the work revert to the author if the book does not remain in print for a specified number of years. Why is that significant to schools? It's not uncommon for a teacher to have a favorite book of short stories or a spelling workbook, or other teaching tool, that is many years old. The work will likely be out of print. Nevertheless, the teacher would like to use several sections of the work in class. Because the use will be repeated from term to term, the plans she has for the material exceed the permitted educational limits, and the teacher would need to get permission to use the materials or pay a royalty. The choice of permission or royalty belongs to the copyright owner. However, suppose that the publishing company is out of business, and there appears to be no one from whom to get permission or to whom to pay a royalty. In such a case, it would be worth investigating the author of the work because the copyright may have reverted to the author when the work went out of print.

In discussing the various rights in the following discussion, consider that this is only a *baseline* discussion of what the copyright owner owns and does not take into consideration any possible exemptions found in the law or in associated guidelines. In addition, rights may be modified with permission or license. When granted a license to do any of the actions prohibited in the discussions of the rights, the end user can do whatever he or she has received permission, or paid a license, to do. Likewise, a license can limit those things that you might otherwise be able to do under law. In other words, you may give up some of your copyright use rights if you agree to a license making that limitation.

Reproduction

The right of reproduction is the fundamental right of copyright and was the initial impetus for the law. Reproduction in all formats is controlled by the copyright owner or his assigns/agents. The law specifically mentions various formats when identifying this right by indicating that nonprint reproduction ("phonorecords") is also a right reserved to the copyright holder.

An important fact to remember is that copies need not be exact to be considered reproductions. If you were to make a drawing of Mickey Mouse on a piece of paper, and if such drawing were recognizable as Mickey Mouse, for the purposes of this portion of the law, the drawing would be of Mickey Mouse. Just because a few details (colors, words, notes) have been changed doesn't mean that the use is beyond the restrictions of this right. Making a change in format such as recording a book or digitizing a photo could also be considered to be making a copy or an adaptation or derivative work. Don't assume that the word "copy" means only photocopy. The law was written in this form long before photocopiers were in common use. In the case *Hearn v. Meyer* (1987), the court ruled that manual copying was as much an infringement as photocopying. More details on this aspect are covered in the chapter on fair use.

Adaptation

Adaptation is changing a work in some way or creating a derivative work based on the original. Derivative works are new works created from older, possibly protected works. J. K. Rowling gets paid a lot of money to write books, but she gets paid a lot more when those books are adapted into screenplays and produced as movies or plays. Some authors are very protective of this right, whereas others take the notion that "imitation is the most sincere form of flattery" to heart. Taking a popular song and writing new words is adaptation. Turning a picture book into a play for the second grade to perform for the PTA is adaptation. Taking the characters of a book and extending the story is adaptation. Scanning a print work into a digital copy is both reproduction (making a copy) and adaptation (changing the format). The same thing happens when a student modifies the work of an artist

Question: How do copyright laws apply to translation of materials? We have a growing number of Spanish-speaking students and families, so we translate all of the documents we create. What are the rules for translating a copyrighted document such a PDF file on the Internet?

Answer: A translation is a derivative work or adaptation, and the right to create translations is a right owned by the copyright owner. Many copyright owners vigorously guard that right because they don't want just anyone making a translation that might be inaccurate or less literary than the original work. Although there are laws that allow works to be converted into formats accessible to the print disabled, there are not similar laws regarding other languages. Your best bet is to ask permission, but don't be surprised if you are turned down, especially if the work is a creative work.

to create a new piece of art, or a teacher converts a cartoon into digital format for a PowerPoint presentation. All of these acts create derivative works. Not all of these uses are necessarily illegal, depending on the surrounding circumstances, but on the surface all these activities potentially infringe on the author's right of adaptation and should be examined by the user.

Other common derivatives are indexes, translations, concordances, abridgements, and recordings of musical works. Some derivative works, however, are entitled to copyright protection themselves (at least on the added value portions of the work and especially when the original work has fallen into the public domain), so one must not assume that all derivatives are under the control of the original copyright owner.

Distribution

When a teacher creates copies of a graphic in a book, the right of reproduction comes into play. When the teacher passes out those copies to her class, the right of distribution becomes an issue. Distribution can occur in many ways. Mailing home newsletters is distribution. Loaning books from the library is distribution. Sending video around the building using the video distribution system is distribution. Putting computer software on the campus network is distribution. Forwarding an e-mail is distribution. Putting student work on the Web is distribution to the world.

Limitation on right of distribution: First sale doctrine. If the right of distribution were absolute, you couldn't give a book to your niece for Christmas, nor could you have a yard sale. Cutting up a calendar with lovely photos would not be possible, nor would weeding a library of obsolete materials. In fact, loaning books from the library would be a violation of the author's right of distribution as well. So how can we do all of those things and still stay within the law? We rely on a nifty piece of legal doctrine known colloquially as the "right of first sale."

Before we can understand the first sale doctrine, however, we must understand what one owns when one owns a book, for example. When you purchase a book at the local bookstore, you have purchased paper, ink, binding, and a license to read the words until the book wears out. You have not purchased the words themselves or the expression of the ideas discussed within. First sale doctrine means that the right of distribution ceases with an item's first sale, meaning that you can do whatever you wish, physically, with the book. You can wrap it up and give it to your niece; you can rip out the pages and wallpaper your study; you can try to get a decent price for the book at a yard sale; you can donate it to the Friends of the Library book sale; you can even toss that book into the dumpster if you are so inclined. You own that one *physical* (as opposed to *intellectual*) copy of that book, and the copyright owner can do nothing at all to stop whatever private use you make of that physical copy. The copyright owner could, however, attempt to stop you from using that work for commercial advantage if, for example, you were to carefully remove the plates in a book of photography and frame them to sell in an art gallery. Attempting to stop you and succeeding may be two different stories, however. Two separate courts of appeals have ruled differently in similar cases on this issue: *Mirage Editions, Inc. v. Albuquerque A.R.T. Co.*, 856 F.2d 1341 (9th Cir. 1988) and *Lee v. A.R.T. Company*, 125 F.3d 580 (7th Cir. 1997). It will take the Supreme Court to straighten out the confusion.

A group of recording artists challenged the first sale doctrine several years ago when they tried to boycott used CD stores. They claimed that the stores were making money on their previously sold works, without paying royalties. The protest died, however, when it was pointed out that they had received their sales royalties the first time the CD was sold, and they no longer held any control over those copies. A case that was controversial and troubling for librarians was decided in 1997. The court held that a library could be found guilty of infringement via distribution. The LDS Church had received a single set of research materials and then made copies, which it distributed to its branch libraries. The branch libraries allowed researchers to use those materials only within the confines of the branch library. The distributed materials were later found to be illegal copies, and the library was held to be liable for distribution of the illegal materials even though the copies were never removed from the library (*Hotaling v. Church of Jesus Christ of Latter-Day Saints*, 1997). The ruling stated, "When a public library adds a work to its collection, lists the work in its index or catalog system, and makes the work available to the borrowing or browsing public, it has completed all the steps necessary for distribution to the public. At that point, members of the public can visit the library and use the work" (p. 203). Such a ruling makes libraries, in particular, concerned that the materials they hold are legal and legitimate.

Public performance

The right to perform a work publicly is reserved to a copyright owner. "Performance" indicates a work of film, video, dance, theater, music, and so on. A work need not be performed in its entirety to be considered "performed." In fact, a posting on the CNI-Copyright e-mail list discussed the amount of a work that must be used to be considered significant. One lawyer replied that if the work is recognizable, enough has been performed to be considered "significant." Naturally, disagreements over that amount would abound, which is why such definitions are hoped for in court rulings.

What is "public." Key to understanding both public performance and public display is comprehension of the legal definition of the term "public." The law defines a public performance as follows:

> *To perform or display it at a place open to the public or at any place where a substantial number of persons outside of a normal circle of a family and its social acquaintances is*

Question: A magazine article encouraged students to use discarded books by using them to create covers and new artwork. Some of the books almost didn't even look like books when the students were finished! However, what about the copyright issue of changing the format of an existing work?

Answer: Actually, the students in this project weren't changing the format of the work. They were using the book itself as a building block of a work of art. Because of the first sale doctrine, the physical copy of the book belongs to the first person who buys it. Without the first sale doctrine, libraries wouldn't be able to loan books to patrons! The copyright owner has no further control over the physical property of that book. The book owner can give the book away, loan it, sell it, destroy it, or rip it apart. The copyright owner still owns the intellectual content of the work, but the paper, ink, and binding belong to another. In this case, the students were using the *physical* book to create new artwork, not using the intellectual content of the book (the part that is protected by copyright).

*gathered; or to transmit or otherwise communicate a performance or display of the work
to a place specified by [the previous] clause or to the public, by means of any device or
process, whether the members of the public capable of receiving the performance or display receive it in the same place or in separate places and at the same time or at different
times.* (17 U.S.C.A. § 101 (West 2009))

What you do in the privacy of your own home, in the company of your family and your intimate friends, is not considered "public" for the purposes of our discussions of copyright. So when
discussing a performance of a movie, for example, if you were to have the showing in your home,
with your spouse and your children present, such a showing would not be considered a public performance, and the showing would not be controlled by the copyright owner. Inviting the next-door
neighbor, his wife, and their two children over to your home to see the same movie would also likely
not be considered "public." However, the farther you reach beyond an intimate group such as this,
the more "public" you become. If you invite your entire class from church and their spouses over for
a party, and you show *Angels and Demons,* you may be skating on thin ice regarding the public performance right. Certainly, a public school classroom is considered "public." That we may want our students to view the school as "home" and "family-like" is of no matter; the fact remains that the school
is a public place. Gatherings such as a Boy Scout or PTA meeting would
be considered public. In fact, an important federal court ruling known as
Redd Horne set the standard for private and public when the court ruled
that a performance of a video in a private, closed viewing room in a commercial video store was, in fact, a public performance (*Columbia Pictures
Industries v. Redd Horne,* 1984). Performances in public places are controlled by the copyright owner under the right of public performance.

Public display

Like the right of public performance, the right of public display controls
works displayed in public places. Displays outside the home are controlled
by the copyright owner. A display is of something static, such as a painting, photograph, or sculpture. It could also apply to literature if the work
were exposed to public viewing, such as on the Internet. Section 109(c)
of the law allows legally acquired copies of artwork to be displayed where
that work is located; so you can hang a poster you have purchased, or you
can display the books that the library owns, but you can't scan those into
a Web page and display them around the world. This limited exception
to public display does not carry over into public performances of movies,
videos, sound recordings or music, and so on.

Digital transmission of sound recordings

The newest of the copyright owner's rights, the right of digital transmission of sound recording, came into being with the enactment of the Digital
Millennium Copyright Act. The right is a reaction to the loss of control
over sound recordings when they are in digital formats. Users began listening to Internet radio stations that streamed pristine digital recordings, and
while listening, they would capture the audio files. Because each digital
copy is just as perfect as the original, users could burn their own CDs of
their favorite songs rather than going to the music store to purchase copies.

Question: *I have some volunteers who want to scan all our new
book covers into our online catalog.
Given that it is a single image from
a work, is that within fair use for
teaching purposes? Or could we just
download high-quality images from
Amazon?*

Answer: Maybe. Putting
something in the catalog is not
"teaching" as typically defined because there is no curriculum for
which this would be a material part,
so the single-copy teaching exception (which is for print materials
only) would not apply. Many online
catalogs have the capability to put
digital images within the catalog display, and there are services that scan
and license those images for that
purpose. (See Syndetic Solutions,
http://www.bowker.com/syndetics/
options/cover_images.htm.) Making thumbnail images (low-quality,
small-size, and low-resolution images) of book covers is probably
an acceptable use. Downloading
high-quality images from Amazon is
probably not.

As a result, earnings in the music industry began to decline. Users were getting the music without paying any fees whatsoever.

Now, based on the number of listeners, Internet radio stations are required to pay hefty royalties to record companies (the copyright owners) through rights brokering organizations. Such fees are not new. Analog (AM and FM) radio stations have paid licensing fees for many years. However, the mandatory fees imposed on digital transmission are many times higher than those paid by analog stations, primarily because of the ability to copy perfect-quality transmissions. Record companies felt that they should get their share of the profits one way or another. This new right allows them to do just that.

Moral rights

A new group of rights was defined by Congress in 1990 as "moral rights." These rights apply to certain types of visual artwork (painting, sculpture, etc.) that are produced in limited quantities (fewer than 200). In such cases the author can require that his or her name remain with the object. In addition, the artists have some power to prevent their artworks from being defaced or destroyed. In one case a sculptor successfully sued a municipality when a large sculpture, installed on city property, was destroyed without his permission. Moral rights would be significant for a school if the school had students paint a mural or create other artwork. The students would own the copyright in the work and could demand that their names be displayed with the work. In addition, if the work were damaged or destroyed, intentionally or unintentionally, the students would have grounds to sue the school for a violation of moral rights. Painting over the work, remodeling the building, or even allowing other students to deface the work with graffiti could be taken as potential causes for action. The same would hold true if you hired a professional artist to paint a mural, unless the artist waived moral rights or copyright in the contract. Censoring copies of a work, such as putting pants on the naked boy in Maurice Sendak's *In the Night Kitchen,* would not fall under this aspect of copyright because the copy would not be the original artwork. It would, however, be an act of censorship, but that is a topic for another discussion.

How does one get a copyright?

In the years up to 1976, authors had to proactively register their works in order to achieve copyright protection. There were certain requirements for a copyright notice, paperwork to be filed with the Copyright Office, a limited amount of time to file for the copyright, a determination of whether the work had been published prior to registration, and appropriate fees to be paid. If any of the requirements were not accomplished in exactly the prescribed manner, the copyright registration was null and void, and the work then fell into the public domain.

With the enactment of the 1976 copyright law, a work became protected as soon as it was "fixed in tangible form." The term "tangible form" means that the work is retrievable—that it isn't ephemeral. A work may be fixed by being

- *written on paper,*
- *painted on canvas,*
- *saved to disk,*
- *recorded on tape or other recording medium, or*
- *exposed on film,*
- *or by any other method that creates a permanent record of the creation.*

Question: Why would I want to go to the trouble to register my creation?

Answer: Although registration is not required to achieve a copyright, it is needed before a suit is filed. You can register the copyright after you discover an infringement, but your remedy will be limited to actual damages (mostly lost profits) rather than statutory damages (damages assigned by law). If your work was used by a nonprofit organization, there are probably no profits to receive, so your remedy of choice would typically be statutory damages.

Any creative work that is recorded in such a manner is automatically granted the protection of copyright for the author/creator. Other types of creation, such as skywriting or extemporaneous performances that are not recorded, cannot be protected by copyright. In order to get the protection of copyright, no notice is required, nor is registration essential.

These changes came about as a result of the United States signing the Berne Convention in 1988, a worldwide treaty in which nations agreed to protect the copyrights of the others under a country's own laws. This agreement made copyright enforcement easier because one needed to know the copyright laws only of one's own country rather than those of hundreds of nations. For example, if you were to write a book and publish it in the United States, you would have to make appropriate registration only here in the United States. France, Germany, and Egypt (among many others) would protect your work under their laws as if the work had been registered in all of those countries. This agreement also makes copyright compliance easier from a user's point of view in that we have to know the copyright laws of only one country—our own. The United States protects the copyrights of all the Berne signatories under the laws of the United States. In most instances, we needn't learn the copyright rules of France, Germany, and Egypt or any of the other countries signing the treaty.

However, if one wishes to be able to sue for damages should the copyright be infringed, "timely" registration of the copyright is required. The necessary information on registration of a copyright is available from the Copyright Office in Washington, DC (http://www.copyright.gov).

Registration requires submission of a number of copies of the work to the Copyright Office, along with a completed form and the necessary fee. The fee varies from time to time and according to type of work registered, but typically it is between $35 and $60 per work, and the fee is higher and registration takes longer if the work cannot be submitted online. Works can be registered as a "collection," so someone who writes short stories or haiku can rest assured that they won't go broke registering each small item. If the registration is approved, several months after the registration is submitted, the registrant will receive a certificate in the mail (Figure 1.1).

Question: Do students own the copyright on the works they create?

Answer: Yes. Original student works are protected by copyright just as any other creative work. Because most public school students are minors, however, parents or legal guardians must grant permission *in writing* for schools to use student work in publications or exhibits and for other public uses. Displays inside a child's classroom don't require permission, but retaining the child's work for display after the child is no longer in the class would.

What can't be protected by copyright?

An important concept in copyright law is that facts are not protectable. Facts are owned by all humankind, and no one person owns, for example, the multiplication tables or the list of the 10 longest rivers in the world. However, if someone were to write a narrative about either of those two factual representations, as long as there was a modicum of creativity involved, the expression of those facts would be protected by copyright to the extent that the expression was creative.

Works that are not fixed in a tangible medium of expression, such as dance that has not been codified or recorded, or an improvisational speech that has not been transcribed or recorded, cannot be protected by copyright. Recent upheaval about university note-taking services such as Nittany Notes have emphasized that course lecture notes are protected by copyright because they are fixed, but the actual delivery

Figure 1.1. Sample copyright registration

Certificate of Registration

This Certificate issued under the seal of the Copyright Office in accordance with title 17, *United States Code*, attests that registration has been made for the work identified below. The information on this certificate has been made a part of the Copyright Office records.

Marybeth Peters

Register of Copyrights, United States of America

Registration Number:

TXu 1-594-183

Effective date of registration:

November 7, 2008

Title

Title of Work: Audiovisual performance worksheet

Completion/ Publication

Year of Completion: 2008

Author

■ **Author:** Carol Simpson

Author Created: text

Work made for hire: No

Citizen of: United States   **Domiciled in:** United States

Year Born: 1949

Copyright claimant

Copyright Claimant: Carol Simpson
███████████, TX, ███, United States

Rights and Permissions

Name: Carol Simpson

Address: ████████

██████, TX ████

Certification

Name: Carol Simpson

Date: November 7, 2008

Question: *I'd like to copy an outline map of my state. What copyright implications do I face?*

Answer: Simple outline diagrams and maps are not eligible for copyright protection. You may copy these types of materials at will. More complex diagrams and maps require the same fair-use evaluation process as graphics.

of the lecture (unless the notes are read verbatim) is not protected. Professors who record their lectures or who have them transcribed in real time may own the copyright on those lectures. Because elementary and secondary school teachers are less likely to lecture, who owns the rights to class notes is much less of an issue.

Titles, short phrases, names, common symbols or designs (e.g., a stop sign); slight variations on type styles, lettering, or coloring; or lists of ingredients cannot be protected by copyright. Ideas, procedures, methods, and discoveries are not protectable, but descriptions or illustrations of these items may be protected by copyright. Works containing only nonprotected material with no original authorship, such as plain calendars, lists of common facts, charts of measures, and so on, are not protected.

Works created by U.S. government employees for their jobs are not protected by copyright. This prohibition on copyright involves works created by members of Congress within their congressional duties or employees of federal agencies as part of their job responsibilities. Some federally funded projects written by nonfederal employees *may* have copyright protection, so it is always wise to investigate the copyright status of any work before making free use of it. The works of state and local governmental agencies may or may not be protected by copyright, as their governing bodies may choose. Check thoroughly.

Works that are not creative cannot be protected by copyright. In 1991, the Supreme Court held that a traditional alphabetical telephone directory did not contain enough original, nonfactual materials to be considered eligible for copyright protection (*Feist Publications, Inc. v. Rural Telephone Service Co., Inc.,* 1991). The creativity of a work also must be *human* creativity. A work painted by an elephant or typed by a chimpanzee cannot receive copyright protection. Blank forms and useful articles also may not be protected by copyright. The term "useful article" can be illustrated by a case where a court found that a buckle was not protected by copyright because it was

Question: *We'd like to print and sell a recipe book for a fundraiser. What copyright implications are there?*

Answer: Recipes consisting of lists of ingredients and simple assembly instructions may be freely reproduced because they are not protectable by copyright. In fact, similar recipes in published cookbooks may be used. The copyright on many cookbooks is primarily a "compilation copyright"—a copyright on the selection and arrangement of the recipes, not on the recipes themselves. Narrative introductions and transitions may also be protected by copyright.

a "useful article," but a sculptural buckle used as body ornamentation could be protected (*Kieselstein-Cord v. Accessories by Pearl, Inc.,* 1980.) One type of work not protected may surprise you: sound recordings, but only if they were recorded before February 15, 1972. The sheet music played in the recording is still protected by copyright, but the actual recording is not, in contrast to recordings made *after* February 15, 1972, which have *two* copyrights: the copyright in the sheet music and the copyright in the sound recording. See the chapter on music for more details.

Work for hire

Although it is true that a copyright vests at the moment of creation, the copyright doesn't always go to the creator. Take, for example, a classroom teacher who teaches fourth-grade science. For her class, she creates a series of science worksheets. The worksheets are particularly effective, so the teacher would like to compile the worksheets into a book that she will offer to a publisher. The only catch to this plan is that the teacher's *district* owns the copyright in the worksheets, unless the teacher has a contract or agreement that would allow the teacher to own the copyright herself. This is true because the worksheets were created as part of the teacher's job as a fourth-grade science teacher. The concept is known as "work for hire." A district could claim as the intellectual property of the school just about anything a teacher does within the context of his or her job.

What constitutes a "job" may not be what you expect. Contrary to the assumption that your job ends when the final bell rings for the day, for salaried personnel the job may be close to 24/7. A common question is to inquire whether doing the work at home or on weekends or vacation makes any difference in the work-for-hire rules. It probably makes no difference in the case of a salaried employee such as a teacher, but it might make a difference for an hourly employee or someone hired as an independent contractor. If the teacher's work was done "within the scope of employment," it matters little where or when the work was done. So if the work was for fourth-grade science, as in this example, the school could make a very good case that the work belonged to the district because the teacher was hired to teach fourth-grade science. However, if you teach fourth-grade science but write a college physics textbook in your spare time at home, the school would be hard-pressed to convince a court that this work was part of your work as a fourth-grade science teacher.

Because a teacher doesn't own the copyright in the work made for hire, he has the same limitations and fair use options on materials he created as any other teacher on the street. If the teacher changes districts, he should ask the district he is leaving for permission to continue to use and/or adapt those materials. Get that permission in writing.

In these tight economic times, schools are seeking ways to capitalize on their creative capital. The *New York Times* reported on some teachers who are making considerable money selling the lesson plans they created for their school jobs (Hu, 2009). Such publicity just brings to the attention of school districts how much money they, themselves, could be making from the material created by their employees in the course of their employment.

Ideas

A bare idea to create something isn't sufficient to achieve a copyright because ideas themselves are not protectable, but the actual creation of the work or some notation about the idea is protectable. So if you came up with an idea for some exam review materials or flash cards, but someone else actually wrote the items, you would likely not have a claim on the copyright in those items. If there are other contributors to the work, to the point that no single person is responsible, you would have difficulty claiming sole ownership of the copyright even if the initial idea were yours. If this work were mounted within an online site, for example, Web designers, instructional designers, and so on could all be considered partial "authors," and if they were district employees, there would be a strong case for the district as the owner of the work. A clause in teacher contracts regarding copyright ownership can forestall later disagreements about who owns what.

For teachers who do work on a contract basis, such as writing curriculum, a specific work may or may not be work for hire, depending on the contract written. Specific types of work, such as parts of a collective work (e.g., book chapters), part of a movie or other audiovisual work, a test, an instructional text, a translation, and so on (though not a sound recording), can be considered works for hire but only if there is a written contract so stating. So a teacher who works over the summer under a supplemental, piecework contract to produce a curriculum guide might, in fact, own the copyright to the guide produced. The school would need to have a written agreement, signed by all parties, to assure that the copyright of the resulting product

> **Did you know?**
> All transactions transferring copyright ownership or any exclusive right in copyrights must be done in writing. Verbal agreements and simple statements such as "I claim no copyright in this work" are not binding unless they are signed. Non-exclusive licenses (limited permission given to many people) need not be written.

belongs, in fact, to the school. Some schools have encountered problems with this facet of copyright law when dealing with volunteers (adult or student) who work on school Web pages and other special projects. The school cannot count on just the spoken word or the handshake to protect its material. Forewarned is forearmed.

Duration of copyright

Copyright, as of the publication date of this book, lasts for the life of the author, plus 70 years. If there are two or more authors, the work is protected for the life of the longest-lived author, plus 70 years. For works of corporate authorship (something written under the name of a corporation), works for hire, and pseudonymous works, copyright protection extends for 95 years from the date a work is published or 120 years from the date it was created, whichever is shorter. For works published by a group (the National Education Association or the Association for Supervision and Curriculum Development, for example) or works of diffuse authorship, such as a movie (producer, director, actors, editors, musicians, set designers, wardrobe, makeup, and others all contribute to the final product), the duration of copyright is 95 years from the date of creation of the work. Works published before 1923 are currently in the public domain in the United States. Those created prior to 1923 but never published may still be protected. Those created between 1923 and 1978 have varying periods of copyright protection. The time of creation (or registration) determines whether, and how long, a work is protected. Laura Gasaway, librarian and law professor, has a Web page that explains in very simple terms when works pass out of the protection of copyright: http://www.unc.edu/~unclng/public-d. htm. A more detailed and complete chart resides on the Cornell Copyright Information Center Web site at http://www.copyright.cornell.edu/resources/publicdomain.cfm (note the Creative Commons permissions at the foot of the page). This page also has a friendly PDF version for use in manuals and trainings. For a fast-and-dirty Web site that gives you a ballpark estimate, try the Digital Copyright Slider at http://librarycopyright.net/digitalslider/, but be aware that the "maybe" answer will require a lot more analysis. My current favorite copyright resource is the flowchart from Sunstein Kann Murphy & Timbers to determine copyright duration found at http://www.sunsteinlaw.com/practices/copyright-portfolio-development/flowchart.htm.

The durations previously identified pertain to works created after October 27, 1998 (or still under copyright protection), when the Sonny Bono Copyright Term Extension Act (CTEA) went into effect. A work created today will not be in the public domain within our lifetimes if the effective term of protection is not shortened. In fact, under this law the work will not be out of copyright protection until almost every human currently alive on the planet has died. Considering the constitutional wording of "by securing for *limited times*" (emphasis added), life plus 70 years certainly seems like forever.

A lawsuit filed by publisher Eric Eldred prompted a Supreme Court ruling on the constitutionality of the law. Publisher Eldred contended that the term of copyright no longer met the "limited time" requirement now that the term had been extended for 20 years. The Supreme Court ruled that as long as there is a finite time imposed by the law, the law meets the constitutional requirement (*Eldred v. Ashcroft,* 2003). Subsequent rulings have upheld *Eldred,* so the length of copyright protection is settled law until Congress changes it again.

Protected or not?

How do you know whether a work is protected? Truthfully, it is not an easy task. You can find out if a work is *eligible* for protection by finding out (1) when the work was created, (2) the circumstances of its creation, (3) whether the work was published, (4) whether there was a "proper" notice of copyright on the original publication, and (5) whether the creator donated the work to the public domain. That's a lot of information to gather, and for some classes of works, you might need even more information. That's what court cases are made of. Nevertheless, those items should help you determine with some amount of reliability the copyright status of most works you encounter. What follows is a general discussion of copyright status and some of the information you will need to collect.

If a work was created in the United States after January 1, 1978, you know that the work was automatically protected by copyright at the moment it was "fixed" or written down, saved to disk, painted on canvas, and so on. The creator need not have taken any specific action to qualify for a valid copyright. After 1989, the author did not need a "C-in-a-circle" mark (©) or other notification of copyright, and the author need not have registered his work with the Copyright Office in order to own a life-plus-70-years copyright on the work. For works created prior to January 1, 1978, both a proper notice of copyright and registration with the Copyright Office were required to obtain valid copyright protection for published works. Those works published without such notice were considered to be in the public domain—without formal copyright protection. In other words, copyright registration prior to publication had to be an intentional act on the part of the creator. For various other periods of time back to 1923, different rules and durations of copyright protection were in effect. See the previously mentioned Cornell chart (http://www.copyright.cornell.edu/resources/publicdomain.cfm) for more detailed information. For unpublished works (such as private letters and diaries, manuscripts, family photos, etc.), however, notice and registration were not required, and the works retained their copyright protection for many years. Many previously unpublished materials went into the public domain in 2002, so be sure to check individual materials against the Cornell chart if you are unsure of the status of a given work.

Registering a work

The process for registering a copyright is set out by type of material. All require a registration fee (which varies depending on the way you file the registration), plus some copy of the material being registered. The requirements for the various types of registrable materials can be found online at http://www.loc.gov/copyright/circs/ (look for circulars 40 through 66).

Because notice of copyright can be an important factor in determining responsibility for willful infringement, the Digital Millennium Copyright Act (DMCA) included strict new regulations regarding removal of what the act calls "copyright management information." Such information can include the actual copyright notice affixed but also might include the names of the author and copyright holder, performers, writers, title, and so on. Removal of copyright information is especially important in cases of school and library photocopying. Under previous

Question: I want to use a book, but it is out of print, and the publisher is out of business. Is the book now free to reproduce?

Answer: "Out of print" is not the same as "out of copyright" (also called "public domain"). If the work is (or might be) still protected by copyright based on its original date of publication (after 1922) or the author's death date, *someone* may own the copyright. Even if the publisher is out of business or the author is dead, those assets went to someone. Use the Copyright Office files to locate the current owner for permission. As a plan B, some publishing contracts allow out-of-print books to revert to the author. Try contacting the author as well. The original creator may still own the copyright, especially if there is no copyright notice.

iterations of the law, a simple notice of possible copyright was sufficient to protect from complicity in copy infringements. Most libraries used a basic ALA-approved stamp "NOTICE: This material may be protected by Copyright Law (Title 17 U.S. Code)." Under DMCA, this warning would no longer be sufficient. If a work's copyright notice can be found, the entire notice must be included (either photocopied or handwritten) with the copies. If no copyright notice can be found on the work, the former stamp would be sufficient.

Recent laws

Copyright law hasn't stayed static since the passage of the 1976 revision. In virtually every session of Congress, someone introduces (and often passes) a bill that tweaks copyright law in some fashion. Recent changes have brought significant changes to how copyright is administered and interpreted. Supreme Court and other federal court rulings have created de facto law under which some or all of the country has to live. (U.S. district and circuit court rulings are binding only for the area of the country each court covers, though courts in other areas may look to the rulings of sister courts for advice. Only U.S. Supreme Court rulings are binding for the entire United States.)

The United States also signs treaties that impact copyright practice. Most require matching legislation to make U.S. law dovetail with the requirements of the treaty. As mentioned earlier, the Berne Convention agreed to protect the works of other signatory countries under the laws of the country that signed the agreement. Therefore, the United States Congress enacts legislation to make United States law conform to the treaty requirements. Even though the United States joined the Berne Convention in 1989, it has yet to fully implement the Convention treaty by making all United States law parallel the treaty requirements.

Some of the more important school-related copyright laws passed since 1976 include the No Electronic Theft Act, the Visual Artists Rights Act, the Digital Millennium Copyright Act, the Sonny Bono Copyright Term Extension Act, the Digital Performance Right in Sound Recordings Act, the TEACH Act, and the Family Entertainment and Copyright Act. Following are discussions of each:

No Electronic Theft Act

The No Electronic Theft (NET) Act, signed into law on December 16, 1997, closed a loophole in earlier criminal law that allowed those who intentionally shared copyrighted computer software via the Internet to be exempt from criminal prosecution if the suspect made no profit on the exchange. Reproduction of copies worth, in total, over $1,000 brings the act into play. Trading software with a total value of more than $1,000 also is covered under this law. NET first declared that reproduction and distribution may be by electronic as well as physical means (UCLA, 1998; United States Department of Justice, 1998). "Computer software" in this law includes MP3 files, so those who trade illegal digital audio files over the Internet could fall into the criminal category established in this act.

Visual Artists Rights Act

Passed in 1990, the Visual Artists Rights Act (VARA) puts artists in control of their works in more ways than standard copyright allows. It is significant for those who create derivative works because the artist has complete control over attribution of his work, even when the physical work has been sold. It is also significant if you have art, even student-produced art, in your school.

The artist has the right both to claim authorship in his work when such attribution has been denied and to deny authorship when work has been misattributed or when the artist's own work has been changed to the point that the artist feels attribution would be harmful to his reputation. In addition, the artist has the right to prevent the intentional modification of a work or the destruction of a work of "recognized stature."

Rights granted by VARA exist until the close of the calendar year in which the artist dies and are not transferable to anyone. Even if the artist sells the physical art and/or the copyright in the art, the artist retains the rights granted by VARA. The rights apply to paintings, drawings, prints, photographs, or sculpture created as unique items or in limited editions of 200 or fewer copies. Certain types of art are specifically excluded from the grant of rights under this act, mostly commercial and mass-produced art (Hoffman, 2002).

Digital Millennium Copyright Act

Signed into law in October 1998, the Digital Millennium Copyright Act (DMCA) was opposed from its inception. Library, scientific, and academic groups have long found the provisions of the act to be overbroad and far-reaching.

Basically, the DMCA updated copyright law to account for the Internet and digital technologies. Key provisions include the following:

- *You may not "break" copy protection on software (computer or DVD) (known as the "anti-circumvention" section).*

- *Schools that provide Internet access can be protected from copyright infringement claims if they register an employee as the district's agent with the Copyright Office and follow a set of procedures in the event of a claim.[2]*

- *You must pay a statutory fee to "Webcast" sound recordings.*

- *The Register of Copyrights was ordered to undertake an overview of digital distance-learning provisions and prepare a report of recommendations to Congress (UCLA, 2001). Note: this was accomplished and the resulting report developed into the TEACH Act.*

- *You must include the complete copyright notice from the original on copies of protected materials (Lutzker, 1999).*

- *A computer technician may make a RAM or backup copy of computer software while doing computer hardware repair.*

- *Libraries and archives can make up to three digital copies of works for preservation purposes if the works are out of print and in danger of destruction from age or condition, but the works may not be used or distributed outside the premises of the library or archives.*

- *The act establishes statutory fees for digital transmission of sound recordings and for making the ephemeral copies that are necessary for such transmission (Band, 2001).*

- *Libraries (only) may migrate works held on obsolete media to current technologies, but the transfers may be made only if the library can't buy the same work in a non-obsolete format. "Obsolete" means that the hardware to perform or display the work must no longer be available for purchase in the marketplace. Eight-track tapes and Beta format videotapes are obsolete. VHS videotapes and phonograph records are not—yet. (Note that this permission is given to libraries, but not to schools or other organizations. A school library can claim both the library and educational exemptions of the law, but only for those items controlled by the library. This rule would not apply to materials purchased by the school for a department or classroom, for example, if they were not considered part of the library.)*

Regularly, the Register of Copyrights conducts hearings on what uses of works the Librarian of Congress might need to exempt for a three year period from the anti-circumvention rules under the DMCA. In the years since the passage of DMCA, fewer than a dozen exemptions have been granted. Most notably, libraries and schools *may* crack software to access purchased/licensed software that is not working properly or to view the list of blocked Web sites in an Internet filter. New exemptions in 2010 include being able to circumvent copy protection to include video clips in noncommercial or documentary video and making an ebook accessible for handicapped readers if there is no commercial accessible ebook available.

As you can see, the DMCA created extensive changes in copyright practice as far as digital materials are concerned. Libraries and other groups were not pleased about many of the provisions reported here and still seek modification of the law.

Sonny Bono Copyright Term Extension Act

The Sonny Bono Copyright Term Extension Act (CTEA) went into effect after it was signed by President Clinton in October 1998. The act extended the copyright of all items under copyright as of the date of the implementation of the act. Because of the impact of this act, no published works will enter the public domain until January 1, 2019, at which time all works published in 1923 will enter the public domain. Before the implementation of this act, the term of copyright was life of the author plus 50 years. The act extended the term of copyright to life of the author plus 70 years, or 95 years from the date of creation for corporate works, movies, and so on. The bill was heavily promoted by the Disney companies because Mickey Mouse would have entered the public domain (through the expiration of the copyright in *Steamboat Willie*) on January 1, 2003.

The act was heavily opposed by librarians and publishers of public domain works, and publisher Eric Eldred chose to challenge the act by requesting an injunction. In January 2003, the U.S. Supreme Court ruled that the act was constitutional, paving the way for its implementation (*Eldred v. Ashcroft*, 2003).

Digital Performance Right in Sound Recordings Act

This act, passed in 1995, granted the sixth right to copyright holders. The right limits the digital transmission performance of a sound recording. Digital transmission would include Internet transmissions and certain digital satellite transmissions.

TEACH Act

The Technology, Education and Copyright Harmonization Act (TEACH Act) established the rules under which copyright-protected materials could be used in online education. The act is the result of a requirement of the DMCA under which the register of copyrights conducted hearings around the country to determine what legislative action was needed to facilitate the use of copyright-protected materials in distance learning. Under the 1976 iteration of copyright law, "transmission" of a copyright-protected work was prohibited, therefore rendering online transmission of copyrighted works illegal without explicit permission, even when a face-to-face showing of the same work for educational use would meet the fair use exemptions. The TEACH Act established a set of criteria that, if followed by schools, would allow the use of limited amounts of copyright-protected materials when used in qualifying educational situations.

Family Entertainment and Copyright Act

The Family Entertainment and Copyright Act included *four* separate acts. The first, the Artists' Rights and Theft Prevention Act of 2005, or the ART Act, criminalized making a recording of a motion picture in a movie theater, as well as prematurely releasing a motion picture being prepared for commercial distribution. The second, the Family Movie Act of 2005, legalized a technology for private homes that allows DVD viewers to filter out offensive content as long as the technology does not make a copy of the video.[1] The third act reauthorizes the National Film Preservation Board. And the final act, the Preservation of Orphan Works Act, allows a library to make up to three digital copies for the purposes of preservation of an *un*published work held in the library collection as long as the copies do not leave the library premises. The act also allows libraries to make copies of published works (allowed under the DMCA) but limits digital copies to the library premises. Most important in this act is the section that allows a nonprofit school library to make copies of a published work *if* (1) the work is in the last 20 years of its copyright term; (2) the use is for preservation, scholarship, or research; (3) the library has investigated and found the work is not in print; (4) the work is not available in the marketplace at a reasonable price; and (5) the copyright owner has not given notice to the Copyright Office that the work is either in print or available for sale.

Penalties for infringement

Should a person choose to ignore the law, the penalty for copyright infringement is not a minor inconvenience. Damages can be actual (true financial damages suffered) or statutory (set by law), depending on how the suit is filed and whether the copyright to the infringed work was registered before the infringement commenced. Statutory damages range from $750 to $30,000 per infringement, with each individual work or event constituting a separate act of infringement. A limited exception permits truly unwary infringers (also called innocent infringers) to have their fines reduced to as little as $200 per work infringed, but such reduction in penalty is at the discretion of the court. To qualify for such an exception, an infringer would have to present a strong case that he or she truly believed (with reasonable justification) that his or her use of the work was not infringing. The presence of a copyright notice would, for example, be an excellent reason to believe that an infringement was intentional. If the court decides the infringement was knowledgeable and intentional, statutory damages can run as high as $150,000 per instance. Legal fees and court costs can escalate the true cost of losing a copyright infringement case because an infringer may be required to pay the copyright holder's attorney fees and court costs as well as the statutory penalties. Of course, there is no cost that can be put on lost sleep and worry.

Most copyright suits are civil matters, but in 1992 the penalty for criminal infringement of computer software copyright (commonly called "piracy") was raised to felony status, with fines up to $250,000! All that is required for an infringement to become a criminal offense is 10 illegal copies with a total software value of $2,500+. For complete information about potential penalties and liabilities, see chapter 5 of U.S. copyright law at http://www.copyright.gov/title17/92chap5.pdf. See Brad Templeton's *Ten Big Myths about Copyright Explained* for more surprising information about copyright.

Following are some examples of different types of infringement:

Innocent infringement—*A teacher reads in a journal that an item has fallen into public domain and makes copies. In truth, the journal confused two items with similar titles, so the item the teacher copied was actually still protected by copyright.*

Standard infringement—*A librarian makes copies of an article for a class many months in advance without making any attempt to contact the copyright holder and obtain permission.*

Willful infringement—*A principal asks permission to reproduce copies of a journal issue for the faculty and is denied. He makes the copies anyway without a reasonable basis to believe he didn't need permission.*

When a court finds that a copyright has been infringed, it may take one of several courses of action. An injunction prohibits the infringer from making any further use or copies of the work infringed. This penalty is used primarily in cases of large-scale use or copying for profit. The court might also impound or destroy infringing copies. Of course, the copyright owner generally seeks monetary damages, and those damages may be actual or statutory. Actual damages are usually requested only in large-scale piracy cases because the copyright holder must prove lost profits. However, if a school were to do something egregious, such as making mass copies of workbooks, lost profits might be more appropriate than the legally established fines. Statutory damages are the type most often requested in suits against schools and school personnel, and because the costs are applied per item copied, they can mount up quickly. Court costs may be assessed to the loser of a copyright action. Attorneys' fees of the prevailing party may also be charged to the loser of an infringement suit, but a prevailing plaintiff will get the fees only if the copyrighted work in dispute was registered with the Copyright Office within the time frame prescribed by law. A prevailing defendant can get fees and costs whether or not the copyright was filed in a timely manner. The court must make the determination of fees.

Is there an easily accessible record of suits against schools that one may consult? No. Although it is true that court decisions are generally public records, the vast majority (maybe 99.9%) of copyright infringement actions are settled out of court. Out-of-court settlements are between the parties involved, especially when there are no criminal actions. The parties may choose to keep the negotiations private, in which case neither party may talk about the events. For that reason, it is difficult to determine how much a school is typically fined for copyright violations. One hears of schools that have been required to purchase legal copies of all software found to be installed illegally, or to purchase a license to show entertainment videos when those had been shown without public performance rights. Other situations may involve punitive fines for illegal reproduction of workbooks or other print materials.

If someone in the district or building violates copyright, that person pays the fine, right? Well, not exactly. Copyright watchdog groups report the results of infringement actions, both as spoils of victory and as warnings to potential infringers. Most of the reported cases indicate that the classroom teacher or librarian is only the beginning in naming liable parties. Many suits go right up the chain of command, from librarian to principal to curriculum director to superintendent to the board of education, under the assumption that these parties are aware of and responsible for the actions of their employees. The copyright owner looks for the "deep pockets" in most instances, but when suing schools, the copyright owner is more likely to be making a statement or setting a precedent. Copyright owners want to make an impact on all educators who will hear of the suit.

Two supplemental forms of liability enter the picture at this point. School employees can be considered contributory infringers if they assisted or helped the infringer to do the infringing act or if they were in a position to control the use of the copyrighted work. An example of such a situation would be a librarian who loaned two DVR recorders and a set of patch cords with knowledge that they would be used to copy a copyrighted video. The librarian helped the infringer to perform the act by providing equipment to aid the infringement. Why would someone want two DVRs and patch cords except to copy a video? The new dual-deck VCRs or DVD-R machines present a problem. Although a VCR-DVD player is convenient to check out because it can handle every technology, if the machine can copy media from one format to the other, you are presenting an infringement technology when you check it out. In addition, the librarian may have provided the program that will be copied with knowledge that the recording will be infringed. If the librarian is in a position to refuse the loan but makes the loan anyway while knowing that an infringement will occur, she can be considered a contributory infringer. A similar situation would exist if the school technician assisted students to use Bit Torrent to download infringing video or audio.

Employers would be vicarious infringers if they had reason to know an employee was violating copyright and had the power to stop the action but took no action. An example of vicarious infringement would be a principal who had been notified that an infringement was taking place but who took no action to stop the theft. Both vicarious and contributory infringers are just as liable as the person who actually made the copies or used the material.

Liability

The teacher's liability—*Teachers control many copyrighted works: books, workbooks, video, computer software. Misusing copyright-protected materials puts the teacher at the center of a copyright controversy. The teacher may or may not need assistance to violate copyright, but for the most part, the teacher will be the beginning of a chain of copyright liability.*

The technician's liability—*Technicians exert control over many aspects of technology. During the course of their jobs, they are aware of certain file transactions, programs installed, and other activities of the network environment. If technicians know that students (or teachers) are trafficking in illegal materials of any kind but take no action to stop the activity (such as informing administrators of the problem or disabling access), they may be found to be complicit.*

The librarian's liability—*We've all heard of "chain of command." Liability works in much the same way. If infringing copies are made on library-owned equipment, it's a good bet that the librarian who loaned the equipment could be involved in the infringement action. A case could be made that the librarian knew (or should have known) that the event would be an infringing action. Only with the support of a strong copyright policy, good record keeping, and thorough staff training would the librarian (and administrators) be able to show that the infringer was acting as an individual.*

The principal's liability—*The principal is the instructional and administrative leader in the school. As such, the principal must be aware of curriculum, student issues, staffing and personnel responsibilities, extracurricular activities, equipment and resources, and dozens of other issues affecting the building and the educational program. With responsibility for such a vast array of knowledge, it's understandable that when a copyright infringement occurs in a school, the copyright owner will presume that the principal had at least passing knowledge of the event or control over those persons committing the infringement. In either case, the principal could be at minimum a vicarious or contributory infringer. Such a possibility raises the likelihood that the principal will be named in any potential infringement action against the school.*

As you can see, the technician, librarian, and administrator are at some risk from the illegal activities of others. To that end, it is worthwhile to establish and maintain clear and thorough copyright records and to inform school personnel and patrons of their obligations under the copyright law.

Administrators, once schooled on copyright, would probably appreciate notification when violations are observed. This isn't to say that the librarian, teacher, or computer technician becomes the "copyright police." On the contrary, these staff members aren't charged with enforcing the copyright law. That falls to the copyright owner, the FBI, and the Justice Department. But the teacher, the librarian, and the technician are doing the students and staff of the school and the district a disservice if they ignore a potentially damaging and embarrassing legal situation. Apprising a principal of a legal violation is akin to notifying her of a fire code violation so that it may be corrected before the fire inspector arrives for inspection. Forewarned is forearmed.

Further, school employees are at more risk of violation of school policy than even of violation of copyright law. Virtually every school district has an extensive list of policies drafted and approved by the Board of Trustees. Almost every district has some form of copyright policy to protect the board when some employee or student goes "rogue" and knowingly violates copyright law. Even if the district is not held liable for an infringement as the result of the actions of the employee, the board is likely to find that the employee has violated the district's copyright policy. As you should be aware, violation of district policy can be grounds for contract termination or other adverse employment action. So although Washington, DC, may be far away, your local school board may be the enforcement agency about which you should have the most apprehension.

State copyright laws

Until 1978, both the state and the federal governments could prosecute most copyright infringement cases. When 17 U.S.C. § 301 came into effect, anything within the scope of copyright became part of the federal jurisdiction. The legislative history of this section states that "as long as a work fits within one of the general subject matter categories (of federal statutory copyrights), the bill prevents the states from protecting it even if it fails to achieve federal statutory copyright because it is too minimal or lacking in originality to qualify, or because it has fallen into the public domain." States do retain some laws to protect sales of sound recordings (some of which are not covered in federal copyright protection, although the underlying printed music is) and videos under piracy statutes (U.S. Department of Justice, 1997).

Related laws

Copyright law doesn't exist in a vacuum. Other types of laws may be factored into any analysis of a situation involving copyright. Those other aspects of the law may include state contract laws, state and federal privacy laws, federal trademark law, and trade secret law, among others.

Contract law

Contract law is the big gun when it comes to trumping an issue of copyright. U.S. copyright law provides certain rights and obligations on the part of copyright owners and those who would use copyrighted materials, but any of those may be swept away by a valid contract. Contract law is, of itself, quite complex; however, it is important to understand that one may sign away virtually all fair use rights given under copyright law just by signing a license (a form of contract) that abrogates those rights.

Some libraries have discovered, to their surprise, that they gave away the right to loan certain items when they purchased the materials under a license rather than as a sale (Simpson, 2007). Particularly in book/software sets, computer software, and audiovisuals, libraries are encountering licensing terms such as the following, which was actually attached to a purchased item: "Libraries may permit reading of this material by patrons of the library through installation on one or more computers owned by the library, but may not lend or sell the disk itself. The library may not allow patrons to print or copy any of this material in any way." As you can see, in this case the library's use of the material has been highly restricted. If the library accepts the license, it is bound by the conditions. In the case of this license, the library would be bound to monitor all use of the materials to make sure the patron did not make any copies of the material. The license here was not referenced in the catalog from which the material was ordered and came to light only when the materials arrived shrink-wrapped. Fortunately, the seller offered to take back the materials if the license was not acceptable as long as the materials were returned with the shrink wrap intact.

Privacy statutes

There are a few federal privacy statutes; most deal with how the government can use and control information that it keeps on citizens and with the release of health information or educational records. But there are dozens of state laws that protect privacy. Laws in states such as California and New York, where many celebrities live, tend to be more restrictive of personal information than those in states with fewer notable persons. Whereas copyright may protect a photograph, privacy laws protect a person's likeness and image. So although a photo of Marilyn Monroe, for example, may be in the public domain, the privacy statutes of California might prevent anyone from using that photograph (and hence her likeness) for commercial advantage without the permission of Monroe's estate (Electronic Privacy Information Center, 2004).

Trademark law

Akin to copyright, but dealing with identifiable items related to business, short phrases, symbols, logos, and so on, trademarks are their own universe of intellectual property. Administered by the United States Patent and Trademark Office, these marks may be maintained perpetually. As long as the trademark owner uses the mark actively and defends it from falling into common use as a generic term (such as what happened to the trade name Aspirin), the mark may be reserved for the trademark owner. Trademarks, just like copyrights, may be sold, traded, and so on. Service marks, identifying services rather than products, are also part of the body of trademarks (Legal Information Institute, 2004).

Trade secret law

Trade secret law is both a state law cause of action and a standardized law that typically protects business methods, processes, and formulas. For example, the formula for Coca-Cola is not protected by patent or copyright because the term of both would expire and allow the formula to enter the public domain where anyone could make it. Instead, the formula is protected by trade secret. All a company has to do to maintain a trade secret is have a process that is not generally known (i.e., secret) and make an effort to keep the process secret. Trade secrets can even be a unique combination of public domain elements that no one else has ever thought of. To violate a trade secret, someone must acquire the secret by "improper means" and use or disclose the secret to the disadvantage or potential disadvantage of the secret's owner. It is not a violation of a trade secret to reverse engineer a legally acquired product to see how it works or to come up with the same process, device, or product independently (though if challenged, you will have to prove that you didn't have access to the other company's information).

Trade secrets can (and sometimes must) be disclosed in order for the owner to use its own secret. For example, a company may design a new machine that has a unique set of parts inside. The company may have designed the machine or may assemble the machine but may not be able to manufacture the parts themselves. It must give the specifications for those parts or assembly to someone else in order to manufacture that machine or device. Typically, a trade secret owner will require anyone who must know about the secret to sign a confidentiality agreement. (You may sign one of these if you take a market research survey on a new product someone is contemplating.) The confidentiality agreement says that you will not use or disclose anything about this secret item, product, or process.

Two forms of law protect trade secrets: state unfair competition laws and the Uniform Trade Secrets Act—a form of standardized law that states may adapt and adopt rather than writing their own law from scratch. Because these laws necessarily vary from state to state, it's difficult to generalize exactly what rules apply in a given location. However, in general, courts look at the following factors to see whether a trade secret exists: (1) the extent to which the information is known outside of the secret's owner's business; (2) the extent to which it is known by employees and others involved in the business; (3) the extent of the measures taken by the secret's owner to guard the secrecy of the information; (4) the value of the information to the secret's owner and its competitors; (5) the amount of effort or money expended by the secret's owner in developing the information; and (6) the ease or difficulty with which the information could be properly acquired or duplicated by others (Peterson, 2008).

Can schools have trade secrets? They can, though it is an unlikely scenario. Nevertheless, if a school found some really whiz-bang way to motivate students or teach algebra, it might claim a trade secret in the process. You would know if your district claimed trade secrets in its teaching methods because the district would ask you to sign a confidentiality agreement. Read such an agreement carefully because if you transfer school districts, you will not be able to use what you learned while at the owning district.

More likely, a school might be the *user* of trade secrets. For example, if a school district purchased a large software package, it might have to know something proprietary about the package in order convert its data to work with the software. In such a case, anyone who had to know the secret of the process would have to sign a confidentiality agreement.

Why is any of this significant for schools?

A school may find itself in copyright hot water in any of several ways. Most common is to receive a cease and desist letter. Such a letter may be sent from a company or its attorneys and generally states that the company is aware that you have violated copyright in some manner. The letter usually goes on to state what you are alleged to have done and what demands the company is making for its supposed damages. (See Figure 1.2.)

It is not a good idea to ignore such a letter. In most cases the letter will demand some response from you by a given date. If the company does not receive a response to its allegations by that date, further legal action may be taken. If you feel that the allegations are unfounded, you should take this opportunity to present your side of the case to the company or other representative of the copyright holder. But don't take such a step without advising your administrators so that they can be prepared for possible legal action. They will likely want to involve the school's legal counsel in any discussions with a potential litigant. One word of caution: copyright courses are *not* required in most law schools. Your school's counsel may have taken many courses in education law, but none at all in copyright. Urge a consultation with a copyright specialist if you are uncomfortable with the advice your counsel provides.

Schools could also find themselves in trouble when a representative of a copyright holder directly contacts someone in the school who is believed to be a wrongdoer. I was once paid a visit by a software company representative who alleged that the library in which I was working used illegal copies of a popular computer program. When I produced appropriately licensed copies of the program, the company representative politely left. If one can easily resolve the potential conflict with a little cooperation and open discourse, that should be the appropriate tack.

The least likely way to discover copyright problems is to be served with a lawsuit. Preparing and filing a lawsuit is an expensive proposition. Most in-house attorneys (attorneys who work directly

Figure 1.2. Example cease and desist letter

Big Law Firm
123 High Rise Office Building
New York City, NY

October 31, 2009

Supt. John Doe
Local School District
456 Main Street
Your Town, Anystate

VIA FEDERAL EXPRESS

Re: ***Copyright Owner v. Local School District***
Our File No. 123-456.78

To Whom It May Concern:

Please be advised that we represent Copyright Owner ("Owner"), the owner of all right, title and interest in and to a copyrighted line of products known as "Series." Copyright Owner is the owner of copyright registrations with the United States Copyright Office for many different variations of its Series line of products. Attached please find copies of several of Copyright Owner's copyright registrations for the Series line.

It has come to the attention of our client that you have been transferring copies of our client's copyrighted Series to a video streaming server and streaming these products to other school districts. Attached please find a web page screen shot of your online catalog of video available to all schools in the XYZ consortium through your streaming server. It is thus our opinion that your product is an infringement of our client's copyright rights.

Our client will be substantially and irreparably damaged should this infringement continue. We therefore request that you immediately cease and desist from the ongoing provision of these infringing products. In order to mitigate further damage to our client, the following actions on your part are required:
- immediate discontinuance of providing access to infringing products;
- turning over to our client's representative of all infringing products in your possession;
- an accounting of all sales, leases, subscriptions or rentals made to date of the infringing products;
- an award of damages for all lost sales and profits or, in the alternative, statutory damages in an amount between $500 and $20,000; and
- an award of attorneys' fees.

Unless we receive your reply by November 15, 2009 we will presume that you do not intend to voluntarily take the necessary actions outlined above and we will have no alternative but to commence immediate legal action against your company in which we will seek all available legal remedies under the Copyright Act, including, but not limited to, an injunction against further access to the infringing product and substantial monetary damages for each act of infringement. We await your prompt response.

Very truly yours,

John Q. Legaleagle, Esq.

for the copyright owner rather than with a law firm engaged by the copyright owner) will do the initial negotiations with potential infringers but probably won't actually file the lawsuit. For that task the copyright owner will engage litigation counsel. Lawsuits are filed directly with a court that has jurisdiction over the matter and the defendant, which would likely be the U.S. district court nearest your town. Your first notice that a lawsuit has been filed may be a certified letter from the court.

The last way a school might find itself in trouble is to have an attorney or process server appear at the school. He or she may be accompanied by or be represented by the FBI and/or federal marshals. Situations such as this require the immediate attention of your administration and legal counsel. As a rule, such incidents do not occur without cause, and there is generally sufficient evidence—the plaintiff has convinced a federal judge that there is likelihood of wrongdoing on the part of your building or district and that evidence will likely be concealed or destroyed if not seized. This is the most serious of cases. Do not ignore this situation; make sure your supervisors are aware of the situation and that they contact your district's legal counsel.

How is a school prosecuted?

Schools may be sued for real or actual damages (typically lost profits), or they may be sued for the fines set forth within the law (statutory damages). It would be highly unusual for a school to be sued for real or actual damages. For real damages to be worthwhile to the copyright owner, the amount of material used and the possible loss in value (tangible or intangible) to the copyright holder would likely have to exceed the allowable statutory damages. That situation generally does not arise unless there has been a large-scale infringement. Because most cases of use in schools don't involve amounts over $30,000, few cases demand actual damages. Cases where schools systematically duplicate workbooks without paying royalties or have vast amounts of illegal computer software are two types of copyright actions in which actual damages would be more beneficial to the copyright holder. Attorneys' fees and court costs can be added to the amount of damages or fine.

Question: I have a teacher who is making CD copies of our library audiobooks for the other special education teachers and their students. (This is so that they do not have to share one audiobook.) Is this a copyright infringement; if so, what is the argument against it?

Answer: Yes, it is likely a violation. It violates the right of reproduction, a right reserved to the copyright owner. There are some *limited* educational exemptions for *performance* of audiobooks, but anything such as this that smacks of what courts call "systematic" copying (buying one copy and duplicating it for multiple teachers to avoid purchasing legal copies) would be seriously frowned on.

What if there is no trial?

The vast majority of copyright cases (involving both schools and others) are settled out of court. Although such a settlement is always a relief to the school, the rest of us are disappointed because a definitive court ruling helps to define the boundaries of copyright. Copyright is an ever-changing landscape, with shifting borders. A court ruling helps attorneys and consumers to understand what can be considered appropriate behavior regarding copyright-protected materials.

Out-of-court settlements aren't necessarily inexpensive, however. A case against Los Angeles Unified School District was settled out of court for $300,000 in fines plus attorneys' fees (Blair, 1998). In addition, the school was required to purchase at retail value all the computer software that had been installed illegally. The total cost for the incident amounted to about $5 million! So although an out-of-court settlement may reduce stress and get the situation behind the school, the option may not be a good one in terms of finances. A good attorney who specializes in intellectual property is the best person to consult in such a situation. He or she can analyze the situation and determine whether the likelihood of winning a court case might make out-of-court settlement a poor idea.

Why worry? Why bother?

So your school doesn't comply with copyright. What difference does it make? Do you feel that no one will ever know in most cases, and no one will even care? Perhaps you have heard that schools are such "small potatoes" that big producers and publishers don't really care because a school doesn't have deep enough pockets for anyone to get a big settlement. You may have even heard that schools are exempt from copyright suits.

Don't believe it! Schools encounter copyright actions on a daily basis. Most are quickly resolved in a professional manner, and no public record exists. These are types of actions for which one can do no research. However, the Business Software Alliance (Business Software Alliance, 2009) reports that schools are among the top 10 industries for which the BSA receives the most reports of software piracy (and awards bounties for those reports). A database of copyright infringement actions against schools is available at http://www.carolsimpson.com. There you can see a sampling of a variety of copyright actions told in the voices of those close to the situations. If you know of a copyright action, from a cease and desist letter to a full-blown lawsuit, please add it to the database of cases so that we can all share in the information of what is actionable and learn how other school districts dealt with the situation.

Copyright compliance is as much an ethical issue as a legal one. Does one take something that belongs to another and appropriate it? Of course not! One also would not walk into the crowded lunch line in the cafeteria and take a dessert without paying for it. "Taking something that doesn't belong to me?" the teacher declares indignantly. "I would *never* do such a thing, especially with students watching!" But the same person might stand in front of a class and instruct, "See how we can right click on this graphic and save it to our disk to use however we desire?" From the viewpoint of a disinterested observer, taking the work of others appears to be inappropriate only in certain circumstances.

Copyright law is federal law. Perhaps you live a long way from the District of Columbia, and you don't think anyone there will know what is going on in your small district. You think the law is a pain to keep up with, and there are few clear-cut rules, so you might just as well pretend it doesn't exist. However, your district probably has a policy regarding copyright compliance. If you feel that Washington is too far away to be a threat, what about your local school board? The penalty for violating a school board policy can be loss of your job. If Washington doesn't frighten you, perhaps the fear of being caught violating board policy does. The fact remains that the law is still the law, even if we don't like it. Those who don't like the law should work to change it, not just ignore it.

Works cited

Band, J. (2001). *The Digital Millennium Copyright Act.* Washington, DC: Association of Research Libraries. Retrieved from http://www.arl.org/bm~doc/dmca_band.pdf.

Blair, J. (1998, August 5). Pirated software could prove costly to L.A. district. *Education Week, 17*(43), 3.

Business Software Alliance. (2009, May 28). *BSA reveals top 10 industries with highest reports of software piracy.* Retrieved from http://www.bsa.org/country/News%20and%20Events/News%20Archives/en/2009/en-05282009-tenindustries.aspx.

Columbia Pictures Indus. v. Redd Horne, 749 F.2d 154 (3d Cir. 1984).

Hoffman, I. (2002). *The Visual Artists Rights Act.* Retrieved from http://www.ivanhoffman.com/vara.html.

Eldred v. Ashcroft, 537 U.S. 186 (2003).

Electronic Privacy Information Center (2004). *EPIC archive—privacy.* Retrieved from http://www.epic.org/privacy/.

Feather, J. (1980). The book trade in politics: The making of the Copyright Act of 1710. *Publishing History, 19*(8), 39.

Feist Publications, Inc. v. Rural Telephone Service Co., Inc., 499 U.S. 340 (1991).

Hearn v. Meyer, 664 F. Supp. 832 (S.D.N.Y. 1987).

Hotaling v. Church of Jesus Christ of Latter-Day Saints, 118 F.3d 199 (4th Cir. 1997).

Hu, W. (2009, November 14). Selling lessons online raises cash and questions. *New York Times.* Retrieved from http://www.nytimes.com.

Kieselstein-Cord v. Accessories by Pearl, Inc., 632 F.2d 989 (2d Cir. 1980).

Lee v. A.R.T. Company, 125 F.3d 580 (7th Cir. 1997).

Legal Information Institute. (2004). *LII: Law about . . . trademark.* Retrieved from http://www.law.cornell.edu/topics/trademark.html.

Lutzker, A. (1999). *Memorandum.* Retrieved from http://www.arl.org/bm~doc/notice.pdf.

Mirage Editions, Inc. v. Albuquerque A.R.T. Co., 856 F.2d 1341 (9th Cir. 1988).

Peterson, G. R. (2008). Trade secret law update 2008: Including restrictive post-employment covenants. In *14th Annual Institute on Intellectual Property Law.* New York: Practicing Law Institute.

Simpson, C. (2007). An ILL wind: Libraries and the interlibrary loan of audiovisuals. *SMU Science and Technology Law Review, 11,* 163–194.

Templeton, B. *Ten big myths about copyright explained.* Retrieved from http://www.templetons.com/brad/copymyths.html.

UCLA Online Institute for Cyberspace Law and Policy. (1998). *The "No Electronic Theft" Act.* Retrieved from http://www.gseis.ucla.edu/iclp/hr2265.html.

UCLA Online Institute for Cyberspace Law and Policy. (2001). *The Digital Millennium Copyright Act.* Retrieved from http://www.gseis.ucla.edu/iclp/dmca1.htm.

U.S. Department of Justice. (1997). *Criminal resource manual 1844 copyright law—Preemption of state law.* Retrieved from http://www.usdoj.gov/usao/eousa/foia_reading_room/usam/title9/crm01844.htm.

U.S. Department of Justice. (1998). *The "No Electronic Theft" Act.* Retrieved from http://www.cybercrime.gov/netsum.htm.

Notes

1. This authorized technology is sold under the trade name of ClearPlay.
2. The Librarian of Congress in July 2010 made a limited exception for circumventing the copy protection of audio or video. The exception applies to amateur filmmakers who may incorporate an excerpt into a new documentary or work of cultural commentary. A previous exception for higher education professors of film studies was broadened to students of film and media and to faculty in all higher education subjects, but was specifically not extended to teachers or students in K–12.

Chapter 2

Public Domain

What is it?

A work not protected by copyright is considered to be in the public domain. Because the latest copyright act made copyright automatic once a work is created, getting a work into the public domain can be a little difficult (or time-consuming). A work can lose its copyright protection in any of several ways.

How does something get into the public domain?

A work can become part of the public domain (PD) through different means. First, some works may not qualify for copyright protection in the first place. A work might not be "creative," or it might not have been created by a person. Other factors come into play when considering copyrightability as well.

A work must be considered "creative" in order to qualify for copyright protection. For that reason, facts are not eligible for the protection of copyright and are therefore in the public domain. For example, a simple list of the 10 longest rivers in the world is factual and not eligible for the protection of copyright. However, if you were to write an essay about the 10 longest rivers and describe their surroundings and their ecology and talk about the important economic benefits each provides for its watershed, the expression of the facts regarding the rivers would be creative and protectable. However, anyone is free to make use of the factual material included within the essay. The most important court case opinion to discuss this concept is known as the *Feist* decision, handed down by the U.S. Supreme Court (see the "Related cases" section at the end of this chapter). In this case the Supreme Court found that simply alphabetizing a list of names and phone numbers was not sufficient creativity to garner copyright protection for the work.

Also, a work created by a gorilla or an elephant, for example, could be highly creative, but because it was not created by a human, the work would not qualify for copyright protection and therefore would be in the public domain. To be protected, the work must be created by a human being. In this day of computer-generated text, questions may arise about works created by computers.

Works created by U.S. federal government employees during the course of their duties are not eligible for copyright protection and so are in the public domain. Speeches of the U.S. president, acts of Congress, booklets prepared for various federal agencies, and U.S. government Web pages all would be free from copyright protection. Use caution in gathering material from government sites, however, because they may have used licensed art (such as from Microsoft Office) or other materials in their works. Also, it is a common misconception that because federal government documents are in the public domain, all governmental entities also place their materials in the public domain. This is not the case, and the matter should be investigated on a case-by-case, agency-by-agency basis. Some school districts and state agencies claim no copyright in their curriculum guides, policies, and so on. Others protect and defend their documents strongly. When in doubt, ask.

Additionally, works that once were protected by copyright may lose that protection through one of several ways. Works created during the period when a specific type of copyright notice was required fell into the public domain if the notice was defective. For example, a copyright notice had to have the c-in-a-circle mark or the word "copyright" to be considered valid. If your typewriter didn't have a copyright symbol, and you typed a letter "c" between parentheses instead, your notice was considered to be defective and your copyright invalid. In such cases, the work immediately fell into the public domain if the work was published with the defective notice.

Works whose term of copyright has run the full course are no longer eligible for copyright protection, so they too fall into the public domain. This class of works would include all those published before January 1, 1923. Shakespeare's plays, for example, aren't protected by copyright in their original form because they were published before 1923. If notes, commentary, or background information have been added to the play, however, those portions of the works may be covered by copyright (provided they were written after 1923 and, if appropriate for the time the additions were published, registered), as would be contemporary illustrations. Reprints of old novels or classic fiction may have new copyrights based on new illustrations or new introductory matter, but the copyright covers only the new additions. Some unpublished works—previously protected under common-law copyright but now released under new legislation—started entering the public domain in 2003 if their 70-years-after-death period had lapsed. Watch for diaries, photographs, manuscripts, and so on to appear in the future as the terms of life plus 70 years run their course.

Works whose copyrights were not renewed, if they were protected by copyright during a period when copyright renewal was required, lost their copyright protection when the copyright was not renewed. Many silent films were not renewed after talking pictures became popular, so they are now in the public domain. Some other materials post-1923 are also now in the public domain as a result of nonrenewal, such as the John Wayne film *McClintock!* The nonrenewal may have been a slip-up on the part of the copyright owner or his agent, but the results are the same. One must research to find which post-1923 works are not protected.

Some materials are dedicated to the public domain by their authors, but there is a caveat: since 1989, the fact that a work has no copyright notice should *not* be taken to mean that the work is not protected by copyright. In fact, because the World Wide Web was created after 1978, most things you see on the Web are protected by copyright unless they were created by some entity forbidden to hold copyrights (such as U.S. government agencies) or are a verbatim reprint of some public domain work, such as old (pre-1923) literature. Some scholars and philanthropists also state on their Web pages that works published there are in the public domain.

How long does public domain last?

Just because a work has no notice of copyright does not mean that the author has put the work in the public domain.

Because "public domain" means that a work is not covered by copyright, the rules regarding the length of copyright coverage do not apply. Currently, once a work has lost its copyright protection and has passed into the public domain, copyright protection cannot be regained on that work. Therefore, the public domain lasts, in effect, forever. There is an exception in section 104(a) that covers a particular class of unpublished works by foreign authors, but that exception will seldom apply in a K–12 school situation.

What can you do with public domain materials?

Public domain materials have no copyright restrictions. If a work is in the public domain, it may be reproduced, adapted, distributed, performed, displayed, and transmitted. However, it is essential to understand that only the *original* public domain work has these options. Subsequent modifications and adaptations may gain for their adaptors or creators a copyright on the additions or changes. For example, the original works of Beethoven are long in the public domain. However, few high school orchestras perform the *original* works of Beethoven. In the first place, Beethoven wrote for instruments that are no longer used. In the second place (and even more relevant), the original scores are far too difficult for most high school orchestras. Someone has *adapted* the works into versions that are less complex and less difficult without losing the original melody and tone of the piece. Although the original parts of the piece are still in the public domain, anything new that is added or modified in the derivative work may be protected by copyright. A simple change of key does not qualify as sufficiently creative to earn a new copyright in a work; there must be more creativity involved to get a new copyright, but the amount of creativity is only minimal. The new copyright applies only to anything new added to the work.

> *Question:* Is the Bible considered public domain? If it is copyright-protected, who would own the copyright?
>
> *Answer:* The answer depends on the version. The King James Version is in the public domain—at least in the original translation. New translations may still be protected. Check the copyright date of the version you are using. Anything copyrighted before 1923 is public domain. (Watch out for "enhanced" versions, though. The Bible text itself may be public domain, but the notes, illustrations, and so on may still be protected.)

How do you find public domain materials?

Public domain materials are everywhere! There are even publishers that specialize in public domain materials. Educational publishers use many public domain materials because there are no costs to use them, and the publishers can edit the materials as they choose. English textbooks, for example, use materials by Shakespeare, Keats, and others because they are free as well as notable.

There are several sources for locating public domain materials. But not all the sources are free to use, though the public domain materials they help you locate are free to use once you locate them in the original versions. Some of the best, such as Pub Domain (http://www.pubdomain.com), are subscription or donation Web sites. But they do offer samples of music, art, children's literature, drama, movies, and literature. All have been scrupulously researched as to PD status. The company has a service for public domain sheet music and public domain photographs as well. Remember, you can arrange, translate, modify, and publish any of the public domain materials they provide, so the cost is negligible if you use the service to any degree. Use caution with photographs because the right of publicity may come into play for any recognizable human images (i.e., models or celebrities), and trademark issues can complicate use of product images.

It is possible to do your own searches for public domain status, but that really means not finding anything in the Copyright Office database and not having definitive information about actual publication date so that you are certain that the version you are working with is the original. Be cautious, especially if you plan to sell or adapt material for public performance. Make certain the version you are using is in the public domain.

Related cases

In *Feist Publications, Inc. v. Rural Telephone Service Co.,* 499 U.S. 340 (1991), a publishing company was collecting listings of names, addresses, and telephone numbers to publish in a private telephone directory. The telephone company objected, contending that the work was their creative property. The Court held that collections of facts, by themselves, are not copyrightable and that some modicum of creativity is required. A simple alphabetical arrangement of names and telephone numbers was insufficient to qualify as "original."

Chapter 3

Licensed and Royalty-Free Materials

Not everything that the educator may wish to use is in the public domain, but what other options exist beyond paying through the nose for material? There are numerous options for locating materials that may be available for little or no cost. But you want to know exactly what you are getting and what reciprocal responsibilities you have regarding the materials you use.

How do "copyright-free," "royalty-free," "license," and "lease" differ?

A work that is "copyright-free" is in the public domain (see chapter 2). There are no restrictions on its use. It may be copied, adapted, distributed, publicly performed or displayed, and transmitted digitally if it is a sound recording. You do not have to ask anyone for permission to use the work. Citation is another matter entirely (see the section on plagiarism). A work that is "royalty-free" is still protected by copyright, but the copyright owner has elected to forgo collection of royalties for certain uses of the material. The copyright owner may impose some restrictions on your use that are allowed royalty-free, so you may not be able to use royalty-free materials in every application you would like. A "license" is similar to restricted, royalty-free use, but generally you pay for the privilege. You can arrange any type of license that you can get the copyright owner to permit. Essentially, anything you can get permission to do, you may do under a license. Permission = license. And finally, a "lease" is a contract through which the owner of the copyrighted work conveys the right to use that work for a limited period of time in exchange for some type of payment. Increasing amounts of educational materials are available by lease, such as certain videos and video libraries. Because you may not recognize that some producers have switched from sale to lease, it is important to check catalogs carefully before ordering and to propose different terms if you discover that the work will not belong to you when you receive it.

How can I use royalty-free materials?

Royalty-free materials are usually governed by license. The license will explain in detail how the collection of materials can be used in your case. Typically, you can use royalty-free art or music in standard broadcast situations or productions/publications without additional payment. The most usual

> **Question:** *Teachers want to have students collaborate on a publicly accessible wiki on a given topic. The thought is that students can cite sources the same way they would for a paper. They would also link to the quoted/paraphrased material if it is online already. However, I noticed that one of our databases restricts reusing content without permission, but would this be educational fair use (scholarship and criticism)?*
>
> **Answer:** Remember that through license, you can give up some of your standard fair use rights. Your database license may have done just that. You need to have your district's legal counsel review the language and see if that is what has indeed happened. Also remember that citation has nothing to do with fair use. Although citation is an academic ethics concept, it is not necessarily required for fair use. Even items from the public domain should be cited.

prohibition on use of royalty-free material is to employ the items in another collection of similar items. For example, many collections of clip art are royalty-free, but they are not copyright-free. The artist or copyright owner does claim a copyright in the works, but the owner does not elect to charge a per-use fee on the art as long as the person using the art abides by license restrictions. Upon reading the software license for the clip art, one may discover that use of the art in publication, Web pages, derivative works, and so on is permitted but that use of the work in another collection of clip art is expressly *prohibited*. Such a common prohibition might cause problems for teachers or librarians who are in the habit of collecting art from various free Web sites or clip art collections and gathering them together by theme, to provide their students with a one-stop-shopping location for project art. A teacher may put up a page of elephant clip art, for example, if her third graders are doing multimedia projects on elephants. But putting the royalty-free art into a clip art collection for her class may violate the license and the copyright of the art.

Sources of royalty-free materials

More and more materials are becoming available under various licenses that allow use without payment of royalties. The Creative Commons license (http://www.creativecommons.org) is a good example. People attach Creative Commons licenses to their works in the hope that the liberal licensing will benefit scholarship and society as a whole. But materials with a Creative Commons designation are not all in the public domain. In fact, most of the materials covered under a Creative Commons license are protected by a valid (if perhaps not registered) copyright. They are made available to the public at large without a fee, subject only to the conditions assigned by the author.

Creative Commons offers four types of licenses that authors may assign to their works, and an author may choose one, some, or all of the licenses. Works may even be tagged as in the public domain, in which case the author will have no more rights to that work, but public domain is not a license. The four Creative Commons licenses are as follows:

- Attribution—*others may copy, distribute, display, and perform the copyrighted work and derivative works based on it, but only if the original work is attributed to the original author.*

- Share alike—*the author allows others to distribute derivative works only under a license identical to the license of the original.*

- Noncommercial—*others may copy, distribute, display, and perform the copyrighted work and derivative works based on it, but only for noncommercial purposes.*

- No derivative works—*others may copy, distribute, display, and perform only verbatim copies of the original work and may not create other works made from the original.*

In addition to the four Creative Commons licenses that you may combine and assort, there are four other Creative Commons tools to help creators license their works for general use without royalties. Those license tools include the following:

- **Public Domain**—*the author claims no rights at all in the work.*

- **CC GNU LGPL**—*The author licenses the work with the Free Software Foundation's Lesser GNU public license along with a Creative Commons metadata and deed. This is primarily for software.*

- **CC GNU GPL**—*The author licenses the work with the Free Software Foundation's GNU public license along with a Creative Commons metadata and deed. This is also only for software.*

- **BSD** *(Berkeley Software Distribution)—The author licenses the work under the Open Source Initiative's BSD license, allowing others to copy, distribute, transmit, and remix the work as long as the name of the author is not used to endorse or promote products derived from the original.*

Several sources of materials (typically images, video, and music) are available to educators and/or the general public under these types of licenses. The following list is simply illustrative:

A1 Free Sound Effects—http://www.a1freesoundeffects.com

AudioFeeds.org—http://audiofeeds.org

Authentic History—http://www.authentichistory.com

Brainy Betty—http://www.brainybetty.com/soundsforpower point.htm

CCmixter—http://ccmixter.org

E-Z Tracks—http://www.ez-tracks.com

Flickr—http://www.flickr.com (use the Creative Commons search)

Freeplay Music—http://www.freeplaymusic.com

Internet Audio Guy—http://www.internetaudioguy.com/iag/freemusic/freemusic.htm

PD Photo.org—http://pdphoto.org

Royalty Free Music—http://www.royaltyfreemusic.com

Stock Footage for Free—http://www.stockfootageforfree.com

Wikimedia Commons—http://commons.wikimedia.org

Many other sites offer a different free clip or image each week.

Note that you should carefully review the terms of service of each site to be certain you fully understand the license you are accepting to use the materials.

Question: When using Creative Commons, is it sufficient to provide documentation by including "Images Courtesy of the Creative Commons Community," or should each image owner be cited?

Answer: Because you are using the images under license, standard copyright assessments don't apply. The license will control. Look at the license for each image. Most require attribution at the least, which means you must identify each creator. Typically, I identify the author of each image on the page where it is used (usually in a small text box); plus, at the end of a Power-Point, I put a mediagraphy page that has thumbnails of each image with the creator's name (or handle if that is all I can find) and the source (such as Flickr). If your source makes other requirements (such as including a certain logo), you must comply with the directions to fulfill your license.

Chapter 4

Fair Use

The copyright law—Title 17, United States Code, Public Law 94-553, 90 Stat. 2541, as amended—gives citizens special exceptions to its strict legal copyright requirements. The purpose of these limited exceptions to the exclusive rights of copyright holders is so that knowledge and scholarship might advance. These special exceptions are called "fair use." Fair use, as defined in the law, has certain aspects that apply to everyone and others that apply only to certain classes of use, such as some uses in nonprofit schools and libraries.

Copyright law provides several instances in which reproduction of copyrighted items is permissible. These exceptions to Section 106 (the section where the rights are defined) are considered the "fair use exemptions" and are found in section 107 of the law. This section is brief enough to be reprinted here:

> *Notwithstanding the provisions of sections 106 and 106A, the fair use of a copyrighted work, including such use by reproduction in copies or phonorecords or by any other means specified by that section, for purposes such as criticism, comment, news reporting, teaching (including multiple copies for classroom use), scholarship, or research, is not an infringement of copyright. In determining whether the use made of a work in any particular case is a fair use the factors to be considered shall include:*
>
> 1. *The purpose and character of the use, including whether such use is of a commercial nature, or is for nonprofit educational purposes;*
>
> 2. *The nature of the copyrighted work;*
>
> 3. *The amount and substantiality of the portion used in relation to the copyrighted work as a whole; and*
>
> 4. *The effect of the use upon the potential market for or value of the copyrighted work.*
>   (17 U.S.C.A. § 107)

These four factors are also known as the four tests or factors of fair use. Basically, the law is saying that Congress intends to protect the rights of the author while still allowing legitimate educational and research uses of copyrighted materials.

Fair use is the most misunderstood aspect of copyright law, at least as far as schools are concerned. Common misconceptions about fair use include the following:

- *Misconception #1—Schools can use any copyright-protected materials they wish because they are schools.*

- *Misconception #2—Using materials is okay if you don't make a profit.*

- *Misconception #3—Promoting someone's work by distributing copies is justification for free use.*

- *Misconception #4—Using materials "for the good of kids" absolves one of copyright liability.*

All of the circumstances identified in the list of misconceptions *could* lead to a finding of fair use, but without other specific facts on which to rely, no one can come to a reliable conclusion. In other words, don't leap to conclusions about fair use with only a partial understanding of the facts. And anyone who tries to convince you that one fact or factor will always give a favorable (or unfavorable) outcome on a fair use analysis is someone to whom you should not be listening. It just isn't so.

Fair use is a balancing act. The idea is to balance carefully the need for an author to protect his right to exploit his work commercially (or privately) and the need for the public to have access to the fruits of knowledge so that we (the public) can advance scientific and creative endeavors. If authors were not able to profit from their creations and discoveries, few would create or research. However, in exchange for a limited-time exclusive right, the author or discoverer must allow limited use of the work so that others may build on the creation or discovery in an effort to increase human knowledge. It is a noble effort and one with which the courts struggle. To preserve as many of the rights of each side of the equation as possible is a Herculean task.

What is it?

Fair use provisions in the copyright law grant users conditional permission to use or reproduce certain copyrighted materials as long as the reproduction or use of those materials meets defined guidelines. Fair use goes hand in glove with the intent of copyright "to promote the progress of Science and Useful Arts." As defined in the law, fair use also balances the First Amendment free speech right with the rights of the author to control the use of his or her copyrighted work.

Fair use is not a right given to educators or any other person. Fair use is a defense applied in court to a charge of infringement. When a court considers a claim of fair use, it considers both the exemptions of the user and the rights of the author. The burden of proving fair use falls to the person using the material, so thorough knowledge of copyright law and associated guidelines is essential for librarians and educators using copyrighted works. Because there is seldom a clear-cut fair use situation, it is incumbent upon the educator to know the conditions under which one may claim fair use.

Difference between statutory fair use and guidelines

Essentially, there are two kinds of fair use:

1. Fair use as defined in the Copyright Act (statutory fair use). *All persons in the United States can avail themselves of this concept of fair use. The law defines the factors that you must consider when making a claim of fair use. Four factors are defined in the law, and the rights of both the creator and the person wishing to use the material are considered. Although the law does not indicate that any of the factors is to be considered with any more weight than any of the others, in practice, courts have weighted some of the factors as more significant than others.*

2. Fair use as defined by several sets of guidelines designed for educators and librarians. *These guidelines apply only to educational and library use of materials and are agreements between producers and consumers of various types of materials. All recognized guidelines were developed at the request of Congress, either through a congressionally appointed committee (e.g., Kastenmeier Report committees) or through a deliberative process organized through Congress*

(e.g., CONTU committees). Some other groups have attempted to generate their own sets of guidelines, but because the groups did not have input from stakeholders on both sides of the equation, the results of their efforts may be suspect. And because there is no congressional history on these ad hoc "guidelines" or "codes of best practices," courts are not obligated to take them into account when considering cases. On the other hand, courts will consider the involvement of Congress in the development of the CONTU guidelines and the Kastenmeier report as expressing the intent of Congress.

If the guidelines you are using don't permit a projected use, you can always fall back on the "four factors" fair use assessment to determine whether a particular use might still be fair, regardless of the limits suggested by the guidelines. You can take the best outcome of the two options.

For purposes of simplicity, it is easier to learn and administer guidelines than to go through the fair use tests. But if the guidelines do not permit a projected use, one can always fall back on the "four tests" fair use assessment to determine whether a particular use might be fair, regardless of the limits suggested by the guidelines. For example, the multimedia guidelines permit teachers and students to use video clips of 3 minutes or 10% of the whole if used in a multimedia presentation (additional requirements figure in this analysis). If the teacher or student wants to use a clip that lasts 3 minutes and 15 seconds, is that use possible? Because this use exceeds the multimedia guidelines, the educator or student can then apply the four tests of fair use to determine whether the use might be fair under that assessment. The guidelines are just that—guidelines, not absolutes. When using the specific limits in the guidelines, remember that they are clearly fair. But that doesn't mean more would not be fair. You just need to go through the more abstract assessment to determine your use.

Because educators have two avenues of fair use available (statutory fair use and guidelines), assess a proposed use from both aspects to see if one will allow the proposed use before abandoning the idea or attempting to license the material. Keeping the maximum fair uses available to educators is essential if there is a wish to avoid a period when fair use is abandoned in favor of licensing.

Examples of fair use analysis

Making a fair use assessment based on the factors outlined in the law (statutory fair use) is not a simple prospect. The law identifies four factors that must be considered in any fair use assessment. Some of the factors have subfactors that must also be considered. As noted previously, although the law doesn't specify that any one of the factors has a greater weight than any of the others, in actual practice. courts have given more consideration to at least one of the four (*Harper & Row v. Nation Enterprises,* 1985). Here we discuss the four factors and then go through a sample analysis.

It may be easier to visualize this as a process of weighing. Imagine a scale, with a plate on each side. One plate is "us" (the educators), and the other is "them" (the copyright owners). Between the two plates are four weights that freely slide from side to side, similar to the scales you remember from the doctor's office. The first three weights are not much different in size, but the last weight is bigger than the others. You don't want to move that one, just as at the doctor's office you get very apprehensive when the nurse moves that large weight at the back!

The weights are the four factors that affect a decision on fair use. Following are common-sense definitions to help you understand how to adjust those weights. Remember, one must evaluate *all* four factors before deciding which way the scales will tip. And a weight needn't be pushed all the way to one end of the scale or the other. Precious little in copyright is black or white, pro or con, and fair use is no exception. It isn't necessary to "win" on all four factors to get a favorable fair-use conclusion. To come to a reasonable conclusion, it is essential to apply the tests in the way a court would

Figure 4.1. Example of fair use test in action

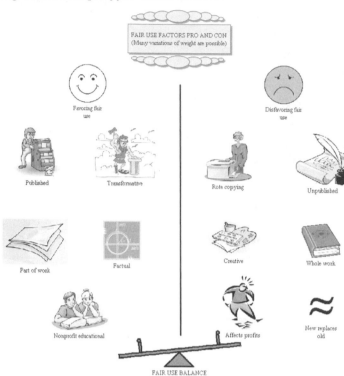

apply them, not as we might wish they would be applied. Gratuitous justification is the surest way to get oneself and one's organization in hot water.

Factor 1: Purpose and character of use

This first factor of fair use is probably the easiest one to assess. It is a two-part test, and either half could result in a determination of a favorable outcome on this test. As with all the tests, apply this one objectively.

The first test of fair use encourages educational use of materials, but it has been interpreted to favor "transformative" uses, such as putting a quotation in a term paper. In *Campbell v. Acuff-Rose Music, Inc.*, the Supreme Court defined "transformative" according to whether the new work merely "supersede[s] the . . . original creation, or instead adds something new, with a further purpose or different character, altering the first with new expression, meaning, or message; it asks, in other words, whether and to what extent the new work is 'transformative'" (1994, p. 579). Another relatively recent court case stated that making low-resolution thumbnail-sized copies of images available elsewhere on the Internet as part of an image search engine was a "transformative" use (*Kelly v. Arriba Soft Corp*, 2002). Even multiple copies of nontransformative uses can be acceptable in limited numbers. See the chapter on print materials for more details on multiple print copies. Keep in mind that, in the absence of or in addition to specific guidelines, all four tests of fair use will be considered in determining an appropriate application of the fair use doctrine. Factor 1 is actually fairly insignificant when all four factors are applied to a given situation.

Factor 1, part 1: Nonprofit educational use

Are you in a nonprofit public or private school, and is the use you are proposing for this entity? Such a use would get a favorable assessment on this portion of this factor; however, you must continue through the remaining three factors before you have a reasonable assessment of your use. But even with a negative result here, one may continue to the other half of this factor as well as to the other three. For-profit schools, such as Edison Schools, some charter schools, and some private schools, would not receive a favorable assessment on this portion of factor 1. No matter what result you get on this portion of the test, continue to the rest of the assessments.

Factor 1, part 2: Criticism, commentary, news reporting

Any of these—criticism, commentary, or news reporting—can qualify a use on this half of the first factor. For example, if a for-profit newspaper uses an excerpt from a novel when publishing a book review, this portion of the first factor can be met. Criticism involves making critical judgments about a work, and the critic usually includes portions of the work to make her points. Commentary involves writing explanations of a work and may or may not be critical. News reporting is exactly what it states. Although intended to apply to the news industry, this selection could apply to the school newspaper, school television reports, and so on.

Note that you do not need to satisfy *both* halves of this factor to move this factor to your side of our metaphorical scale. For example, the local television station can still use a portion of a movie in a review under this factor (taking into account the rest of the factors, of course) even though it does not satisfy the first half of this factor regarding nonprofit educational setting.

Factor 2: Nature of copyrighted work

Factor two of the four is a two-pronged question. Neither half eliminates consideration as fair use, but having both on your side greatly enhances your fair use defense.

Factor 2, part 1: Factual or creative?

This question pertains to the content of the material being used. As discussed before, facts cannot receive copyright protection. Therefore, appropriating facts from a copyright-protected work would be less hazardous than taking portions from something creative. Materials that would lose on this factor would be literature (novels, poems, drama), art, music, and so on. Materials that would tend to draw this factor to your side of an evaluation would be newspaper accounts, almanacs, maps, and other factual representations of information. An important point to note is that although the *facts* themselves are free to use, the *expression* of those facts is not, except in the excerpts that could qualify for a fair use assessment. For example, an encyclopedia article is written from and about factual material. The facts contained in the article are free to use, but the way the author of the encyclopedia article has expressed those facts is not, unless you are taking a brief quote. Also, a work such as an almanac is composed primarily of facts. The facts themselves are free to use, but the selection and arrangement of those facts, plus the expression of the facts if presented in narrative or graphic form, is the basis for the copyright in the almanac.

Factor 2, part 2: Published or not published?

The second half of this factor asks whether the work is published. One might assume that because an author/creator who has published a work expects it to be seen and used by the public, there would be slightly more protection given to published works than to unpublished ones. In reality, unpublished works are more closely protected because the author/creator obviously did not wish the material to be made public. Unpublished materials would include such things as letters, diaries, family photographs, e-mails, and unpublished manuscripts.

"Published" in copyright parlance may not have the meaning generally attributed to the word. The 1976 law defines "publication" as "the distribution of copies or phonorecords of a work to the public by sale or other transfer of ownership, or by rental, lease, or lending. The offering to distribute copies or phonorecords to a group of persons for purposes of further distribution, public performance, or public display constitutes publication. A public performance or display of a work does not of itself constitute publication" (17 U.S.C.A. § 101). Something offered for sale in the marketplace is obviously "published," even if no one buys it. But a speech of Dr. Martin Luther King Jr. was found to be *un*published even though his organization had distributed copies of the speech to the press on the day the speech was given (*Estate of Martin Luther King, Jr. v. CBS, Inc.*, 1999). In contrast, author J. D. Salinger successfully defeated a fair use defense by a Salinger biographer who published some of his unpublished letters, even when the author did not quote directly from the letters but only closely paraphrased them (*Salinger v. Random House,* 1987). The *Salinger* court explained that "protected expression has been 'used' whether it has been quoted verbatim or only paraphrased" (p. 97). There has been no clear legal assessment of whether a Web page is published when it is mounted on the Web or whether something distributed to family, to friends, or even within an organization such as your school is officially "published." (Note that out-of-print is not the same as unpublished.)

Factor 3: Amount of work used?

This factor is a little clearer to understand. The question is, basically, how much of the work will you use? As a matter of practicality, the less you use, the better. If you want to use a short paragraph from a large Tom Clancy novel as an example of a metaphor, you are probably okay here. However, if you want to use a haiku, you will undoubtedly use *all* of it. Anytime you use *all* of something, there are going to be questions about this factor. Anytime you use *most* of something, you will also probably get an unfavorable evaluation on this factor, as well. Remember, it is only one factor of four, so complete the analysis before you give up.

When there are analyses of this factor, the phrase "significant amount" appears frequently. For example, when asked how much of a musical recording would be considered "significant," a copyright attorney explained that if one can tell what song is being used, the amount is "significant." That amount could be even a few bars and in some cases even a few notes. How much of a work is "significant" is a judgment call and one that a court would adjudicate. A case involving film is illustrative. Television network CBS used short excerpts from several Charlie Chaplin films in creating a retrospective of the work of the legendary comedian. From one film, approximately an hour and a half long, CBS extracted about 55 seconds. Similar extracts of up to about 3 minutes were taken from other films. The court found that the use of the excerpts was "qualitatively substantial" and found against CBS (*Roy Export v. Columbia Broadcast System, Inc.,* 1980, p. 1146). Common sense would tell you that copying 10 pages from a picture book constitutes a far more significant extract than copying 10 pages from a novel. If someone has told you that you can always copy 10 percent of something ("the 10 percent rule") under a claim of fair use, please discard that misconception. There is no such thing as a 10 percent rule as part of a fair use determination (though you will see that figure referenced later in the multimedia guidelines). Every fair use assessment is individual based on the facts of the particular use.

Essence of work

The term "essence of the work" is often tossed about when discussing how much one may use under the fair use defense. This term is used to explain a short segment of a work that embodies the spirit of an entire work. A scene of a movie or a phrase of a song or a section of a book might all be considered to represent the "message" or "spirit" of that work. If one uses something that embodies the entire piece within a small segment, one has—in essence—used the entire work.

This concept may be explained with some examples. If you are aware of the book *Rosie's Walk* (Aladdin, 1971), you will recall that the entire text of the book is spread across two pages at the beginning. The rest of the book consists of pictures of Rosie the hen being pursued across the barnyard by a fox, blithely ignorant that she is on his dinner agenda. The mishaps that befall the fox in his pursuit of Rosie are featured in the pictures, but there is no text to describe what happens. So if you were to copy the two textual pages from this 32-page book, you would have copied a small portion of the book, yet you would have copied the text in its entirety! These two pages would easily be considered the "essence" of the work.

An important Supreme Court case on this issue involved former U.S. president Gerald R. Ford. President Ford, after he left office, wrote his memoirs under the title *A Time to Heal* (Harper & Row, 1979). His publisher, Harper & Row, negotiated an agreement with *Time* magazine to publish an excerpt from the book, at or near the time of publication of the book. The excerpt was to be from the section of the book in which former President Ford explained why he had pardoned former President Richard Nixon. This was a hot issue of the day and much-sought-after information. *The Nation* magazine managed to get a copy of the unpublished manuscript, from which they published a 300-word excerpt before the *Time* article could appear. This scooped *Time*'s article.

Harper & Row sued *The Nation*, claiming *The Nation* had violated copyright law. *The Nation* claimed that its use of the excerpt was a fair use. The U.S. Supreme Court held that *The Nation* had indeed violated the copyright of the work, ruling that the 300 words chosen were sufficient to be considered "the essence of the work" and that the use of unpublished material was significant in the assessment (*Harper & Row v. Nation Enterprises,* 1985).

There is one exception for this "essence of the work" rule: true parody. The Supreme Court held that the band 2 Live Crew could use a substantial part of the song "Pretty Woman" in a parody of the song, so it is apparent that how much is "too much" varies from case to case (*Campbell v. Acuff-Rose Music,* 1994). The fairness of excessive copying can be determined only after taking into account the other three factors and the circumstances as a whole. Just remember that this is only one of four factors, so the use of a large portion of a work is not always a completely disqualifying point. This case also cited the "transformative" nature of the resulting work as significant in the analysis. A transformative work is one that puts the borrowed material to a new or novel use. The Supreme Court explained why this type of parody was an exception to what would otherwise require license or permission:

> *Indeed, as to parody pure and simple, it is more likely that the new work will not affect the market for the original . . . by acting as a substitute for it . . . The market for potential derivative uses includes only those that creators of original works would in general develop or license others to develop. Yet the unlikelihood that creators of imaginative works will license critical reviews or lampoons of their own productions removes such uses from the very notion of a potential licensing market. "People ask . . . for criticism, but they only want praise."*

In still another case, a schoolteacher copied 11 pages of a 24-page handout from another teacher's copyrighted work on cake decorating. The courts held that the 11 pages constituted too much of the copied work to be classified as fair use and that the 11 pages also constituted the most important sections of the work copied. Furthermore, the new work competed directly with the original because both were educational for a similar audience (*Marcus v. Rowley,* 1983).

Schools will want to note that common problems under this factor include using identifiable portions of songs, using graphics (because generally the entire graphic is used), and using poetry. Of course, anytime you use *all* of anything, you should seriously consider this factor. Having an unfavorable outcome on this single factor doesn't mean you won't prevail on the other three, but it is worth significant deliberation.

Factor 4: Effect of use on market for or value of work

This factor is the "eggplant that ate Chicago" of the four factors. Some courts have given this sole factor more importance than the other three even though the law does not indicate that one of the four factors is more significant in a fair use assessment. In fact, the U.S. Supreme Court has said that this factor "is undoubtedly the single most important element of fair use" (*Harper & Row v. Nation*

Enterprises, 1985, p. 566). Essentially, if your use would deprive someone of sales of the item or other items the copyright owner might reasonably develop, this factor would come into play. Courts actually consider potential damage, rather than actual damages, when weighing this factor. The Supreme Court explained that "to negate fair use one need only show that if the challenged use 'should become widespread, it would adversely affect the *potential* market for the copyrighted work'" (p. 568) (citing *Sony Corp. of America v. Universal City Studios, Inc.,* 464 U.S.417, 451 (1984) (emphasis added); *id.,* at 484, and n.36 (collecting cases) (dissenting opinion).

One must also consider that the "value of" fits in here. If your use would somehow harm the original author, or his ability to capitalize on his work, even in ways you might not imagine or agree with, this factor can become significant. Some people like to rationalize by saying that their use of a work actually *promotes* the original work. However, it is not up to you, the person borrowing the original work, to make that decision. The copyright owner alone has the right to decide where and when his work will be promoted. A wise person once advised, "If the copyright owner wants you to help promote his work, I promise you he will contact you!"

Commercial use

In general, any commercial use of a work or portion of a work will yield a poor result on this factor. For schools, that would mean any use that transfers money, even if there is no net profit. For example, if you sell yearbooks, and you have used unlicensed/unpermissioned copyrighted graphics in the yearbook, this use would be considered "commercial." The same would hold true if you are selling CDs of the band concert or t-shirts with a cartoon on them or making any other transaction involving copyright-protected materials used without license or permission.

Misrepresentation

An important case to understand regarding "loss of value" is the *Ticketmaster v. Microsoft* case (1997). In this case, Microsoft had created a link to the Ticketmaster ticket-ordering page, a page buried deep within the Ticketmaster Web site. Ticketmaster sold advertising on its home page, but not on the pages deep within its site. Ticketmaster and Microsoft had negotiated a relationship in which Ticketmaster links would be included within a new Microsoft Web site, but negotiations had broken down. Microsoft went ahead and made the link to the Ticketmaster ordering page anyway. Ticketmaster claimed that Microsoft was using the Ticketmaster trademark and logos without permission, implying a relationship that did not exist. Microsoft contended that the use of the link was fair use.

Because Microsoft used frames on the Web site, Web pages belonging to Ticketmaster appeared to be part of the Microsoft Web site. The direct URLs do not appear in the browser location window when frames are in use; only the URL of the master site displays, in this case Microsoft's Seattle Sidewalk. Ticketmaster contended that such obscuring of the origin of the Web pages and the use of the Ticketmaster trademark and logo were misrepresentations and not subject to a claim of fair use (*Ticketmaster v. Microsoft,* 2007). This case was eventually settled out of court. In the settlement Microsoft agreed to link only to the top page of Ticketmaster's site, where there advertising and other indications of the ownership of the content were visible.

The significance of this case for schools lies in the fact that there are often Web pages deep within online sites that may be useful for schools. Although most links to deep content will be for instructional purposes, creating links to deep pages may result in implied relationships and/or misrepresentation of relationships that are offensive to the owners of the sites to whose pages are linked, especially if the linking school uses framing technology that hides the URL of the original site. To be sure, it is always safe to ask permission to deep link, but relying on fair use when your link implies association or obscures the source of the material can be problematic (Bailey, 2008). Even further, owners of sites to which you link may pull some nasty tricks if they are unhappy with your link.

What would happen if everyone were to . . .

In analyzing a complex copyright situation, a copyright attorney once advised that the court, in assessing the final factor of fair use, must assess what would happen to the "market for or value of" the work as if *everyone* were to do what one person or entity is proposing to do. The Supreme Court agreed in *Harper & Row v. The Nation* (1985, p. 568). In other words, that you are just a small classroom in a rural school in middle America isn't the issue. The question is, if everybody were to repeat this same behavior with the same fair use defense, what effect would *that* use have on the market for or value of the work?

Looking at a case from this standpoint makes sense. For example, if an English teacher duplicated an editorial in today's newspaper for her class, the use is minimal for that class. But if every English teacher across the country were to do the same thing, would that affect the market for the newspaper? Likely not. People would still want to read the comics, check out the want ads, and get the scores from the ballgame last night. Making copies of that editorial would not likely affect the market for the paper.

However, suppose a second-grade teacher made copies of an entire picture book for her class. The court would ask, "What would happen if every teacher were to distribute copies of the entire picture book to his or her class?" You can easily see how the broad reproduction might affect the market for the book. Why purchase a book when your teacher is going to give you a copy for free? In addition, there is the issue of the value of the work. The copyright owner may want that book printed only in hardback because the cost cutting that must occur to get an affordable paperback copy reduces the quality of the outstanding illustrations—a significant part of the book. The copyright owner does not want the reputation (or value) of the book to be abridged by substandard reproduction.

This same rationale applies to translations. Making a foreign-language translation of a work is a foreseeable type of exploitation of a work that would typically be reserved for the copyright owner. Publishers are exceptionally picky about their translations and usually discourage translations by amateurs. Particularly for fiction and poetry, language is key. Publishers seek out noted authors to do translations of other authors' materials so that they can be certain that the translation retains the same subtle language effects as the original. The Supreme Court explained that "because individual words carry 'a life and force of their own,' translations never fully capture the sense of the original" (*San Francisco Arts & Athletics, Inc., v. U.S. Olympic Committee,* 1987, pp. 559–560). Therefore, publishers are not typically generous about permissions for translations. A poor translation could ruin the market for the work in the segment of the market where such a poor translation is made available.

Various types of guidelines

In addition to the statutory fair-use tests, various sets of guidelines have developed over the years. The first appeared not long after the 1976 law was passed. Because the text of the law was too vague to be of much help in deciding whether a particular use was permitted, the U.S. House of Representatives and the Senate issued reports in an effort to determine an equitable balance between the rights of copyright owners (who may or may not be the actual creators of the copyrighted works) and those of the general public.

The House report included a set of guidelines (often referred to as the "congressional guidelines" or the "fair use guidelines," http://www.copyright.gov/circs/circ21.pdf, pp. 5–7) developed at the suggestion of the House Judiciary Committee by the Ad Hoc Committee of Educational Institutions and Organizations on Copyright Law Revision, the Authors League of America, and the Association of American Publishers. The courts may take this statement of intent into account when deciding cases of copyright infringement in an educational context. The House report was quite explicit on the amount and types of copying that could be considered fair use, but it went on to say that additional copying might be fair if it could meet the four factors of fair use. These specific limits are discussed in the section on print. At the same time, a similar committee developed guidelines for educational uses of music (the Music Publishers Association of the United States, the National Music Publishers' Association, the Music Teachers National Association, the Music Educators National Conference, the National Association of Schools of Music, and the Ad Hoc Committee on Copyright Law Revision). Both guidelines were accepted by the House and Senate conference committee that drafted the final version of the law, and the acceptance is documented in the Congressional Record of September 21 and 22, 1976). Those guidelines are discussed in detail in the sections on video and music, respectively. In 1979, a similar committee, gathered at the request of Congress, developed guidelines for off-air taping of television programming (United States Copyright Office, 2009).

In addition to the early congressional guidelines came regulations on interlibrary loans and resource sharing, components of an active library program (United States Copyright Office, 2009). As technology advanced, presentation packages such as PowerPoint® and KidPix™ stretched the limits of fair use. Pressure from educators on producers finally yielded a set of congressionally sanctioned guidelines to govern the use of copyright-protected materials in these types of presentations (see chapter 8 for details).

The passage of the TEACH Act, codifying rules for using copyrighted materials in distance learning situations, represented a giant leap forward. The new advance in course distribution required a parallel reorganization of fair use permissions to enable online classes to have fair use of materials similar to that which face-to-face classes had enjoyed for many years.

Each time technology took a leap forward, fair use guidelines followed behind, trying to keep up. Unfortunately, when guidelines were created to handle the newer technologies, older guidelines were not updated to match. Hence, you will find that what is okay in one medium is not okay in another. This disconnect is a major reason that so many people find understanding and administering copyright to be so confusing!

To whom does it apply?

As you go through the various guidelines, there are several things to keep in mind. The first will be, to whom does this apply? As we discussed before, the statutory "four tests" of fair use may be applied to any citizen at any time. Some of the guidelines that we discuss in upcoming chapters may apply only to teachers, or only to librarians, or only to students. When making assessments, it is very important to remain clear about whom you are discussing.

Situation will also be an important consideration. Where, when, and how will these materials be used? What may be fair use in one instance may not be fair use in another. Pay particular attention to the situation when you are looking at the guidelines that will follow.

Remember, it is permissible to "shop" for the fair use evaluation that is most favorable to your use. If guidelines don't permit the needed use, you can always fall back to the standard fair-use assessment to see if your additional use can be justified. It is important to always press for the maximum permitted use because those rights not used will eventually erode away.

And finally, the guidelines were written by educators and publishers, not by Congress, so they are typically easier to understand than the statute. Guidelines are certainly easier to apply than the fair use balancing test. Sometimes the restrictions of guidelines will not allow enough of some medium to meet the teaching need of a student or teacher. For example, the multimedia guidelines allow using up to 30 seconds or 10 percent of a song in a multimedia presentation, whichever is less. For a typical rock song, 10 percent is 18 seconds, so the limit is the lower of 18 and 30. However, suppose that a musical phrase that the teacher wants to use is 20 seconds in length. Does that mean the segment is out because it exceeds the 18-second limitation? Or does it mean that the teacher must truncate the phrase to be able to use it? Not necessarily. The teacher can go through the four-test analysis that is available to all citizens. If the use can pass the four tests, she can use the 20 seconds with confidence.

So for easiest use, begin with any guidelines that apply to your particular situation. If you are not able to justify your use under that set of guidelines, fall back to the standard four-factor fair use assessment. If you fail on both options, your use may not be fair, and you will want to investigate permission or a license.

Schools versus libraries

As pointed out earlier, everyone has certain fair use rights. Schools get a special set of fair use rights to help them educate students. Libraries get another set of special guidelines to help them achieve their civic mission. School libraries get the best of all possible worlds because they can claim the school exemptions, the library exemptions, and the fair use exemptions afforded all citizens. The school library exemptions don't extend to the parent school, however. Only activities within the library are acceptable candidates for the library exemptions.

The best part of having the library exemptions may be that if you have a library, you probably have a librarian. School librarians are the only educators who routinely receive an education on copyright law during their training. Even school administrators seldom get more than a cursory copyright education. Of course, having an education doesn't make the librarian the copyright police. The librarian is a resource person who is able to help students, faculty, and administrators to puzzle out the conundrum that is copyright. Look at your librarian as the copyright *consultant*, not the copyright cop. But whatever role the librarian plays, the librarian is a perfect choice to help explain the various guidelines and statutory exemptions.

Question: In a cooking class, there is a collection of cookbooks in an office area. Each student selects and copies a recipe from a book in the office. They use their chosen recipe in preparing a meal in class. Cookbooks are not allowed into the classroom/lab area. Each student copies only one recipe, and the students are choosing from a variety of books. With repeated use by a large number of students, and over the course of a semester, a large percentage of any book might be copied. Is this practice "fair use"?

Answer: Recipes, or at least recipes that are a list of ingredients and simple assembly instructions, are not protectable by copyright. The copyright that you see on the cookbook is a "compilation copyright" meaning that the selection and arrangement (and any prefatory material) is what is protected, not the recipes themselves. However, even without this limited copyright on recipes, this type of copying would likely be fair use because each student chooses what he copies and makes only a single copy for personal use. In that respect, this type of copying is similar to a class of students coming to the library to do research on the same topic. There is a high likelihood that many of them will make copies of similar material, but as long as they choose the copies to make and make only one copy for personal use, there should be no problem under fair use.

Works cited

Bailey, J. (2008). Is "deep linking" in trouble? *The Blog Herald.* Retrieved June 6, 2009, from http://www.blogherald.com/2008/12/29/is-deep-linking-in-trouble/.

Campbell v. Acuff-Rose Music, 510 U.S. 569 (1994).

Estate of Martin Luther King, Jr. v. CBS, Inc., 194 F.3d 1211 (11th Cir. 1999).

Harper & Row, Publishers, Inc. v. Nation Enterprises, 471 U.S. 539 (1985).

Kelly v. Arriba Soft Corp., 280 F.3d 937 (9th Cir. 2002).

Marcus v. Rowley, 695 F.2d 1171 (9th Cir. 1983).

Roy Export Co. v. Columbia Broadcast System, Inc., 503 F. Supp. 1137 (D.C.N.Y. 1980).

Salinger v. Random House, Inc., 811 F.2d 90 (2d Cir. 1987).

San Francisco Arts & Athletics, Inc. v. U.S. Olympic Committee, 483 U.S. 522 (1987).

Ticketmaster v. Microsoft, C.D. Calif., Civil Action No. 97-3055DPP, filed 1997.

Ticketmaster v. Microsoft. (2007). Retrieved June 6, 2009, from http://www.netlitigation.com/netlitigation/cases/ticketmaster.htm.

United States Copyright Office. (2009). *Circular 21: Reproduction of copyrighted works by educators and librarians.*

Chapter 5

Print Materials in Schools

Because the four factors cited in section 107 were less than clear, representatives of affected education and publishing groups met to work out much more specific explanations of the law. The result was endorsed by Congress when it was accepted by the conference committee charged with reconciling the House and Senate versions of the 1976 Copyright Act (United States Copyright Office, 2009). These congressional guidelines, as they are called, are not law per se, but they indicate agreement between educators and publishers, and they are used as benchmarks against which copyright infringement may be gauged. The congressional conference committee explained about the guidelines, "The Committee believes the guidelines are a reasonable interpretation of the minimum standards of fair use. Teachers will know that copying within the guidelines is fair use (United States Copyright Office, 2009, p. 8). Courts use legislative intent when they try to determine exactly what Congress meant when it enacted a law. The idea is to have a court case resolved in the way that Congress intended when it passed the applicable law. Because the guidelines were read into the record as the expressed intent of Congress when it passed the 1976 law, courts can put a lot of stock in the report.

The guidelines state minimum standards of fair use; certain other types of copying may be permitted. Exactly what those other types of copying are and how much is tolerated would vary depending on the judge and jury hearing the case. Yes, the final arbiter of what is permitted is a court of law. Although you might be convinced that the pages you plan to copy fall under the fair use exemption, the copyright owner may have entirely different views. The most conservative line is generally safe, whereas straying very far afield of these guidelines is an open invitation to litigation (though not necessarily unfair). One might make an analogy to driving. Going 31 miles per hour in a 30-mile-per-hour zone probably wouldn't merit a ticket, but going 50 miles per hour in the same zone would likely alert even the most laid-back officer. In a school situation, sometimes one is more comfortable giving teachers and students clear directions and numbers on which to judge appropriate behavior. These congressional guidelines do just that—provide specific limits to acceptable behavior. That doesn't mean that more is not fair or that more will necessarily land you in court.

These guidelines were developed primarily for print materials because print material was predominant in 1976 when the guidelines were written. Although there are specific limits and restrictions based on the format of material, there are also some general tests imposed on all educational uses of copyrighted works. These tests are more concrete and easier to apply to educational and library copying than are the fair use factors. The additional tests are those of brevity (defined by specific lengths and numbers of items), spontaneity (see following questions), and cumulative effect.

You must give an affirmative answer to both of the following questions before a claim of fair use may be made under these guidelines:

1. *Reproduction or display is at the instance and inspiration of the individual teacher.*

2. *The inspiration and decision to use the work and the moment of its use for maximum teaching effectiveness are so close in time that it would be unreasonable to expect a timely reply to a request for permission.*

Essentially, these spontaneity questions restrict educators from having materials (or television programs) copied in anticipation of demand. All requests for duplication, whether photocopies or off-air recording, must come directly from the teacher involved. In other words, an administrator, department head, librarian, or other person in a position of authority may not direct teachers or librarians to copy materials under the fair use exemption. In addition, a teacher's superior may not dictate to the teacher that copyright-protected materials must be copied. A supervisor may *suggest* specific materials, but it is the responsibility of the individual teacher to decide to make the copies. This requirement is often called a "bottom up" copying scheme as opposed to a "top down" order. See the chapter on managing copyright for appropriate responses when told by a superior to make copies.

What typical activities are covered?

The photocopy machine is probably the biggest danger spot in the school from the standpoint of print copying. Teachers photocopy materials at an astounding rate, and they do not always have the authority to make multiple copies of the items they are copying. Although the print guidelines are very specific about how much and how many times something may be copied, and also specify items that may *never* be copied, few teachers or administrators have ever seen the guidelines. If someone were to do an audit of the copies made at the copy machine in a given week of the second semester of school (or possibly even the second marking period), one would find that the vast majority of the copies being made were infringing.

Typical school activities (permitted and not permitted) that are addressed by the rules in this chapter include the following:

- *copying teacher-made tests/worksheets/letters*
- *copying commercial workbook pages/worksheets*
- *copying coloring book pages/sheets*
- *copying sheet music*
- *copying graphics onto bulletin boards freehand or via a projection device*

- *copying articles from professional magazines to distribute at faculty meetings*

- *copying graphics/maps/charts onto transparency film*

- *copying test booklets for assessment*

- *copying textbooks when there are not enough for every student*

- *copying magazine articles/newsletters for students (Weekly Reader, etc.)*

- *copying activity cards and instructional materials when there are not enough for every student*

- *copying test sheets (SRA kit sheets, etc.) when the original supply runs out*

- *copying flyers with graphics for PTA, etc.*

- *scanning book covers for library Web pages*

This is not a complete list of the types of print copying activities that are possible or even common in schools. But knowing the rules for these activities will provide guidance to other types of activities.

Photocopying—issues

Typical photocopying issues to which schools will want to pay particular attention are as follows:

- *photocopying consumable materials such as workbooks (whether or not the book is still in print or in adoption)*

- *photocopying more materials per term or year (depending on the length of the course) than allowed in the guidelines*

- *using photocopies to substitute for purchase of materials (as in making copies of textbook chapters rather than buying a copy of the text when you are a few short)*

- *administrators or curriculum coordinators directing teachers or entire grade levels or courses to photocopy protected materials (when such decisions may be made only by the teachers themselves, individually)*

- *not getting permission to repeatedly copy materials after the first fair use*

- *copying student work to retain as exemplars*

These items are not all fair or unfair. Each just needs a thorough assessment.

its planned earnings. If a publisher wanted to sell photocopy masters, it would have created the book differently and certainly would have priced it differently.

Under the guidelines, though, if you suddenly find yourself a few workbooks short, as soon as you put in an order for enough copies for all the students, you may make copies from a purchased copy you have (one page at a time) until your purchased copies arrive. Even if it takes six months for the order to arrive, you can legally make the interim copies.

If your boss tells you that the school has no plans to purchase the workbooks, and you must make copies, you have a couple of options. You can attempt to educate your boss on copyright law. That may or may not be a successful strategy. If the boss rejects your attempts to comply with copyright law, investigate your school policies. Chances are you have a copyright policy that requires all personnel to comply with copyright law (most schools do). Then you can bring up the problem of violating board policy. For some bosses, violation of policy is a more immediate threat than violating federal law. There may also be a state law that says a school or government employee cannot be ordered to violate any law. That, too, may have some impact on your boss.

If all those options still fail, I recommend you put your objections (on any of the bases identified here) in writing (dated and signed) and hand them to your boss. Keep a copy for yourself. Then do as you are told. If the district gets in trouble for your actions, you will have ample evidence that you tried everything you could to do the right thing.

Phonorecords—issues

No, we aren't talking about 12-inch black vinyl discs. Not all copying involves the photocopier. An audio-recording of a print work is called a "phonorecord." It is important to note that reading a book onto a tape or disc is exactly the same thing, according to the law, as putting that book on the photocopier and copying every page. Most educators recognize that photocopying an entire book is not usually a fair use, yet they feel entitled to make an audio recording of a book for a student who is a struggling reader and to retain that copy to put in the library.

The types of phonorecord issues that will interest schools include

- *reading library books onto cassette tapes or digital media to assist struggling readers,*

- *reading books onto cassette tapes or digital media to assist visually impaired students, and*

- *reading the newspaper onto tapes or digital media to take to senior citizens, as a service project.*

Again, not all these uses are fair or unfair, but they merit close investigation.

Graphics—issues

Nothing perks up a tired worksheet like clip art or other graphics. However, using graphics can be problematic in certain situations. Although the guidelines do address graphics for instruction, many of the graphics used in schools are for decoration, not for instruction. The guidelines and the fair use tests are designed to support use of copyright-protected materials for direct instruction, but making your school or classroom look "cute" or "welcoming" is not a stated purpose of fair use.

The types of graphics issues that schools will need to pay particular attention to include the following:

- *copying/enlarging cartoon characters, greeting card graphics, and images from books/coloring books for the purpose of decoration of bulletin boards, classroom walls, etc.*

- *using graphic characters on school t-shirts, book bags, signs, etc.*

- *using characters from library books to create murals or other decorative elements*

Murals—issues

Murals are lovely ways to decorate school walls. They warm up walls that otherwise would have a definite "institutional" feel. As long as students, teachers, or outside artists are creating or copying their own work, murals are not a problem. When you need to be concerned is when the mural artist uses the work of others in the mural. The work of others can be famous paintings (painted after 1923 and not in the public domain) or—more commonly—representations of famous book characters such as the

Cat in the Hat or Disney characters. These instantly recognizable characters are protected not only by copyright but also by trademark in most cases. The artists/copyright owners/trademark owners may aggressively protect these characters. In fact, a librarian in Florida reported that representatives from Disney actually arrived with paint and painted over a mural that contained Disney characters. Insist that paid artists create their own works in any murals they create for your schools. See http://www.eyeful-art.com for some excellent examples.

Scanning—issues

Changing format on the scan is the biggest problem you will encounter with this method of reproduction. When you create a scan, you create not only a copy but a *digital* copy of an analog work. Digital copies may be copied infinitely without any of the degradation that is common to analog copies such as photocopies. Producers are exceptionally nervous about allowing their material to be digitized, fearing that it will "escape" and be lost forever.

Here are common activities involving scanning that you will want to watch:

- *scanning photos for yearbooks, Web pages, and newspapers*

- *scanning book covers for library catalogs and Web pages*

- *scanning maps for Web pages*

What rights are affected?

Of the reserved rights of the copyright holder, several are of particular import in issues of print reproduction. Those rights include the following.

Reproduction

- *Making copies is how a print copyright owner makes money. If you make the copies locally, the copyright owner gets no money from your copies.*

Distribution

- *Where do the copies you make go? Copyright owners get to decide where (or if) their works will be distributed. Especially in matters of out-of-print works, copyright owners may not wish these materials to be available because they are out-of-date or not fashionable, or the publisher has other materials with which this work may compete. All would be valid reasons not to have the work available in the marketplace. Perhaps the*

recording medium of any type is exactly the same thing, copyright-wise, as putting the book on the photocopier and copying every page. And you are going to do this multiple times. The publisher could make a good case that there are audio recordings of the book that could be used in place of the homemade recordings, so this is replacing an authorized copy of the work. The use isn't transformative in any way—the teacher is copying the book exactly as it was written. There is no "value added," no interpretation, and no criticism or commentary. The work is creative, not factual. And the teacher is reading the book in its entirety. A homemade recording of the whole work would certainly replace a purchased recording of the work. I can't see any of the four fair use factors falling in your favor except for the educational purpose, but that standing alone is not sufficient to support a finding of fair use.

Question: A teacher has plastered his walls with newspaper cartoons. Is it a copyright violation for teachers to cut out cartoons and display them?

Answer: Presuming that the teacher bought the book or newspaper, she may cut it up and post the cartoons on her wall. The teacher may also make a single copy of a cartoon for her personal use or for teaching. That single copy can be on transparency film. The cartoon may also be scanned into a multimedia authoring program (see chapter 8 on multimedia for details).

publisher feels the work is inappropriate for the venue in which you propose to distribute the work. Such decisions are reserved for the copyright owner, alone, to make.

Adaptation

- *When you make changes in print materials, you are adapting them. Perhaps you want to take a book and turn it into a play to present to parents for a PTA meeting. Or you wish to translate a work into Spanish for your Hispanic students. Or you wish to take a cartoon and turn it into a large paper "run through" for the football or basketball team. Naturally, you will want to adjust the picture to put the characters in the team uniform. You might write new words to go with a piece of sheet music. All these typical activities are considered adaptation and are within the rights of the copyright owner.*

Display

- *Print materials are displayed when they are put in a public place. Display could include book covers on bulletin boards, student work posted in the halls or on a Web page, and newsletters and yearbooks.*

What guidelines affect print materials?

When considering what fair uses one may make of print materials, there are several things to keep in mind. First, is the material protected at all? Remember that anything published before 1923 is in the public domain in the United States. Materials published after 1923 but before 1976 that were not registered appropriately, or not renewed, are also in the public domain. You may use public domain materials for any purpose whatsoever.

If you find that the material is indeed protected, you may decide to seek a fair use defense for your use of the materials. You have two choices: find a set of guidelines that applies to the materials you wish to use, or apply the statutory four tests of fair use. Finding that the materials are print, you may elect to use the print guidelines to see whether your proposed use is within the limits of the guidelines. If your use exceeds the guidelines, you may go through a fair use analysis to determine whether your use may be considered fair via that route.

When the 1976 law was passed, there were no guidelines. There was only the fair use section of the law (section 107). The law is cryptic and difficult for laypeople to understand. Representative Kastenmeier of the House Judiciary Subcommittee headed a House committee that worked with publishers and education representatives to clarify the fair use definitions codified in the law and to give educators understandable, workable limits for fair use. These limits are known collectively as the Kastenmeier report or the classroom photocopying guidelines, or sometimes the print guidelines.

Kastenmeier report

The first half of the report covers print works (specifically books and periodicals), and the second half includes guidelines on the use of printed music. Also appended are short guidelines on replacement copying and repair of damaged materials (Special Interest Video Sales Group, 1995).

Details of report
Single copies for teachers

A teacher may copy (or ask to have copied) for the purposes of research, teaching, or preparation for teaching any of the following:

- *a single copy of a chapter from a book*
- *a single copy of an article from a periodical or newspaper*
- *a single copy of a short story, short essay, or short poem, even if it is contained in a collection*
- *a single copy of a chart, graph, diagram, drawing, cartoon, or picture from a book, periodical, or newspaper* (United States Copyright Office)

The teacher may retain the single copies of these materials in files for personal or research use or for use in teaching. This interpretation would permit reading the material to a class. A liberal, but not unjustifiable, interpretation of the guidelines would allow the teacher to write the material on the blackboard or overhead projector for use in teaching as well. In addition, a librarian could make a photocopy of a book cover for use on bulletin boards promoting reading or special events and could retain that copy for use in future displays.

The preceding permissions seem reasonable. The congressional guidelines, however, provide some limitations on these options. There are four significant prohibitions to the print permission, three of which have application to single copies for teachers:

"Copying shall not be used to create or to replace or substitute for anthologies, compilations, or collective works. Such replacement or substitution may occur whether copies of various works or excerpts therefrom are accumulated or reproduced and used separately." [Note: In other words, you can't create your own books by gathering bits and pieces from other sources. This would include notebooks of editorial cartoons, comic strips, poems, series of essays, and the like.]

"There shall be no copying from works intended to be 'consumable' in the course of study or of teaching. These include workbooks, exercises, standardized tests and test booklets and answer sheets, and like consumable material."

"Copying shall not: substitute for the purchase of books, publishers' reprints or periodicals; be directed by higher authority; or be repeated with respect to the same item by the same teacher from term to term." (United States Copyright Office, 2009)

The prohibitions are significant because they deal with guidelines often breached in daily school and library practice. A teacher may find some particular item that seems relevant to a course. Although copying some portion of the text is acceptable, copying more than the limited chapter, article, essay, or chart described in this law would be considered to be substituting for the personal purchase of the work and would therefore be in violation of the congressional guidelines and of the copyright law itself. Financial loss to the copyright holder is the overriding consideration when a court is asked to consider a ruling of fair use, so anything beyond minimal copying would tend to tip the scales

Question: We have a new poster-making machine. If a teacher makes a photocopy of a page out of a textbook and uses the copy to make a poster with this machine (for display in the classroom during the unit being taught), is it violating any copyright laws?

Answer: A single copy of something for personal research or *use in teaching* is okay, so if the teacher *discards* the original photocopy and just keeps the poster, there should be a reasonable claim of fair use because the teacher has just one copy of the material. It is true that the copy is an adaptation, but there is no commercial purpose (unless the teacher is making the copy to avoid purchasing a copy of the same material), and the work isn't being redistributed, so the impact should be minimal.

Question: The speech and debate team would like to make several copies of numerous pages from books that state "no portion of this book may be reproduced or copied without written permission of . . ." Is this "fair use"?

Answer: A notice in a book cannot override federal law regarding fair use. However, a signed contract or license can. It is impossible to answer the question without knowing the book, where it came from, how it was acquired, and so on. Here are some things to consider:

Copying for classroom use, in limited amounts as suggested in the print guidelines, is permissible. Going far beyond that limit may *not* be fair use. This appears to be, from the description in your question, an extracurricular use. In that case, all the classroom guidelines go out the window, and you fall back on standard fair use—the four tests. You have to consider whether this work is creative, whether it is published, whether the use is nonprofit, whether the use is transformative, how much you are using of the work, and what effect the use will have on the market for or value of the work. However, if you have licensed these materials, and the license says they can't be copied, all bets are off. The license controls.

Question: *A class has a textbook for each student, but the teacher wants to copy some of the pages for the students. One reason is the books are harder to give out and for the students to work with. Another reason is she wants the students to be able to write on the pages and doesn't want them to write in the books. Is it okay for her to copy some of the pages given that we have a copy of the book for each student? I know we're not supposed to make copies to keep from purchasing books, but we have a copy for each student, so that excuse would not apply.*

Answer: Some multiple copying for educational purposes is certainly fair use, but you are correct that if you were copying to avoid purchasing books, your copying probably would not be fair. To assess whether you are exceeding what would be considered "fair," figure out how much you are copying. Start looking at the print guide-

away from a justifiable claim of fair use on the fourth factor. Though the law doesn't specify that any of the four factors of fair use is "more equal" than others, in reality, courts hold the "value" test to be more significant in application (*Harper & Row,* 1985, p. 566). Sometimes a work may be out of print, and a teacher will attempt to justify copying the entire work because it is not available in the marketplace. However, "out of print" is not the same as "out of copyright." As noted previously, there may be many reasons a work goes out of print: perhaps demand for the work has dwindled, and it isn't economically reasonable for the publisher to keep the work in print. Or the publisher may have a similar work by a different author that it would prefer to promote, having decided to let the earlier one lapse out of print. The book you have may be inaccurate. Whatever the reason, it is the prerogative of the publisher to print or not print a work the publisher owns. By making unauthorized copies beyond the chapter/essay/article limit, the teacher bypasses the permissions and royalty to which the copyright owner would be entitled. Significantly, if the teacher needs only a little more than the article or chapter, the use will probably pass the four-factor fair use tests. The more the teacher uses, the less likely the use will pass the four-factor assessment.

Similarly, because copying may not be "directed by higher authority," an administrator, curriculum director, supervisor, or department head cannot direct a teacher or other staff member to copy copyrighted materials under fair use for whatever purpose. An individual teacher must initiate the copying for that teacher's use. An example of violation of this aspect of the guidelines would be a principal telling a teacher to copy a specific article on an aspect of classroom management. The principal may ask the teacher to *read* the article but cannot order the teacher to *copy* the article. The teacher may, however, decide to copy the article for files or for reading at a more convenient time. This decision in this case would originate with the teacher; hence, there would be no problem.

Another example of deviation from the guidelines would be a department head directing teachers to copy the instructions from a set of standardized tests so that only one set of instructions would need to be purchased. Not only is this a violation of the prohibition on copy orders coming from a higher authority; it also is a direct attempt to deprive the copyright holder of sales, violating the fourth fair use factor: "the effect of the use upon the potential market for . . . the copyrighted work."

Multiple copies for classroom use

Copying in multiple units for student use in a classroom setting is completely permissible if certain tests are met. An instructor may not make more than one copy of the item for each student in the course, and each item copied must be used for classroom use or for discussion. Additionally, each copy must include a notice of copyright. To clarify this point, if a teacher has 30 students, she may not make 45 copies under the assumption that some of the students will lose or mutilate their copies before the assignment is finished. The teacher must actually use the copies for a specific activity or discussion. She may not make the copies just to include them for their literary or cultural value or as a nonrequired (enrichment) supplement.

The requirement of notice of copyright is the most–often-neglected aspect of this section of the guidelines. Failure to include this notice is a violation of the Digital Millennium Copyright Act (DMCA) because it removes what is known as "copyright management information." The DMCA prohibits removal of copyright management information in any reproduction, performance, or display of a copyrighted work. Copyright management information includes the work's title, author, copyright owner, recording performer, credited movie director, credited movie producer, and credited movie writer, any terms or conditions that apply to the use of the work, and any identifying numbers associated with the work (17 U.S.C.A. § 1202). Sometimes this can be as simple as a notation on the margin of the page, such as "Copyright 2001, Big Publishing Co.," because the rest of the information is included somewhere on the reproduced document. It also means that when you record a program off-air, you must include all the credits as part of your recording. See the section on audiovisuals for more details on recording video.

The three tests that each instance of copying must meet are brevity, spontaneity, and cumulative effect. These tests are very specific in nature, and each copy must meet all the criteria for each test. This wording is specified in the guidelines and indicates legislative intent, so fudging significantly on the limits is probably not a good idea.

Brevity

Poetry: If a poem is fewer than 250 words and is printed on not more than two pages, it may be copied in its entirety. If the poem is longer than 250 words, only 250 words may be copied. The law does allow an unfinished line to be included if the 250-word limit should happen to fall in the middle of a line.

Prose: If a complete article, story, or essay is less than 2,500 words, it may be copied in its entirety. For other types of prose, such as a play, a novel, or a letter, a copy must not be more than 1,000 words or 10 percent of the whole, whichever is less. No matter how short the work, one may legitimately copy an excerpt of 500 words. In other words, if a work is only 1,000 words in total, a teacher may copy 500 words even though that amount exceeds the 10 percent guideline.

Exception: The type of literature composed of text and significant illustrations, commonly called "picture books," is generally much shorter than the 2,500-word limit for complete copying. The law provides a specific prohibition against copying works of this type in their entirety (and it specifically includes

---

lines to see where you may cross over the line. Typically, the Guidelines for Educational Uses allow one chapter from a book. Depending on what your teacher is planning to copy, she may exceed that guideline. Of course, guidelines are guidelines, and a slight variation is probably not fatal. But you will have to make the assessment based on what she actually plans to copy. And of course, given that you did purchase the books, the publisher may just give you permission to make the copies you would like to make. It's certainly worth a phone call or e-mail.

Question: Can teachers make multiple (more than nine) copies of pages from workbooks that are no longer in print?

Answer: First, Congress gave us fairly clear guidance on what it thought would be "fair" when it comes to making photocopies. Under that guidance, a "copy" could be a chapter, an essay, a poem, a short story, an article, and so on. From the nonexclusive list of items, you can infer that something long, such as an entire book, wasn't within Congress's contemplation. Also, Congress made it clear that "consumable" items—items designed to be used up, such as workbooks— are not fair targets for multiple copying.

The key to your question is that the workbooks are out of print. "Out of print" is not the same as "out of copyright." So someone owns the rights in those workbooks. And it is that person's right *not* to offer that book for sale. Maybe it is inaccurate or outdated. But for whatever reason, the publisher does not want to offer the book for sale.

If this were a book chapter or a magazine article, you could fall back on the congressional guidelines and make up to nine "copies" (with one physical copy per student of whatever you choose to copy). But it isn't. It's a workbook—one of the things to which Congress told us you may *not* apply fair use. Copying consumables is not "fair" according to Congress. Of course, you could probably make a short quotation from something consumable as a fair use, but that's not what you are proposing. You are proposing "multiple copies for classroom use," which is exactly what the congressional guidelines are about.

Question: Is it okay for a teacher to record a picture book and let kindergarten students listen to the recorded story while looking at the book?

Answer: There is a special exception to copyright law for handicapped users that allows this practice, but the person for whom you are recording the book must be blind or otherwise physically unable to use a book. The copy must also be made on a special recorder designed for handicapped users (see 17 U.S.C § 121). Making a copy of a book by recording it is the same (according to the law) as making a copy by photocopying it. Remember that for picture books there is a copy limitation (under the classroom guidelines) of two pages or 10 percent of the text, whichever is less.

similar works intended for adults). Only two pages of a picture book may be copied as long as those two pages do not make up more than 10 percent of the text of the book. Graphic novels were not invented when these guidelines were written, but one could make a good case that they would fall into a similar exception.

Illustration: One chart, graph, drawing, cartoon, diagram, or picture may be copied per book or periodical issue. These copies must be photocopies or other exact copies. Modifying the illustration in any way violates the author's right of adaptation. Note that teachers *may* make a single copy of an illustration or chart for use in teaching under the rules regarding single copies for teachers. That single copy can be on a transparency or scanned into PowerPoint and used in that format.

Spontaneity

The idea to make multiple copies must be initiated by the individual teacher. In other words, the department head cannot make copies to give to each teacher to use in class, nor can the principal copy copyright-protected materials to hand out in certain classes. The guidelines even go so far as to state that the making of multiple copies must be at the inspiration of the individual teacher, implying that the department head or supervisor cannot even give the classroom teacher a list of appropriate items to be copied without violating the letter of the law. This doctrine is consistent with the prohibition of copying directed by a higher authority, as discussed earlier.

The rationale for the spontaneity rule is that the idea and decision to use the work and the moment it will be used for maximum teaching effectiveness are so close in time that it would be unreasonable to expect a timely reply to a request for permission. "Unreasonable" and "timely" are subject to some degree of latitude. How long should one expect to wait for permission to reproduce? Are two weeks enough? A month? A semester? As a rule of thumb, allow about four weeks for a reply. If teachers know at least four weeks ahead of time that they will need to copy something for use in class, they should write for permission. If they do not receive a reply in time, they could then proceed with the copying given that there is not sufficient time to send a second query. Obviously, if an article, illustration, poem, or other printed matter comes to the attention of the teacher a matter of days before the time of optimum use, the teacher could make multiple copies for the class without writing for permission. The teacher may not, however, use that same article, illustration, or poem in subsequent semesters or years without permission because then there would have been ample time to request and receive permission for the use.

Cumulative effect

The last test that an instance of multiple copying must pass is that of cumulative effect. The guidelines are intended to assure that copying is not substituting for purchase of books and periodicals. Again, the law seeks to protect authors and publishers to assure there is a market for materials. To comply with this test, the copying must be done for only one course. For example, a teacher may make copies of a poem for all freshman English classes (one copy per student) but may not copy the same poem for her sophomore English classes.

The guidelines limit the number of copies that may be made from a single source or author during a school year (or a semester or quarter if this isn't a full-year class). A teacher may make class copies of one short poem, article, story, or essay or two excerpts from the same author during one term (year or semester or quarter). If the copies are taken from a collective work (a book of poetry or essays by multiple authors, for example), the teacher is limited to three or fewer items during a class term. Periodical articles are also limited to three or fewer items copied from one periodical volume (not issue) during one term. Current news articles from newspapers and magazines are exempt from this requirement. When an item ceases to become "current news" is not defined, but a two-month window would be generous. Although the preceding rules are very specific, you must also consider the four prohibitions on print permissions when determining fair use. (Three of them were quoted in this chapter, on p. 53.)

1. *"Copying shall not be used to create or to replace or substitute for anthologies, compilations, or collective works. Such replacement or substitution may occur whether copies of various works or excerpts therefrom are accumulated or reproduced and used separately."*

2. *"There shall be no copying from works intended to be 'consumable' in the course of study or of teaching. These include workbooks, exercises, standardized tests and test booklets and answer sheets and like consumable material."*

3. *"Copying shall not*
   - *substitute for the purchase of books, publishers' reprints or periodicals;*
   - *be directed by higher authority; or*
   - *be repeated with respect to the same item by the same teacher from term to term."*

4. *"No charge shall be made to the student beyond the actual cost of the photocopying."*

In addition, no more than nine instances of such multiple copying can occur for one course during one class term.

The intent of these prohibitions is to protect authors and publishers from teachers who would substitute copies for purchased books or workbooks.

Question: Our 10th-grade English teachers require their students to create an anthology of poetry, essays, short stories, and articles on one thematic aspect of the Holocaust. Because the law states that copying should not be used to create or be a substitute for anthologies, compilations, or collective works, is this a violation of copyright law?

Answer: The print anthologies restriction is addressed more to teachers who simply photocopy the world rather than purchase textbooks. If the students make only a single copy of the materials for their own projects, the students make the choice of what to copy, and the projects revert to the students at the end of the assignment, there should be no problem.

Question: We have 60 copies of a small book. We have ordered 40+ more, but they have not come in yet. The teacher wants to photocopy the first two chapters plus introduction for the 40+ students without books so that she can get started on the unit. Those pages (17) are more than 10 percent of the total work (150 pages). The closest I come to any similar example is under music when the teacher may copy pieces if the performance time is here, but the purchased copies have not yet arrived. Is it okay for the teacher to make these copies?

Answer: As a general rule, when you have sufficient copies of books on order, you can copy—one chapter at a time—material that you need in class until the ordered books arrive. But you can't start copying until the purchase order goes out. Just sending the purchase order to the central office isn't sufficient because the order may not be approved and sent.

Question: If we have a purchased a copy of a book for each student, but we do not want the books to go home, may we make copies of these books to send home? Should they be shredded after one use?

Answer: This is probably not a fair use because the intent is to deprive the copyright owner of a sale. This type of copying is making a backup copy in case the student forgets the book at home or loses/damages the book. The only medium for which a backup copy is allowed is computer software. There is no exception for print, for educational use for books, and so on.

Question: In creating an anthology of poetry for our different grade levels to use in writing, one teacher suggested that we collect different complete poems from different poetry collections, retype them, and reprint them within our district. Is it okay to do this if each poem is no more than 1/12 of the collection it came from? We think this should be okay because of fair use. Or is each poem is a complete work?

Examples of acceptable multiple copying

As a result of confusing reports about a nominee to the Supreme Court, a teacher requests the librarian to make 32 copies (one per student enrolled in the course) of a one-page excerpt (approximately 475 words) from a book to give to each student. The students will use the excerpt as a basis for a written exercise in editorial writing. Each student's copy is free, and each copy includes a notice of copyright.

An elementary teacher asks the clerical aide to make 19 copies (one per student) of a time line of the American Revolution. The students will include the diagram in a notebook they are creating to follow the events of the Revolution from beginning to end. Each copy includes notice of copyright.

An English coordinator suggests that a particular poem might be good to teach the skill of identification of meter. The decision to use the poem is left up to the individual teacher.

Last year, a first-grade teacher copied a word game out of a children's magazine for her students to use as they studied a specific letter sequence. This year she wants to use the same game. She plans in advance and writes for, and receives, permission.

Examples of unacceptable multiple copying

A teacher copies a column from five consecutive issues of a magazine, making a booklet of articles for each student in a class. This practice violates the prohibition against creating anthologies as well as the cumulative effect test against copying more than three articles from a periodical volume.

Every year an elementary teacher makes copies of the poem "There's a New Kid on the Block" to give to students on the day that a new student arrives in class. Using this poem every year violates the prohibition against copying the same item from term to term.

A teacher wishes to teach the concept of sequencing. To help students visualize the process, the teacher copies a short picture book for each student and then mixes up the pages. The students must put the book back into the correct sequence. This practice violates the limit on brevity in that only two pages or 10 percent may be copied from a picture book.

A debate teacher requests copies of several selected articles for students to use in preparing a defense. The copies cost $4.57 at a local copy shop. To make matters simpler, the teacher charges the students $5. The extra money goes into the fund used to buy ribbons for the debate tournament. This practice violates the fourth prohibition regarding multiple copies. The student may not be charged beyond the actual cost of the copies.

A month before the school year started, the school decided to teach a new class. There wasn't time to order textbooks. The teacher had to come up with all the teaching materials herself. She copied chapters from different books plus articles from magazines in order to give students learning materials. This example violates the admonition against more than nine instances of multiple copying per year or term (depending on the length of the class).

A principal reads an article appropriate to a staff development concept. She asks the secretary to make copies for all the teachers and place the copies in their mailboxes. This instance violates several regulations including "top down" prohibitions. Also, the teachers aren't students enrolled in a class—they are employees. Copying for the purpose of staff development seldom merits a fair use exemption. It could be a fair use, however, if the four factors of section 107 are met.

Copies for handicapped students

A modification to the rule against copying and adaptation permits institutions serving the blind and physically handicapped to acquire or make adaptive copies in Braille or other formats (17 U.S.C.A. § 121). There are specific regulations about the format of the copies and who may use them (36 C.F.R. § 701.10). These rules cover students who are unable to use standard print works because of visual deficiencies or because they are physically handicapped and cannot hold a book or turn its pages. Those students who qualify under this law must be identified through the Library of Congress Division of Blind and Physically Handicapped or through one of the state library branches. Application requires certification of the disability by medical personnel. The needs of the dyslexic students may be served through this service if a medical doctor certifies that the person has a reading disability resulting from organic dysfunction and of sufficient severity to prevent their reading printed material in a normal manner (§ 701.10(b)(1)(iv)). It does not address the needs of the slow learner or students with primary languages other than English.

The "other formats" referenced in the law include reading books onto cassette tapes or other media, but the law discusses only magnetic tape formats. When using cassette tape, one must pay particular attention to the format of tape specified in the law. Although consumer-grade cassette tape plays at 1⅞ inches per second (i.p.s.) using two-track tapes, the format specified in the regulation is 15/16 i.p.s., using four-track tapes. The 15/16 i.p.s. four- track standard is used in the Recording for the Blind program that is established through the Library of Congress and the various state libraries. Special players are required to play these slow, multi-tracks. The players are available for free when the application is approved. This section of the law also permits digital copies, such as those made for Kurzweil machines. The law cautions that copies in whatever format made under this exception may be used only with students certified as eligible (§ 701.10(e)). So although other students could profit from the audio recordings or other formats you may employ for sight-disabled students, you may not—under fair use—use those same adapted materials with students who have not been prequalified for the exemption.

As of December 3, 2004, a new amendment to copyright law came via the Individuals with Disabilities Education

Answer: The copyright guidelines (aka the print guidelines, given that print was really all there was back in 1976 when the guidelines were negotiated and adopted by Congress) are quite specific that you are not able to make an "anthology" if doing so takes the place of textbooks or purchased reprints. That is part of the "cumulative effect" test. Also, under those guidelines each class may engage in only nine instances of "free" multiple copying per course, so if you planned to use more than nine poems, you would be over that allowance anyway.

Question: If it is a violation of multiple copying to copy the same poem for your class year after year, is it a violation of copyright law to show the same video to your class year after year? I've heard that it is okay to show the same video every year as long as the school has purchased a legal copy of it. But, I've heard that practice is not acceptable without a performance license.

Answer: No, it isn't a violation to show the same film in subsequent years. Print copying is covered under the Kastenmeier report, whereas audiovisual (AV) use is covered under section 106 of the law. The print guidelines (the Kastenmeier report) specifically state that copying may not be repeated from term to term. But the AV use guidelines do not address reuse. Perhaps the act of copying is what they feel makes the two uses different, but they are treated differently for school-use purposes.

Question: I have been trying to figure out whether we can legally copy To Kill a Mockingbird on CD for a student who is entitled to have it according to her individualized educational program (IEP). It is not available for purchase, and we do not own a copy. It is currently out of print at the author's request. The audiobook can be purchased from secondary sources for usually well over $100.

A teacher borrowed the CD from a public library over the summer and made a copy. Is she allowed to give this to the student to take home? Also, are other students allowed to borrow it even if it's not in their IEP? Other schools in the district have this audiobook title that can be borrowed via interlibrary loan. We can borrow it for her, but last year there were no copies available to borrow from the public libraries in our area during the time that the students needed it.

Would I be correct to tell her that, even though the recording is unavailable (out of print), it is not out of copyright, and because the audiobook is available from other sources (from other schools or via purchase from secondary sources), she would be in violation of the law if she copied it? I called the publishing company, and they said they didn't think copying was legal, but didn't seem too sure.

Answer: Copyright law does not address IEPs. A school can put anything in an IEP, such as "If the student has no behavioral demerits in a week, the student is allowed to choose one video of his choice to watch on Friday afternoon." However, this showing does not meet the direct teaching requirement of sec-

Improvement Act of 2004. The new requirements allow certain technologies to be employed to assist "print disabled" (which would include diagnosed dyslexic) students. These materials can be produced locally only if such materials are not available for purchase. The law also provided for the establishment of the National Instructional Materials Access Center under the auspices of the American Printing House for the Blind. The law directs a new standard, the National Instructional Materials Accessibility Standard, solely for the conversion of print materials into accessible formats for print-disabled students. However, the new standard and exemptions apply only to required textbooks. Library materials and supplementary materials are not addressed in the new law. Authorization for services under this law still must come via certification through the State Library or the Library of Congress Division of Blind and Physically Handicapped. Both require certification by a medical professional that the individual is unable to use standard print materials (Individuals, 2005).

Print permission issues

If a teacher knows that a particular item will be used year to year or term to term, the safest course is to write for permission. The same holds true if the teacher plans in September, for example, to use a particular poem at Thanksgiving. This knowledge gives the teacher ample time to request permission from the copyright holder, likely the publisher. In such an instance, under the congressional guidelines, requesting and receiving permission is mandatory prior to copying, not optional. However, if the teacher requests permission but gets no response by the time the material is needed, the teacher may make the needed copies—once. If the teacher hasn't gotten permission to make copies by the second time the materials are needed, she needs to locate something else to use.

Always remember: a copyright owner is not required to respond to your request for permission. If you don't get an affirmative response, the safest course is to assume the answer is "no" (Gasaway, 2006, p. 126). The important *Kinko's* case (see the section on related cases in this chapter) supports that notion; in this case, the court explained that Basic Book's failure to respond to requests for permission was not to be interpreted as a license to copy (*Basic Books, Inc. v. Kinko's Graphics Corp*, 1991).

Consumable materials

Consumable materials include much more than workbooks. The category includes workbooks, tests, standardized tests, answer sheets, and worksheets among other forms of consumables such as cut-outs, templates, and patterns intended to be destroyed in making the item. The prohibitions on multiple copying state that "there shall be no copying of or from materials intended to be consumable" (United States Copyright Office, 2009a, p. 7). Pattern books, such as knitting books or woodworking plans, probably don't qualify as consumable and would likely be afforded the protection of other printed works, but dress patterns printed on tissue are likely intended to be destroyed to an extent in making the item.

The problem with consumables is that there are multiple items in the schoolteacher's bag of tricks that can be considered consumable yet are still copied, albeit illegally. Schools often draw on the "no-profit" defense when copying consumables, but such a defense doesn't take into consideration the other tests of fair use. All aspects of the fair use exemption must be considered when making copies under fair use. Here are some common examples of improper use of consumables:

- *A teacher buys a single copy of a book of worksheets and copies one of the worksheets for students to use when they have a substitute teacher.*

- *A teacher buys a book of worksheets and then cuts the worksheets apart to create a new sheet, duplicating that new worksheet for the class.*

- *A computer program provides a package of questionnaires on which to record responses to questions. These sheets may or may not be suitable for insertion into an automatic scoring machine. The publishing company sells replacement packages of the required questionnaires. When the supply of questionnaires runs low, the librarian photocopies a new supply from one of the originals, keeping an original on file to make future copies.*

- *A new math series comes with a package of standardized tests. In order to stretch a limited budget to buy a set of manipulatives, the school buys one package of the tests (enough for one classroom) and duplicates enough additional copies so that all students in the grade level can take the test on the same day.*

These uses (and infinite variations) are all out of compliance. In each of these violations, the teacher could come into compliance simply by receiving permission from the publisher of the material. Because the publishers are in the business of selling consumable materials, it is unlikely they would grant blanket permission to reproduce their consumables. However, because printing their products involves materials and labor costs to them, they might be willing to work out a discount arrangement for a school to undertake the actual duplication of the material under a license agreement. It can't hurt to ask. The worst they can do is say no.

tion 110(1) and therefore would require a public performance license.

In this scenario, the teacher's copy is illegal. If you are making another copy, you will be compounding the illegality. There is a provision in the law allowing you to make a *replacement* copy (meaning that you already own it, but it has become damaged), but there is no provision for making an original copy because the work is out of print. I have gotten this question on this particular title at least a dozen times recently, so there is demand there. However, if one were allowed to make original copies, the demand would go away, and there would be no economic incentive for the publisher to renegotiate the rights with the copyright holder. As you are aware, copyright is an economic law, and economic motives are the basis for its existence. I don't see any changes in that view forthcoming.

I'm not sure why the student needs the audio copy. If he is blind or physically handicapped (unable to use standard print) or severely dyslexic (with a medical diagnosis of same), the student can qualify for the services of your state library. That institution will certainly have this work on tape in the specialized format required for Recording for the Blind and Dyslexic. The loans are free, as are the special players required.

Periodicals

Copying periodical articles (including newspaper articles) falls into the same basket as copying most print materials. Periodical articles are mentioned specifically in the guidelines concerning making single copies for teachers. An article from a periodical or newspaper is considered to be within limits of acceptable copying for that purpose. In addition, making a single copy of a chart, graph, diagram, drawing, cartoon, or picture from a periodical or newspaper is also legal. Under the guidelines, current news articles are exempt from permissions requirements; however, an item is only "current" for a short time. The two-month suggested lead time for permission requests is probably sufficient for this use as well. It's important to acknowledge that news doesn't stay "current news" forever.

The guidelines on multiple copies for classroom use are much more specific with regard to types of acceptable copies, whether from books or periodicals. The guidelines for brevity apply equally to items copied from periodicals and newspapers.

Poetry taken from periodicals must meet the guidelines for poetry in general: if a poem is shorter than 250 words and is printed on not more than two pages, it may be copied in its entirety. If the poem is longer than 250 words, only 250 words may be copied. The law does allow an unfinished line to be included if the 250-word limit should happen to fall in the middle of a line (United States Copyright Office, 2009a).

Prose taken from periodicals must meet the test for all other prose: If a complete article, story, or essay is shorter than 2,500 words, it may be copied in its entirety. For other types of prose, a copy must not be more than 1,000 words or 10 percent of the whole, whichever is less, with a minimum acceptable copy limit of 500 words (United States Copyright Office). In other words, if a work is only 1,000 words long, a teacher may copy 500 words even though that amount exceeds the 10 percent guideline.

Graphic material in periodicals may also be copied, provided the copying meets the test for illustrations: one chart, graph, drawing, cartoon, diagram, or picture may be copied per periodical issue (United States Copyright Office). Beware of copying an item—a cartoon, for example—from several issues of a periodical. The allowed limit is three per periodical volume. The number of issues making up a volume varies from periodical to periodical. A volume could be one month, three months, six months, or a year period, as defined by the publisher.

The test of spontaneity is also applicable to copies from periodicals. The making of multiple copies must be at the "instance and inspiration" of the individual teacher. A supervisor may not direct a teacher to make multiple copies of material from any periodical. In addition, the decision to use the work and the time of its use in class must be so close that it would be unreasonable to expect a reply of permission from a copyright holder. Again, the four-week window for permission would appear to be adequate.

The guidelines also specify a test of "cumulative effect" to limit the number of instances of copying allowed. Those guidelines affecting the copying of periodical materials are as follows:

- *The copying must be done for only one course.*

- *Only one entire article or two excerpts may be copied from the same author.*

- *No more than three items from the same periodical volume may be copied during one class term (year or semester, depending on the course).*

- *No more than nine items may be copied in multiples per course during one class term.*

Following are some examples of these rules applied to typical classroom uses of periodical copies

- *The American history and American government teacher finds an article that would be applicable to both courses. She may not reproduce the article for both classes. She may post the original article on the class bulletin board, however, and ask students to read it there.*

- *A biology teacher has already handed out two excerpts of works from Stephen Jay Gould for her class's study of evolution when she finds a new article in the journal Science that is even more enlightening. She may not make multiple copies of the work without permission. She may, however, place her copy of the magazine on reserve in the library and require students to read it.*

- *A third-grade teacher has copied two different articles from this year's Zoo Books for her science class. In preparing a unit on poetry, she finds a poem in one of this year's issues. She may copy the poem but may not copy any additional items from that volume of the periodical for this term.*

- *A sociology teacher uses magazines as a primary resource, copying articles to use as discussion starters and essay support. So far this term, he has copied eight articles to hand out to his classes. In a new issue of National Geographic, there are two articles about primitive societies that he would like his students to compare and contrast. He may not copy both these articles because that would exceed the nine-items-per-term limitation.*

Documents in the public domain, such as periodicals or monographs from the Department of Education or ERIC, do not count in the total copies per year because there is no restriction on duplication of public domain materials.

The general prohibitions on multiple copying apply to periodicals also. Those prohibitions specify that copies may not be used to create or substitute for anthologies or compilations. The prohibitions state that the copies do not have to be "accumulated" to fall under this rule. "Accumulated" in this case refers to collecting the copies and distributing them all at the same time, as if they were together in a booklet. The articles may be copied and used separately and still violate this prohibition.

Additionally, copying must not substitute for the purchase of a subscription to the periodical or for a publisher's reprints, it must not be ordered by a higher authority, and the same items may not be copied in succeeding class terms. Of course, the student may not be charged for the copies beyond the actual cost of the copies. The most significant consideration in making the fair use assessment is that of financial impact on the copyright owner. If the proposed fair-use copying were to be repeated widely by many others, would such copying have an adverse effect on the copyright holder's revenues? If so, the use is undoubtedly not fair.

The lone exception to the rules on copying from periodicals is that of articles from current news periodicals (e.g. *Time, Newsweek*) and newspapers and the current news sections of other periodicals. When the guidelines are followed, copying such articles is in compliance. The only question would be how "current" the article is. Although no guidelines exist to specify the amount of time allotted to "currency," a window of two months would not be inappropriate and would certainly be justifiable, especially around vacation periods when an article might be published but the class does not meet for a span of time.

Graphics

The term "graphics" can cover a lot of territory: paintings, photographs, lithographs, serigraphs, etchings, maps, diagrams, and charts, for example. Posters and illustrations can all be considered graphics. Graphics pose a major source of potential copyright problems for schools. Section 106 of the copyright law reserves six rights to the copyright owner: reproduction, adaptation, distribution, performance, display, and digital transmission of sound recordings. The rights of reproduction, adaptation, and display are the most problematic for schools as far as graphics are concerned. In certain instances, reproduction of graphic material may fall under the "fair use" provisions. Making a single copy of a graph or illustration from a book is acceptable if the copy is for personal research or study, and multiple copies of a single graphic are authorized for a class under the standard print fair-use guidelines:

- *Copying must be at the instance and inspiration of the teacher and so close in time to the required use that receipt of permission would be impossible.*

- *The copy is for only one course in the school.*

- *There are not more than nine occurrences of multiple copying for that course.*

- *Not more than one graphic is copied per book or periodical.*

Adaptation (also known as a derivative work) is a bigger dilemma. A "derivative work" is a work based on one or more preexisting works, such as a translation, musical arrangement, dramatization, fictionalization, motion picture version, sound recording, art reproduction, abridgment, condensation, or any other form in which a work may be recast, transformed, or adapted. A work consisting of editorial revisions, annotations, elaborations, or other modifications that, as a whole, represents an original work of authorship is a "derivative work" (17 U.S.C. § 101). Graphics producers make much money from adapting their works for other media. Disney characters adorn everything from drinking cups to nightshirts to posters. Cartoon and advertising graphics decorate paper goods, greeting cards, and billboards. All of these appealing images are attractive to children, and teachers wish to capitalize on their students' recognition of the popular characters and themes. This desire is made all the more realizable because virtually every teacher has available the means to incorporate these designs into bulletin boards, handouts, notes to parents, and other decorative uses in the classroom or library. But copyright law doesn't look kindly on such unauthorized uses. By taking an artist's work and enlarging, modifying, or converting it to another medium, a teacher usurps the creator's (or more accurately, the copyright holder's) right to determine how the image will be used.

The library may be a contributory infringer in some school-based instances of copyright violation in this area. The primary tool in this misdeed is the document camera, the overhead projector, or the opaque projector (if you still have one of those around). If the librarian lends that equipment with the knowledge that it will be used to infringe copyright, the librarian could be considered a contributory infringer because he or she has knowledge that copyright is being or will be infringed and contributes to the infringement. A contributory infringer could be liable for damages. A good plan would be to post the standard copyright warning notice usually affixed to photocopiers on all equipment that could potentially be used to make contraband copies, adaptations,

---

Question: The art teacher at our school would like to put samples of famous artworks on her Web page. If the artist is long dead (e.g., Van Gogh, Renoir, etc.), can she copy the work from another Web page and put it on her own in order to provide samples for her students to view?

Answer: She can copy the artwork itself (because the work is in the public domain if the work was published before 1923), but the image from someone's Web page *may* be protected by copyright. And if it is protected by copyright, and the owner has watermarked the image, your art teacher friend could get into a lot of hot water for taking and redistributing an image.

The court in *Bridgeman Art Library v. Corel Corp.* held that a photo of a public domain work that employs no creativity in angle, lighting, and so on cannot be protected by copyright because the photograph doesn't meet the requirement for minimal creativity. Some photographers and museums, however, don't believe that and insist their works are protected. They can be very litigious if they find you are using their digital images. That would mean a lot of expense and stress to fight the suit, even though you would be likely to win in court. Depending on your aversion to risk, you might want to scan your own images from photographs as long as they meet the previously stated requirements.

or derivations. The wording of these notices is specified by law and is reprinted in Appendix E. Preprinted adhesive labels and stand-up signs are sold by the major library supply houses. In this instance, one could make a case that the document camera and the overhead projector could be considered "unsupervised reproduction equipment." Libraries (as opposed to schools) aren't held liable for unsupervised reproduction equipment, so the librarian might have a viable defense against contributory liability if the standard disclaimer is attached to any library-owned equipment capable of making reproductions.

Graphic infringements occur in the following instances, among others:

- *A teacher uses the document camera to enlarge a greeting card illustration for a bulletin board decoration.*

- *A librarian photocopies an image from a coloring book as part of a worksheet she is creating.*

- *The PTA uses a pantograph (a device that traces an image in a larger size) or overhead projector to enlarge a poster to wall size as a hall decoration.*

- *The art teacher creates stuffed animals of popular picture book characters.*

- *The principal scans a cartoon from a magazine into the PTA newsletter.*

- *The cheerleading squad creates a paper "run-through," featuring a popular cartoon character dressed in the team uniform, for the basketball team.*

- *The librarian scans images from books (rather than book covers) to put on the library Web site (a single copy from a book for use in the library is fine, but distributing copies to the world is likely beyond the scope of fair use).*

Student work

Students fall into a little different category than teachers and the school in general. Under fair use, a student can make a single copy for his own research and education of just about anything within reason: an illustration, an article, a chapter, and so on. The same "top down" prohibition on directed copying would likely apply if a teacher tells a student that he must make a copy of a specific item, such as when a teacher has exhausted her nine instances of multiple copying and then directs the students to make their own copies of something she would make if given the opportunity. In the Related Cases section of this chapter, see the description of a higher education court case of top down copying: *Blackwell Publishing Group v. Excel Research Group, LLC.*

Teachers are sometimes very cavalier with student work

Question: Our art teacher would like to have her elementary students paint a mural in the library combining characters from children's literature. These would not be a direct copy from a book but rather a combination of characters within an original setting. None of the characters would be Disney, but rather from artists such as Tomie DePaola. This would be an educational effort, to teach art skills. There would be no financial gain to this. Is it okay?

Answer: Financial gain isn't the big consideration here. Note that many artists are just as aggressive about protecting characters as are Disney and Shel Silverstein, for example. What you are doing is creating a derivative work. Students have the right to do this for their own education (such as copying the work of an artist to develop the student's art skills), but the copies must belong to the student. For this mural, you are planning to do a daily public display of these characters, and the daily display has nothing to do with coursework. The copies will not be with the students; rather they will stay at the school, and the purpose of the copying is to avoid paying for licensed copies of artwork. None of these is a reason in your favor.

I wouldn't recommend this project to you. As an alternative idea, the students can read several versions of a tale (Cinderella, for example) and then draw *their own* versions of the characters. However, remember that the students own the copyrights to their own work, and you will want signed releases from the students' parents (because the students are minors) to retain and display the work. I would probably add to the permission form that the school has all rights to the work, so that at some point in the future, you can decide to paint over the mural, thereby destroying it.

and retain copies of work for use as exemplars. Although a student (if the student is over 18) or the student's parents (if the student is a minor) may give permission for a teacher to retain and use a copy of the student's work, there is no generalized educational permission for such use. Standard fair use would apply, meaning that a teacher could take a sentence, for example, from a student's paper and use that sentence to demonstrate a common grammatical error. To really muddy the waters, however, remember that under the Family Education Rights and Privacy Act (FERPA), a teacher may not disclose a "student record" without permission of the student's parents or the student (if the student is of age). By using the portion under fair use and attributing the erroneous sentence, the teacher may have violated FERPA!

A 2009 court case involving the plagiarism detection service Turnitin.com found that commercial use of an entire student paper was a fair use, but the court emphasized that the use was not of the creative aspect of the paper. Turnitin converted the paper into a digital thumbprint against which it compared newly submitted papers, and Turnitin did not even read the papers (*A. V. v. iParadigms*, 2009). That qualification would be significant if a teacher were using previous student work in a way that others could see the creative aspect of the work, especially if the teacher used the entire work.

Scanners

The scanner jolted the world of print copyright. Virtually any image can now be transformed into bits and bytes for incorporation into graphics packages, desktop publishing documents, and multimedia presentations. As stated previously, the original copyright holder retains the rights of reproduction, adaptation, and display, among others. Scanning a copyrighted illustration may be a copyright violation of any of those three rights. A student may use a scanned copyrighted image in a report, but the student must retain ownership of the report once it is graded. The teacher may not retain that report (or a copy of it in paper or electronic format) for her own purposes, nor may she reproduce it for a workshop without the permission of the student or the student's parents *and* permission from the copyright owner of the original work used in the student's report. If the work is a multimedia presentation, it may be displayed only for the students and teachers in the class for which it was prepared, as directed in the multimedia guidelines, plus uses personal to the student (see the section on multimedia for more details). Presentation before what would amount to an open audience is considered a public performance. The student may not grant permission for such a performance because although he owns the copyright to his own portion of the work, he may not give permission for that which he does not own—the copyrighted material he has "borrowed" to enhance his own work.

A staff member cannot scan a cartoon or article into a newsletter for distribution to the faculty or parents. A scanned copy of a famous photograph cannot legally be modified by computer graphics into a similar, or even quite different, image. There is no amount of modification that can be made to an original image to make the format conversion okay. In short, the technology to reproduce an item electronically may exist, but this does not mean that the user of the technology has the right to do so. A case ongoing in 2010 points out the hazards of such conversion. An artist converted a photograph of then-candidate Barack Obama into a poster upon which he superimposed the word "Hope" or "Change" (depending on the version). The photograph was made by a news photographer and was copyrighted by a news syndication agency. The artist did not ask the permission of either the photographer or the news agency to create the poster, and then he sold the rights to the poster to others who made clothing and other items (*Shepard Fairey v. Assoc. Press*).

As you can see, potential for copyright infringement of graphics is quite broad. The best prevention is to insist on original or public domain graphics.

Resources for understanding

Fair use of print materials glossary

Accumulation: Gathering together reproductions to be distributed at one time. Accumulated copies do not count as one; they count as the total of the parts. Also, copies do not have to be distributed at once to be considered an anthology.

Collective work: A work written by two or more authors, each of whom contributes separate, identified portions of the work.

Current news: Descriptions of events that have happened in the recent past. Some magazines and newspapers contain nothing but current news, whereas others mix current news with commentary, essays, and personality pieces. Only current news is offered a special exemption from copy limits.

Notice of copyright: Required notice on fair-use reproductions of copyrighted material. The notice must include the name of the copyright holder and the date of copyright, such as "Copyright 2010, Linworth Publishing." The notice must appear on each copy.

Periodical volume: The binding increment of a periodical. Most periodicals assemble volumes based on a 12-month period (though the volume may start in January, July, or any other month), but others use a two-volume-per-calendar-year arrangement or other increment.

Term: The length of time to complete a course. An English class may span an entire school year, whereas an elective class such as psychology may meet only for a semester or quarter. The term of the English class is a year, and the term for the elective is either a semester or quarter. One must consider the term of the course when evaluating the ability to reproduce materials for that course

Related cases

Some landmark cases have been ruled on in recent years. Understanding these cases will help develop a mental framework for understanding the scope of fair use.

American Geophysical Union v. Texaco Inc., 37 F.3d 881 (2d Cir. 1994)

One of the most important cases regarding photocopying, this case involved a corporate library (Texaco) that made photocopies of magazine articles at the request of scientists who worked for the company. American Geophysical Union and 82 other publishers of scientific and technical journals sued, claiming that photocopying was not within the bounds of fair use. The courts agreed, citing that this was "institutional, systemic" copying, with the intent to avoid paying for additional copies of the magazines.

Princeton University Press v. Michigan Document Services, Inc., 99 F.3d 1381 (6th Cir. 1996)

The ruling in this case found that using photocopies of copyright-protected excerpts of works to assemble "course packs" for college courses is a copyright infringement and does not meet the tests of fair use. The course packs were assembled by a for-profit copy shop near the university campus, and no permissions were sought, and no permission fees were paid through third-party clearinghouses.

Bridgeman Art Library Ltd. v. Corel Corp., 36 F. Supp. 2d 191 (S.D.N.Y. 1999)

Bridgeman marketed high-quality photographic reproductions (both prints and digital copies) of public domain paintings owned by various museums. It sued Corel for selling a CD with some of

Bridgeman's digital reproductions. Bridgeman admitted that it put considerable effort into making exact copies of the original works of art. The court explained that when the copy is "slavish," there is insufficient creativity (such as in camera angle, lighting, facial expression, etc.) to qualify for a copyright, so Bridgeman's digital copies were not protected by copyright. Just because the person taking the photo expends a lot of effort in making the work, as the Bridgeman photographer had done here, does not mean that the work contains a "creative spark" required to support a claim of copyright.

Basic Books, Inc. v. Kinko's Graphics Corp., 758 F. Supp. 1522 (S.D.N.Y. 1991)

The court held that Kinko's violated the copyright of several works by making copies for course packs without requesting permission or paying appropriate fees. The decision lists the actual works copied and the pages copied. Most of the works were out of print and out of stock, but copying a single chapter from a book was found to be excessive. Note that Kinko's is a for-profit enterprise, even though the use was nonprofit. This case has significant implications for school and library copying. The court stated, "Plaintiffs in copyright infringement action had burden of showing defendant's 'willfulness' in order to receive statutory damages, and could sustain that burden by showing that defendant recklessly disregarded plaintiffs' rights or that defendant knew or should have known it infringed their copyrights." Pay particular attention to the "should have known." In this context, the court defines "willful" as "with knowledge," not necessarily meaning malicious. If a reasonable person might figure out that an action was infringing, everyone will be held to that standard. This case is also a good example of the courts upholding use of the classroom guidelines when considering an infringement case.

Blackwell Publishing Group v. Excel Research Group, LLC, No. 07-12731, 2009 WL 3287403 (E.D. Mich. Oct. 14, 2009)

Rather than paying royalties and having a local copy shop create a course pack of readings for a course, the university put the copies of the readings for the course at a local copy shop. Students were required to go to the copy shop and make copies of their readings in the class. The publishers sued the copy shop for direct infringement and won. The court based its finding on the fact that the copy shop kept the masters; provided the masters to the students; provided the copiers, the space, and the utilities; and even assisted the students if asked. Under those circumstances, the court held, it was really the copy shop making the copies, not the students.

Hotaling v. Church of Jesus Christ of Latter-Day Saints, 118 F.3d 199 (4th Cir. 1997)

This court held that a library could be found guilty of infringement if it allowed researchers to use materials only on the premises. The materials were later found to be illegal copies, and the library was held to be responsible for distribution even though the copies were never removed from the library. The court declared that simply listing an item in the library catalog was distribution under the definition in the law.

Works cited

American Geophysical Union v. Texaco Inc., 60 F.3d 913 (2d Cir. 1994). Retrieved from http://www.law.cornell.edu/copyright/cases/60_F3d_913.htm.

A.V. v. iParadigms LLC, 562 F.3d 630 (4th Cir. 2009).

Basic Books, Inc. v. Kinko's Graphics Corp. 758 F. Supp. 1522 (S.D.N.Y. 1991). Retrieved from http://
fairuse.stanford.edu/primary_materials/cases/c758FSupp1522.html.

Blackwell Publishing Group v. Excel Research Group, LLC, No. 07-12731, 2009 WL 3287403
(E.D. Mich. Oct. 14, 2009). Retrieved from http://www.exclusiverights.net/wp-content/
uploads/2009/10/Blackwell-Publishing-Inc.-v.-Excel-Research-Group-LLC.pdf.

Gasaway, L. N. (2006). *Copyright law and the practice of law in the digital age.* In *The Law Library
2006: Skills, Strategies & Solutions, 125-139* (PLI Patents, Copyrights, Trademarks, and Literary Property Course Handbook Series No. 8345).

Harper & Row, Publishers, Inc. v. Nation Enterprises, 471 U.S. 539 (1985).

Hotaling v. Church of Jesus Christ of Latter-Day Saints, 118 F.3d 199 (4th Cir. 1997). Retrieved
from http://caselaw.lp.findlaw.com/scripts/getcase.pl?navby=search&case=/data2/
circs/4th/961399p.html.

Individuals with Disabilities Education Improvement Act of 2004, PL 108-446, December 3, 2004,
118 Stat. 2647 (2005).

Princeton Univ. Press v. Michigan Doc. Servs., 99 F.3d 1381 (6th Cir. 1996). Retrieved from http://
fairuse.stanford.edu/primary_materials/cases/michigan_document_services.

Shepard Fairey v. Assoc. Press, No. 1:2009cv01123 (S.D.N.Y. 2009). Retrieved from http://news.justia.
com/cases/featured/new-york/nysdce/1:2009cv01123/340121/.

Special Interest Video Sales Group. (1995). *Fair use doctrine: Excerpts from the Copyright Act.* Retrieved from http://www.sivideo.com/9fstsleb.htm.

United States Copyright Office. (2009a). *Circular 21: Reproduction of copyrighted works by educators
and librarians.*

United States Copyright Office. (2009b). *Fair use.* Retrieved from http://www.copyright.gov/fls/
fl102.html.

Chapter 6

Audiovisual Materials in Schools

The law defines audiovisual as follows:

> *"Audiovisual works" are works that consist of a series of related images which are intrinsically intended to be shown by the use of machines, or devices such as projectors, viewers, or electronic equipment, together with accompanying sounds, if any, regardless of the nature of the material objects, such as films, videos, or DVDs, in which the works are embodied.* (17 U.S.C. § 101)

Section 110 of the Copyright Act of 1976 was written, in part, to address the needs of producers of audiovisual materials who were concerned that their property was not being adequately protected under the old law. The new law clarified many ambiguities, though often not in favor of educators.

The same fair use guidelines that apply to print materials do not apply to audiovisuals. There are differing guidelines for print, multimedia, and distance learning, and the guidelines are not at all consistent. But educational exemption for use of audiovisuals is described within the law itself. Because of the nature of the audiovisual medium, producers worry not only about unauthorized copies but also about losing profits from unauthorized performances of the protected works. Unauthorized performances aren't generally a concern of print publishers, with the exception of those who publish plays and music. But producers of music recordings, movies, and television programs make their money from licensing those works for public exhibition and broadcast as well as from direct sales, so they are especially wary about what end users will do with the copy they have purchased. Had Congress allowed as free rein for copying audiovisuals as they permitted for print materials through the congressional guidelines, these media producers feared they would be cheated of profits that were rightfully theirs.

Aside from playwrights and composers, copyright owners of print materials needn't worry much about their performance rights because performance of print materials is not much of a problem. The right of adaptation is reserved for the copyright holder in all circumstances, and mounting a performance of a print work is no simple feat. In order for a print work to be "performed," it must be adapted for a play or painting or sound recording—a straightforward violation of copyright. But if graphic or illustrative materials are involved, a "performance" is as simple as a display. Simply tacking up a copyrighted work, when not associated with an educational fair use exemption, would be a technical violation of copyright if the display was intended for others to view.

Fundamental concept: The key to understanding the audiovisual guidelines is recognizing that Congress, when writing the law, wished to provide support to teachers in a classroom while presenting content to students. Beyond that, they had little sympathy for a school's request to be exempt from the requirements of copyright. The key element to remember is this: as long as the direct-teaching piece is in place, teachers are fairly free to use video and its cousins within the classroom. The primary problems teachers have with the guidelines are that teachers know there is more to school than just class, and there is more to learning than the set curriculum. Enrichment, reward, and relaxation are all valid parts of the educational experience, but they are not ones that Congress elected to support through exemption from the requirements of copyright law. Once that basic concept is internalized, the audiovisual exemptions fall into place.

What typical activities are covered?

It is very important to remember that this section of the law covers video, filmstrips, sound recordings, animated graphics, and all other nonprint formats that are not multimedia or distance learning.

Because school is a public place (in other words, it is not a private home), any performance of a copyrighted work in a school is considered a public performance. Public performance is a right reserved to the copyright holder. Certain types of public performances, however, are permitted under the exemptions for audiovisual performances included in section 110(1). If a particular showing should happen not to meet the requirements for exemption, does that mean the teacher cannot show the audiovisual work? Not at all. It just means that the showing isn't exempt from the requirements of public performance. Public performance of audiovisual media requires one of three things:

1. *permission from the copyright owner to hold a public performance,*

2. *a license from a rights broker that covers the work to be shown, or*

3. *payment of royalties to the copyright owner or his agent.*

The kinds of school activities covered by the guidelines in this chapter include the following:

- *showing films/video/television to present or summarize content*

- *showing films/video/television to reward students*

- *showing films/video/television to entertain/babysit students*

- *showing films/video/television in connection with extracurricular events*

"Video" in this context means any kind of video—analog or digital—whether on tape, on disc, or downloaded from the Internet from a site such as Netflix or YouTube. If you still have material on film, consider that "video" too. The same rules apply to all, regardless of physical format.

Movies—issues

The primary issue involved with showing movies is non-instructional showings or peri-instructional showings. A secondary issue involves archival copies. The following are examples:

violated, both the teacher and the principal could face dismissal for violation of district policy. Doesn't sound very pretty, does it?

- *Rainy day recess—What do you do with a group of squirmy third graders who can't go outside? Show them a movie! It will keep them quiet and still.*

- *General cultural-value showings—After lunch each day, some students finish fast and get restless. So to keep everyone in one location, you show a movie on some educational topic, even though it may have no relation to their classwork.*

- *Entertainment showings—The PTA offers a babysitting service during the PTA meetings. They show cartoons to keep the little children occupied and quiet in another room.*

- *Peri-instructional showings—The band must take a commercial bus to the state band competition. The bus is equipped with a video player and monitors, so the band director plans to show the movie* Mr. Holland's Opus *on the long drive.*

- *Extracurricular activities—The middle school cheerleaders are having a lock-in in the gym, and the sponsor plans to show the movie* Cheer.

- *Copies of video—Video is perceived as being fragile and expensive, and owners want to protect their investments. Some teachers and librarians want to make backup copies of videos they own so that they will have a replacement copy if something should happen to the original.*

The preceding scenarios are all common, typical school uses of audiovisuals (mostly video), and they all make management and economic sense. Unfortunately, they are all copyright violations! The key thing to keep in mind as you go through the explanations and rationale for the audiovisual rules is that the members of Congress who passed these rules must report to both educators and publishers/producers. Alas, because educators *consume* resources and publishers/producers *create* them and pay taxes on the income derived from them, Congress leaned toward the side of producers in this aspect of fair use.

TV/cable/satellite—issues

The issues surrounding television and cable programming are similar to those involving film and video. Non-curricular and peri-curricular showings are common, though non-permitted under section 110(1). Because many of the useful curriculum-related programs show at night and on weekends, teachers would like to record programs for showing at a better time of day, or a better time of the school year (when they are studying the topic of the program). Recording programs and retaining them is a different issue from just showing the program, as in the case of video and film. With off-air recording, you are actually making a *copy* of the program as well as performing it.

Typical scenarios include the following:

- *Recording news programs—A 20/20 program on gang warfare is appropriate for a Home and Family Living class.*

- *Recording movies—The English teacher wants to record*

Question: Can staff show video in their classrooms that they have purchased from the iTunes store and now have on their iPods or laptops?

Answer: Barring some specific license for an individual video (which sometimes happens), any legally acquired video may be used for direct instruction if you meet all the requirements of section 110(1) of copyright law. Section 110(1) is the five-factor assessment for exempt use of video for direct instruction.

Question: *Our school will charter large, commercial buses for an extended field trip. The buses have DVD players and TVs. We would like to show a movie owned by one of the teachers to keep the children occupied while we make this lengthy trip. Is this legal?*

Answer: Probably not, unless performance rights were acquired with the recording. This use of video is not face-to-face instruction. It probably involves some people who are not students and teachers in the class, such as a bus driver or chaperones, and the bus might be considered a bit strange for an instructional locale. The copyright holder, however, could grant (or sell) you one-time public performance rights. Additionally, the bus company may have a public performance license that will cover your use, or if your school has a performance license, your license may cover use in a school bus. Investigate your options.

this weekend's NBC playing of *Mel Gibson's* Hamlet *to show to her class at the conclusion of the current unit on the play.*

- *Recording sports programs—The gymnastics coach wants to record all the Olympics gymnastics events to show students proper form. She will retain the recording and use it every year.*

- *Recording cable broadcasts—The drama teacher wishes to record an A&E broadcast of* Rent *to show her advanced technical theater class.*

Recording is the major issue here, given that most schools don't subscribe to premium satellite and cable channels. Occasionally, the local cable company will provide a feed of the basic cable lineup, and showing those programs *live* is perfectly okay because you are a subscriber. However, subscribing at home allows you to record and retain programs for use at your convenience, but use at school (of programs recorded at home or at school) is public performance and therefore does not enjoy the same permissions as recording for private use at home. See more about recording from cable/satellite in the section on off-air recording.

Web—issues

Until the TEACH Act was enacted, "transmissions" of audiovisual works were prohibited. Now, under the requirements of TEACH, some transmissions of audiovisual materials are allowed. See the chapters on the Internet and distance learning for complete details.

Sound recordings—issues

Sound recordings include both music and spoken word recordings. The recordings may be on any type of medium, from wire recordings to vinyl to digital recordings. Although digital recordings have amazing clarity and depth of sound, a person can copy a digital sound recording with perfect reproduction an infinite number of times. The recording industry felt the effects of this simple technique as far back as 2002, citing significant drops in sales and profits (Recording Industry Association of America, 2002).

Typical activities involving sound recordings include the following:

- *Choir director purchases one copy of a CD of a musical that the school will perform and makes a copy for each cast member so that they all can review the songs before rehearsals start.*

- *The school webmaster streams a copy of the song the senior class has chosen as senior song.*

- *The reading resource teacher makes a backup copy of the recordings in all the book/recording sets in the reading resource room.*

What rights are affected?

Producers of audiovisual materials are anxious about their materials. They apply various technical protection measures to prevent copying or illegal performance of their works. Their reasons include potential violation of the following rights.

Reproduction

Copies, especially digital copies, mean unlimited reproduction at perfect quality. With the history of the decline of the recording industry after MP3 file-sharing, producers are understandably nervous about allowing copies for *any* reason.

Distribution

Going hand in hand with reproduction, distribution of copies is the copyright owner's biggest worry. The copies made could be distributed via networks like MP3 files are or on tape/CD/DVD. Distribution of television programs and video can occur through use of a video distribution system or through cable networks or microwave transmission.

Adaptation

Anytime you change the format of a work, you have created an adaptation. Changing a work from VHS to DVD or streaming video is an adaptation. So is taking clips and making a separate recording of excerpts (equivalent to an anthology of print works). If you expurgate a work (remove offensive words or scenes), you have also created an adaptation. Creative people, including directors, are highly offended when someone dares to change their work (see *Gilliam v. Am. Broad. Cos.* and *Clean Flicks of Colo. v. Soderbergh* in the section on relevant cases). Moral rights, though not terribly strong in the United States, may come into play in such a situation.

Public performance

Any performance that happens in a school is a public performance. The key to understanding what is public and what is not is who attends and where it occurs. A performance that occurs in your home *may* be private, depending on who attends (certainly an open house would not be a private event). A showing that occurs where the public may go cannot be private. Courts have ruled that a private viewing booth at a video store is a public place (*Columbia Pictures Indus. v. Redd Horne,* 1984), so a room in a public school is certainly public.

Virtually any copyrighted audiovisual work is capable of being publicly performed, be it music, drama, dance, motion picture, literary work, or other audiovisual expression. A public performance need not be a gala event in an auditorium. Something as seemingly trivial as playing your MP3 player through a set of speakers can be classed as a public performance, given the proper circumstances. Those circumstances are clearly defined in the law:

> *(1) . . . a place open to the public or at any place where a substantial number of persons outside of a normal circle of a family and its social acquaintances is gathered or (2) to transmit or otherwise communicate a performance or display of a work to a place specified by clause (1) or to the public, by means of any device or process, whether the members of the public capable of receiving the performance or display receive it in the same place or in separate places and at the same time or at different times.* (17 U.S.C. § 101)

Any performance of a copyrighted work under these circumstances would require a license. The gray area of this definition is the "substantial number." How many people outside the normal circle of a family does it take to cross the line into public performance? The *Columbia Pictures v. Redd Horne* case indicates that no one in addition to the viewer need be present to create a public performance, especially when various people view the material sequentially. Only one person viewing a video in the private viewing room of a public video store created a "public performance" according to the ruling in that case, so a classroom of unrelated students viewing a movie in a public school would certainly be a public performance as well. Putting motion media onto the open Web can certainly be considered a public performance because you have made it accessible to the world via the Web, which would meet the requirements of clause 2 in the preceding extract.

Public display

Section 101 of 17 U.S.C. defines a display:

> To "display" a work means to show a copy of it, either directly or by means of a film, slide, television image, or any other device or process or, in the case of a motion picture or other audiovisual work, to show individual images nonsequentially.

Where a display becomes "public" has always been an issue of concern. Obviously, the same definition of "public" applies here as it does for public performance. A place open to the public or anything beyond a family and its circle of social acquaintances is public, and therefore, any display at a public school would also be public. So would any display on the Internet. Remember, however, that there will be some fair-use and guideline exemptions that could come into play.

Digital transmission

Digital transmission was added to the rights of the copyright holder with the passage of the Digital Millennium Copyright Act. Digital transmission became a concern of music producers once they realized that Internet radio was streaming perfect digital copies of their songs to anyone who cared to save the files on their local computer systems. Because (and this is said with tongue firmly in cheek) a CD has perhaps only *one* good cut, why pay for an entire CD when you can grab the "good one" for no cost via Internet radio?

As a result of this concern, significant royalties must be collected for each listener of a recording digitally transmitted. The Register of Copyright periodically has hearings on the rate and then sets what the rate will be. The DMCA did not provide for any specific educational exemptions for digital transmission, but the various media would still fall under the existing TEACH Act if they met the act's requirements.

What guidelines affect AV materials?

Rules for using audiovisual materials are included in section 110(1) of 17 U.S.C., the current copyright law, so this will be a question of law, not one of externally developed guidelines. The actual wording says,

> Notwithstanding the provisions of section 106, the following are not infringements of copyright:
>
> (1) performance or display of a work by instructors or pupils in the course of face-to-face teaching activities of a nonprofit educational institution, in a classroom or similar place devoted to instruction, unless, in the case of a motion picture or other audiovisual work, the performance, or the display of individual images, is given by means of a copy that was not lawfully made under this title, and that the person responsible for the performance knew or had reason to believe was not lawfully made.

The rules are written in legalese, not in edu-speak, so it may take a bit of translation to explain the significance of the five factors included.

5 yes/no questions

Explaining how to base an audiovisual fair-use assessment on the paragraph excerpted here is really fairly simple. The result can be condensed into five yes/no questions, based on the factors set forth in the law. The form in this section (see Figure 6.1) gives you a shorthand way for a teacher to go through the fair use analysis, but because rationalization often justifies a recreational showing, an instructional leader is always a good check to verify appropriate use. See the following definitions for details on how to answer the questions on the form. *Any* answer of no on the form means that public performance rights are required to show the movie in that circumstance.

Nonprofit educational

The use here must truly be nonprofit. Interestingly, you don't have to make a profit to be "for profit." You only have to *try* to make a profit. So if your school hires a band for a school dance and charges admission, or the film/video club is taking donations to watch the Oscar-nominated films from 10 years ago, they are "for profit" even if they don't break even. This also means that for-profit day care centers and schools don't qualify for this factor.

Classroom or similar place

A "similar place" could be the auditorium, gymnasium, cafeteria, multipurpose room, library, theater, band hall, natatorium, or field house. A "similar place" probably would not be the local pizza parlor (unless this were a business class, and students were watching a movie on restaurant management) or on a bus on the way to a band competition.

Instructors and pupils in the course of face-to-face teaching activities

This factor means that the use must be for direct teaching in class. Reward, enrichment, and supplemental activities (unless directed by the teacher to the class) are not qualifying activities. Extracurricular and babysitting activities are also not covered here.

Legally acquired copy

There are many ways to legally acquire a copy of an audiovisual work. Basically, this factor is about assuring that the copy isn't pirated. As long as someone has legitimately paid for the copy, you are probably clear on this factor. Ways you can get a "legally acquired" copy include the following:

Library. You may use a copy of an audiovisual work owned by your school library.

Student or teacher. You may legally use a copy of a work owned by a teacher, a student, or a student's parents, as long as the work isn't recorded from cable or off-air beyond the recording guidelines (see the off-air recording section).

Borrowed from library. You may use a copy borrowed from the public library, from a university or community college library, or from a regional media library.

Figure 6.1. Audiovisual performance worksheet

Audiovisual Performance Worksheet

Answer the five questions below with YES or NO.

_____ 1. Are you a non-profit educational institution?
You are not non-profit educational if you are an Edison school, or if you work for a proprietary or some charter schools.

_____ 2. Will the showing be only for students and teachers in a regularly scheduled class?
You aren't in a regularly scheduled class if you are in an extracurricular activity, doing staff development, or having an all-school assembly

_____ 3. Will the showing take place in a classroom or other instructional place?
Instructional places can include the library, gym, auditorium, and cafeteria, but probably not a bus.

_____ 4. Is the showing made from a legally-acquired copy of the work?
Legally acquired copies can come from the library, the teacher, the student, a public library, a university, or a rental outlet unless the contract with the rental outlet prevents an exempt showing. A copy recorded off-air (or from a cable-only channel) outside of the permissions for that type of recording is not legally acquired.

_____ 5. Will the showing be used for direct teaching and of material use in presenting a lesson on your curriculum?
A showing is not used for direct teaching when it is not on a topic of the assigned curriculum for that class, when it is for entertainment, or for reward.

Do you have five YES answers? Congratulations! You may use the video without getting public performance rights.

You have a NO? Here is how to fix each NO (if you can fix it at all):

On #1 – You will need public performance rights for every showing.

On #2 – Eliminate the extra people for your showing.

On #3 – Move the showing to an instructional place.

On #4 – Borrow or rent a copy from one of the qualifying locations.

On #5 – Tie your showing tightly to the curriculum for the class in which you will show the program. Forget the entertainment, rainy day recess, and pass-the-big-test movie parties.

Copyright Carol Simpson, 2008.

Rented from video store. A copy rented from your local video store may be used as long as the teacher can answer yes to all five of the AV exemption questions. Long ago, video stores required you to sign a contract before you could check out videos. That contract sometimes restricted what you could do with the video you rented. If your video store still requires such a contract, check it to see if you might be in violation of the contract if you show the video to students at a public school. If your store doesn't require a contract at all, the videos are legally acquired, so they would be okay to use.

Caveat: digital downloads. A new wrinkle in audiovisual purchase arrived when iTunes began to sell downloadable video. Ordinarily, you could say that yes, a copy purchased from an online service is a legally acquired copy of the work. Nevertheless, when dealing with digital copies of anything, you should closely check to see if at the moment of purchase, or perhaps when you signed up for the service, you agreed to some terms that would restrict your use. In the case of iTunes and other video providers such as YouTube, you should look to see if you have agreed to a license on the works you purchase there that indicates you will use these works only for personal use. Although a qualifying school showing does not require public performance rights, your license may limit your ability to use that video outside your home or with a public group. In other words, you may have agreed to a license that tosses the traditional fair use assessments out the window. In that case, you will need to investigate the license under which you received the video to see what rights you do have. License always trumps.

Recorded off-air. A video recorded from an over-air channel under the off-air recording guidelines or from a cable/satellite channel with permission of the copyright holder is an acceptable source allowing you to answer yes to the question "Is the showing made from a legally acquired source?" (See off-air recording guidelines section.)

> *Question:* What do you know about companies that edit R-rated movies to remove sex, drugs, and inappropriate language and then sell the edited version? The companies to which I have been referred are Cleanflicks.com, Editmymovies.com, and Familyflix.net.
>
> *Answer:* Use caution with those companies. Several were targets of copyright infringement suits filed by the copyright owners of the edited films. The U.S. District Court for the District of Colorado (where the suit was filed) ruled that the copies the companies sold infringed the copyright of the various movie studios that owned the copyrights. None of the companies had permission to edit the films, and the copies they sold were illegal. Remember that one of the factors in doing a copyright fair-use evaluation to use video is using a copy that is "legally acquired," so using one of the illegal copies could be risky.
>
> If you want an expurgated movie that is legal, the *only* legitimate company I know of is Swank. Go to http://www.swank.com and choose "other group showings" from the options.

Although the librarian needn't demand receipts from students and teachers, a cautious approach would dictate that outside videos owned by students and teachers be accompanied by a statement from the owner verifying ownership (Figure 6.2). Should the copy later be determined to be fraudulent, the school and library then have a solid case that they had no knowledge that the recording was in violation (one of the requirements for a fair use determination under section 110(1)).

Of course, common sense would tell you that if the recording is not in a standard commercial case or is obviously re-recorded, the program is probably not legally acquired. In such a case, the librarian would be wise to refuse to show such a program, or to provide equipment to do so. A school or district policy addressing videos not owned by the school is an essential part of effective copyright compliance. The policy should be approved by the board, supported by the principal, and annually

Figure 6.2. Copyright verification form

I, _____, certify that the videotape/film,

_____

belongs to me/my household. This tape was purchased by/for me, and is a legally acquired copy of this
program.

I am lending this program to _____

as part of the educational program with the understanding that the program will be used for instructional

purposes only. I release the staff and students of _____

liability for damages that may occur to my tape.

Signed _____

Date _____

Question: A special education class regularly shows Disney movies (a student brings them from home) on Fridays as part of their curriculum. The teacher says that watching movies is part of their individual education plans (IEPs). These are very low-level students whose educational experience seems to be centered on social skills. Does an IEP override copyright law?

Answer: An IEP cannot stipulate that the teacher violate federal law. A school where I once served had a class of emotionally disturbed students who watched feature movies on a regular basis for "social skills." However, these were movies such as *License to Drive* and *Ferris Bueller's Day Off*, where the characters were forced to make decisions. The teacher would stop the movie, and the kids would discuss what the options were and what the possible repercussions are. Then they would watch the rest of the movie and see

called to the attention of the faculty. Such a policy would give the librarian a firm foundation to deny a faculty member's request to use questionable material.

Face-to-face teaching activities

This factor of AV fair use is generally the most difficult to meet; this is where in the analysis Congress expects to see the direct teaching. In other words, the display of the work must be related to the lesson at hand, not simply related to some type of lesson-past or a lesson-to-come. For example, the freshman English curriculum might require the students to read Shakespeare's *Romeo and Juliet* in September each year. However, the English teacher needs some time to prepare final exams later in the semester, so she decides to show the Franco Zefferelli movie of the play to occupy her students while she works on the exam months after the class has studied the play. Such use of the video would probably not be within the fair use exemption because the class is no longer studying the play. A good rule of thumb is to ask, "Is this an integral part of the unit I am teaching right now?" If the answer is "no," then the showing is probably a public performance. Beware of loose or questionable links from audiovisual material to lessons. Showing *Babe* because the class has been studying the farm is not a reasonable tie-in unless your local farms have talking animals. The same rationale would apply to showing *The Lion King* during a study of Africa or the great cats. There are many more curriculum-appropriate materials you could select. Showing at least portions of those films for a class studying digital animation would undoubtedly be a fair use.

Applying this factor kicks out the most common uses of media in schools: reward ("If you work hard on this project all week, we will have a movie on Friday afternoon"), recreation ("It is too cold/hot/rainy to go out for recess today, so we will watch an educational movie instead"), and babysitting ("We need to talk to the parents to-night at the PTA meeting, so let's send the little kids to the gym and let them watch a movie while we discuss the bond issue"). Extracurricular activities are also suspect under this factor because they are not direct teaching. Extracurricular activities such as film/video clubs are valuable recreations, but they are just that: recreations. Some universities have been cited for similar activities, so it is possible that public schools could also be targeted. You might just want to mark this factor as "unknown" on the assessment checklist, but that doesn't yield the five yes answers required for an affirmative decision. At that point, you want to assess your aversion to risk. Do you want to take a chance that no one associated with the movie producers will ever find out? Ask yourself whether students will tell parents what film they watched at school, or whether you are putting your plan to have "entertainment for the kids" in the PTA newsletter or are putting the film on the school marquee. Putting any mention of films in the local newspaper is a recipe for confrontation. Film companies and licensing watchdog agencies subscribe to clipping services that send them articles from small local and regional newspapers and links to Web pages mentioning their products.

> what happened. At the end, they discussed what had happened and why. This could qualify as fair use. Showing cartoons for reward (which is what this appears to be) is specifically prohibited—no matter *what* someone writes down in a lesson plan or IEP. Such uses require public performance rights.

Umbrella licenses

Unless a video use relies on a specific teaching goal documented in a district curriculum guide or state standard, one may reliably count on the need for a performance license. Several vendors sell so-called umbrella licenses or blanket licenses that permit the school or library to show non-curricular movies and videos from limited lists of producers. There are pros and cons to these licenses. A library-only license makes the librarian (and the library) the local "babysitter." Whenever the P.E. teacher is out, the kids are sent to the library to see movies to keep them entertained. If you have a building-wide license, teachers become lax in their use of video. The primary vendor of these licenses is Movie Licensing USA because they are the exclusive licensor of Disney works for public schools, but Motion Picture Licensing Corporation also licenses public schools for some film producers, and Christian Video Licensing International licenses churches and parochial schools. See Appendix D for contact information.

Additionally, beware of what might be called "general cultural value." Certainly there are many wonderfully educational videos on the market and perhaps in your library or personal video collection. However, showing these types of videos to a class without a specific curricular objective is not permitted under the "face-to-face" rule except when you own public performance rights on that video. If the objective isn't specified in the curriculum guide for this particular class, showing a video on that topic is a public performance, and license or permission is required.

> *Question:* Our student council plans to sponsor an event called "Flick on the Field." This event entails showing a movie on the large video screen on the scoreboard after the football game is over. I told the student council sponsor that because we do not hold public performance rights to the movie, it is a violation of copyright law, but she insists that because we are not charging admission, then we are permitted to show the movie. I have addressed this with our principal, and his stance is that because only students from our school will be viewing the movie, it is not considered a public performance. Is there any other information you can give me to help them understand the situation?

> *Answer:* The sponsor and the principal are both wrong. *Any* showing at a place open to the public (which is your football stadium) is a public performance. Any showing in a school is a public performance regardless of admission charge. Some

public performances are exempt by law. See the AV performance worksheet, and answer the five yes/no questions. If you can't answer yes to all of them, you have a non-exempt public performance, and you must pay royalties or get permission. Swank (http://www.swank.com) will license one-time showings for many of the more popular video producers. Choose "other group showings" at the main page.

Keep in mind that what is "curricular" for one class might not be part of the curriculum for another, no matter how "educational" the topic might be. For example, a French class might be able to show the movie *The Red Balloon* as an example of French culture (part of the curriculum for that class), but an English class would have difficulty tying in this wordless movie to its literature objectives.

Home use only

Many videos have a "home use only" notice. Some libraries and schools are fearful that using recordings so labeled will place them in jeopardy. The truth is that simply placing a "home use only" notice on a video does not restrict a school from lending a copy owned by the library or using the program if the use otherwise meets all of the fair use criteria set forth previously. The only exception to this rule of thumb would be if the video is shrink-wrapped with some sort of notice that opening the wrapping indicates acceptance of a limitation on the use of the video. License always trumps.

Once a recording has been sold, the "right of first sale" states that the copyright owner's exclusive distribution right to that copy has ceased (Reed, 1989, p. 2). The transfer of the right of distribution is the essential transaction that allows libraries to lend books and other materials. Note that only the right of distribution has ceased. The right of performance and display still resides with the copyright owner. In other words, the purchaser of a movie or video may lend, sell, or give the copy to whomever she wishes without worry. Performances of the movie, however, must still comply with the law regarding performances or displays.

Caution: Watch carefully for producers or suppliers who sell you a license to a program rather than sell you the program itself. Licensing a program is a way for a copyright owner to retain the distribution right because there is no actual sale. If you purchase a license to a program, you will be subject to any restrictions the copyright owner may choose to impose, including restricting your right to lend the program.

Mary Hutchings Reed, former consultant to the American Library Association, recommended that "home use only" labels be allowed to remain on movies owned by a library (Reed, 1989). A library would not want to appear to encourage copyright infringement, lest it be considered a contributory or vicarious infringer. The "home use only" label reminds patrons that the movie is not licensed for public performance, and although any lawfully acquired movie may be used in a qualifying educational setting, these movies are still subject to copyright restrictions in the matter of public performance.

Movie cautions

Following are some practices that are almost never acceptable with movies:

- *Making an anthology or collection from clips or excerpts (unless you are a film studies professor)*
- *Transferring the work to another medium—for example, film to video (analog) or video (analog) to digital video—unless the medium on which the work is stored is obsolete based on the legal definition of "obsolete" and the work is not available for purchase in a newer medium (with a small exception for some distance-learning uses under the TEACH act—see chapter 9)*
- *Using a program for recreation or reward without acquiring performance rights*

Examples of analysis

Situation: Students exempt from state standardized testing need something to keep them occupied for several hours. Principal decides to show a movie.

Analysis:

1. *Nonprofit educational: yes.*

2. *Classroom or other instructional place: yes, he plans to use the cafeteria.*

3. *Instructors and pupils in a class: no, these students are from several different classes.*

You can end the five-point analysis here because you encountered a no response. A public performance license is required for this showing.

Situation: You want to show a movie on the bus as the students in your class are on their way to a choir concert in the state capital.

Analysis:

1. *Nonprofit educational: yes.*

2. *Classroom or other instructional place: no, it would be difficult to justify the bus as a classroom.*

You can end the analysis here because you encountered a no response. A public performance license is required for this showing. Check with the bus company. Some have a blanket license that will permit this showing. If you have a license from Movie Licensing USA or one of the other licensing agencies, check your contract to see if it includes bus showings. Some do. If bus showings are something you contemplate doing frequently, discuss with your licensing agency what it would cost to include that permission in your contract.

Situation: The teacher shows a video from the library about the "age of plants" as enrichment for a unit on the "age of reptiles" so that she can work with students who are behind on their dinosaur reports. Only students in the class will watch the showing.

Analysis:

1. *Nonprofit educational: yes.*

2. *Classroom or other instructional place: yes.*

3. *Instructors and pupils in a class: yes, all those viewing the movie are students and teachers in this specific class.*

4. *Legal copy: yes, the video is owned by the school library.*

5. *Face-to-face teaching: No. This is not part of a regular lesson. It is being used for enrichment/ babysitting/reward for students whom the teacher needs to keep busy while she does something else.*

Situation: The PTA wishes to sponsor a family movie night at school in the cafetorium. Those in attendance will include students, their parents and siblings, and some teachers. Students and their families will not pay admission.

Question: For the days that teachers use movies for nothing but babysitting or "rewards," isn't it a violation to air something on our network that is a home-use-only recording from a video store such as Blockbuster and is an entertainment video?

Answer: Generally, it makes no difference *where* the recording is from, for either curricular or reward showings, as long as the source is legal. The only significant concern is whether you have public performance rights for the recording. Blockbuster doesn't sell or rent public performance rights; hence, you can use the recordings only in curricular situations. If your library owns the recording, for instance, and you have received or purchased public performance rights with the program, you can show it for whatever purpose you want. If you don't own public performance rights, however, you can legally show it only in curricular situations. A showing that meets the five yes/no tests for video does not require public performance rights. (See caveat about downloaded copies.)

Analysis:

1. *Nonprofit educational: yes.*

2. *Classroom or other instructional place: yes.*

3. *Instructors and pupils in a class: No. Not all of the attendees are students and teachers in a class. Parents and non-school siblings are not students in the class.*

You can end your analysis here because you got a no response to this question. This performance will require payment of royalties or permission of the copyright holder. Contact one of the rights brokers such as Movie Licensing USA, Motion Picture Licensing Corporation, or Swank.

Off-air recording guidelines

To the average classroom teacher, a video is a video—you stuff it into a player and press "play." A lot of misinformation floats around about what may be recorded and what may be retained. The number one consideration to keep in mind when trying to determine a recording's status is "who recorded this and when?" Court cases have determined that a private individual may record—for the purposes of "time shifting"—anything broadcast over the public airwaves or from cable channels to which the individual subscribes. The person may then retain the recordings without penalty. But the recording is only for the use of that individual and his or her immediate family and circle of friends (*Sony Corp. of America v. Universal City Studios,* 1984). Schools and libraries are not permitted such liberal recording. Recording for school is controlled by the off-air taping guidelines, which were part of a similar negotiation process from which came the print guidelines and the Guidelines for Educational Uses of Music (United States Copyright Office, 2009). The guidelines do not address recording original video broadcasts from the Internet, so that is an open point of discussion. One could easily analogize that a broadcast open to everyone online is similar to an off-air broadcast over the airwaves and that a broadcast from a channel that requires a subscription (either free or for some cost) is similar to cable. But no court has addressed this situation to date. The remainder of our discussion focuses on more traditional television broadcasts.

Recording programs from television can be simple or highly complicated. The key to knowing what you may record and what you may not record is how the program is getting to your television. For school use, programs may be freely recorded from regular broadcast channels. Broadcast channels are those local channels one can ordinarily receive via a television antenna as opposed to only via a satellite dish or cable. Some local channels are available both via an antenna and through the local cable system or through a satellite provider. If a particular channel is simultaneously rebroadcast on cable or satellite, the actual recording may be made from the cable or satellite transmission. This exception can be an advantage in instances when the cable/satellite signal is better than the broadcast signal or when the recorder is already hooked up to the cable or satellite instead of an antenna.

"Air" versus cable versus satellite

But what about all those wonderful cable channels: Disney Channel or Nickelodeon or Discovery or Lifetime? There are no recording exemptions for exclusively cable channels. Decisions to record a particular pro-

Question: May a program recorded off the air be shown twice in 10 days? For example, if a teacher has four sections of a class, can he show the recorded program to only two of them? Must he show the program to those four sections as part of the same lesson, or may he be divide the program into two (or more) class days?

Answer: Under the off-air guidelines, a program recorded off the air may be shown twice in a 10-day period. If the recording cannot be *shown* in a single class period, the showings certainly may be divided. As long as each class sees the entire program no more than twice in the 10-day period, you should be okay. All four sections may see the recording.

gram must be researched on the basis of granted rights. Because reproduction rights reside with the copyright holder, the ability of a school to record a program and retain it for any amount of time is wholly at the whim of the copyright holder. Many of these channels offer educators' guides that enumerate the available rights on a program-by-program basis. The Web sites *Kidsnet* (currently offline, but updated periodically), *Discovery Networks' Classroom Resources,* and *Cable in the Classroom* also offer retention rights information and addresses of producers so that permissions and supplemental materials may be requested. See Appendix M for addresses and phone numbers of these reference sources.

Satellite programming will have the same restrictions as cable broadcasts. Programs broadcast by satellite may not be recorded for school use without specific permission of the copyright holder. Deliberately de-scrambling encrypted satellite signals is a federal offense. If you have access to a streaming video source, your ability to record and retain the videos will be totally dependent on your license with the provider.

The location where you record has no effect on the legality of school use. A teacher or librarian or student may record programs at school or at home. If a librarian is recording a program, that recording must be at the request of a specific teacher or student. In other words, a librarian cannot record a program just because she knows someone will ask for it after the fact. We all know a teacher who will come into the library the day after a program airs, saying something like, "Gee, it was so good! You wouldn't happen to have that recorded, would you?" If you have recorded the program at the specific request of another teacher, you may fulfill the appeal; otherwise, you will have to disappoint. Maybe the next time a program airs, the teacher will be better prepared. (See the section on recording in anticipation.) The librarian or administrator can certainly remind teachers that a potentially useful program is approaching, and if a teacher wishes the library to make a copy, the teacher should put in a request.

Copies recorded off-air *must* include all copyright information, usually included in the credits at the end of the program. The program need not be shown in its entirety, but the program itself must not be edited or altered from its original content. See the discussion of *Gilliam v. American Broadcasting Companies* in the section on related cases. In other words, using the fast forward button on the player is acceptable, but editing or shortening the program is not always legal, especially if it removes the copyright information.

As the librarian or technologist accepts recording requests from teachers, keep one requirement in mind: the same teacher may not record (or request to be recorded) the same program multiple times, no matter how many times the program is rebroadcast. A common example would be a teacher's recording a program and showing it to his class. He erases or destroys the recording when the 45-day limit expires as the guidelines

Question: Okay, I know I can't record a cable or satellite program and retain the recording under the off-air taping guidelines. But can I show the program live to my class?

Answer: If your showing meets the requirements of the five factors for audiovisual performance, you may show the program to your students live unless you are under some license or other contract that says you may not.

Question: I already taught a unit earlier in the school year, but now a program is on TV about that topic. I know I will want to use the program with the unit next year when I teach the topic again. Can I record it and save it to use for the next year?

Answer: Your question raises several additional questions: What channel is it? If it is ABC, CBS, NBC, or Fox, for example (normal channels you can get with an antenna), you have 10 *school days* from the date of recording to use the program. You can keep the recorded program for 45 *calendar* days, but only for evaluation for possible purchase. After that time, you must erase the recording. If the channel is a cable or satellite channel, you have no automatic recording rights. Check http://www.ciconline.org for possible permissions and retention rights.

require. The next year, the program is rebroadcast, and he records the program again. This second recording may not be used with students unless specific, written permission is received from the copyright holder.

Is this significant? Certainly. An Arizona school district settled a copyright infringement suit alleging that recordings had been made off-air and had not been erased or destroyed at the end of the 45-day retention period. The Association for Information Media and Equipment (AIME) vigorously pursued the district, eventually receiving significant monetary damages from the district as well as a commitment to follow copyright regulations strictly in the future (AIME, 1990). AIME is known as an industry watchdog, and given the slightest inkling that a district is in violation of copyright, it will intervene on behalf of its member companies.

So how does one protect oneself and the school from inadvertent infringement in this area? The best suggestion would be to create and maintain a log of recording and use requests (Figures 6.3 and 6.4). This database will contain a history of all off-air recordings used by a particular teacher. Although it is possible to manually log recordings, a computer database is the most efficient method of maintaining this type of record. Create fields for teacher, program, channel or network, broadcast date or date recorded, and retention rights. When a teacher submits another recording request (or presents a home-recorded video), sort the database according to the teacher's name and check earlier requests. It will be easy to find a duplication by that teacher. Remember that this database will grow. It isn't a database that can be trashed at the end of each school year. Recordings are cumulative. Once a teacher has recorded a particular program (meaning episode or single broadcast), that teacher may not record the same program again without express permission, even if the program is rebroadcast many months or years later.

Retention. Once you record a program, when must you use it? The retention restrictions are explicit. You may keep a recorded program for a maximum of 45 consecutive (calendar) days. Of those 45 days, students may view the program only during the first 10 school days. (Note that student use considers school days, but total time counts consecutive days, including weekends and holidays.) Even those first 10 days are prescribed: once for instruction, once for reinforcement. No other viewings are possible under the fair use guidelines. During the other 35 days of the 45-day period, you may use the program only for teachers to evaluate the program for possible purchase or request for permission. You may retain the program beyond the 45-day period only if you receive explicit, written permission from the copyright holder. Lacking such permission, erase or destroy the recording at the end of the 45-day period.

Note that these so-called fair use rules apply only to programs recorded off regular broadcast channels. Cable or satellite programs that permit limited school use may impose specific retention restrictions that may be more liberal or more narrow than the standard 10/45-day fair use (e.g., three days, one year, or life-of-recording). Check program guides and cable-in-education periodicals for specific details on each program, such as the guidelines identified at Cable in the Classroom: http://www.ciconline.org/copyright.

There are, of course, "special" situations that must be dealt with vis-à-vis copyright. What about a student who was ill and missed an

Question: A teacher has some TV broadcasts recorded off-air several years ago. He has not been able to find a source from which we may purchase a copy. How do we determine that a program is no longer available for purchase? And if it is no longer available for purchase and/or broadcast, is he able to use his recorded version in school?

Answer: The teacher may not retain those programs more than 45 days post-broadcast, so the recordings are illegal for school use (personal use at home doesn't have this restriction). This isn't the same situation ("not available at a reasonable price") as replacing a book that has been damaged. This is part of the off-air recording guidelines. These recordings may have *never* been available for sale, and that decision is the prerogative of the copyright owner. If the program is not available for sale, and the recordings are older than 45 days past the broadcast from which they were recorded, your only option will be to track down the copyright owner to request permission to use the recordings.

Figure 6.3. Off-air video log sample

Teacher	Program	Channel	Date	Rts.
Miller	Whale watch	PBS	9/3/05	fair use
Armand	Using a ruler	NBC	9/5/05	fair use
Raney	The Vietnam experience	Life	9/16/05	7 day
Kyser	National Geographic special	PBS	9/17/05	life/tape
Miller	Oprah	NBC	9/20/05	fair use

Figure 6.4. Off-air video log

Teacher	Program	Channel	Date	Rts.

in-class showing? Could another showing be arranged for that student? Probably. Because the library is a place for instruction, and the librarian is certainly an instructor or is directed by the regular instructor, the librarian could arrange a makeup showing of the recording to the student, but only during the first 10 days after the program is recorded. The fair use guidelines still apply to the 10-day play limit. If the student does not return until after the 10-day limit has expired, the student will have to rely on other methods to get the information presented in the program.

Home recording. As long as a program is recorded and housed in the library, the librarian can be assured that the recording will be properly logged and will be erased at the end of the 45-day period. But what about home-recorded programs brought to school by teachers and students? The location of the physical act of recording makes no difference at all. What affects school use of recorded television programming is the source of the broadcast (broadcast, cable, or satellite) and the date of the recording. The 10/45-day rules apply to recordings from regular broadcast channels, no matter who makes the recording or where they are recorded. In other words, if a teacher records a program from a local broadcast channel in December but wants to show it in May, such a showing would not be permitted under the off-air guidelines, and specific, written permission from the copyright holder would be required. A recording from a cable or satellite channel would be governed solely by the retention and use periods allocated by the copyright owner, if any.

Figure 6.5. Off-air recording verification

This tape_____

was recorded off-air _____ *by me / for me* _____ on channel_____

on (date) _____. The 10th consecutive school day from the

recording date is _____. I may use this recording only once in

relevant teaching activities. I may repeat the showing only once for reinforcement.

The 45th day after the recording date will be _____. Between the 11th

and the 45th day, this tape may be used for teacher evaluation only. It will not be shown to students during

this period unless permission has been received from the copyright owner.

I made _____copies of this recording. Each copy is accompanied by this statement.

This recording will be erased/destroyed no later than the 45th day indicated above.

Teacher_____

Library staff_____

Date _____

Signature indicates the statement above has been read and understood.

Figure 6.6. Off-air recording label

Teacher's Name:_____

Program Title:_____

Date Recorded:_____ Erase/destroy By:_____

Teacher's Guide: _____YES _____NO

To order a video copy of this program (after this recording has been erased), call
_____.

So how does the librarian or technologist know the specific details of recordings brought into the building by teachers and students? Although it is certainly possible to follow a "don't ask, don't tell" policy concerning outside video, you would have no documentation should a recording ever be challenged. The best alternative is to require a signed affidavit stating the date and channel on which the program was recorded (Figure 6.5). In addition, each copy should have a label attached similar to that in Figure 6.6.

Copies of off-air recordings. In some cases, one program might be appropriate for more than one class at a time; for example, a documentary might be suitable for all the American history classes to view. Not all school buildings are fortunate enough to have a centralized video distribution system that allows a single recording to flow to multiple classrooms. In such an instance, the school may make copies of the off-air recording, one for each classroom that would need to view the program at the same time. Each copy must have the same off-air recording notices and copyright information attached, and each copy is subject to the same time restrictions as the original. For example, if a recording were made on Sunday, the third day of the month, and the copies of the original recording were made on Tuesday, the fifth day of the month, all showings to students from all of the recordings would have to be counted as if all the recordings were made on Sunday the third. The 45-day requirement would also apply to all of the copies, counted from the date of the original recording.

Recording in anticipation

Persons in authority may not forecast that teachers will request copies of a particular resource and record that item so that it will be available on the chance that a teacher might ask for it. This type of situation frequently occurs when a principal or librarian notices that there is a television program scheduled to air that would relate to some curriculum. The educator decides to copy the program in expectation that teachers will ask for the program after the fact. In order to comply with the off-air guidelines, the request for recording must come from the teacher who wishes to use the program. This is often described as a "bottom up" rule: the person at the point of use (the classroom) is the one who must make the request for copying.

Public performance rights

Because many audiovisual materials may be purchased with public performance rights, wise librarians track which of their materials have such rights. Entries in the catalog, stickers on individual items, and log books all successfully inform library patrons of the items for which rights have been purchased. A notation on how the rights were acquired would be helpful, as well as the duration of the rights—for example, "via catalog," "life-of-recording," or "on P.O. #123456, 2 years (exp. 11-15-13)."

A file of performance rights documentation would also be a good idea. A few suppliers, especially video producers, provide blanket public performance rights in the prices of all videos in their catalogs. A photocopy of this statement from the catalog attached to the purchase order for the videos should be sufficient documentation. Another supplier includes a statement on the order envelope stating, "The video cassettes you purchase from XYZ Company are sold for school and library use. Broadcast rights are not included. Programs may not be reproduced, copied, or transmitted without written permission." An extra-thorough method of ensuring a complete understanding would be to include a line on the purchase order stating, "All materials to include public performance rights" (or archival rights, if you wish to make backup copies of the programs). Acceptance of the order with this statement included would contractually obligate the supplier to provide public performance rights as well *unless the supplier responds that the order is being shipped as an accommodation, and they do not provide such rights* (Figure 6.7). Make sure that whoever receives arriving purchases forwards to the ultimate user a copy of any communication (including boilerplate language on the packing slip) that arrives with the product. That language may reject your request for public performance

Figure 6.7. Sample purchase order

PURCHASE ORDER #12345123
SMALLVILLE INDEPENDENT SCHOOL DISTRICT
4321 S. Front Street
Middletown, USA

To: Video Supplier
    1234 Main Street
    Hollywood, CA

Please accept our order for the following:

Quantity	Title	Price
1	Copyright and you (VHS)	$25.00
1	A school librarian's view of copyright (VHS)	$50.00
	shipping	$ 5.00

Note: All videos will include public performance rights. If additional charges are required confirmation must be received before shipment.

	TOTAL	$80.00

rights, and you may be unaware of the change. Depending on the law in your state, if you keep the item with the change in the terms, you may have accepted their changes. *Caveat:* Be certain that you are sending the order to a company that is able to broker such licenses. Some AV jobbers will supply the recordings on the purchase order even though they are not able to broker the performance rights.

The sale of public performance rights is a contractual obligation, so the purchaser and the copyright owner (usually through a supplier or distributor) can negotiate whatever rights package the owner would like to sell and the purchaser can afford. Don't be afraid to propose the type of performance rights you need. The worst the copyright owner can do is say no. Just make sure you prepare your proposal far in advance of your anticipated performance date. The educational fair use exemptions don't apply to non-instructional public performances, and if you have not acquired the necessary rights before your public performance, you are on hazardous ground.

Examples of acceptable performances

A teacher shows a library-owned video to his sixth-grade science class to demonstrate the effects of water pollution as part of a lesson on ecology. This use is protected under the educational exemption because it meets all of the necessary criteria: it is presented for enrolled students by an instructor in face-to-face teaching in a classroom, and the copy is legally owned by the library (or at least the teacher has no reason to think it is not legally acquired).

An English teacher's classes have been studying *Romeo and Juliet.* To conclude the unit, the teacher shows the English department's recording of the Franco Zefferelli version of the play in class, spreading the program over three class days. This use is also protected under the educational exemption. The teacher is showing the program; it is an integral portion of the lesson; the performance is taking place in the classroom; and the copy has been purchased by the English department.

An elementary school music teacher plays a recording of a performance of John Philip Sousa's "Stars and Stripes Forever" as part of a unit on patriotic music for third graders. The recording accompanied the music text. This is a performance in class, by a teacher, within a lesson plan, with a legally acquired copy.

Examples of unacceptable performances

The PTA shows a library-owned copy of *The Little Mermaid* to the children of members in a classroom while the officers have a meeting in the library. The copy is legally acquired, the performance takes place in a classroom, and the performance may be presented by a teacher or pupil, but this

Question: A language arts teacher is teaching a unit on science fiction. She would like to use short clips from several science fiction movies. Can this be handled in a legal manner?

Answer: The answer is "it depends." If she has the clips cued up on the recordings, and she punches play, runs the clips, and then pops out the media and does the same to the next one, sure. If she wants to make a new recording with just the clips in question, then the answer is no—that is considered making an anthology and is not permitted unless she is a professor of film studies. However, if she is making a multimedia program (PowerPoint, etc.), she can use up to three-minute clips of video in that presentation, but she will need to check the new multimedia guidelines for the specific limits, retention times, reuse limits, and so on. For use in teaching their classes, university-level teachers of film studies (but not K–12 teachers of the same topic) may circumvent copy protection to make anthologies of movie clips from movies owned by the school (37 C.F.R. 201.40).

performance is not a part of face-to-face teaching activities. This would be considered entertainment or reward and as such would not be permitted without public performance rights. This example would require payment of royalties for the performance. Renting a copy of the video would have no effect on the legality of the performance, and the school may be liable for providing equipment for an infringing performance. The same prohibition would apply to movies or recordings used to reward classes for good grades, commendable behavior, or perfect attendance.

On the last day of the semester, the American history teacher decides to play for his class a record on the Cuban missile crisis so that he can calculate grades while the students are occupied. The class is not currently studying that portion of the curriculum. This use is not acceptable because the face-to-face teaching requirement is not met. Although a weak case can be made for the fact that the topic will eventually be covered, this topic is not under the current lesson plan. Public performance rights would be recommended in this case.

Because the drama teacher gives such hard tests, a group of drama students decides to rent a video of a play they have been studying and show it in the drama room after school to review for the upcoming exam. Several of the students plan to bring friends to watch the movie with them. This would definitely be considered a public performance because non-students (the friends) would be involved in the session. This also would not be considered face-to-face teaching because the instructor would not participate in the meeting. The students could do the same performance at one of their homes with no copyright implications for the school.

Archiving audiovisual works

Copyright law pertaining to computer software allows the purchaser to make a single backup copy (also called archival copy) of the diskettes in case something unfortunate should happen to the original diskettes. Unfortunately, audiovisual materials do not come with the same archival permission as does computer software under 17 U.S.C. § 117(a). Owners of film, video, or audio may not make backup copies of the works unless they have some license that grants such rights. The usual terms of purchase are similar to that of a book: you may use the material until it wears out or breaks. At that point you may attempt to repair it, but usually the best alternative is to replace the work. In the case of video and audio, this is called "life of tape" (though it should probably now be called "life of recording"). You have the right to use the program as long as the recording works. When the recording breaks, corrupts, or wears out, it is probably time to look for a replacement. The good news is that recording costs are usually quite reasonable, at least for works available from more than one source. Some educational producers offer low-cost or lifetime replacements, as well. If you still have film materials, film producers often sell replacement footage at a very reasonable cost. Because you cannot easily splice videotape, it is not possible to replace a few feet damaged when "eaten" by a video player. And a non-technical person generally cannot repair a damaged DVD, MP4, or MP3 file.

When a film breaks, given that backup onto tape or digitization is permitted only in limited circumstances, the only alternatives consistent with copyright law are to splice the film or to purchase replacement footage if the damage is extensive. The same holds true with audiotape. Backups onto other tapes or digital media (compact disc or digital audio storage) are not allowed unless an unused replacement is unavailable in the marketplace at a "reasonable price." The law waives this prohibition when a copyrighted work is recorded on a medium that is no longer in regular use, such as Beta format videotape or reel-to-reel video. Because Beta format is obsolete, you may transfer your Beta programs onto VHS tape or digital storage without specific permission for each program. The DMCA defines a format as obsolete "if the machine or device necessary to render perceptible a work stored in that format is no longer manufactured or is no longer reasonably available in the commercial marketplace." So if you can no longer buy a Beta-format player, you can transfer your work onto DVD or VHS tape or digital storage. But if you can still buy a VHS player at a "reasonable price," you may not legally transfer your VHS programs to the streaming server or to DVD. *Important note:* if the work is available for sale in a modern format, the law demands purchase rather than copying.

Closed captioning

There has been much discussion of the legality of adding closed captions to existing video. Some experts argue that adding the special digital coding required for this feature results in a "derivative work" (Sinofsky, 1993; Kruppenbacher, 1993). Such a derivative work would not be in compliance with copyright. Frank Kruppenbacher, ITV program coordinator at the National Technical Institute for the Deaf, argues that in order to make a closed-captioned copy, one must make a working copy to which one adds the necessary encoding. He contends that the working copy is, in itself, a violation of copyright.

However, Congressman Robert Kastenmeier stated during congressional arguments on the Copyright Revision Act of 1976 that the legislative intent of the law would specifically allow the making of a working copy with closed captioning in an institution serving the hearing impaired, as long as the copy stayed within the institution requiring it. The copy must necessarily be restricted from general use, but it might be shared among other institutions serving hearing-impaired populations (United States Copyright Office, 2009).

If your building has a population of hearing-impaired patrons, you would probably be safe in closed-captioning your videos that aren't already so encoded. Keep in mind the guidelines Congressman Kastenmeier set forth as parameters, and you will probably not be challenged. If still in doubt, consult a copyright attorney.

Question: The orchestra director would like to have a concert using movie theme songs. We would like to play video of the movie while the orchestra is playing. Our question is, how can we use the video without breaking any copyright laws?

Answer: This isn't face-to-face instruction, and simply answering "no" to that qualifying question means that you don't qualify for an automatic fair use exemption on the use of the movie. You can, however, go through the four tests of fair use to see if you qualify on those grounds.

Question: I have some very expensive videos in my library collection and I'm afraid to circulate them for fear that something might happen to them. May I make an archival copy of the video as I do with the computer diskettes we circulate?

Answer: No, you can't make backup or archival copies of video without specific permission to do so. Copyright laws give express permission to make archival copies of computer software only. No other medium is granted such permission. However, if the video is on, for example, Beta tape (now obsolete) and not for sale in newer formats, the DMCA allows you to transfer the recording to a current technology (VHS or digital). That means you can transfer a Beta tape if you cannot buy that same program in VHS or DVD. But if your program is available in a current format, you are obliged to purchase a replacement if you want a copy: no gratis transfers if the producer has the work for sale.

Video distribution

Video distribution is a type of closed-circuit network in which a classroom teacher (usually) controls video being sent from centralized equipment in the building. Videos are loaded into centrally housed players and are either started at a predetermined time or started by the particular teacher requesting the program. The advantage of the technology is that one doesn't have to roll equipment all over a building, and there is some control over the amount and type of video being used in a building. Additionally, the software that controls the players can track and record usage and generate reports of which programs and players were used most often and which programs were played by which teachers. The primary disadvantage is that because the librarian (usually) is the person loading and perhaps starting the videos, the librarian becomes a part of the copyright compliance loop.

According to Mary Brandt Jensen, law librarian and law professor, the library or librarian can be considered a contributory infringer if "the library caused, assisted, encouraged, or authorized the patron to do the infringing act or was in a position to control the use of the copyrighted work by the patron" (Jensen, 1992, p. 150). Obviously, if the library is the site of a video being infringed, the library would have to produce considerable evidence that it was unaware of the nature of the video in order to be held blameless. Are the copyright police going to come get you? Probably not. But could you be required to give deposition testimony against your fellow teachers or administrators if a copyright owner suspected an infringement and sued? Certainly.

Librarians can solve the problem of questionable video recordings in the video distribution system by requesting certain documents from teachers before the recordings are played:

- *If the recording to be played is owned by the library, the teacher need only submit a copy of the lesson plan showing the link between the lesson and the video. Because the building librarian is familiar with the curriculum of the various grades and classes, it is obvious if someone is showing video that is outside his assigned curriculum. The librarian could also request the assistance of the administrative staff in assessing the appropriateness of the showing.*

- *If the recording to be shown was rented from a local video store, the teacher still must meet the fair use requirements of the law in order to use the recording in class.*

- *If the program was recorded off-air, the teacher must submit a verification of compliance with the off-air guidelines.*

Recording off-air, in contrast to recording from cable, is permissible within strict fair-use guidelines. Those guidelines were discussed in the section on off-air recording. Programs recorded by the library staff at the request of teachers should be clearly labeled as copyrighted material, with both the recording date and erasure date explicitly noted on the medium. To assume that all recordings brought to the library for play in the retrieval system are within the legal limits for fair use is naïve. If the teacher were to play an illegal recording and be caught, the copyright owner would have a potential case against the librarian as a contributory infringer because the librarian assisted in the illegal performance.

Having a copy of the teacher's lesson plan showing direct correlation of the movie to the day's lesson is a good idea.

Digital video servers/video streaming servers

When converting analog (tape) videos into digital (hard disk) storage, one must first convert the format of the video. Format conversion is an adaptation, creating a derivative work. Although there are a few limited exceptions for works no longer available in the marketplace (see previous section), most conversions are a violation of one of the rights of the copyright holder. In addition, the purpose of the conversion is to distribute the video, another right of the copyright holder. Naturally, you also have made a copy of the work, and you have copied all of it. The work is creative, and you have done the copying to avoid paying for a digital copy of the work. So a fair use assessment here doesn't look good either. Use extreme caution in making these conversions. Many of the educational video producers are now offering digital versions specifically for streaming servers, so investigate that option. Educational media producers are actively looking for streaming cases. See, for example, the explanation of the Association of Instructional Media and Equipment to a university's plan to stream video to classes (Lutzker, 2010). As you can tell from the tone of the piece, the group is not happy about the practice and is threatening litigation. Its position is that the university's streaming of videos it had purchased "was a violation of copyright that raised a very serious threat to the educational video publishing community" (p. 1).

Sound recordings

Sound recordings, as used in this section, include phonograph records, audio recordings in analog (cassette), digital (e.g., MP3) and proprietary (e.g. Playaway) formats, compact discs, reel-to-reel tape, and hard disk–based recordings. These types of media are distinct from the section on music because music also includes the print music notation, as well as performance of the printed music. This section deals only with recorded aspects of music but also includes all other types of recordings, such as spoken word.

All the formats listed in the preceding paragraph can be and are protected by copyright. Even if you do not see a copyright

Question: If we have a situation that otherwise meets the conditions of fair use, and we have three separate classrooms that need to see the same video, can we stick a home-use video into our media distribution system and send it out to the three rooms simultaneously?

Answer: This is likely a fair use. Providing all the classes are studying the same topic, and teachers and students are present, this type of showing is not significantly different from hooking three TV monitors to one video player—a use which is generally accepted to be fair. When video distribution leaves the campus, however, a court might decide that you are doing closed-circuit broadcasting, which requires a completely different set of licenses.

Question: Our district is looking at a system for video delivery. To make this work, every analog video must be transferred to a new, digital format and stored on a server. Not only would this be changing format, but also, because the video would be placed on the server, multiple users could then use the video. The district people and sales people are saying they think it's legal because we would only be transferring the image of videos we have bought.

Answer: Just because you own the analog recordings doesn't mean you can do anything with them you choose. You have no inherent right to make a copy of the videos in analog format, much less in digital format. Note that often in licenses you will see a prohibition about "storage in any digital retrieval system." This proposed use potentially violates the right of duplication, the right of adaptation, and the right of distribution. Remember: a sales person wants to sell you an expensive new toy, not necessarily advise you that the use of that toy might be illegal. Get permission to digitize those analog recordings if they are in VHS format as long as VHS players are still on the market. Once you can no longer purchase a VHS player, it will be safe to make a transfer. Remember, though, that being able to make a transfer because the medium is obsolete and the work is not for sale in another format does not mean the video is in the public domain, and it doesn't mean you can make multiple copies of the transferred video.

Question: Our assistant principal wants to purchase a high-speed cassette-duplicating machine. He wants to get recordings of various types and pick songs or stories from them to make a collection. He will copy all these cassettes so that teachers can have them in their classrooms. Isn't this an anthology?

Answer: Not only is this making an anthology; it is also reproduction (a protected right) and distribution (yet another protected right). The suggested use says anything about curriculum, classroom teaching, or any of the other triggers that *might* bring in a discussion of fair use. Of course, at the scope suggested, fair use would likely be out the window anyway.

Playing the *original* recordings in the classroom—as long as

symbol on the item itself, you must assume all sound recordings published after February 15, 1972, to be copyrighted unless specifically shown otherwise because the law no longer requires notice of copyright. Some recordings use the special symbol assigned to phonorecords (also known as phonograms)—a "p" in a circle, ℗, similar to the "c" in a circle, ©, commonly understood to be the symbol designating copyrighted print materials. Remember that *neither* symbol is required, so the absence of a symbol really tells you nothing about the copyright status of a work.

In earlier times, when a sound recording was played publicly, the *composer* of the music was entitled to a royalty, but the *performer* of the music was not. The performers did receive royalties from sales of recordings, but not from public performances of the recordings. The reasoning here was that sound recordings did not have public performance rights. However, some jazz and blues recordings are performances that have always been covered by copyright. These styles of music rely heavily on improvisation. Because the work is "fixed" only at the time of recording, there is a dual copyright—that of the composer who wrote the basic song and that of the performer who improvised a section of the performance. However, since February 15, 1972, all sound recordings now carry a dual copyright: for the composer and for the performance. The rights to the performance are typically owned by the record company. This expansion of the earlier rights explains why you may see a copyright notice on a recording of a public domain work, such as classical music. Recordings fixed prior to February 15, 1972, may have had some copyright protection under state copyright laws, but such protection was highly variable, and the 1976 copyright act eliminated all state copyright laws.

Because the Internet has become an active medium in the transmission of sound recordings, and because many people are substituting Internet transmissions of performances for the *purchase* of CDs or tapes (think Pandora), in 1995 Congress granted public performance rights to "digital audio performances." Web pages that deliver recordings on the request of the viewer may be in violation of the new right (17 U.S.C. § 114(d–f)). The No Electronic Theft (NET) Act (P.L. 105-147) provides criminal penalties for those who violate copyright of sound recordings via the Internet, even if the violator makes no profit from the transaction (UCLA, 1998).

Sound recordings have the same requirements and permissions as do all audiovisual materials. Sound recordings of music add an extra onus to the mix. A work may involve three copyrights: one for the sheet music, a second for the recording, and possibly a third for the arrangement. For example, a current hit record may have music and lyrics copyrighted by the author and an arrangement of the music copyrighted by someone completely different, and the actual recording of the performance of that music and lyrics may be covered by an entirely different copyright owned by the record company that made the recording. Or a public domain work may have been recently arranged, and the creative elements of the new arrangement may be protected by a copyright (Kohn & Kohn, 2010). In order to receive permission to use the recording in any derivative work, video, or public performance, you must get permission from all copyright holders or qualify for some sort of fair use defense. Occasionally a teacher will ask students to perform music and record the performance to use as background music for a multimedia presentation. Even if the music is in the public domain, the arrangement of the music may not be. Additionally, the students now own the copyright to their own performance of the music. You will need clearance for any use beyond use by the students involved.

Three organizations do most of the copyright clearances for professional music recordings: the American Society of Composers, Authors and Publishers (ASCAP); Broadcast Music, Inc. (BMI); and SESAC, Inc. Following is the contact information for these organizations:

ASCAP
One Lincoln Plaza
New York, NY 10023
212-621-6000
http://www.ascap.com

BMI (Broadcast Music, Inc.)
320 W. 57th St.
New York, NY 10019
212-586-2000
http://www.bmi.com

SESAC, Inc.
421 W. 54th St.
New York, NY 10019
212-586-3450
http://www.sesac.com

See the chapter on music for more details about recording sheet music.

Non-instructional performances of sound recordings

There is an exemption in the law for non-instructional performances of sound recordings in schools. Section 110(4) grants schools an exception to the performance rights requirement when the performance meets four factors. First, the performance of the sound recording (or print music, for that matter) may not be made by transmission. In other words, the performance must be made directly to an audience and not sent via a public address system or cable television system to people in locations that would not be able to hear the initial performance without the aid of the technology, such as people in a different room or building. Second, the performance must be nonprofit in nature.

they are directly tied to the lesson at hand in that specific classroom, *and* as long as the teacher is the one to make the decision to use the recordings (remember: a bottom-up scheme), *and* the only ones to hear the recording are the students and teachers in the class, *and* you are in a nonprofit educational institution, *and* you are working with a legally acquired (i.e., someone bought it) copy of the work—should be okay. The problem here is that under the AV guidelines (basically summarized here), you must comply with *all* of the provisions. If you say "no" to any of the conditions just listed, you don't qualify for fair use.

Question: Is it okay for a teacher to take an audiobook on CD that the school owns, copy it to iTunes, and have the student listen to it on an iTouch (or iPod or MP3 player)?

Answer: Although individuals have the ability to make those types of transfers under the Audio Home Recording Act, for schools and school libraries (which have differing rules) those provisions do not apply. Under section 108, *libraries* have the capability to make a single copy of a phonorecord (which is the technical name for an audiobook) if the copy is not for the purpose of commercial advantage (you aren't making an extra copy to avoid purchasing another copy), your library is open to the public, and you include the same copyright notice on the copy that was on the original (17 U.S.C.A. 108(a)). However, the section excludes copies of musical works (which includes music CDs), audiovisual works (movies would fall into this category) and graphics (17 U.S.C.A. 108(i)). Further, § 108 says that any library that has accepted a contract (such as a shrink-wrap contract or accepting terms of service) is bound by that contract (17 U.S.C.A. 108(f)(2)). This provision would apply if you download recordings from a Web site such as iTunes or Audible.com, where you must accept terms of service to make the download. You will be bound by any contract you agree to (typically by clicking "I accept" somewhere on the Web site, maybe only when you first set up your account).

Question: We would like to play commercial music such as CDs in the library as background. This would be done with a sound system that could be heard in all parts of the library. Are there any restrictions or guidelines that we should consider?

Answer: This is a performance of a sound recording, so you must look at public performance rules. This type of performance may fall under the exemptions of section 110(4) of the copyright act if you can meet four requirements:

1. There can be no transmission of the performance. The performance of the recordings must be made directly in the presence of the audience. How big your "sound system" is might affect the analysis here. A simple boom box would likely be okay, but a PA system that carries sound into several rooms of the library might not.

There cannot be any direct or indirect commercial advantage given by the performance, and this does not refer only to profits from admission fees, either. Sometimes the profit can be from selling refreshments or other items that would not be sold except for the lure of the "free" performance. Third, none of the performers, organizers, or promoters of the performance can receive any compensation for the performance. So if you are having a school dance, and you are paying the DJ, you will not qualify for this exemption. Finally, any direct or indirect admission charge (e.g., donations for attendance, payment for a dinner at which the music is performed) must go only to educational purposes (Moser, 2006). This exemption applies only to nondramatic performances, so don't plan to use this for a performance of a musical or even the music from a musical performed in the same order as orchestrated in a dramatic performance.

There is one small caveat that goes along with this exemption. If the copyright owner objects to your potential use, the owner can voice that objection to your use at least seven days in advance. If the owner makes such an objection, you may not use the work. How does this apply in real life? It's unlikely that a copyright owner will know in advance of your use of a specific work unless you advertise it. But there is a small catch: copyright owners (or more likely the broker of the copyright owner's rights) may give a blanket objection in advance. For example, ASCAP or some similar rights holder may give notice to a school district that it objects to all potential performances of the works in its catalogs. Such notice will not apply to standard classroom instructional uses; it would apply only to these uses outlined in section 110(4).

Copyright owners can send notice, in advance, including blanket notice, that they do not wish their recordings used as well, and you must abide by their wishes. Typically, that notice would be from a performing rights society such as ASCAP or BMI, but it could be from an individual copyright owner. As a general rule, copyright owners won't know that you plan to play a particular work and so will not be able to effectively object in advance. However, performing rights societies may send your district a blanket objection to such performances, and that notice would be effective until rescinded. You may need to see if your district has ever received an objection, though I don't personally know any school that has received such a notice.

Copying sound recordings

As with all audiovisual materials, a school owner of a copy of a sound recording may not make copies of the original, even archival copies. Library owners (as opposed to the school in general) may make a copy of a damaged or deteriorating recording that is not available in the marketplace at a fair price (17 U.S.C. § 108). Private owners may, for personal (not school) use, make analog or digital transfers to different media under the Audio Home Recording Act (17 U.S.C. §§ 1001–1010). The senate report during the debate on the act made clear that copies of a work owned by one family member and made for another family member and copies for use in a car or on a portable audio device are acceptable exceptions under this act. Those same exceptions do not apply to school users. Also, the act applies only to copies of standard physical works such as CDs and records and does not address songs fixed on computer hard drives, such as songs downloaded from iTunes (*Recording Indus. Ass'n of Am. v. Diamond Multimedia Sys., Inc.,* 1999). Copies of those works would be governed by the license accepted when the copies were acquired.

Some recordings may be purchased with duplication rights, especially foreign-language education recordings (e.g., tapes or other recordings that accompany a foreign-language textbook). Be sure to retain the paperwork granting the duplication rights and any restrictions that may accompany them (e.g., duplication of one copy per student or one copy per textbook purchased). If numerical restrictions apply, create and maintain a log of duplications (Figures 6.8 and 6.9). A bit of extra time spent in the process can save many hours of research compiling records at a later date, should you be challenged on compliance.

2. There can be no direct or indirect commercial purpose for the performance. An example of a commercial purpose would be if you are playing music in the library during the time you are selling donuts or bagels or coffee in the mornings. The idea of the music in this case is to encourage the students to come into the library to purchase those items.

3. The performers, promoters, or organizers of the performance cannot receive any compensation. An example of this would be hiring someone to come to the library to choose and play the music.

4. There cannot be any direct or indirect admission charge unless all the proceeds go to educational or charitable purposes.

Sampling

The amazing capabilities of digital editing equipment make all sorts of creative work with audio not only possible but also simple. This equipment is so sophisticated that individual wave forms can be edited, copied, modified, or erased. The technology is called "sampling." Several lawsuits have been filed and won as a result of one

Figure 6.8. Sample duplication log

Date	Tape	Copies	Comments
7/22	Un jour en France	15	Dubonet – 235 remain
8/15	Un jour en France	10	Martin – 225 remain
8/16	Habla espanol	13	Spanish 4 1/student

Figure 6.9. Audio-recording duplication log

Date	Tape	Copies	Comments

party extracting selected sounds from a copyrighted work and inserting them into a new, derivative work. For a detailed explanation of several of the more notable sampling cases, see *Moser on Music Licensing* (2006). Kohn (2010) explains,

> *Though artists will use samples of existing recordings to save money and time, a more common and compelling reason why sampling is often employed stems from a desire to use the distinctive sound of a successful song or recording artist for the express purpose of giving sampling artist's original work a familiar element that listeners will quickly recognize.* (p. 1598)

Some courts have likened sampling to laziness and cheapness on the part of recording companies and artists. The judge in an important trial on sampling in the rap music industry stated it simply:

> *Get a license or do not sample. We do not see this as stifling creativity in any significant way. It must be remembered that if an artist wants to incorporate a "riff" from another*

work in his or her recording, he is free to duplicate the sound of that "riff" in the studio. Second, the market will control the license price and keep it within bounds. The sound recording copyright holder cannot exact a license fee greater than what it would cost the person seeking the license to just duplicate the sample in the course of making the new recording. Third, sampling is never accidental. It is not like the case of a composer who has a melody in his head, perhaps not even realizing that the reason he hears this melody is that it is the work of another which he had heard before. When you sample a sound recording you know you are taking another's work product. (Bridgeport Music v. Dimension Films, et al., 2005)

How were samplers in this case caught? Does it make any difference? They were caught, found guilty in an expensive trial, and forced to pay the appropriate penalties. But if you need ammunition to convince crafty audiophiles, there are certain digital "signatures" that enable audio (especially digital audio) to be quite simply identified (with the necessary equipment and expertise).

How much sampling is too much in a fair use assessment? A copyright attorney posted on a copyright discussion list that if a consumer can recognize a snippet of a song as being from the original, that is too much. When you think of game shows such as *Name That Tune,* where contestants could name a song from three or four notes, you realize that it doesn't take a lot of song before you have run into the "significant amount" issue. Kohn describes a situation where 6 notes are repeated 10 times throughout the sampler's work and explains that such sampling is "clearly" infringement (Kohn, 2010, p. 1600). If the part copied is the part of the original work that makes it artistically or musically valuable, the copying can be considered infringement (*Boosey v. Empire Music Co.,* 1915). Although sampling for student work used only within the classroom or for the student's personal use at home is more than likely fair, once material sampled is distributed far and wide via the Internet, the copyright owner can make a much more vigorous case that the use is not fair. The more transformative the use of the sampled material and the less the use of the new material affects the market for the original work, the more likely the student use would be considered fair (Moser, 2006). Students should pay particular attention to their sampling and make notes of what they sampled, especially if the students have any musical ambitions. It is entirely possible that the student will further develop schoolwork as part of a band, and the result may end up in commercial distribution or as an example on the band's Web site. Cautioning students early on about sampling and pointing them to the cases discussed in Moser can save them many headaches later.

Sampling tips:

Sample from your own recordings (ones recorded by you or your students). You will still need permission from music publishers if you are sampling from recorded music, voices, or environmental sounds. One federal circuit (6th Circuit covering Michigan, Ohio, Kentucky, and Tennessee) has held that *no amount* of sampling is legal without permission (*Bridgeport Music v. Dimension Films, et al.,* 2005).

The MP3 dilemma

As the Napster case (*A&M Records, Inc. v. Napster, Inc.,* 2002) the Grokster case (*MGM Studios, Inc. v. Grokster, Ltd.,* 2004), and the subsequent Recording Industry Association of America (RIAA) campaign against individuals using peer-to-peer file-sharing have shown, some trading of copyright-protected material via file-sharing networks is illegal. School technical personnel will want to watch for packets associated with various file-sharing software packages given that the RIAA has declared its intent to sue educational institutions for contributory and/or vicarious infringement if shared files are traced back to those organizations. The RIAA declared (as reported by the University of Massachusetts, 2009),

> *A copyright is infringed when a song is made available to the public by uploading it to an Internet site for other people to download, sending it through an e-mail or chat service, or otherwise reproducing or distributing copies without authorization from the copyright owner. In civil cases copyright infringement can occur whether or not money was exchanged for the music, and in criminal cases there only needs to be a possibility of financial loss to the copyright holder or financial gain to the infringer [emphasis added]. The NET Act sets penalties for willful copyright infringement.*

The NET Act imposes criminal penalties of up to five years in prison and up to $250,000 in statutory fines if the infringement included an expectation of financial gain. That expectation could be as little as expecting another file in return, as is the case with file sharing. Certainly, liability for these types of actions is something you and your district want to avoid. The Electronic Frontier Foundation offers a plethora of tips to manage access to music files while staying out of the line of fire with the RIAA (Electronic Frontier Foundation, 2006).

Related cases

A&M Records, Inc. v. Napster, Inc., 239 F.3d 1004 (9th Cir. 2001)

Internet service that allowed users to share digital audio files (mostly music) was found to infringe the copyright of the works' owners in this case. The court noted that "[c]ourts have been reluctant to find fair use when an original work is merely retransmitted in a different medium." It further found that users who upload or share copyrighted musical works without permission violate the copyright owner's right of distribution, and those who download copyrighted musical works without permission violate the copyright owner's right of reproduction.

Clean Flicks of Colo. v. Soderbergh, 433 F. Supp. 2d 1236 (D. Colo. 2006)

A company that removed profanity, drugs, sex, and nudity from popular entertainment films and resold the expurgated copies was found to infringe the copyright of the movies. The court found that the edits were not transformative as they added nothing new. In addition, the creative nature of the movies coupled with the non-transformative edits and the fact that the expurgators took all (or almost all) of the original movies. The court commented that the right to control the content of a copyrighted work is the essence of copyright law, and removing the expression of the idea by censoring the movies violated that right.

Columbia Pictures Industries v. Redd Horne, 749 F.2d 154 (3d Cir. 1984)

The Redd Horne company was found guilty of copyright infringement by charging patrons to perform copyright-protected videos. Officers of the company were found liable for contributory infringement. The case showed that even performances in closed rooms may be considered to be public under the definition of the law. The court said, "A defendant is not immune from liability for copyright infringement simply because the technologies are of recent origin or are being applied to innovative uses."

Encyclopaedia Britannica Educational Corp. v. Crooks, 542 F. Supp. 1156 (W.D.N.Y. 1982)

A regional educational agency converted films to video and distributed them to member districts. The agency remains under a permanent injunction preventing it from making copies of programs.

Gilliam v. American Broadcasting Companies, Inc., 538 F.2d 14 (2d Cir. 1976)

The comedy troupe Monty Python performed regularly on the British television network BBC. Monty Python made an agreement with the BBC to syndicate its performances to ABC on the condition that ABC not make any changes in the program other than inserting commercials and editing to conform with applicable censorship requirements. ABC then made significant edits to some episodes before they were aired. The court found that the unauthorized editing of potentially offensive material by ABC infringed the Monty Python copyright in the programs by "mutilating" them.

Works cited

A&M Records, Inc. v. Napster, Inc., 239 F.3d 1004 (9th Cir. 2001).

Association for Information Media and Equipment. (1990). *Press release.* Elkader, IA: AIME.

Boosey v. Empire Music Co., 224 F. 646 (S.D.N.Y. 1915).

Bridgeport Music v. Dimension Films, et al., 410 F. 3d 792 (6th Cir. 2005).

Columbia Pictures Industries v. Redd Horne, 749 F.2d 154 (3d Cir. 1984).

Electronic Frontier Foundation. (2006). *How not to get sued by the RIAA for file-sharing.* Retrieved from http://www.eff.org/IP/P2P/howto-notgetsued.php.

Gilliam v. American Broadcasting Companies, Inc., 538 F.2d 14 (2d Cir. 1976).

Jensen, M. B. (1992, Winter). I'm not my brother's keeper: Why libraries shouldn't worry too much about what patrons do with library materials at home. *The Bookmark, 50,* 150–154.

Kohn, A., & Kohn, B. (2010). *Kohn on music licensing* (4th ed.). Austin, TX: Wolters Kluwer.

Kruppenbacher, F. (1993, June 14). Re: CC and copyright. Message posted to CNI-COPYRIGHT electronic mailing list.

Lutzker, A. (2010). Educational video streaming: A short primer. *AIME News, 24*(1), 1–3. Retrieved from http://www.aime.org/news.php.

MGM Studios, Inc. v. Grokster, Ltd., 380 F.3d 1154 (9th Cir. 2004)

Moser, D. J. (2006). *Moser on music licensing.* Boston, MA: Thomson.

Official fair-use guidelines: Complete texts of four official documents arranged for use by educators (4th ed.). (1985/1987). Friday Harbor, WA: Copyright Information Services.

Recording Indus. Ass'n of Am. v. Diamond Multimedia Sys., Inc., 180 F.3d 1073 (9th Cir. 1999).

Recording Industry Association of America. (2002). *RIAA releases mid-year snapshot of music industry.* Retrieved from http://www.riaa.com/news/newsletter/082602.asp.

Reed, M. H. (1989). *Videotapes: Copyright and licensing considerations for schools and libraries.* Syracuse, NY: ERIC Clearinghouse on Information Resources. (ERIC Document Reproduction Service No. ED 308 855).

Sinofsky, E. (1993, June 14). Re: Closed-caption videotape conversion. Message posted to CNI-COPYRIGHT electronic mailing list.

Sony Corp. of Am. v. Universal City Studios, 464 U.S. 417 (1984).

UCLA Online Institute for Cyberspace Law and Policy. (1998). *The "No Electronic Theft" Act.* Retrieved from http://www.gseis.ucla.edu/iclp/hr2265.html.

United States Copyright Office. (2009). *Circular 21: Reproduction of copyrighted works by educators and librarians.* Washington, DC: Author.

University of Massachusetts. (2009). *Security awareness: Laws FAQ.* Retrieved from http://www.massachusetts.edu/lawsfaq/faq.cfm#28.

Chapter 7

Music Materials in Schools (Print and Recorded)

Music, as with most other media, has its own set of guidelines. Music, in the context used here, means sheet music, not sound recordings. However, making sound recordings of sheet music falls under these guidelines in certain circumstances as well.

What typical activities are covered?

Typical activities in schools include reproduction and performance to some extent. Keep in mind that printed music is always covered by the print guidelines. However, certain uses of music in education are exempt from the print requirements in ways that standard prose are not.

Reproduction of sheet music—issues

Sheet music publishers make their livelihood from selling copies of sheet music. They are highly protective of their one product. With photocopiers able to make fast, high-quality copies, this method of piracy is a serious threat to music publishers.

Examples of typical questionable activities involving reproduction of sheet music include the following:

- *An elementary music teacher finds a song in a book. She makes enough copies for her entire choir and saves the copies for use in future years.*

- *The high school band director buys one copy of music for each type of instrument in the band (e.g., one trumpet part, one flute part, one drum part, etc.). He duplicates enough copies of the music for each person in the band to have the appropriate music.*

- *The choir director purchased a set of music for his choir. A set includes eight of each part: soprano, alto, tenor, and baritone. However, this year he has 12 sopranos but only 3 altos. He would like to make 4 extra copies of the soprano part to make up for the alto parts he won't be using.*

Performances of sheet music—issues

Even if students are expected to memorize music before performance, the music being played originated with sheet music. Performances of music beyond the classroom are public performances. However, for nondramatic performances in school where there is no admission charged, or where all of the admission proceeds go to the educational institution, most use is permitted unless the copyright owner objects at least seven days in advance.

Following are examples of typical acceptable and possibly questionable performances of sheet music:

- *The band will be performing copyright-protected sheet music as it marches in the homecoming parade. The use is not in school and not part of a class.*

- *The choir performs copyright-protected sheet music as it sings holiday songs at a local nursing home.*

- *The junior/senior-class musical is not a classroom activity, but it does use copyright-protected sheet music. The classes charge admission to raise money for the junior/senior prom.*

Reproduction of recorded music—issues

Occasionally, music teachers need to make copies of recorded music for their students. This type of situation occurs more frequently at the college level, but if you have a music theory class or a history of music class, similar things may happen at a high school. Teachers may make copies of complete works or portions of works and may make anthologies of such excerpts for the purpose of conducting "aural exercises or examinations."

Typical acceptable and questionable reproductions of recorded music might include the following:

- *The band has a concert, and the assistant principal records the performance. To raise money for new band instruments, the band makes copies of the recording and sells them to band members and their parents.*

- *The music teacher wants to demonstrate syncopation to his class. He makes copies of several examples of the technique from differing decades to show how different composers treated it.*

- *The band director wants to make copies of a recording of the work the band will play in the next concert, so that the students may practice at home with a full ensemble.*

Performances of recorded music—issues

Performing recorded, copyright-protected sheet music is a common occurrence. Most of these issues are addressed in the chapter on audiovisual materials under the section on sound recording. However, some additional topics come into play. Non-instructional public performances of recorded music always require a license. The difficulty is in getting a license for a secondary or elementary school.

Examples of typical acceptable and possibly questionable recording performance issues include the following:

- *The communications director wishes to put the video of the recent band concert on the local cable public access channel that is available to every home in the district and beyond.*

- *The principal wishes to play recorded music over the PA system during passing period and lunchtime and during the closed circuit announcements.*

- *The district technology director decides she wants "music on hold" over the telephone system.*

- *A fifth-grade teacher wishes to play relaxing music in the background while her students work on projects. The music does not relate to the instructional goal; it just provides a tranquil environment for productive work.*

Adaptation of sheet music—issues

All adaptations are within the rights of the copyright owner. However, schools do have some limited exemptions to create adapted works within an educational context.

Typical questionable music adaptation issues in schools might include the following:

- *The choir teacher purchased music for a female duet but would like to adapt the music to include two male parts. The publisher sells a four-part version of this piece, but the teacher has no budget to purchase new music, so he writes the two needed parts.*

- *The marching band director wants to have an innovative performance for the regional contest, so he writes an arrangement of a new off-Broadway musical.*

- *An arrangement of a Beethoven sonata for modern instruments is too difficult for the beginning orchestra to play, so the middle school director simplifies the piece.*

Question: Our high school recently staged a musical and legitimately purchased the production rights for this event. A parent video-recorded the performance and now would like to make copies of the video to sell to parents of cast members at exactly the cost of making the copies. These recordings would be used only for the enjoyment of the students' families. Will this violate copyright law?

Answer: Unless the school (or the parent) also purchased rights to distribute the production, this use would likely be a violation of copyright. The law doesn't address this specific situation, but it does address performances of music. A school may make a single recording of a musical performance, but that copy can be used only in class to critique the performance.

What guidelines affect music?

There is no section of current copyright law that identifies specific guidelines for permitted educational uses of music, either printed or recorded. However, several groups collaborated to draw up a set of guidelines that address the unique aspects of using music in schools. In 1976, at the same time Congress was developing the fair use guidelines, several music industry groups and music educators developed the Guidelines for Educational Uses of Music as part of the same process. The groups participating included the Music Publishers Association of the United States, the National Music Publishers' Association, the Music Teachers National Association, the Music Educators National Conference, the National Association of Schools of Music, and the Ad Hoc Committee on Copyright Law Revision. Because these guidelines aren't law, they are more of a "gentlemen's agreement" than a belief that the uses described are acceptable by all parties. Staying within these guidelines is a sensible fair practice. Someone might be able to make a case for slight extensions of the limits detailed here, but just as in speeding, the more one exceeds the limits, the more one is at risk of penalty.

In addition, standard tests of fair use always apply, as do the print guidelines, audiovisual guidelines, TEACH act, and multimedia guidelines. Always look at all aspects of a given situation to assess all the possible angles before making a determination as to whether a use is fair or not.

There are actually *three* sets of guidelines covering educational use of music. The longer-lived of the guidelines, the Guidelines for Educational Uses of Music, are generally accepted because they evolved from the same congressional process that generated the print guidelines. Following guidelines promulgated by such a collaborative group (composed of copyright owners and end users) forms a reasonable basis to make decisions on what types of use are appropriate. Beyond what these guidelines offer, the Music Publishers Association has some additional guidelines, as does the National Association for Music Education. Both these supplemental guidelines expand on the original set of rules and add supplemental information on new technologies that were not available when the original guidelines were written in 1976. The expansions are not endorsed by copyright owner groups, however, so use caution in their application.

Print music

Types of copying of printed music that are acceptable include the following:

- *Emergency copying when purchased copies have not arrived in time for a performance, with the understanding that the emergency copies will be replaced with purchased copies.*

- *For non-performance classroom purposes, the teacher may make one or more copies of portions of works, as long as the parts are not a part that would constitute a "performable unit such as a section, movement or aria." The copied portion may not exceed 10 percent of the whole work. You may make only one copy per pupil.*

- *If the school buys sufficient copies of printed music, those copies may be edited or simplified as long as the fundamental character of the work is not changed (e.g., jazz stays jazz), or the lyrics are not altered or added if none exist.*

According to the Guidelines, there are several prohibited types of music copying:

- *Any copying that substitutes for purchasing a collection, anthology, or collection of music.*

- *Any copying of "consumable" materials such as workbooks, tests, and exercises.*

- *Copying music for performance, except as explained in the first permission regarding emergency copying.*

- *Copying with the intention of not purchasing music, except as explained in the first and second permissions*

- *Copying without including the copyright notice that appears on the printed copy.*

Question: The music teacher wants to copy an old music workbook because the work is now out of print, and she cannot locate the publisher. Because the work is not available for purchase, is this permitted?

Answer: The Guidelines for Educational Uses of Music state that copying of consumables is never fair.

Recorded music

Under certain circumstances, school users may make copies of recorded music. Those circumstances include the following:

- *You may make a single copy of recordings of performances by students, but it may be used only for evaluation or rehearsal. This recording may be kept by the school or the individual teacher.*

- *You may make a single copy of a sound recording of copyrighted music (as long as the recording is owned by the school or an individual teacher) for the purpose of constructing "aural exercises or examinations." This derivative recording may be retained by the school or teacher. (This permission pertains only to the copyright of the printed music and not to any copyright that may exist in the sound recording.)*

What rules/laws are different about recordings?

Recordings of music are treated no differently than spoken-word recordings. The five yes/no tests still apply to using copyrighted recordings of music in the classroom. The direct teaching aspect is an essential element of the fair use assessment, so entertainment, ambience, or enrichment are not sufficient to get the nod on the face-to-face teaching question. The bad news about using sound recordings is that two copyrights apply to sound recordings created after February 1, 1972. Prior to 1972, there was no copyright in the actual recording, so a recording of public domain music (such as much of classical music) would be in the public domain. No copyright in the sheet music plus no copyright in the recording equals no copyright in any of it. Since 1972, however, there has been a copyright in the underlying composition (sheet music) plus a copyright in the recorded performance. For that reason, recent recordings of Bach, Beethoven, and the great masters (in fact, any music published before 1923 as long as it is in the original form) are protected by copyright even though the underlying work is long in the public domain.

A hot topic in the recording industry today involves peer-to-peer file sharing. Individual users, for private use, may make copies of works they lawfully own. So someone might copy a song from a compact disc to an MP3 player in a completely lawful manner. However, schools are not individual users, and making copies of recordings must follow the requirements set forth in this section. Sharing digital files with others who do not own legal copies of recordings is not legal, for either individual users or schools. Few cases actually go through the entire legal process to a verdict (most are settled out of court), but the few cases that have gone to trial do not present a favorable picture for those transferring files (Jury, 2009). In addition, the RIAA announced its intention to sue those who enable users to share software (Norah, 2004). If peer-to-peer file-sharing software is installed on school computers, and users distribute a significant amount of music, the host and the individual may be named in suits.

Music in performance

The performing of music can happen in a classroom setting, or it can happen in such circumstances as a concert, sports event, talent

---

Question: Teachers come back from workshops in which the presenter used music throughout and recommended that participants do too. The music is owned by the presenter (or teacher) and is used for transitions in instruction, for example. Is this fair use for the presenter, when participants are not students and the presenter is making money from the presentation? Is this a fair use for a teacher in a classroom when it is part of the instructional process?

Answer: Using music for direct instruction is certainly permissible. An example of that type of instruction is a music teacher who plays a song before the students sing it, or a teacher who plays a Civil War march as an example of the culture of the Civil War era. Simply owning music does not give the purchaser public performance rights, however, just as owning a video does not give you public performance rights in the video, either. The fact that the presenter is being paid is not dispositive. Teachers get paid to teach school, but that doesn't disqualify their use of video if the showing meets the requirements of section 110(1). Uses of more than minimal amounts of music that are for entertainment purposes (such as transition) are not covered by fair use. Instructional use is use for direct teaching. Transitions are between teaching segments and are simply "filler." There are assorted producers of royalty-free music that can be used in such situations, or the district can purchase a municipal umbrella license from the American Society of Composers, Authors and Publishers (ASCAP) to cover all

Question: *Can popular music be played during intermission, time-outs, and so on at a basketball game if there is an admission charge (which is not for profit and will be given directly back to sports)?*

Answer: Is the music being performed by the band or other students? If so, this is probably a fair use. There is a performance exemption for *sheet music* for school performances when none of the performers are paid and any admission fees go back to the school. There is no similar exemption for recorded music (which is a separate copyright on the recording). For that you will need a municipal performance license from the performing rights organization that represents the music you wish to perform, either through your city (if your city government controls your school system) or through your district (if your school district is its own governmental entity). Alternatively, you can get permission directly through the copyright owner, but as a rule, the performing rights organizations are much easier to reach (though there will *always* be a fee for permissions through those agencies, whereas there is a slim chance a copyright owner might give *gratis* permission).

show, dance recital, musical, or other event. Some key questions to ask when assessing potential for liability in music performance include the following:

- *Is the work a musical, opera, operetta, or other dramatic work (or a song from one of those)? Dramatic works have no exemptions under the guidelines, and permission from a rights holder or broker is always required, even for no-charge performances. Ordinarily, one gets the rights at the time one purchases the scripts, scores, and so on. If you wish to record and sell copies of the performance, be sure to negotiate those rights at the same time.*

- *Is the performance part of face-to-face teaching? Following the audiovisual guidelines, the five yes/no tests give guidance regarding the appropriate setting to use music. Enrichment, reward, general cultural value ("every student should know this piece of music!"), and entertainment are not qualifying situations for performance of copyrighted music.*

- *Is the performance live, with no commercial advantage? This strange phrase means that no performers, promoters, or organizers get any money from the event and that there is no direct or indirect admission charge (Frankel, 2009). There is a small exception for this rule, however. If all proceeds go to educational, religious, or charitable purposes, an admission fee is acceptable. However, making copies of the performance to sell would not be within the limits because that goes beyond a live performance. Note that the copyright owner of any works to be performed can object to the performance and prevent use of the work(s) if the objection is registered seven days in advance. Such an event isn't likely, however, because unless you advertise the program, the copyright owner probably will never know you are using the work. Note that this exemption applies only to nondramatic works. Plays, musicals, operas, and so on don't count, so a musical play by the third grade before the PTA may need permission or license; check with the publisher. A performance by a DJ or a live band at a school dance would not meet this exemption because the performers are paid.*

Broadcasting music

Broadcasting music or any other copyrighted material takes it out of most of the educational exemptions, though standard fair use may apply in some circumstances. An example of a fair use of music in broadcast might be a music appreciation program where a teacher plays a short segment from a recorded piece to demonstrate what "staccato" sounds like.

Broadcasting for "noncommercial" entities is covered in section 118 of the copyright act (17 U.S.C. § 118). Subsection (b) explains that copyright owners and public broadcasting entities "may negotiate and agree upon the terms and rates of royalty payments." Absent such an agreement, a panel of judges, serving as the Copyright Royalty Board, sets appropriate royalty rates for broadcast use of copyrighted material.

This concept would apply when a school band records its performance and wishes to play the recording on the local public cable channel. Note that § 118 qualifies its use of musical work to include only "nondramatic" music. These rules would exclude broadcasting the school musical. Any dramatic production will require broadcast rights from the copyright owner. Such rights are typically negotiated with the copyright owner at the time the school purchases the rights to perform the work. If you forget to include those rights in your original contract, you can certainly add them later, but the publisher knows it has you over a barrel, and your rate will likely not be as favorable as it would have been if you had included that in the original negotiations.

Performance rights organizations

Suppose you have determined that you need permission or license to copy or arrange music, to have a dance with a DJ, or to perform music where the performers are paid, though the proceeds will go to the booster club or the PTA. A performing rights organization will be a convenient place to get those rights. Virtually every nightclub, honky tonk, city stadium, theater, country club, coliseum, or other venue where music might be performed for commercial purposes can obtain a venue license to cover performances in that location from one of the performing rights organizations. The two primary sources for performance rights are ASCAP and Broadcast Music, Inc. (BMI; see Appendix D for contact information). Though many performances in schools are exempt, there are entertainment performances that require a performance license. With such a license, a school would be able to play music on the telephone, offer background music in the lunchroom, perform music at athletic events, and hire a local band to perform for the student dance.

A blanket license that covers everything on the campus is not the only way to comply with the law, however. For example, if the band boosters should decide to hire a local band to perform a concert to raise money for new band instruments, a school would need to contact one of the organizations for a single performance license in order to be within the limitations of the law (Frankel, 2009).

Permissions and licenses

To get permission to make new arrangements of music, to translate or adapt music, to perform music in a broadcast setting, or for any of the many other times that exemptions do not cover the activities in a school, one should contact either the rights

Question: At the sports awards banquets, the coaches want to have a slide show of team photos with music from a CD. Even though PowerPoint allows this option, is it within copyright guidelines? This is for entertainment purposes. Is it legal to play a CD on a boom box while the slide show plays (rather than adding the songs to the slide show on the computer)?

Answer: It makes no difference whether the performance runs through PowerPoint or a boom box for the purposes of determining that this is a public performance. They are both copyright problems. Copyright allows plenty of permissions for using materials *in class* to *teach content* to *enrolled students*. However, once you extend beyond those limits, copyright permissions drop back to the limited fair use that is allowed for you, me, and the man-on-the-street. The fairly liberal multimedia guidelines would permit some music in a PowerPoint presentation, but only for private use of students, staff development, or classroom assignments. This use wouldn't qualify under that standard. The four statutory fair use tests wouldn't give the needed permission here because the work being used is creative, you are using all of it, and the use is to avoid purchasing a license for performance. You have a public performance and need permission or a license. *However,* if that banquet is taking place at the local country club, or some venue that has an ASCAP/BMI license, your performance might be covered under the venue license. Check with the building management for their available licenses.

broker or the copyright owner for permission. When requesting permission, it is important to be explicit in what you plan to do, how many times, how many copies, what use will be made of the resulting material, and so on. The publisher or copyright owner is not required to reply to your request. If the answer is no, or you do not get a response, you have the same result: don't use the work. Some copyright owners will allow use of out-of-print works at no charge, but others feel a responsibility to exploit works to their maximum. They are the ones in the driver's seat in this situation.

What you want to do will determine the type of license or permission you need. Public performances and the copying of sheet music need permissions from ASCAP or BMI. If you plan to record sheet music (such as making copies of a band or choir performance), you need what is known as a "mechanical license" from the Harry Fox Agency (see Appendix D for contact information). The Music Publishers Association has several useful forms for requesting permission or license to copy or perform music (Music Publishers Association, 2010).

Many different types of licenses apply to copyrighted music. Some licenses are not required for schools under an educational fair use exemption, but other types of licenses are required. Note that for many uses you will need multiple licenses. For example, to record music in a video and show the program on television, you would need mechanical, synchronization, broadcast, and possibly grand rights. Here is a brief synopsis of the most common types of music licenses.

- Arrangement—*For creation of a new version of a composition other than a simple change of key. Included: new instrumentation, simplified chords, shortening a lengthy composition, changing lyrics, changing musical style (from jazz to hip-hop, for example).*

- Broadcast—*For use of a recorded performance on radio, television, satellite, or cable. Typically, even short excerpts must have a broadcast license.*

- Festival use (adjudication)—*For use of photocopies of out-of-print sheet music for judges in a musical competition.*

- Grand—*For staging a musical play, ballet, or opera or for performing any song in a dramatic manner. These rights are available directly from the publisher of the sheet music or the producer of the show.*

- Master—*To use an existing recording. These rights are usually available directly from the recording company.*

- Mechanical—*For an audio recording of a composition on tape, CD, or digital download format, whether or not the recording is sold. You need this license to sell or give recordings of student concerts to students, parents, and friends. Mechanical rights are mandatory—a music publisher cannot prevent you from recording a cover of its song once the publisher has recorded and released the song. Royalty rates are set by law. Mechanical rights are brokered through the Harry Fox Agency (http:// www.harryfox.com) and are available for small runs. You can try to negotiate a reduced rate through individual copyright owners, but the reduced rates must still be submitted to Harry Fox. See the Web site for details. You will need master use rights and mechanical rights if you wish to make copies of existing recordings.*

- Performance—*For a public performance of a musical work. For schools, many exceptions apply to public performance. If it is to be used in direct teaching, apply the five-part AV fair use guidelines. If the performance is to be a public performance by students (such as a band concert), some exemptions apply. Entertainment and reward performances require performance licenses. Performance rights are available from one of the performing rights societies ASCAP, BMI, or SESAC.*

- Photocopy—*For making photocopies of out-of-print sheet music. Not for copies for festival adjudication. These rights are available directly from the sheet music publisher.*

- Reprint (lyrics or music)—*For use of music or lyrics in a book, magazine, or printed publication. Some uses may be covered under the print exemptions for schools. These rights are available directly from the music publisher.*

- Sub-out—*For selling a new arrangement of an existing composition. Most likely covered under the arrangement license agreement as well.*

- Synchronization (synch)—*For including a performance of a musical composition in film or video, such as background music in a film or a recording of a band performing copyright-protected music in a music video. Synch rights must be negotiated directly with the publisher of the underlying sheet music.*

- Web posting/digital downloads—*For posting print music (including lyrics) and recorded material on the Internet. Digital downloads are licensed through Harry Fox Agency. Web posting of print material is negotiated directly with the publisher of the underlying sheet music.* (Alfred Publishing Co., 2008; ASCAP, 2008; Harry Fox, 2009)

It is helpful to understand which license you need before you contact the publishing company so that you will be quoted the correct fee for the rights you need.

of events allowed by your license. Check over the license carefully to be certain it contains the permissions you anticipate needing (school dances, parades, between-class PA music, music in the lunchroom, etc.).

Question: When I contacted one of the rights organizations for permission to broadcast our band concert on the local cable channel, the price they quoted was very high for our limited use. I then sent a letter directly to the copyright owner, saying, "If I do not receive a response by [date], we will assume you grant the permission and will broadcast the performance as described." Are we okay?

Answer: No, you may not be okay. First of all, do you know that the copyright owner actually received your request? Even if you sent the letter certified and have received the return receipt, a copyright owner is not required to respond to requests. Compare this to walking up to Donald Trump on the street in New York and saying, "May we have a party in the boardroom in Trump Tower?" Then Mr. Trump turns around and walks off. Would you believe you have permission to have the party? If you show up with balloons and a birthday cake, would you be surprised if the security guards don't let you in? Your complaint that "Mr. Trump didn't say no!" would probably not move the security guards to let you in. Always get permissions in writing.

Resources for understanding

Artists House Music—http://www.artistshousemusic.com/legal. Includes exceptional explanations of the legal aspects of music, including videos of lawyers, musicians, and those in the music industry discussing the use, licensing, and adaptation of music.

Columbia Law School Music Plagiarism Project—http://www.ccnmtl.columbia.edu/projects/law/library/entrance.html. Includes hundreds of documents (texts, scores, audio, and video) about music copyright infringement cases in the United States from 1845 forward.

Kendor Music—http://www.kendormusic.com/licensing/photocopies.htm. Outlines required permissions for sheet music. Though specific to this company, it is a good overview.

Music Library Association, Copyright for Music Librarians—http://www.musiclibraryassoc.org/copyright/. A complete source for all the guidelines that affect music, from copying to library archives. Not just for librarians.

Music Publishers Association Copyright Resource Center—http://www.mpa.org/copyright/copyresc.html. Includes forms and other tips on working with music publishers to get hard-to-find music.

Related cases

A&M Records, Inc. v. Napster, Inc., *239 F.3d 1004 (9th Cir. 2001)*

In this case, Internet service that allowed users to share digital audio files (mostly music) was found to infringe the copyright of the works' owners. The court noted that "[c]ourts have been reluctant to find fair use when an original work is merely retransmitted in a different medium." It further found that users who upload or share copyrighted musical works without permission violate the copyright owner's right of distribution, and those who download copyrighted musical works without permission violate the copyright owner's right of reproduction.

Works cited

Alfred Publishing Co. (2008). *Licensing and permission requests.* Retrieved from http://www.alfred.com/alfredWeb/front/General.aspx?pageid=296&catid=55.

ASCAP. (2008). *Common music licensing terms.* Retrieved from http://www.ascap.com/licensing/termsdefined.html.

Frankel, J. (2009). *The teacher's guide to music, media, and copyright law.* New York: Hal Leonard.

Harry Fox Agency. (2009). *Mechanical licensing.* Retrieved from http://www.harryfox.com/public/MechanicalLicenseslic.jsp.

Jury awards $675K in music downloading case. (2009, August 3). *E-school News.* Retrieved from http://www.eschoolnews.com/2009/08/03/jury-awards-675k-in-music-downloading-case/.

Music Publishers Association. (2010). *Making a record: Do I have to obtain a mechanical license?* Retrieved from http://www.mpa.org/copyright/you.html#record.

Norah, L. (2004, May 1). *RIAA sue another 477 music sharers.* Retrieved from http://itvibe.com/news/2501/.

Chapter 8

Multimedia in Schools

Multimedia was invented after the latest revision of copyright law. There are no definitive court cases in this arena, but thanks to the hard work of a group of media producers, publishers, and media consumers, a set of reasonably clear-cut guidelines on the use of multimedia in education was approved in late 1996. The guidelines are not law, but they came from the Clinton administration–sponsored CONTU process (Office of General Counsel, 1997). They are certainly lower-end limits, but they are at least a beginning point in looking for what is an appropriate amount of material to include in multimedia presentations. Under these guidelines, "multimedia" includes such common programs as PowerPoint and KidPix and various other presentation systems.

What typical activities are covered?

In creating a multimedia presentation, the user is likely to deal with copyrights on all aspects of the production that aren't actually originated by the author: video, graphics, music or other sound recording, and computer software. Here are some typical things that happen in a school that would fall under the class of activities known as "multimedia":

- *A teacher prepares a PowerPoint presentation using clip art graphics.*
- *Students create a KidPix presentation using video clips downloaded from the Internet.*

Student multimedia projects—issues

When students include copyrighted material in their multimedia projects, copyright issues such as the following may appear:

- *Students play a current popular song in its entirety as background on their PowerPoint project.*
- *Students find popular cartoon images online, and they wish to include them in a Hyperstudio project that they will display for the PTA.*
- *Students create a project in Flash, and they wish to mount the project on the school Web site.*
- *A student wishes to attach an award-winning PowerPoint project from freshman English to his college application.*

Teacher multimedia projects—issues

- *The teacher wishes to create a PowerPoint presentation on the play* Hamlet, *using multiple clips from Mel Gibson's and Laurence Olivier's movies.*

- *The teacher plans to retain a well-executed instructional multimedia program he created that includes graphics harvested from the Internet and to use the program for the foreseeable future.*

- *The teacher wishes to post an instructional multimedia program on the class Web site, for students to access at any time during the semester. The program includes images scanned from several supplemental texts.*

What rights are affected?

Reproduction

Any work included in a multimedia program must be copied in order to be included. Because multimedia programs are, by definition, computer driven, the works must be digital. Copyright owners are, as a rule, nervous about digital reproduction because all copies are identical in every detail to the original and can be reproduced indefinitely.

Adaptation

Adaptation would include editing, cropping, and excerpting from complete works. Including something in a multimedia work creates a derivative work, which is an adaptation. Copyright owners are cautious about their works being used as the basis for other works over which they might have no control.

Distribution

Multimedia works may be distributed by disk, CD, or file transfer. Mounting a multimedia program on the Web also distributes the work to the world, or to all those who have access.

Public performance

Because a school is a public place, any performance of a multimedia program is a public performance. Using the copyrighted works of others in a multimedia program means those works are performed whenever the multimedia work is performed.

Public display

For works of art and other copyrighted static images, display occurs any time the program is viewed.

Digital transmission

Mounting multimedia with audio on the Web means that any accompanying audio will be transmitted digitally. Copyright owners are highly suspicious of digital transmissions of audio.

What guidelines affect multimedia?

Standard fair use applies to *anyone's* use of copyright-protected materials, so even if the following educational guidelines don't result in an allowable amount of media sufficient for a specific application, one can always fall back on the four tests of fair use to determine possible permitted use. The Fair Use Guidelines for Educational Multimedia appeared in 1997 and provided a set of rules that were specific to this then-emerging technology. However, in reading the specific requirements that follow, never fail to remember that standard fair use tests may also apply. Because the multimedia guidelines are easier to interpret than the fair-use four-factor assessment, apply the multimedia guidelines first. If those don't meet your needs, you can fall back on the general fair use tests.

Multimedia guidelines

When multimedia first emerged as an educational medium, there were no copyright rules that addressed the types of uses required for the technology. Falling back on the print guidelines or the § 110 audiovisual rules just didn't address the unique needs of this technology. In order to create a multimedia work, virtually all the relevant material must be transferred to digital format. Music, video or still images, and graphics all have different copyright rules. And although you may own a CD recording, for example, all you really own is the right to listen to the music until the disc breaks or wears out. You have only limited rights to convert any of that material into another format such as tape or computer disc. The Audio Home Recording Act of 1992 permits such actions for your personal use at home, but use in school doesn't fall under that legislation. Even some material considered to be in the public domain may have restrictions. Many movie stars made films promoting war bonds, for example. And those films are in the public domain—but only for the purpose of selling war bonds. To use the likeness of any of the stars, you would need to get permission from whoever owns the rights to the likeness (Goldstein, 2009).

In order to clarify exactly what uses of traditional media would be considered "fair" in this new technology, the Conference on Fair Use (CONFU) set about to gather potential stakeholders to negotiate fair use guidelines for several different areas of electronic access, including multimedia. Few of the other groups achieved agreement on guidelines, but the multimedia group at least gained a goodly consensus of opinion that the guidelines drafted are fair (Office of General Counsel, 2004). One notable group, the American Library Association (ALA), refused to endorse the guidelines because they felt the guidelines were not liberal enough. So although the ALA does not accept the limits imposed by the guidelines as maximums, they do accept them as fair.

These guidelines outline suggested limits of acceptable use of copyrighted materials in fair use situations. The guidelines are not law, just as the classroom guidelines are not law. The guidelines are simply an agreement between those who own the copyrights and those who wish to use the copyrighted materials on what will be permitted under a claim of fair use. Compliance under the guidelines doesn't mean the use is "legal." It means that the copyright holders agree that someone who uses their materials within these limits has not exceeded fair use. As with all claims of fair use, the claim is an affirmative defense to infringement. "Affirmative defense" in this context means that the use being defended is an infringement of one or more of the six rights of the copyright holder, but the claim of fair use is a permissible defense to that infringement. Because the guidelines are not actually part of the law, an infringer would point to the guidelines as evidence of reasonableness in use of material in an educational context.

The agreed-to Fair Use Guidelines for Educational Multimedia provide concrete limits on the types and amounts of material that may be included in works created by teachers and students. The guidelines are far easier to understand and follow than the highly subjective statutory fair use assessment. The Guidelines give educators and students the closest thing available to a "bright line" test—a clear-cut limit on what is acceptable.

One of the first notations in the guidelines is that all materials used in derivative works should be properly cited as being taken from the works of others. That means everyone—students and teachers—must attribute the sources of the materials they use in the creation of their multimedia projects. The guidelines also state that multimedia works made from the copyrighted materials of others may be used only in support of the education of students in nonprofit educational institutions. That doesn't mean that there is no personal use available; it means only that these guidelines are designed only for educational situations. For personal use, or non-educational use, the person using the works of others will have to rely on standard statutory fair use for his justifications.

Special definitions for multimedia

Educational institutions: "nonprofit organizations whose primary focus is supporting research and instructional activities of educators and students for noncommercial purposes" (Office of General Counsel, 2007).

Educational multimedia projects: programs that "incorporate students' or educators' original material, such as course notes or commentary, together with various copyrighted media formats including but not limited to, motion media, music, text material, graphics, illustrations, photographs and digital software which are combined into an integrated presentation" (Office of General Counsel, 2007).

Educational purposes: "systematic learning activities including use in connection with non-commercial curriculum-based learning and teaching activities by educators to students enrolled in courses at nonprofit educational institutions" (Office of General Counsel, 2007).

Educators: "faculty, teachers, instructors, and others who engage in scholarly, research and instructional activities for educational institutions" (Office of General Counsel, 2007).

Lawfully acquired: "obtained by the institution or individual through lawful means such as purchase, gift or license agreement but not pirated copies" (Office of General Counsel, 2007).

Multimedia: "Material is stored so that it may be retrieved in a nonlinear fashion, depending on the needs or interests of learners" (Office of General Counsel, 2007).

Multimedia—covered or not?

All references to multimedia works are to productions that include copyrighted materials. Obviously, any multimedia production in which the teacher or student creates all the text, data, sounds, and graphics would be totally under the control of the creator. The guidelines permit multimedia works made by students to be used in the class for which they were created and also to be retained in portfolios maintained by the student for job interviews, college applications, and other purposes. Teachers may use the multimedia presentations they create in face-to-face instruction, or they may assign students to view the presentations on their own. Repeatedly in the guidelines, you see the phrase "educator

Question: As our district moves along with our student-produced book trailers, we are doing proper mediagraphy and attribution pages along with the fair-use wording on the first slide of all of our trailers. If we are using images only from Creative Commons and music from freeplaymusic (freeplaymusic.com), can our trailers stay up on our school page for an indefinite amount of time, or is there a time limit?

Answer: Look at the type of Creative Commons license you have for each image. There are multiple licenses available from Creative Commons. Some will allow you to do anything if you only attribute the source. Others say you cannot redistribute or modify the image. So that is your first task—identify the license attached to the material you will use. Then look at the license with Freeplay as well. It may allow you to use the music in school but not allow you to put the music up on an open Web page. If you put the trailers up on a limited-access page, you could be under the TEACH Act or the multimedia guidelines, depending on how access is restricted. Neither will allow you to leave the trailers up indefinitely if they contain certain amounts of copyright-protected materials.

use for curriculum-based instruction." That phrase should remind you of the statutory guidelines for use of audiovisuals. The multimedia guidelines are very much in the same vein as the audiovisual guidelines (§ 110(1)) and the print guidelines in that they support direct teaching but not the supplemental, extracurricular activities so often seen in schools.

Retention and access

Teachers may display their own multimedia programs at conferences and workshops, and they may retain the programs they create in portfolios for job interviews, evaluations, and other uses. There is a finite limit to an educator's right to keep a work created from the copyrighted material of others, however. Although a student may keep a work indefinitely, a teacher may keep a work for only two years from the time of its first use with a class. Beyond the two-year window, you need permission to retain or use *each* portion of copyrighted material used in the presentation. In other words, for teachers, after two years there is no more fair use (under the multimedia guidelines, at least) of the material used in that particular production.

If you will use a multimedia work over a network for students at a distant location, several factors come into play. To ensure that only students enrolled in the course may see the program, you need some type of security. Students must log in or provide some other evidence of identity (see the discussion of secure networks in the next sections). In addition, the network over which you transmit the program must have in place a means to prohibit copying the program. If there is no such safeguard, the program may be used on the network for only 15 days. After that time, the program disc may be checked out to students, but only with a warning that the program may not be copied.

Secure network

A secure network meets two requirements. It requires a login or PIN to access network resources, and it restricts copying of the materials on the network.

Insecure network

An insecure network requires a login or PIN but does not have the ability to prevent copying of materials posted there.

Here are some typical scenarios that illustrate the retention guidelines:

> A teacher creates a multimedia presentation to illustrate a point of his curriculum. The production uses some copyrighted sounds and graphics. The presentation is so successful that the teacher wishes to demonstrate his work at a national conference of teachers. Such a use is within the guidelines, provided that the display is within two years of the teacher's first use of this production for his classes.

> A student creates a multimedia work utilizing copyrighted materials. The presentation is such an excellent example of student work on this topic that the teacher would like to put the presentation up on the school's network for other students to view in the future for reference, and as an example of how to make a presentation. This use is permitted only if the audience

Question: Can I take a student's multimedia project to a teacher's workshop outside the school district to use as an example if I obtain the student's and parent's permission?

Answer: If the student did all the work on the project—that is, there is no copyrighted material that the student did not create included in the project—the permission of the student and parent is all that you require. If, however, the project includes copyrighted material used by the student under the multimedia fair use guidelines, only the student may use the project for workshops. The teacher may not retain copies of the work for any reason. Teachers may use projects *they create themselves* for workshops per the guidelines, however.

for this presentation is limited to students enrolled in the current class. Some type of network security (passwords, access restrictions) must be in place to prevent access by students outside the class. The student's parents may give permission to use the student's contributions in future semesters, but neither the student nor her parents have authority to give permission for the portions created by others. If the use of those elements passes a standard fair use assessment, the student's use of those works may be fair and can be included in the student's work for future use.

A teacher wishes to display at an open house, technology fair, or science fair an exemplary student multimedia production that incorporates some copyrighted material. Use of copyrighted materials is permitted for class use only. The guidelines do not allow public performances of materials under fair use. You would need to rely on a standard fair use assessment for those portions.

Quantity limits

The guidelines specify the amounts of different types of copyrighted materials from a single source that may be used in all multimedia projects created in the course of a term. In other words, from any one video, book, audio recording, or database, a student or teacher may not exceed a specific limit in a single year or term. Should a teacher reach this theoretical limit, any additional material in a presentation would require permission. Students, especially students in grades K–6, are granted more leeway in their limits of copyrighted material, so that if a younger child exceeds the limits slightly, he is forgiven his lack of finesse.

The limits outlined in the guidelines are as follows:

Motion media *(film, video, television): Up to 10 percent or 3 minutes, whichever is less, of an individual program. Example: A student wishes to use a 20-second clip of a Mickey Mouse cartoon. The total length of the cartoon is 3 minutes (180 seconds). The maximum limit under the guidelines is 10 percent, or 18 seconds. Could the student make a case for the extra time? Quite possibly, yes. If the student is a fifth grader or younger, the extra 2 seconds would probably be ignored.*

Text *(prose, poetry, drama): Up to 10 percent or 1,000 words, whichever is less, of a novel, story, play, or long poem. Poems shorter than 250 words may be used in their entirety; only three poems by one poet or five poems by different poets from an anthology may be used. For poems longer than 250 words, only three excerpts from one poet or five from works by different poets in an anthology are permitted. Example: A teacher creates a learning module containing several segments of poems from modern poets that were not included in the class textbook. The teacher finds several of the poems in a single book of modern poetry. She wishes to use seven excerpts of poems written by different poets in the book, and all of the excerpts are under 500 words. This use likely exceeds the multimedia guidelines. All seven poems are from the same book. But statutory fair use may apply.*

Music, lyrics, and music video: *Up to 10 percent but not more than 30 seconds from a single work (or combined from separate extracts of a work). It makes no difference whether the work is being used as a musical work on its own or is an incidental accompaniment to some visual material. If a video clip has music in the background, and you can't separate the music from the visual material, you will be restricted by the 30-second limitation for music. If the music is altered in any way, the fundamental melody must be maintained, and the basic character of the work should be preserved. Example: A student wishes to use a three-minute clip from* American Graffiti *that has a musical background track of rock and roll songs. The student will be limited by the guideline for music that limits use of music to 30 seconds or 10 percent, whichever is less. But statutory fair use may also apply.*

Illustrations, cartoons, and photographs: *A work may be used in its entirety but only if no more than five images from a single artist or photographer are used in a multimedia work. In addition, if images are taken from a single collective work, no more than 10 percent or 15 images may be used. Example: A teacher creates a PowerPoint presentation on the early years of World War II. On each of the 25 slides, the teacher puts an editorial cartoon of the period. All the cartoons come from the same book. The use exceeds the limit of 15 illustrations from a single book. Statutory fair use might apply if the teacher comments on the cartoons rather than using them as decoration.*

Numerical data sets *(computer databases or spreadsheets): Up to 10 percent or 2,500 fields or cells, whichever is less, may be used from a copyrighted database. Example: A student takes a portion of the Internet Movie Database for use in a paper on Ronald Reagan. As long as the use is less than 10 percent of the work, the use is fair under the guidelines.*

Rule in practice: A concrete example of this rule would be the teacher who uses several images from a library book to create a multimedia presentation for his class. The book is a collection of paintings by different artists. The number of images used reaches the limit assigned in the guidelines for this type of material: 15 images in a collective work. Before the term is finished, the teacher wishes to use additional different materials from the same book for another multimedia presentation to his students. But any use of materials in a single term beyond the limits will require specific permission for each item. The teacher will need to request permission in advance before he may use the additional images. If the teacher wishes to use the *same* materials, in a multimedia test or drill material, for example, this is not additional material. It is the same material he is already using under the fair use exemption and may continue to use for the semester or term. The teacher has not used anything additional beyond the allowed 15 images.

Remember that some producers may provide additional permissions for your use in multimedia. See the Discovery Education terms of use on how students and teachers may use video and images clipped from its Web site: http://connect.discovery-education.com/termsOfUse.cfm.

How many copies?

An educator or student may make only two copies (including the original) of the multimedia work. An additional copy may be made if one of the copies is lost, stolen, or damaged. If more than one person creates the multimedia work, each may have one copy of the work. Each copy may be retained as long as is permitted for the type of author (student or teacher). See the section on retention and access for the specific lengths of time.

Question: The principal in my school would like to use a popular "top 40-type" song, along with a PowerPoint presentation. Do we need special permission?

Answer: Basically, your principal can use up to 30 seconds of the song without permission. He may retain the presentation for two years from the date of its first use. He *must* have, as the first slide in his presentation, a statement similar to this, or with wording to this effect: "This presentation contains copyrighted material used under the educational fair use exemption to U.S. Copyright law. Further use is prohibited." The *last* slide(s) of the program must include a mediagraphy that includes the copyright information (copyright date and copyright holder) for each piece of copyrighted material used in the presentation. Additionally, if the use includes images, they should be documented on the same slide where the image is used. The documentation can be in small type.

Other restrictions

The opening screen of the multimedia work and any accompanying printed materials must contain a notice that the work contains copyrighted materials that have been used under the fair use exemption of U.S. copyright law. Although the guidelines don't specify the wording of the notice, something such as the following would appear to meet the requirement:

> *NOTICE: The following presentation contains copyrighted materials used under the Multimedia Guidelines and Fair Use exemptions of U.S. copyright law. Further use is prohibited.*

However, because this required notice applies to *all* users, even second graders who are creating KidPix presentations would need to have something similar. Obviously, a second grader wouldn't understand anything like this sample notice. However, a notice such as the following would both meet the guideline requirement and be understandable to young students:

> *NOTICE: I borrowed other people's stuff to create my project. I followed the rules. Please don't copy my project.*

Not only does such notice comply with the requirements of the guidelines; it teaches students early on that they are expected to acknowledge the work of others, not hide it. It also promotes respect for the work of others and pride in one's own work.

Attribution

The guidelines, and academic integrity, require complete attribution and acknowledgement of all copyright-protected materials used in a multimedia presentation. How to document images and sounds in a multimedia presentation is sometimes a quandary. Although teachers and students may make alterations to copyrighted material if the purpose is to support specific educational objectives, the author must clearly indicate that such alterations have been made.

Consider the analogy of a documented research paper. In addition to the bibliography or mediagraphy at the end of the paper, the author documents each item used at the point of use in the paper. If the author has made any editorial changes (such as emphasizing text), she notes the changes. The in-text documentation usually takes the form of a short parenthetical reference to the complete information found in the works cited section of the paper, plus any acknowledgement of editorial modification. A multimedia project is no different.

In a multimedia presentation, at the point of insertion of some external, copyright-protected work (video, image, audio, etc.), include a shorthand reference to that item as listed in the complete works cited section. The type of reference can be consistent with whatever style sheet governs the project. In Figure 8.1, the slide has a simple text box added to the page, placed near the location of the item added. The text need not be large or distracting; in fact, the text in the sample was made larger than would normally be used so that it would be easier to read in this book. But small text (though not miniscule) would certainly be acceptable.

In addition to the in-text attribution, the multimedia guidelines require specific information in the entries in the works cited section. The guidelines specify the type of information that must be listed, but not the order, so the required information may be arranged in whatever format the assigned style sheet specifies. Following are the items that must be included:

Figure 8.1. Sample documentation

Image by somtam_girl

- *author*
- *title*
- *publisher*
- *place of publication*
- *date of publication*
- *copyright symbol (©)*
- *year of first publication*
- *name of the copyright holder*

A sample bibliography entry for the work shown in Figure 8.1 might look like this:

Somtam_girl. (2006). *Water lily.* Lewisville, Tex.: self-published. © 2006, Carol Simpson.

This particular work was published online under a pseudonym. But because I'm the author, I knew who the copyright owner is. The copyright owner may not always be the same as the author, but it sometimes is.

Keeping track of the copyright owners would be a good idea, even if the guidelines didn't require that. For teachers, especially, fair use covers only two years of use. Retention after that time requires permission of the copyright holder. Because material may disappear from the Internet, or the source work may be lost or destroyed in the interim, having all that information recorded with the item is essential. You also will have it on hand if the presentation becomes commercially viable, or you want to extend use beyond what is granted in the guidelines.

Multimedia tips

The power of multimedia and the computer applications that support it also provide powerful liability for the users. Although you have the capability to grab a frame from a film or extract a single face from a photograph or isolate an instrument from the accompaniment of a popular song, you may not exceed the limits imposed in the multimedia guidelines (or through statutory fair use) without permission from whoever owns the rights to those items.

Guidelines to remember when creating multimedia presentations:

- *Students and teachers may use copyrighted material in multimedia presentations if they observe quantity limits.*

- *Students and teachers may use copyrighted material in multimedia presentations if they support direct instruction.*

- *Students and teachers may keep the multimedia presentations they create for class, though teachers face a two-year limit without additional permission.*

- *Specific limits govern the amount of material that may be used in multimedia presentations, based on the original medium.*

- *Students and teachers must acknowledge all copyrighted work with a specific format of bibliography or mediagraphy.*

Best advice: Invest in clip art, music, and video sold expressly for multimedia productions, or create your own. The multimedia collections are usually copyright-cleared for such applications, but check anyway. Clip art *books* would fall under the "illustrations" portion of the guidelines because one would have to scan or otherwise digitize the images to include them in a multimedia presentation.

Resources for understanding

See http://www.utsystem.edu/OGC/IntellectualProperty/ccmcguid.htm for the full text of the guidelines. Because the guidelines were written by educators and producers, they are written in readable English, not legalese.

Works cited

Goldstein, P. (2009). *Goldstein on copyright* (3d ed.). Austin: Wolters Kluwer Law and Business.

Office of General Counsel, University of Texas System. (1997, June 11). *CONFU background.* Retrieved from http://www.utsystem.edu/OGC/IntellectualProperty/confu2.htm.

Office of General Counsel, University of Texas System. (2004, December 22). *CONFU: The conference on fair use.* Retrieved from http://www.utsystem.edu/OGC/IntellectualProperty/confu.htm.

Office of General Counsel, University of Texas System. (2007). *Fair use guidelines for educational multimedia.* Retrieved from http://www.utsystem.edu/OGC/IntellectualProperty/ccmcguid.htm.

Chapter 9

Distance Learning in Schools

Distance learning has been a black eye for copyright advocates for a long time. A significant reason is that Congress has a hard time keeping up with the pace of technological change. Add to that the age of most congressional representatives and senators, and you realize that they just don't understand how distance learning works, much less how the use of copyrighted material is just as essential to the success of distance learning as it is to face-to-face instruction. Consider it a generation gap of the educational kind.

History of distance learning and copyright

The 1976 version of the law made *transmission* of any audiovisual work a violation of the law. Though only radio and limited video teaching existed at that time, they could not be used to send copyright-protected materials. So although using recordings, videos, films, and other audiovisual works in face-to-face settings was perfectly legitimate, using those same items in the same quantity to the same students who happened to be in a location apart from their teachers was considered to be an infringement. How were the teachers to reconcile this seemingly odd disparity of regulations?

Enter the new millennium. Entire courses are delivered via satellite or videoconference or Internet. Web pages for teachers have become a primary channel of communication and distribution of exercises, homework assignments, and other supplementary materials. Producers are concerned that their works might be compromised by video, audio, or Internet transmission. These new capabilities didn't mesh with the distance-learning provisions of the 1976 act.

When the Digital Millennium Copyright Act was passed, a provision called for the register of copyrights to hold hearings on the best way to develop fair use guidelines for distance learning. The resulting report was turned into legislation that eventually emerged as the TEACH Act (Technology, Education and Copyright Harmonization Act). The bill was signed into law by President George W. Bush on November 3, 2002, and it went into effect immediately. It provides guidelines on how copyright-protected materials can be used in distance education. The TEACH Act completely revises section 110(2) of U.S. copyright law. The information in this chapter addresses distance education as a support role for K–12 rather than in terms of a full-time online high school, for example. When distance learning becomes a full-time occupation, you need to discuss an overall intellectual property policy with your legal counsel.

Although the act references only "distance education," the definition of that term is nonspecific. Courses may be delivered entirely online, or they may be blended with online modules or activities. As Armatas (2008, p. 2) explains, "[d]istance learning is not necessarily separate and distinct from on-campus education, however. An individual course may contain both classroom and distance components." Anytime a student has online-directed learning components in a course, those components constitute "distance learning," and the TEACH Act guidelines come into play.

TEACH Act guidelines

The TEACH Act provides considerable support for using copyright-protected audio and video materials in online and video-distributed courses as long as they are used in support of direct instruction. The act requires several conditions to be met before the protections of the act are available. Following the lead of the audiovisual guidelines, the TEACH Act requires, in general, the following:

- *That there be a direct connection to the current curriculum.*
- *That only officially registered students view the materials.*
- *That both the transmitting and receiving ends of a transmission see that transient copies of works are removed quickly (by flushing the server cache, etc.).*
- *That the transmitting body be responsible for protecting the copyright of any materials it transmits. (This means the school is ultimately responsible for protecting any copyrighted materials used in distance learning.)*

In order to make the law as forward-looking as possible, the act isn't restricted to the types of distance learning that existed at the time the act was passed. Rather, the teaching activity as a whole must meet the definition of "distance education" as defined in the law:

- *It must occur in discrete installments.*
- *It must occur within a confined span of time (undefined).*
- *Parts must integrate into a "lecture-like" whole.*
- *"Mediated instructional activities" must resemble traditional classroom sessions.*

Despite the fact that schools promote constructivist teaching methods for face-to-face classrooms ("the guide on the side, not the sage on the stage"), only more traditional teaching activities, teacher-directed, qualify for the TEACH Act exemptions. Some pundits have characterized the act's provisions as an attempt to make distance learning resemble Beaver and Miss Landers. But whatever else the act did, it acknowledged distance learning and distance-supported face-to-face learning as valid educational activities that deserved to use copyrighted materials under a fair use defense, just as traditional classrooms had done for so long. Nevertheless, there are a few important things to understand about the enabling conditions cited here.

"Discrete installments" combined with "confined span of time" means that materials created by others cannot go up online and stay up forever. The expectation is that something will be mounted for a limited time and then will come down. Anything created by a teacher or owned by the school district can be used as much as the teacher likes, obviously. The TEACH rules apply to using the works of others. So, for example, if a teacher creates a class wiki, and the wiki contains only work created by the teacher or other district employees, that may stay up indefinitely. However, if the wiki contains material copyrighted by others, under the TEACH rule, the copyrighted material in the wiki can remain up for only a limited period of time.

But don't interpret "traditional classroom sessions" to mean synchronous. The TEACH Act specifically negated the previous requirement that everyone be in attendance at the same time, with a teacher in every location. Nevertheless, total anarchy in learning, such as providing a pile of learning resources and letting students work their way around in any fashion whatsoever, would not meet the "traditional classroom session" requirement either. There should be organization, specific assignments, and some direction on the part of the teacher to generate "mediated instructional activities" that resemble traditional classroom sessions.

However, every silver lining must have its cloud. The following activities are expressly *prohibited* by the TEACH act, no matter how long you plan to keep them up:

- *scanning or uploading complete or long works*
- *storing works on open Web sites (no login/password)*
- *allowing student access at will (such as supplemental material or material with no specific, limited time frame)*

Three groups share statutory responsibility for complying with the requirements of the TEACH Act: policy makers, information technology staff, and instructors/developers. Each group has specific tasks assigned, and unless all three groups do their part, the protections of the act fall away. Compliance must be a carefully considered, well-orchestrated activity.

Policy makers

Policy makers are, in most instances, the Board of Education. This group must be able to verify nonprofit educational status. Generally, the state education agency can certify a district's status, but other methods are possible. The board must have an adopted copyright policy. Most states' education agency or school board association has a set of boilerplate policies that boards can adopt. Those boilerplate policies typically include a copyright policy. A copyright policy must be adopted for a school to take advantage of the TEACH Act provisions.

Policy makers are responsible for seeing that faculty, students, and staff are trained in copyright compliance. Training means more than putting a copy of this book in the library. Just as with sexual harassment training or asbestos abatement, sign-off training documents each individual's attendance and demonstrates that the board takes the training seriously. Similarly, students must be informed that teaching materials may be protected by copyright. An administrative expectation of compliance by all parties is the key.

Finally, the policy makers must direct that access to distance-learning materials be limited to enrolled students only. Restricting access to enrolled students resembles the section 110(1) audiovisual guidelines' directive that only students and teachers in a class be present when copyrighted audiovisuals are shown under the educational exemptions. In the case of distance learning, restricting materials to enrolled students means using passwords or other access-limitation measures. Some districts offer self-enrollment for community education classes, for example, and such access would prohibit the use of materials under the protections of TEACH.

Information technology staff

The information technology (IT) staff bears a significant part of the burden of compliance with TEACH Act provisions. They must assure that only registered students (and designated support staff) can access course materials. As part of that responsibility, IT staff must promptly remove access from students who drop a class or move away. In addition, if a substitute teacher has access to online courseware, that person should also be deleted when no longer instructing that course.

IT staff must prevent students from capturing material for longer than a class session. Preventing capture may mean encrypting materials, in some cases, or streaming materials so that they cannot be saved locally. The IT staff must prevent student redistribution of copyrighted material.

Preventing redistribution may go hand in hand with preventing capture, if streaming technologies are used. Preventing redistribution probably does not extend as far as preventing printing a document, but it could mean preventing downloading the document to retain in digital form.

IT staff must protect digital rights management (DRM) information, which can include verifying that materials have not been cropped or edited to remove copyright notices and that all audiovisual materials include credits and copyright statements. They must make sure only "intended recipients" can access any transmissions. This constraint will require working with internetwork hosts, if any, to see that access to files and data streams is secure.

Finally, the IT staff must make long-term retention (such as time when the course is not being taught) out of student reach. Copyrighted works may be retained from term to term, for example, but they must be stored in access areas that are not available to students or others. This requirement is particularly important for programs where online or broadcast courses are hosted on remote servers or through remote transmission facilities. The IT staff must see that the courses are taken offline and stored where the staff at the hosting facility can't access the copyright-protected materials. A single student could probably be allowed to access course materials for enough time to clear an incomplete, but open-ended storage available to *all* students in the class would likely be over the line.

Instructors/developers

Instructors and developers of courses and course materials bear the biggest burden in TEACH Act compliance. As far as copyrighted materials they may include in a course, they may read stories, poems, essays, and so on. They may play nondramatic music (not musicals or operas). An instructor may show "reasonable and limited" portions of dramatic audiovisual works (movies and operas). The term "reasonable and limited" is given no specific time period; however, in a face-to-face class, a teacher may show an entire movie, if that movie meets the audiovisual guidelines tests. The act goes on to state that the teacher may use other works typical of a classroom session. For example, in a classroom session, a teacher might use a PowerPoint presentation (using the multimedia guidelines to assess use of copyrighted material within the presentation) and narrate it. Similar use in an online course would be work "typical of a classroom session."

An instructor may *not*—under the TEACH Act—include in course materials any work marketed for online learning, such as digital curriculum, electronic databases, or learning systems. All online learning materials are licensed to schools for online learning, and using these materials in an online learning situation under a claim of educational exemption would deprive the copyright owner of a sale of a license for these materials. Don't interpret that prohibition to say that you may not use something for which you have a license or permission, or something in small bits such as quotations. Remember, this is just a prohibition on an educational exemption, not a total prohibition on use. So if you have a license at your campus to use specific databases, and your license says you may deep link into a specific article, you may certainly do what your license allows in the online classroom.

In addition, an instructor or developer may not use anything that is from an illegal copy if he has any reason to think the copy may be illegal. So using a DVD that was purchased from a video supplier and that comes in an appropriate-looking case would not raise any suspicions that the product was manufactured in the Far East in a pirate facility. The

Question: A foreign language teacher would like to read a foreign-language poem (not one she has written) and post it on her Web page. Is this a copyright violation?

Answer: As with all legal questions, the answer is "maybe." Is she teaching online? Do the students log in to the site? If so, this could be covered under the TEACH Act. The TEACH Act allows a teacher to read something such as this and post it for a limited time if it is for direct instruction and if it is encrypted or otherwise fixed (or perhaps streamed) so that the students can't copy it. If this is on an open Web page, this is almost assuredly a violation.

user would likely be exempt from liability in such a situation. But if the instructor gets a downloaded copy from someone who is known for downloading from questionable sites, he has a reasonable suspicion that the video is not a legally acquired copy.

An instructor in distance learning must (a) plan and conduct all use of copyrighted materials; (b) ensure that all use is part of regular, systematic instruction; (c) ensure that all use is directly related to teaching content; and (d) ensure that all use is not entertainment, reward, or enrichment.

Digitizing for online learning

An instructor or designer may digitize materials for use in distance learning if the use meets portion limitations (Armatas, 2008). In addition, the instructor must verify that no digital version of the work is available or that the digital work is inaccessible because of a protection scheme. Finally, the instructor may *not* digitize textbooks, books, workbooks, and so on. Students or schools are expected to purchase books and workbooks in the traditional manner. Some occasional handouts are likely okay in the manner of the original print guidelines.

Many school activities will fall under the TEACH Act's provisions even if they are not a matter of teaching complete courses online. Many teachers use a Web site for course support or to mount today's homework worksheet in case it "gets lost" on the way home. School or library Web pages may use copyright-protected materials in pursuit of their educational goals but do not qualify for the special exemptions permitted under TEACH. A careful analysis of the situation will determine whether the TEACH Act provisions may be relied on for a given situation.

Resources for understanding

TEACH Act—http://thomas.loc.gov/cgi-bin/cpquery/?&dbname=cp107&maxdocs=100&report=hr685.107&sel=TOC_507516&. The full text of the act itself.

Copyright and digital distance education—http://www.copyright.gov/disted/. An explanation from the U.S. Copyright Office.

The TEACH Act and some frequently asked questions—http://www.ala.org/ala/issuesadvocacy/copyright/teachact/faq.cfm. Prepared by Kenneth Crews, lawyer and librarian, regarding provisions of the act.

Basic TEACH checklist for institutional users—http://tilt.colostate.edu/guides/tilt_copyright/checklist.pdf. A condensed, point-by-point review of the requirements of the TEACH Act.

Work cited

Armatas, S.A. (2008). *Distance learning and copyright: A guide to legal issues.* Boston: American Bar Association Section of Intellectual Property Law.

Chapter 10

Internet in Schools

The Internet is the new paper. Resources come to the school via the Internet. Student work is published online. It is only natural that this would be a widely used communications channel in schools. There are no Internet-specific guidelines to regulate our activities with the exception of the TEACH Act, but those limitations are specific to distance learning (Armatas, 2008). Outside of those guidelines, you are on your own, copyright-wise. Much of what students and teachers do online is not within the context of an online course as defined within the act, so that leaves them without a lot of markers for what use is acceptable.

What typical activities are covered?

Because the Internet is so broad in its coverage and style, the list of activities that fall into this area is huge.

Printing pages—issues

Printing pages from the Internet falls under rules similar to those found in the print guidelines. Look to those guidelines for how many copies one may make and what one may do with them. Following are examples of typical activities that would be governed by these rules:

- *A teacher finds a Web page that clearly explains a concept that the class is studying. She makes a copy and duplicates it for each student.*

- *A student locates a poem online for a poetry notebook he is creating. He prints off the copy to include in his notebook.*

- *A librarian finds an image of all the book covers from the nominees for the state reading incentive. She prints multiple copies of the image to broadcast around the school to increase interest in the program.*

- *The PE teacher uses an online catalog to find sports equipment for his upcoming order. He prints copies of the various items he wishes to purchase so that he can comparison shop.*

- *The school webmaster finds a Web site whose style he finds attractive and user-friendly. He prints the entire site so that he can use the design as he reworks the school's Web page.*

Bookmarks—issues

Bookmarks are files of links to frequently visited or not-to-be-forgotten Web pages. Making bookmarks is similar to writing down an address. Addresses are facts and are not generally protectable by copyright. Typical activities that would involve bookmarks include the following:

- *A group of students is working on a WebQuest. They bookmark a group of sites that have relevant information for their final project.*

- *A principal bookmarks sites that have information about a grant program to which he plans to apply.*

- *The librarian bookmarks sites that will be needed by the class coming tomorrow for research. Having the sites pre-identified keeps the students on task and away from surfing potentially off-topic sites.*

Links—issues

Links are similar to bookmarks, in that they are Web page addresses. Links can be problematic when a Web page owner objects to your link to her page. The primary reason owners might object is that they feel you are capitalizing on their site without appropriate attribution or payment. Using frames to access a Web site hides the true origin of a Web page (the URL doesn't show in the address bar), and the actual Web site from which the content is displayed may get no acknowledgement.

Although individual links may be public domain facts, collections of links (especially those collections with significant organization or annotation) gain what is called a "compilation copyright" over the selection, annotation, and organization of those links.

Typical activities that would involve links include the following:

- *A librarian finds another library's list of links on a reference topic. A class will be studying that topic shortly, so she copies all the links and puts them on the school library's Web resource page for this class.*

- *A principal links from the school's Web page to the district's Web page and that of the feeder schools in their vertical path.*

- *The school webmaster finds some online resources that support the school curriculum. He links the resources into a display that uses frames on the school's Web page so that no one can tell where they come from. Each of the resources looks like it was created by the webmaster as part of the school's Web page.*

Copying pages to local servers—issues

It is sometimes easier to copy a Web page or Web site and put the information on a local server than it is to bring the page across the Internet every time a student must get information. Some software will allow you to copy an entire site at once, even collecting outside pages or sites to which the first page is linked. Going through a fair use assessment doesn't provide much support that copying this extensively and then redistributing would be a fair use.

Following are typical activities involving copying pages:

- *A teacher uses special downloading software to collect video from several Web sites that will be important for an upcoming research project. She creates a collection of the videos on her own Web page.*

- *The music teacher copies 200 pages of sheet music from a subscription database. She stores the pages on her local computer and prints copies when her classes need new music.*

- *The principal pays for a single subscription to a Web site that has worksheets for math remediation. He copies the pages using a special harvesting program and installs the copies in the resource room. Students from several grade levels use these pages to practice for the upcoming standardized tests.*

Redistributing pages—issues

Copying a page is not the only potential trouble spot for appropriating Web material. Sometimes teachers or students not only copy material from a Web page but also incorporate that material into a new page. Once the new page has been mounted on the Web, it has been distributed to the world.

Typical activities involving redistributed pages include the following:

- *A teacher finds a WebQuest that is perfect for the unit the class is about to begin. Rather than link to the posted site, the teacher copies the pages and mounts them within her own Web site so that she is in control of the pages.*

- *A district webmaster locates several pages on teen suicide that are particularly appropriate to the situation in that district. To make the pages consistent with the design of the pages on the local Web site, the webmaster reposts the pages using cascading style sheets so that they will look like the rest of the site.*

E-mail—issues

E-mail is probably the most abused Internet property. It is forwarded, edited, copied, and reprinted, sometimes to the point that the original author is long lost. E-mail, as with other written material, is the intellectual property of its author if the contents of the e-mail are minimally creative. Because an e-mail is not published (it is a private communication, just as a letter is), protection for e-mail is much stronger than for typical published materials. The recipient may retain his one copy of the e-mail, but he may not redistribute it, adapt it, or make additional copies of the e-mail without permission.

Typical activities involving e-mail include the following:

- *A student receives an e-mail message from an unwelcome admirer and forwards the e-mail to 25 friends in the band.*

- *The librarian sees a post on a mailing list identifying resources for a commonly taught topic. He forwards the message to all the teachers in the relevant department, asking if they would like him to create a Web page with links to those items.*

- *The principal receives an angry e-mail from a parent. She forwards the e-mail to teachers who have that person's children in class.*

Chat and IM—issues

Chat and instant messenger (IM) applications are blocked in many schools, but for those who allow the practice, the communications in both those applications are usually ephemeral—they exist only briefly and are not saved "in tangible form." When a work is not fixed in tangible form, no copyright exists. However, if the chat is logged or archived, each participant would own the rights to his respective contributions. Even if one participant archives the chat without the knowledge of the other participants, the various speakers own their own input to the conversation, and the archiver may not use their conversation without permission. Depending on the law in your state, it may be illegal to record or archive a conversation without permission of all the participants; but that is a state law issue, not a copyright issue.

Following are typical activities involving chat and IM:

- *A fourth-grade class has a chat with the author of a book they have been reading. The chat log is retained as a record of the experience.*

- *A teacher has an IM discussion with the parents of a problem student. They agree to keep copies of the log in the student's file.*

Question: Can students read a published poem, portion of a story, and so on and post the recording on an iPod, Web site, or network?

Answer: Live, nondramatic reading is possible for personal, school, and library use, but once you start distributing recordings of materials, you quickly get into a quagmire. Remember that publishers get royalties for having their works recorded and sold. Anything that bypasses existing recordings or reduces the incentive for someone to make and sell such licensed recordings is going to be looked at unfavorably. Just reading a poem or story doesn't add any value to the work—it is simply a reproduction of the work. If the student wishes to read the entire work, the more of a work you use, the less likely your use is fair. And the wider you distribute the recording, the less likely the use is fair. The original works are creative, which weighs against a fair use assessment as well. If the student adds some value, such as reading a portion of the work and then commenting on it, your use could lean back toward the fair side of the analysis, depending on the outcome of the other fair use factors such as amount and creativity. Certainly, how far the recording can be accessed (just the class, or the whole world?) would be a factor as well. Always keep in mind that present copyright is a law primarily of *economics*, not a law specifically designed to facilitate education.

What rights are affected?

Virtually all possible rights of a copyright holder are affected by the Internet.

Reproduction

Because the Internet is digital, unlimited perfect copies are possible of any work transmitted by this medium. For that reason, copyright owners are exceptionally sensitive to having their work posted on the Internet without permission.

Adaptation

Capturing digital content makes editing with powerful digital tools a simple process. Copyright owners fear that their work will be appropriated and repurposed against their will or without compensation.

Distribution

Distribution on the Internet is worldwide, instantaneous, and free. Whereas with print distribution, costs and logistics come into play, and distribution may be so minor as to be a non-issue, distribution via the open Internet can be immensely harmful to the value of a work or the market for that work. Why buy it when you can download it for free? Many copyright owners are horrified at the prospect of wide Internet distribution of their work. In fact, as of 2009, around the world, only about 5 percent of downloaded music was paid for—certainly not a bottom line that any company would want! (Gain, 2009)

Public performance

Video or audio programs broadcast across the Internet may be public performances if they meet the criteria for that designation. Copyright owners are just as concerned about Internet performances as face-to-face ones—perhaps more so given that the medium can be played almost indefinitely and to a vast number of persons.

Public display

Public display is the sister right to public performance, and the same concerns apply.

Digital transmission

Performing sound recordings via the Internet is a huge concern for the owners of copyrights in these recordings. Because the recording can be captured in its pure digital form, the person recording has a perfect copy of the original. Why buy a CD when you can capture the one track you like directly from the Internet radio station or other source? Copyright owners have suffered huge losses in revenue because of this practice, and they take extraordinary steps to stop any such use without permission or royalty payment.

The difference between an AUP and copyright

An acceptable use policy (AUP; actually an acceptable use *agreement* because it isn't a policy adopted by the school board, but is a contract signed and accepted by the end user) is a document that sets the rules by which an end user accesses the Internet through his Internet service provider. Schools typically require students and faculty to sign an acceptable use agreement that says they will abide by the rules the school sets for use of its network resources. Often the rules are included in the student or faculty handbook or in the student code of conduct. Copyright is federal law, and its requirements supersede any rules established by the school as a service provider. An AUP may or may not have any stipulations about copyright among its provisions and rules. Even if the AUP is silent on copyright, the law still applies.

Special rules for Internet

The Digital Millennium Copyright Act (DMCA) established some forms of protection from liability that may affect schools. Detailed in section 512 of Title 17 of the United States Code, the many specific requirements to be eligible for protection under this section are quite complex. Essentially, the law states that if an Internet (or online) service provider (ISP or OSP) registers an agent with the Copyright Office, and if it complies with a long string of action items—such as agreeing to remove potentially infringing material once it is brought to the service provider's attention—the copyright infringement exposure of the OSP is limited. Schools, because they provide Internet access to their staff and students, are probably OSPs or ISPs. The protection offered by the DMCA extends only to the school or district, not to the individuals who may have committed the infringements.

Question: We would like to stream video of library story time on the Web. What is the difference between our reading a book at an actual story time or streaming it on the Web?

Answer: Copyright law gives libraries a limitation on enforcement of public performance rights of non-dramatic work (reading books, for example). Rights specific to libraries are covered in section 108. First of all, recording a book on tape or digitally is making a phonorecord. Section 108 says that under certain circumstances, you can make up to three copies of a work, but only if the work is out of print and also damaged, deteriorating, and so on. Additionally, it says that the copy may not be made available outside the premises of the library if the copy is in digital format. So streaming would be out because to stream you must have a digital copy. Further, section 108(i) explains that the library exemptions do not apply to pictorial or graphic works. Those terms are defined as "two-dimensional and three-dimensional works of fine, graphic, and applied art, photographs, prints and art reproductions," among other things (17 U.S.C. § 101). In some instances, picture books could fit that definition. The law does say that licensing is an option, so if you can get permission, all bets are off. There are several mentions in the law of "systemic distribution," which streaming could certainly be considered if you do this on a regular basis.

Under the TEACH Act, a school might be able to make this type of distribution, but TEACH is limited to schools. You wouldn't qualify.

Question: Must I have permission to put a link to another Web page on my own page?

Answer: Links have been likened to cross-references in a library catalog. They are facts (just like street addresses) and cannot be protected by copyright, so making links should be acceptable. Some sites don't like you to "deep link" (linking deeper into the site than the main page) because you might miss advertising, disclaimers, or conditions of use posted there. These sites may object, but it probably won't be on copyright grounds. If you use frames, remember that the site to which you link will appear to be on your server because the address in the address bar will not change. Some sites may object to the relationship implied by their site showing up under your site's address. In lieu of frames, sometimes an offer to open a link in a new window that makes clear the site is external to the school site is sufficient to satisfy the copyright owner. In other cases, you may not be able to link. Some sites, under their terms of use, specifically say you may *not* link to their site or restrict the terms-of-service conditions under which you may link. For instance, they may allow you to link only to the home page of the site. See the conditions of linking for Bloomberg.com, for example: http://www.bloomberg.com/notices/tos.html#linking. Because you are likely

Registered agent

The designation of someone to be the copyright agent for notification of claims of copyright infringement is one step that schools can easily take. The school designates a single person who will respond to claims of copyright infringement and registers that person with the Copyright Office (http://www.copyright.gov/onlinesp/). The school posts complete contact information for this person on the school Web site. If someone should find infringing material on a Web page, he notifies the copyright agent, who will then take down or disable access to the material in question.

Why is this important?

By complying with the requirements of the Digital Millennium Copyright Act OSP provisions, the school is protected against liability for infringements that may happen as a result of students or teachers posting infringing materials on a school Web site. When might that happen? Based on reports to the author, it happens more often than you might imagine. For example, consider that gifted and talented students are in GT classes because they write well (among other reasons). When a GT student turns in a marvelous essay or poem or short story, the teacher praises the student, reads the work to the class, and asks to post the work on the school Web site or online literary magazine. If a student in remedial English were to write the same essay or poem or short story, the teacher would immediately accuse the student of plagiarism. But when the writing comes from an exemplary student, the teacher accepts the paper at face value and posts the work online. About three months later, the real author contacts the school district, threatening to sue for copyright infringement. Through having a registered agent, and following the appropriate takedown provisions, the school is protected from a lawsuit (though the busted student is now in the hot seat). Teachers can be just as guilty. When teachers have their own Web pages, they may post copyrighted worksheets, video, or other material that exceeds a fair use defense or violates a license agreement. The same takedown procedure should apply for teachers' infringing material.

What guidelines affect the Internet?

Unlike print works, music, audiovisuals, multimedia, computer software, and distance learning, there are no set copyright guidelines for the Internet. Partly because the Internet is composed of print, music, audiovisuals, multimedia, and computer software, none of the established guidelines fit perfectly, but *all* of the established guidelines may apply to some extent. For that reason, it is often easier to fall back on the standard four tests of fair use to determine whether the use of material taken from the Internet is fair. Also remember that access to many of the works on the Internet is through license. Articles from online databases and Web sites that require registration predicate access to those items on terms of the license agreement rather than through fair use. Whatever terms you accept through the license are binding as contracts, even if those terms are more restrictive than those of fair use or agreed guidelines. Although your use may be fair under copyright law, you may violate the terms of your contract of use if you apply only the tests of fair use to the materials you use from a licensed Web site. The copyright owner may not have any copyright claim against you if your use would be considered fair, but he would very likely have a valid claim against you for violation of your contract with the copyright owner—the terms of use of the Web site. That suit can be just as expensive and damaging as an action in copyright. This section continues with the assumption that the material under discussion is *not* used under any license or terms of service.

Suppose you write a document on a word processor. Perhaps it is a poem or a chapter of a book. As soon as you save the file on the hard disk, your work is protected under copyright. You can send the chapter to your publisher, you can ask other writers to read the manuscript and give suggestions, and you can pass out copies at workshops. The work is still protected under copyright law. Should one of those people take your manuscript and misuse it, you could sue with a reasonable likelihood of success. You may register your work with the Copyright Office if you like, but registration isn't required. Registration does, however, confer a number of important advantages for enforcement.

Now suppose you put that very same manuscript on your Internet home page. Have you just abandoned the copyright to that work because you put it on the Internet? Not at all. You still own five rights of a copyright holder: reproduction, distribution, adaptation, public performance, and public display (the sixth right won't apply to a print manuscript). And so does every other creator of materials available via the Internet. Every creator? Yes. Every person who writes a document published on the Internet, who creates a graphic or icon, who scans his own photograph or records his own voice into a digital file, who sends an electronic mail message, who creates a document for a newsgroup, or who designs a Web page owns the copyright to his creative work. And because the United States is a signatory to the Berne Convention, no notice of copyright is required on *any* item in order for the item to be protected by copyright law. Even if the work you wish to use is on a Web page hosted in another country, if that country is a Berne signatory, the United States will protect the work under the copyright laws of the United States.

As the creator, that person can decide exactly how he wishes that material to be used. Obviously, the creator has decided to permit display of this work via the Internet because he included it on a Web page, sent it via e-mail, or posted it to a newsgroup. The fact that the copyright holder elected to share

accessing any Web site under a license (terms of service) that you accept if you use the site, you are bound by any restrictions imposed.

Question: Our registered agent received notice that some material posted on the school Web site infringed the copyright of the person who reported it. But after doing an investigation, the agent was not able to verify that the person claiming the copyright actually owned the material. May we repost the material?

Answer: If you have done a thorough investigation, and the person claiming copyright cannot produce any convincing evidence that he owns the copyright in the work, you may remount the material. Don't discard any information you located during your investigation, however. You may need it later.

Question: I print out pages from the Internet, photocopy them, and pass them along to my department heads. I usually include notes for them to "share" this with members of their department. Can I legally print out pages from the Internet by invoking the browser print function?

Answer: Certainly for personal use you may make a copy of a Web page unless the terms of use of that Web site tell you that you may not. School use, however, relies on the terms of use and the various educational exemptions, as well as traditional fair use. The rest of this answer assumes there are no terms of use that have limited your use of the material on the Web site. Under the educational fair use exemptions, you may make a *single* copy of up to a chapter of a book or an article of a magazine (not the entire work) for your own personal use and education, including use in teaching. A Web page probably has the same limitations as an article, so a copy for yourself is within the limits. These teachers aren't your students, so they don't qualify for the educational fair use exemption for multiple copies. (If they were your students, you would have some limited ability to make multiple copies.) The teachers are employees in this case. Go through the four fair use tests to determine whether you can make a case for your multiple copies under that analysis. Because you are copying the entire work, the work is likely creative, and you are making the copies to avoid purchasing reprints, you will likely need permission to make the copies you describe. Or you could e-mail the teachers a link to the page in question and suggest that they each visit the linked page.

Question: One of our teachers has created a beautiful Web site that he has enhanced with 30 seconds of music from the movie Jaws. Is it permissible for him to "loop" that 30 seconds on his site, or must he obtain permission or a license from the copyright holder in order to do so?

Answer: Although it is possible to use 30 seconds of music from a movie in a PowerPoint program under the multimedia guidelines, the right to digitally transmit a sound recording across the Internet

his work in this manner, however, does not mean that anyone can freely appropriate that material for other uses.

As a friend likes to point out, "There is a difference between 'can't' and 'not supposed to.'" The technology exists for someone to view a document or graphic and, by clicking on the appropriate button or menu, grab that item in a pure digital form. From that point it is quite simple to adapt, modify, resend, forward, copy, or display the item. Someone could certainly do those things, but one is not supposed to. Why not? Because the rights to do all those things are reserved for the copyright holder. Without specific permission for more, all the copyright holder permits when an item is displayed on the Internet is for you to view the item as you navigate around the network (Bender, 1996). Naturally, fair use applies in all situations, so a parody of eBay or an academic explanation of the design of a Web page would likely be fair use. Appropriating content without specific permission, when that content is molded into new material, is on shakier ground. A complete assessment is highly fact-dependent, so it is difficult to give hard and fast rules on what is fair and what is not in the making of mash-ups and other modern reconstructions. Much will depend on the amount of the work used and how the resulting product will be used.

Certainly there are some documents that state that they have been dedicated to the public domain or that use for nonprofit purposes is permitted by the copyright holder. Among the billions of documents on the Internet, there are quite a few documents with these types of permissions. Nevertheless, these situations are apart from the average item located on the Internet. And a case may be made for "fair use" of Internet materials, just as one may make a claim of fair use for print and audio-visual materials. Similar situations must apply before a claim of fair use may be considered valid, though. One must analyze and evaluate every use in light of the general guidelines, given there are no specific rules for the Internet. Remember that each of the four tests of fair use must be weighed against every claim:

The purpose of the use. Is the use for nonprofit educational purposes? Displaying a Web page or making a transparency of some information for the purposes of teaching a lesson at a public or nonprofit private school would likely be looked upon favorably.

The character of the use. What type of material is going to be used? Factual material placed on the Internet has little protection of copyright because facts can't be copyrighted. If you are using lists of common facts such as the 10 longest rivers or population figures, you have much more latitude to use the material. Highly creative material, such as artwork, videos, or Web page design, would be much more highly protected.

The amount of material copied (also called the extent). How much of the material are you going to use? If you plan to copy the entire item (whole text file, complete graphic, entire Web page), you'd best have good answers to the other three qualifying questions. The more of an item you plan to use, the less leeway you are permitted. This factor has significant impact on software that can capture entire Web sites for use in an offline situation.

The effect of the use on the market for the work. What effect would your type of use have if everyone made similar use of the material? For example, if everyone were to download the whole Web page, do you think anyone would want to visit the site? Probably not. Given that some sites have advertising or other agendas on their sites, they wouldn't want someone to miss seeing those friendly notices. By downloading the page to an offline machine, one would miss the constantly changing variety of advertisements that the sponsor of the page spends lots of money for you to see. Missing those advertisements would potentially deprive the sponsor of revenue. As far as copyright goes, that is a no-no. What if the page is put up by a nonprofit individual or organization? The same reasoning applies. Perhaps the author of the document will one day develop that information into a book or magazine article. Would the market for the book be as great if everyone were able to capture the material from the Internet? Maybe the nonprofit organization wants Internet explorers to see the wealth of material their members can assemble, and if one captures a document, there would be no point in returning to this site again. Or perhaps the information is quickly dated, and the organization feels it would be harmed if it were identified with outdated material. There are many ways that financial harm could result for the copyright holder of an Internet document or file.

Take as an example the Rainforest Maths site originally put up by Australian teacher Jenny Eather (see Figure 10.1). She had a well-used and highly respected site offering math activities for elementary students. However, others (including government organizations) downloaded her content, translated it into other languages, and put her work up on their own Web sites. Commercial users also appropriated her content without permission or payment. So she removed her site completely for a time (Eather, 2008). It is now back up at http://www.rainforestmaths.com, but under a much more carefully regulated access and licensing plan. This is an example of how inappropriate use of copyrighted information can harm all of us—even those who do not act inappropriately.

Keep in mind that each classroom use of material retrieved from the Internet must be weighed against the four factors listed earlier in this chapter and several other places in this book. Imagine a scale, and each of the factors coming onto the scale on either the side *for* you or the side *against* you. According to some courts, the fourth factor weighs much more than all the others. Consider that when making your analysis.

Web-based material is copyrighted just as print and audiovisual materials are, and notification of copyright status is not required. Small portions of Web documents may be used by teachers in class if there is not sufficient time to secure

to anyone who asks to hear it is still reserved to the copyright holder. If your teacher had this stream behind a password protection scheme and met the other guidelines of the TEACH act, he might have more protection, but as it is, this doesn't look very good. Some transformative use of the music, such as commentary, would also help.

Figure 10.1. Rainforest Maths screenshot

Source: http://www.rainforestmaths.com/

permission, just as with print materials. Large chunks of images, documents, and Web sites should not be taken without prior consent. Watch for Web pages granting permission for use in educational situations. There are many.

Because there is greater latitude for student use of copyrighted materials, they may also use modest portions of Web documents as long as the copies they make belong to them. Teachers may not keep copies or originals of works made by students in which they incorporate materials copied from the Internet. The copies made from the Internet must reside with the student.

Remember that showing a Web document to a class constitutes a public performance or display of that page. Copyright law and its associated guidelines don't speak of the Internet, but common sense can gauge how closely a given use meets the fair use test. And as always, permission can override any limitations imposed by the law or guidelines. The good news is that many educational Web pages grant permission for educational use. Failing an outright grant of permission, the persons responsible for most reliable Web pages have e-mail links built right into the pages, so contacting the proper party for permission is a lot simpler than tracking down print or video copyright holders.

When putting up your own Web page, make sure you have the proper rights for the graphics, designs, logos, and photos you use. Photos are especially touchy. You need permission not only from the photographer but also from any recognizable person in the photograph. When requesting permission, as in all cases of permissions, verify that you are getting rights from the person authorized to grant such rights.

Special considerations for different Internet services

The Internet has several unique services that require analysis for appropriate use in a copyright context. E-mail, news and discussion groups, file transfer (including peer-to-peer file sharing), general Web pages, and Web 2.0 all require specific types of analysis.

E-mail

The author of an e-mail message owns the content of that message. You, as the recipient, may not make copies of that message or distribute it without the consent of the original author. This impacts messages you may forward to third parties without the express consent of the original author. There would probably be allowances to reprint some or all of the message in a reply to the sender. You might also paraphrase the message in the reply. Because you are sending that information back to the copyright holder, there would likely be no problem. One of the critical questions asked in determining whether a use of a copyrighted work is fair is "has the work been published?" Typically, private e-mail has never been published in such a way that many people would likely have seen this particular work. Because the work has not been published, there is less likelihood that use of the work would fall into a situation covered by fair use. Works are often unpublished because an author does not wish them to be published. In addition, if the e-mail is created at work under the scope of employment, there is the possibility that the e-mail is a work for hire (Fishman, 2000). Are there any court cases to support this? Not yet.

For safe parameters, keep private e-mail private unless you have the express permission of the original writer. Don't forward it to newsgroups or email distribution lists, don't include it in a message to a third party, and don't post it on your Web page, unless you receive permission. It's good manners; it's good practice.

Newsgroup and discussion list information

When someone posts a message to a newsgroup or a discussion list, he or she makes an implied decision to "publish" the work. Once a work is published, there is much more latitude to use portions of that work within the fair use exemption. You may, however, negate that implied license simply by noting in the posting that you request the material not be distributed beyond the list. Again, there are no significant court cases to support these assumptions. These are rules derived from the world of print and extrapolated into cyberspace.

For a safe guideline, you can probably copy a few sentences or paragraphs of a newsgroup or discussion list posting because it was published, as long as you aren't going to use it for a money-making purpose. Certainly you would attribute the source just as you would with any other work you did not create, but that is an academic integrity issue, not one of copyright. If you wish to repost the entire article or message to another newsgroup, it is always good manners (and safe legal practice) to ask permission to repost.

Web page information

When deciding how to use a Web page, make your analysis similar to that for a print document or an audiovisual item (depending on what you will be using from the Web). Keep in mind the four tests of fair use. The nonprofit educational use is a given for use in a classroom, but what about the character of the material used and the extent of the material used? The more creative the site (i.e., the less factual), the less of the site may be used without prior permission. As a matter of good teaching, one would want to make the best use of teaching resources. One doesn't use more of a video than is necessary to make a point. Teaching time is too valuable. So one would make optimum use of Web-based resources as well. Use what is necessary; then get on to other things.

Using any Web page involves a display of the material. Display is the right of the copyright holder. The Web page creator elected to display the work on the Web. Viewing the page is what was intended. However, causing the page to be displayed in a way that the creator did not intend, such as through frames that imply the content belongs to your own Web page rather than to that of the creator, could certainly cause copyright and other issues.

In creating Web pages, one must have concerns about using copyrighted materials on those pages given that the pages are distributed to the world. One must make copies to put a page on the Web, and frequently one must also convert materials from an analog format to digital to get the information on the Internet. Music, multimedia elements and other copyrighted information, once mounted on a Web page, are not only copied but also distributed and displayed or performed publicly. All these conditions are cause for concern. In the interest of copyright compliance, some rights brokers have established a "click-through" license for quick, efficient licensing for Web page use (ASCAP, BMI). Note that there is no automatic fair use for these types of elements on Web pages. Each individual use must be subjected to a fair use analysis.

Chat

Chat is as spontaneous as face-to-face conversation. However, few people record (or "fix") conversation. There is no case law regarding the ownership of chat conversations. Extrapolating from other media, one might be able to say that chat is ephemeral, not being "fixed." In such a case, no copyright is vested in a communication that is not fixed in a tangible medium of expression. If the chat is captured, however, fixation automatically generates a copyright for the author of each communication. So each "send" might be construed as a separate "work" protected by copyright, or a series of posts might be taken as a long, possibly disjointed, document, the copyright of which is co-owned by the participants.

Copying Internet code

Although it is possible to download a site's HTML code and adapt the design into your own page, remember that the creative work that went into the design is also copyrighted. Just as copying a drawing or painting requires permission, if you admire the design work of a Web page, ask the creator before you appropriate the result. Use of the HTML code as a reference, such as "I need to know how to make a two column table" and looking at and appropriating the HTML code to create such a table are certainly within fair use. HTML commands are public domain; the intellectual content displayed by the HTML code is not.

Web 2.0 applications

New technologies (or new applications of old technologies) outpace copyright law. Congress generally waits for a particular technology issue that cannot be addressed through the courts and present law before it goes tinkering with the status quo. For the most part, courts handle copyright issues with Web 2.0 applications using the standard fair use assessments, using previous cases as analogies to present-day applications. When courts get confused, they try to correct things themselves. Take, for example, the intersection of Web 2.0 social networking software such as MySpace and Facebook with the U.S. Constitution's First Amendment. Cases involving defamation, libel, and bullying have cropped up in most of the federal circuits. Several of the cases have involved students setting up fake MySpace or Facebook pages defaming teachers or school administrators. The pages have labeled the school personnel as pedophiles, alcoholics, homosexual, fat, or just plain stupid. One even solicited money to hire a hit man to kill a teacher. Those are not copyright issues; they deal with the First Amendment right to speak on topics of interest and where that right crosses the line into slander and libel. However, some of the profiles used school logos, photos, and other material taken from real school Web sites. The materials that the students appropriated were probably protected by a copyright, but copyright is not why the students ended up in court. The real legal issue in these types of cases is the First Amendment issue. Courts have ruled all over the map on these cases. In fact, two panels of the Third Circuit on the same day ruled in opposite directions on two fairly similar cases involving students posting defamatory information about school personnel (including photos) on MySpace (*JS ex rel Snyder v. Blue Mountain School District,* 2010; *Layshock v. Hermitage School District,* 2010). The entire panel of judges for the Third Circuit Court of Appeals (called "en banc") heard oral arguments on the two cases in June 2010 to decide what will be the rule of law for that circuit. As of this writing, the court has not issued its opinion. These cases revolve around First Amendment issues rather than ones of copyright. Nevertheless, copyright issues can come into play in cases such as these.

When you consider the various Web 2.0 (and many of the original Web) applications, the primary concerns of copyright owners are the rights of reproduction and distribution. Digital material is easily and effectively reproducible, and those many digital copies can fly around the world at the click of a mouse. Imagine that you are an auto manufacturer who painstakingly handcrafts automobiles. All of a sudden a new technology appears that allows industrialists in a third world country to purchase a single auto (or perhaps steal the auto from a showroom) and inexpensively mass-produce exact copies that they then use to flood the world market. Worse yet, they decide to give the copies away for free! The same holds true with the Web. The moment something is mounted on the Web, virtually anyone in the world has access to the work. No matter that your page was mounted with the intention of helping your first graders learn to spell. It now shoots electronic, perfect reproductions of the spelling workbook to hundreds of teachers in dozens of countries—none of whom paid the author or publisher for the privilege. Your social networking site or blog, by allowing you to mount photos, music, and video, does essentially the same thing, especially if you allow almost anyone to "friend" you or view your handiwork.

The primary Web 2.0 applications used by schools are social networking, video distribution, photo sharing, bookmark sharing, and wikis and similar relational databases. Each has copyright implications that school personnel should consider as they employ the applications.

Social networking

As far as copyright goes, think about your social network page as just another Web page with nifty features. Social networking is a source of potential copyright infringement, both as a perpetrator and as a victim. Although most social networking sites are for individuals, more schools and school organizations are mounting their own social networking sites to generate fan support. Even if your site is limited to those identified as "friends," your site probably does not meet the requirements of the TEACH Act for publishing liberal amounts of copyright-protected material.

Harvesting material from Facebook or MySpace and their cousins is also something you should evaluate carefully. Although the photos others put up on their pages may be perfect for that open house slide show, they are also protected by copyright even if there is no copyright notice or symbol. Because communication through social networking is so simple, why not just ask if you can use the material and avoid the pesky fair use assessments? Those social Web sites are also perfect for posting student book reviews, art work, and writing. But distributing to those widely viewed pages is also distributing to the world material that is copyrighted by your students. Get permission to post material on your social networking fan site just as you would on your regular Web page.

Podcasting

Podcasts are simply digital audio recordings that users download to an audio player or a computer or perhaps stream online. Just like a print document, if the content of the recording is original, the person making the recording owns the copyright in that recording. So if your students record a story they wrote, they own the copyright in the original written story and a separate copyright in the recording of their reading. If a student reads a book or story written by someone else, the original author owns the copyright in the original, and the student's reading of the work is a phonorecord (an audio copy) of the work. Although students can certainly make such recordings for personal use, putting that copy on the Internet or other network involves distribution to the world. Teachers who create podcasts within the scope of their employment face the same ownership hurdles as do teachers who create print documents within the scope. So, for example, a

Question: A teacher would like to copy and paste other people's podcasts (ones that she has come across via Web searches) to her own district Web page for students to listen to. Is that acceptable?

Answer: The teacher probably should not copy the podcasts without permission. You are redistributing someone else's content (a violation of the right of distribution) and streaming it on the Internet (a violation of the right of distribution of sound recordings). Falling back on the four fair-use factors is also not productive here. The copying is not transformative (she is just copying, not commenting or adding anything). She is copying the whole thing. The work is creative, presumably. Although it is unknown whether the teacher's use would affect the market for or value of the work (more facts would be needed to assess this factor), why can't she just link to the podcasts online rather than copying them? There is no problem linking to them.

librarian who does a weekly podcast of book talks as part of her responsibilities to encourage reading would likely find that she does not own the podcasts, which are instead owned by the school.

In creating a podcast, consider what uses would be fair if you were putting something up on the Internet. Podcasts included within a secure Web site that meets the requirements of the TEACH Act would follow the requirements and limitations of the act. Podcasts available on the open Web should follow the requirements of anything else mounted on the open Web. Even if the podcast is "educational," if it is available to anyone on the Internet, you will have a more difficult time making a strong fair-use case for reproducing a large amount of a written or recorded work within your program. Including copyrighted recorded music in a podcast would bring up the same concerns if you were to put the recording online. The more open the access, the more likely you are to receive a DMCA takedown notice on the podcast host.

In-class listening to a podcast of a non-student or non-employee would be safe if following the audiovisual guidelines of section 110(1). Just as with movies, a podcast performance that meets the requirements of this section would be exempt from the copyright owner's performance right.

Downloading a podcast from a place like iTunes adds another wrinkle. Download and subscription sites generally have some terms of service attached to your use of the site. If you have a login and a password to enter the download site, you can be virtually certain that you agreed to some terms of service to use the site. Although you certainly have fair use privileges to use material published on such a download site, you may have waived that right for all intents and purposes when you accepted the terms of service. Your use of bits of material taken from a podcast may fall within the limits of fair use, but it may be a simultaneous violation of the contract you agreed to when you accepted the terms of service. The question, then, is do you use the material anyway? The ethicist says no. The attorney says maybe. How likely are you to be caught? Would the owner care? What is the worst that can happen if you are caught and the owner does care? Consider where you will use the material. Within your own classroom? If the use is arguably fair, and there is small likelihood that the owner will know, why not? If you plan to put your creation on an insecure Web site where a Web spider will find your material and inform the copyright owner, even if your use is arguably fair, your worldwide distribution may have dampened the argument. You may have to convince a court that your use is fair, and that is expensive in both legal fees and peace of mind. Is your use worth that risk?

YouTube, Teacher Tube, and similar sites

Video sharing and streaming sites offer a unique set of challenges. Issues include uploading either student- or teacher-created video to a site, performing video from the site, and downloading video from the site. The first factor to consider is this: what are the terms of use for the site? Because you are using the site under a license agreement or a terms of service, that contract will have considerable effect on any analysis.

YouTube's terms of service limit what you may upload and download, as do most of the video sharing sites. To upload to YouTube, you must agree that any copyrighted material included in your video is used under license or permission. Remember that usage under fair use would be acceptable to upload. However, the state of the law is very unstable regarding fair use when posting material online. The video of the toddler dancing to the Prince song "Let's Get Crazy!" is informative. Although the mother who posted the video clip eventually won her case in court because she used a very short segment of the song, and the song was of very poor quality in the background, music and movie companies routinely demand that Web hosters remove video containing elements of their products. Such "take down" demands are consistent with the DMCA. New automated scanning (similar to school Web filters) makes simple work of blocking or removing work that may be infringing. Just because the mother won her case does not give a green light to anyone using copyright-protected material in a video posted on a video sharing site. Courts will take into account *all* the fair use factors in making a determination on fair use.

For a teacher who creates videos as supplements to class materials, remember that the teacher likely does not own the rights to the video—the school district owns the copyright. Therefore, unless the teacher has district approval to post the video online, the teacher does not have the rights to distribute the video to the world. Further, if the video contains images of children, posting the video on an insecure Web site may be a violation of state or federal laws regarding privacy of students. A teacher who posts a video created by a student on an open-access video site also needs permission of the copyright owner (the student, through the student's parents).

In-school performance of video from a video hosting site would follow the standard rules for educational public performance of motion media, found in § 110(1). Those are the standard five requirements: (1) nonprofit educational institution, (2) performance by and for students and teachers in a class, (3) performance in a classroom or other instructional place, (4) legally acquired copy of the video, and (5) material part of direct instruction. On an online site, "legally acquired" means that you meet the terms of service for the site. If the site is limited to children, and you have misrepresented yourself as being of the age for the site, your use of the video is not within the terms of use. If you have a hacked password, your copy of the video from the site is not "legally acquired."

The final consideration for using video hosting sites is in downloading the video. Under YouTube's terms of service, users may download only video that is specifically marked as available for download. Other hosting sites may have similar terms of use, but verify exactly what limits you have agreed to before downloading. However, many people have external software that will capture YouTube video (and possibly that of other hosting sites). Using illegally captured video would not be a "legally acquired" video for the purpose of the § 110(1) exemptions. Distributing copies of downloaded videos to other teachers, or mounting them within your own online courses, would be a violation of the terms of service with YouTube and a violation of the distribution right of the copyright owner. YouTube does grant limited permission to embed a YouTube viewer in your own Web page for the purpose of sharing YouTube video, as long as certain other procedures are followed, such as putting a "prominent" link to YouTube. So an acceptable alternative would be to embed the YouTube player in a Web page and view the video through that rather than downloading at all.

Flickr, Picasa, Snapfish, and similar photo-sharing sites

A copyright attaches to a photograph as soon as the photo is fixed in tangible form. "Tangible form" when speaking of digital images means saved to some storage medium. Any image you find on the Internet (other than live, unrecorded video) is saved in some sort of computer file. Most of the photos you find on photo sharing sites are not labeled with any copyright notice, but none is required. Assume that any image you see on an image site is protected unless you know with certainty the photo is not protected. Images marked with some sort of Creative Commons or other copyleft scheme are *not* copyright-free. The images are simply available under a liberal, but standardized, license. Make certain that you understand your responsibilities in using materials under that license. Identify the copyright owners appropriately. And remember that if the license is a "share-alike" license, you are required to make whatever you create with the borrowed material available to others under the same restrictions as the image you received.

Uploading images to an image sharing site typically requires registration and agreement to terms of service. Look in the terms of service for a requirement that you either be the copyright owner of the images you upload or have permission of the copyright owner to upload the images. If you are uploading photos you personally shot, you generally own the images unless the images were made in the course of your employment. In that case, the images likely belong to your employer. Use caution in uploading images to a photo sharing site that were taken by students because the students own the copyright in those images. Most students are minors and are not legally capable of giving permission. Contact a student's parents (and consult your district policies on use of student work) before uploading images students created to an image sharing site.

Using images you find on a photo sharing site requires that you carefully note the license attached to the image. What constitutes "fair use" in using the image of another is not crystal clear in the law. Recent court decisions have found that the more "transformative" the use of images, the more likely the use is fair. But "transformative" generally requires more than just reproducing the image for decoration in a brochure, for example. Including a portion of an image in a collage or new Photoshop creation is much more likely to be considered transformative because the new use gives value added to the original image and does not replace the original. And remember that transformativeness is only a portion of one of the four factors assessed in making a fair use analysis. Fair use does not live or die on transformation alone.

Delicious, Digg, Technorati, and other social bookmarking sites

According to Wikipedia, "in a social bookmarking system, users save links to Web pages that they want to remember and/or share. These bookmarks are usually public, and can be saved privately, shared only with specified people or groups, shared only inside certain networks, or another combination of public and private domains. The allowed people can usually view these bookmarks chronologically, by category or tags, or via a search engine" (Social bookmarking, 2010, para. 3). Web addresses, or "links," are facts. Similar to a street address, a link is a direction for a computer to follow to retrieve a specific file. Facts cannot be protected by copyright. So a given link that someone might find on a social bookmarking page is not protected by copyright. Nevertheless, although facts themselves are not protectable by copyright, collections of facts certainly can be. A social bookmarking page is a collection of facts, just like an almanac is a collection of facts. The almanac is certainly protected by copyright for its collection and organization of the facts it contains, and a social bookmarking site would have a similar protection. Individual page owners generally will have no claim of copyright infringement in the link itself, but they might have some claims of misrepresentation if their pages appear in a frame that implies the page is part of someone else's site.

Posting links you choose to a social bookmarking site has no copyright implications because the links themselves are not protected by copyright. Copying links from someone else's social bookmarking site might have copyright implications only if you copy an amount more than what would be considered fair use. For example, if a teacher has put up a Delicious page of links about the Civil War, and another teacher copies the entire page and its organization and mounts those links on his own page, the creator of the original page might have a viable claim of copyright infringement. And though it is unlikely that the creator would sue, she might send a cease and desist letter, which can get your social networking site pulled from the Web by the hosting company.

Happening to find an interesting link on someone's social bookmarking site does not mean you cannot also make a link to that interesting site. Just make sure that your own collection and organization of links is your own creation. If you find someone who has a terrific set of links, why not link to that page instead of copying the other person's work?

Wikis and other user-contributed online databases

Wikis are the simplest form of online databases, where anyone with access to the wiki site can edit pages within the site (Matias, 2003). Wikipedia is the most famous wiki, but thousands of wikis have been put up by schools and businesses. Because the wiki data is saved into a "tangible form" file for the purpose of Web display, the data within the wiki pages is protected by copyright. Naturally, the wiki software itself is also protected by the copyright owned by the original programmer (or someone to whom the programmer assigned the copyright). Contributions to the wiki, unless assigned to others through the terms of service of a wiki (which is questionable at best because assignments of copyrights must be in signed writing), belong jointly to the contributors. Each person who contributed to a wiki article shares the copyright of the wiki article with the other contributors. If someone's job includes contributing to a wiki (such as an IT person whose job it is to draft wiki articles on tech support issues), those contributions would likely be considered the property of the employer.

What can you add to a wiki? Consider a wiki to be a normal Web page. It is essentially a highly interlinked Web site with indexing. If the wiki is up on the open Web, follow any rules you would apply to publication on the Web. Make certain that any copyrighted material is used within fair use (standard fair use, because any educational exemptions are unlikely to apply in an open Web situation) or has permission. If the wiki is mounted within a secure school site and is part of a regular course, the exemptions of the TEACH Act might apply, depending on the circumstances. If you are relying on the TEACH Act exemptions, consider how long you wish the material to stay available. Remember that copyright-protected material put online under TEACH Act exemptions may not stay up indefinitely. Of course, if you have permission for the copyrighted material, you may do whatever the permission says you may do.

Downloading or copying material from a wiki posted on the open Web would have the same requirements as any other Web-based material. Note that many general wikis such as Wikipedia are put up under Creative Commons licensing, so consider the implications of using material under those terms. If you plan to have a restricted Web page or create material that you might someday market (such as a curriculum guide), you would not want to include material from many of the Creative Commons licenses because they require that any resulting derivative work be distributed under a share-alike license or a noncommercial license. Both of those licenses would be contrary to the purpose of your use.

Kindle and other e-books

Issues involved with e-books include file format conversions, transfers, and copies. E-books have not yet achieved a standard format (eBook Mall, 2010). Some e-book readers will read only proprietary formats; others accept multiple formats. Various formats may or may not include digital rights management (DRM), which can limit the ability to use or transfer copies (Schember, 2010). Circumventing digital rights management to allow an unauthorized reader device to display an e-book file is a violation of the Digital Millennium Copyright Act. Further, transferring an e-book to a different computer or different device than that for which it was purchased may be a violation of the license that came with the e-book. Such transfers are not likely copyright violations because you still have only one installed

Question: Teachers want to have students collaborate on a publicly accessible wiki on a given topic. The thought is that students can cite sources the same way they would for a paper. They would also link to the quoted/paraphrased material if it is online already. However, I noticed that one of our databases restricts reusing content without permission, but would this be educational fair use (scholarship and criticism)?

Answer: Remember that through license, you can give up some of your standard fair use rights. With your database license, you may have done just that. You need to have your district's legal counsel review the license language and see if that is what has indeed happened. Also remember that citation has nothing to do with fair use. Although citation is an academic ethics concept, it is not necessarily required for fair use. Even items from the public domain should be cited. But restricting using whole or complete items from the database does not prevent students from using the facts contained within the database. Facts are not protected by copyright.

version of the e-book. The single installation reflects your terms of use or license that you agreed to when you received the e-book but may limit your use or distribution of that e-book file. One should always look carefully at the terms of service or license when purchasing an e-book because the license will dictate the limitations you accept with the purchase. In July 2010 the Librarian of Congress announced a 3-year option for visually impaired people to bypass copy protection to transfer an audiobook from one e-book reader to one for which there is no audiobook version in order to activate the read-aloud function.

When a school or a library purchases an e-book, sometimes it wishes to make multiple copies of that file. For example, a library may wish to install an e-book on half a dozen e-book readers so that it is available to those who come to check out an e-book reader. Typically, the license that comes with the e-book says that it may be installed on only one device at a time. If the e-book comes on a compact disc or DVD, like computer software, the owner may make a backup (and unused) copy of the actual software, as well as installing the software in workable form on the device in which it will be used. However, it may not be installed on more than one device without a license that allows multiple installs. The fact that only one person may be *accessing* the e-book at a time is not generally what the license controls; it controls how many simultaneous e-book *installations* the user may have. This situation is analogous to installing a single-user program on multiple computers to avoid purchasing multiple copies of the program. Naturally, there may be any number of nuances to this analysis, such as plain text files of public domain works. Such files are not protected by any copyright and cannot be restricted because there is no proprietary or copyrightable content. To make a fair analysis of e-book copies, it is essential to know what the underlying document is, whether any new material has been added (which would generate a new copyright in the added material), what format the material is in, and what license came with the e-book. Of course, fair use would allow an e-book reader to take quotations from and use portions of material in e-books under the same conditions as using similar materials from printed books.

Blogs and other self-publishing

A blog is generally a single Web page, with writings posted in reverse chronological order. Typically, blogs are written by a single author (though some allow interactive comments) and are generally public (Brain, 2003). Because a blog is a Web page, the contents of the blog have been saved in "tangible form" and therefore qualify for copyright protection to the extent that the material is original and creative. Whether a student or a staff member writes the blog, each person owns his or her own contribution to it.

Although some schools elect to establish their own blog-like sites that may just be a collection of links to single Web pages, most true blogs utilize some blog hosting service such as Blogger, WordPress, or TypePad. These blog hosting services require acceptance of terms of service as part of the contract between the hosting service and the owner of the blog. For example, visit http://www.blogger.com/terms.g to see Blogger's terms of service. The terms specify that Google (which owns Blogger) may use posted content in any way it sees fit. It also allows those who post information on the site to set terms of ownership, such as applying Creative Commons licensing to blogs. So what can you post to a blog, and what can you take from someone else's blog?

Posting to a public blog involves rules similar to posting on any public Web page. Naturally, fair use is available, but because the page is public, any educational exemptions are unlikely to apply. Because this is a Web page hosted by an Internet service provider, if a copyright owner finds that you have used his material in a way that would exceed fair use, the copyright owner has the ability to trigger the DMCA takedown provisions. To get your blog re-enabled, you would need to respond to the takedown notice. See http://www.google.com/blogger_dmca.html for an example of the process.

To use some material from someone else's blog, you would have available the standard fair use limitations of print materials, typically. A blog is a form of essay, so the print limits for essays would work well. Rather than copying a blog, however, linking to it might be a better option that would bypass copyright concerns entirely. If you are not copying or distributing the blog entry yourself, there are no copyright concerns that would intrude. Putting someone's blog in its entirety into a commercial product (such as curriculum guides or commercially sold curriculum) would probably exceed the limits of fair use.

Twitter and other microblogging tools

Twitter and its friends are considered "microblogs" because they have the same purpose as a blog but are limited in the size of an individual installment. It is questionable whether a tweet is sufficiently creative to be copyrightable. Because two individuals can independently come up with the same work that is protected by copyright (and thus each owns an independent copyright in the work), it is quite possible that multiple people came up with the same "Just got off the plane in NY" tweet. Tweets issued by school personnel within the scope of their employment (such as snow day alerts) would belong to the school district if there were enough creativity to be protectable by copyright. Certainly any use of someone's public tweets would be available on the same basis as a blog posting.

Second Life, MUDs, MOOs, and other virtual worlds

Second Life and its cousins are virtual worlds in which users create personas called "avatars." The avatars follow the direction of their creators to interact with other personas, places, and objects in the environment (Strickland & Roos, 2007). Users in the environment can generate user-created content, and (unless the site's terms of service say otherwise) users own the copyright of the objects they create. In some virtual worlds, anyone can copy objects he may see, even though those objects may have been created by someone else. In Second Life, users even have virtual businesses selling various goods and services to other virtual residents of the world (Kravets, 2009). Users can upload user-created content, which brings into focus the copyright liability of these types of environments. Just as in the real world, copyright becomes an issue in the virtual world when someone appropriates the intellectual property of others.

When a virtual world is publicly accessible, the environment's Internet service provider will be subject to the Digital Millennium Copyright Act takedown provisions if a copyright owner finds that a user has uploaded or otherwise used the owner's material within the virtual world. A virtual world housed on a school district server and available only to students within a course for the duration of that course would fall under the exemptions of the TEACH Act.

Resources for understanding

YouTube Terms of Service—http://www.youtube.com/t/terms. Covers the agreement a user accepts by using the YouTube site, including what a user may upload, download, and distribute.

Works cited

Armatas, S. A. (2008). *Distance learning and copyright: A guide to legal issues.* Boston: American Bar Association Section of Intellectual Property Law.

Bender, I. (1996, Summer). The Internet—It's not free and never was. *AIME News.*

Brain, M. (2003, August 20). *How blogs work.* Retrieved from http://computer.howstuffworks.com/internet/social-networking/information/blog.htm.

Eather, J. (2008, August 15). Why Jenny has taken it down [Msg 6]. Message posted to http://www.proteacher.net/discussions/showthread.php?t=102053.

eBook Mall. (2010). *Popular eBook formats.* Retrieved from http://www.ebookmall.com/choose-format/.

Fishman, S. (2000). *The copyright handbook* (5th ed.). Berkeley, CA: NOLO.

Gain, B. (2009, May 28). Special report: The future of file sharing. *Intellectual Property Watch.* Retrieved from http://www.ip-watch.org/Weblog/2009/05/28/the-future-of-file-sharing/.

JS ex rel Snyder v. Blue Mountain Sch. Dist., 593 F.3d 286 (3d Cir. 2010).

Kravets, D. (2009, September 17). Linden Lab targeted in Second Life sex-code lawsuit. Retrieved from http://www.wired.com/threatlevel/2009/09/linden/.

Layshock v. Hermitage Sch. Dist., 593 F.3d 249 (3d Cir. 2010).

Matias, N. (2003). *What is a wiki?* Retrieved from http://articles.sitepoint.com/article/what-is-a-wiki.

Schember, J. (2010, January 3). *The ABCs of e-book format conversion: Easy Calibre tips for the Kindle, Sony, and Nook.* Retrieved from http://www.teleread.org/2010/01/03/the-abcs-of-format-conversion-for-the-kindle-sony-and-nook-plus-some-calibre-tips/.

Social bookmarking. (2010, March 28). In *Wikipedia, The Free Encyclopedia.* Retrieved from http://en.wikipedia.org/w/index.php?title=Social_bookmarking&oldid=352577816.

Strickland, J., & Roos, D. (2007, November 8). *How Second Life works.* Retrieved from http://computer.howstuffworks.com/internet/social-networking/networks/second-life.htm.

Chapter 11

Computer Software in Schools

When the present version of the copyright law was adopted in 1976, computers were huge machines in refrigerated rooms. Few but the most visionary foresaw the emergence of computers as a household or personal appliance—certainly not the Congress as it moved through its deliberations. The 1976 copyright law offered protection to computer programs only as a new form of literary work. In 1980, however, computer programs received expanded protection under section 117 of the newly revised statute. Making unauthorized copies of computer software has risen in seriousness in recent years. A revision of the law passed in 1992 brought software piracy to felony status, with fines up to $250,000 and up to five years in prison for systematic violations. The "No Electronic Theft" (NET) Act, passed in 1997, eliminated a loophole for those who provide infringing copies of software via the Internet and other networks. Those who willfully infringe more than $2,500 worth of software are liable for infringement, *whether or not a profit is made.* Noncommercial infringement of one or more copies worth more than $1,000 can result in a sentence of a year in prison and fines.

What typical activities are covered?

School personnel who knowingly lend computer software to persons who intend to copy it and school personnel who knowingly lend the necessary equipment to copy software may also be charged with copyright infringement. This situation is known as contributory infringement. Prosecution under this aspect of the law is uncommon, but not impossible. An example of such an act would be a video store selling recordings it knew to be in violation of copyright. They did not make the infringing copies, but they profited by the sale of copies they knew to be illegally made (Berman, 1993). A school whose educators use videos they know to be improperly made would be at risk of some sort of enforcement action.

Similarly, a principal who had been notified that an employee was violating copyright but who took no action could be

> *Question:* I want to install software I use at work on my computer at home so that I can transfer data back and forth. Can I rely on the 80/20 rule to install this software?
>
> *Answer:* There is no such thing as a blanket 80/20 rule. Some software licenses allow you to install software from a work computer onto a laptop or a computer at home if you are the user of the software at work more than a certain percentage of the time the software is used, but the provisions of the individual software license will determine whether such installations are acceptable.

accused of vicarious infringement if the employee knew the actions violated the law. Naturally, any of these cases would have a vigorous defense on several grounds, but the fact remains that one does not actually have to make the copy to be held liable. One must decide for oneself whether the risk of suit is worth the activity. Here are some common computer software copyright situations and their legal implications:

- *A teacher comes to the library and asks to install her personal copy of a word processing program on one of the school computers. She will be using the program at home in the evenings and at school during the day, so only one copy will be in use at a time.*

- *In the absence of a license provision permitting such uses, having the same software loaded on two computers even if they are not in use at the same time is not permitted.*

- *A student accesses the Internet from the library and downloads a game from a Web site. He proceeds to give copies of the game to all his friends.*

Before you can analyze the action, you need to know whether the software was distributed as shareware, as share-alike, or under some other form of license. Shareware is a type of copyrighted software that may be freely distributed. The user of the software must pay a fee if he decides to keep the software after trying it. Anyone may give copies of shareware software to others. The ultimate users are the people who are obligated to pay the license fee if they decide to retain and use the software. Similarly, some software is available through share-alike licenses from Creative Commons or other copyleft organizations. Many of those, too, may be freely shared. Software distributed under some other provisions may have other restrictions, or none.

Multiple installs—issues

Computer software is so very tempting. It will easily install as many times as you need and will run on all the computers on which you install it. Unfortunately, each installation requires a license. Some software just wants you to type in the license code on the package, which allows an unlimited number of installations. Other software is "smart" and uses an Internet connection to contact the software company. The company verifies the license and checks to see if that particular license code has been installed previously. If the license number has been previously installed, the software will not function. More recent software is in the latter category.

Examples of typical activities involving multiple installs include the following:

- *Student computer assistants tire of checking out DVD-ROMs to students in the library, so they install the program on each library computer. The program comes with a license for only one installation.*

- *A teacher buys a program for his computer at home. The program helps him create interactive tests for his students. Because it is so helpful, the teacher also installs the program on his laptop and his computer at school. The program allows installation on one desktop machine and that same user's laptop.*

- *The industrial arts teacher is required to teach technical drawing. The state urges the use of computer-assisted design (CAD) software. The district has had financial difficulties and can afford only three copies of the software. There are six computers in the lab. The teacher installs the program on the other three computers so that more students can work at once.*

Networking—issues

Putting software on a network can result in distribution of the software beyond the limits allowed by the license. With broad access permitted by internetworked computers, access to site-licensed software can be from anywhere.

Typical examples involving networking include the following:

- *The computer technician put a single-user copy of software on the district Web server where anyone with rights to the server could access it. The software does not have the technological means to prevent more than one person from running the software at the same time.*

- *The webmaster puts a link to the school's contracted periodical database on a public Web page so that students can access from home. The database license specifically states that only access from school is permitted.*

Checking out software—issues

Why would someone want to borrow software? The answer is simple. You need to print one poster and don't want to spend a lot of money for a program to print that one. So you borrow the software, install it, print the poster, uninstall the software, and then return it. It is legal for libraries to circulate software, with some detailed caveats.

Following are typical examples involving circulating software:

- *A teacher borrows a crossword puzzle–making program to create a puzzle with this week's vocabulary words. She enjoys the program so much that she doesn't uninstall the program when she returns the software.*

- *A school secretary borrows a graphics program from the library. As she is walking out, she tells the librarian, "I'm so glad you had this! My pastor has wanted it for the church for a long time. I'll go install it there and have this back by Monday morning!"*

Clip art—issues

Electronic clip art is the panacea for those who cannot draw a straight line. It is also a huge pit of potential copyright infringement. Because clip art is protected by copyright the moment the graphic file is saved to disk by the original artist, very little clip art is in the public domain. Yet the ease of copying digital files tempts even the most honest computer user.

Typical scenarios involving clip art include the following:

- *A computer teacher collects clip art files and mounts them on a Web page for ease of access for his students.*

- *An elementary teacher prefers her students not surf the Internet for images, so she finds a dozen or two appropriate images and mounts them to the class Web page so that students working from home can access the images.*

- *Cheerleaders need clip art for posters, so they find an image of a famous cartoon character. With digital editing software, they put the cartoon character into the school basketball uniform for use on the posters.*

Types of infringement

Infringement actions similar to those that can occur in the realm of print can also occur with computer software. Several types of copying are activities of which to be wary.

Direct infringement

"Anyone who violates any of the exclusive rights of the copyright owner [reproduction, adaptation, distribution to the public, public performance, public display, rental for commercial advantage or importation] is an infringer of the copyright or right of the author" 17 U.S.C.A. § 501(a) (West, 2010).

Activities that typically represent direct infringement of computer software include the following:

- *downloading software*
- *uploading software*
- *making software available for download*
- *transmitting software files*

Remember that you need not be the one actually making the illegal copies to be liable for copyright infringement. Those who knowledgeably control the means necessary to make copies or those who cause others to actually make the copies may be contributory infringers or vicariously liable as well.

Indirect infringement
Contributory infringement

Anyone who knows or should have known that he or she is assisting, inducing, or materially contributing to infringement of any of the exclusive rights by another person is liable for contributory infringement. Activities that typically represent contributory infringement of computer software include the following:

- *posting of serial numbers*
- *posting of cracker utilities*
- *linking to sites were software may be unlawfully obtained*
- *informing others of sites were software may be unlawfully obtained*
- *aiding others in locating or using unauthorized software*
- *supporting sites where the preceding information may be obtained*
- *allowing sites where the preceding information may be obtained to exist on a server*

Vicarious liability for infringement by another person

Anyone who has the authority and ability to control another person who infringes any of the exclusive rights of a copyright holder and who derives a financial benefit is vicariously liable for the infringement of another person (Simpson, 2008). The following are clear cut examples of vicarious infringement:

- *ISPs (Internet service providers) who have warez (proprietary software with copy protection removed illegally) or pirate sites on their system*
- *ISPs who have pirates for customers*
- *system administrators for social networks or online groups where pirate activity takes place*

What rights are affected?

Computer software issues can affect virtually all of the rights reserved to the copyright holder.

Reproduction

Copyright owners are especially concerned about reproduction of software because all copies are identical to the original. Software is expensive to develop, and each copy duplicated illegally is a significant amount of profit/cost recovery.

Adaptation

Digital adaptation is easy and may be undetectable. Copyright owners worry about essential portions of their underlying code being stolen and reproduced in competition.

Distribution

Distribution of software is fast, simple, and inexpensive compared to the costs involved in print distribution, for example. A digital work can be available around the world in a matter of seconds.

Public performance

Performance of digital works can reduce demand for legitimate copies of the work.

Public display

Public display is less possible for computer software, but digital images and other digital works such as Web pages are also displayed.

Special rules that affect computer software

Computer software is unique in many aspects. Because it is digital, copyright owners have developed different forms of distribution and different terms of sale from other, more traditional media. Software can be highly lucrative, and it begins at a high price point. Those who want to be cool want to have the latest toys, but the high price only makes them that much more determined to get the software without paying the high price and resultant benefit to the copyright owner. As a result, software has suffered more piracy than most other media. Copyright owners responded with their own volleys, and the war was on. Various selling methods and distribution channels emerged to address these scuffles.

License versus copyright

Although most software (even "shareware") is copyrighted, the purchase of software is usually governed by a license agreement as well as by copyright law. When purchasing a book, the purchaser does not own the book but merely the paper, the ink and binding, and the right to read the words until that copy of the book wears out. Something similar holds true with software. The purchaser does not own the software but rather has the right to use the software in a manner described in a license agreement, which is usually included in the documentation of the software package. Reading and understanding the license agreement is an important part of acquiring a new package. Once accepted, these restrictions govern all use of the software.

There are several forms of license agreements: signed agreements, usually on some sort of warranty registration; implied licenses; and so-called shrink-wrap licenses. Implied licenses are included in the software packaging, usually as a part of the documentation or as a separate sheet. These licenses usually say something like "use of the software after reading the license terms implies acceptance." If you don't care for the terms of the license, the manufacturer will usually allow return of the package for a refund. Shrink-wrap licenses are often visible through a plastic overwrap on the software package. A similar type of license is called "click wrap" because the license appears when the software is installed. The user must click on an acknowledgement of the license to complete the software installation. The wording of both of these licenses will state that the user is bound by the conditions of the license if the user opens the shrink-wrap or clicks the accept button. There is a degree of controversy about such default contracts (Goldstein, 2009). Some courts indicate that if one is given the opportunity to return software once the details of the license are known, the license may be valid (*ProCD v. Zeidenberg,* 1996). The various circuit courts are split on this issue, so know your rights in your state.

If the signed license agreement is returned to the software company, or if you click on the "I agree" button, you will be legally bound by the restrictions imposed in the license. This license agreement may supersede some standard rights under copyright (Goldstein, 2009). It may also grant some extra privileges, such as the ability for the person on whose computer certain software is installed to also install the software on a laptop or home computer. This permission is by no means a right, but a gracious offer on the part of the software company. Read the fine print to determine whether you have permission to make any additional installations and what permissions you may have.

Some license agreements grant the purchaser the right to duplicate a specified number of copies of the software—commonly called a limited site license. The software producer allows a discount on the software price, and in return, the purchaser uses his own media and labor to make copies. Site licenses are generally specified on purchase orders and hence are legal and binding contracts between the purchaser and the producer. Because the deal involves a contract, producers may be able to work out the exact type of license you desire, even if those particular terms may not be listed on the producer's price sheet. If the producer suspects the purchaser has violated the contract or license agreement, the legal action is more likely to be based on contract law than on copyright, but damages could still be significant if the purchaser is found to have breached the contract. Probably the most significant damage would be the prevailing party's attorney fees, which are often charged to the loser in a contract lawsuit.

Legitimate copying versus piracy

"Piracy" is the illegal copying of computer software (among other things). For teachers and students who have at-home computers compatible with the school computers, the temptation is strong to bring home a copy of the school's software so that they can transfer work back and forth. The rules on making copies of computer programs allow only two instances in which copies may be made of programs outside the scope of a valid license agreement.

You may make a copy or adaptation if the copy is an essential part of the operation of the computer program (17 U.S.C. § 117[a][1]). For example, if the program must be copied to the hard disk of the computer, that copying is acceptable. Because most, if not all, computer programs require the program to copy itself into the computer's memory in order to run, such an "ephemeral" copy is also permitted under this portion of the law. The program erases itself when the program is finished. In addition, modifications such as installing a printer driver or other customizations allowed by the software itself are also within the acceptable limits of adaptation.

A copy or adaptation for archival purposes may be made if the archival copy is not used (17 U.S.C. § 117[a][2]). This copy can be on disk, diskette, backup CD, or tape. Destroy the archival or backup copy if you sell or transfer the program. You may use the backup copy of the software and put the original away for safekeeping, or vice versa. Either is acceptable as long as both copies are not used at the same time. This provision is only for "owners" of software, however, not for licensees, so determine which you are before you make your backups. Your license likely allows the archival copy, but check it to see what limits it may place on the archives. What probably isn't okay is making a copy of a program that you get on a flash drive or a dongle, such as some game programs. Most federal courts (with the exception of the Fifth Circuit) have found that you cannot make archival copies from "read-only memory semiconductor chips since the programs on the chips could be neither reprogrammed nor erased and were not susceptible to destruction or damage through mechanical or electrical failure" (Goldstein, 2009, p. 7:47).

Don't forget that the Digital Millennium Copyright Act requires that one not remove copyright management information from protected works, including computer software. A license agreement may contain the copyright management information for a specific software package, so be wary about discarding all that fine print.

Software for free?

Several forms of software may be freely copied without any licenses or agreements. The first type is known as public domain software. There are several ways a work can enter the public domain. For computer software, the primary way a work comes into the public domain is for the author to abandon the copyright in the work. Public domain software is a computer program that has been released by the author to be freely copied by whoever would like to use it. Such software is often found on Web sites dedicated to the public domain and from computer users' groups and clubs. A Creative Commons Public Domain Dedication or CC0 license will also accomplish copyright abandonment (Creative Commons, 2009b; Peters, 2009). The title screen of the program or the documentation typically will indicate the public domain status of the program.

Another form of software that may be freely copied isn't exactly free. Known as "shareware," this software is copyright-protected. The author or copyright holder has elected to distribute the software through a try-it-before-you-buy-it method. A popular site for shareware is Tucows (http://www.tucows.com). Shareware software is available through similar channels as public domain software, but once the software has been used and evaluated, the user is expected to register the software and pay a fee for the program—anything from a voluntary donation (sometimes to a charitable organization) up to $100 or so. Some authors give a time frame for this trial period. Others limit the features of shareware software so that you are limited in the number of elements—or saves, or records—that the software may create during the trial period. The software may or may not continue to work at the end of the stated period. Others just say "if you like it, send money." It's the honor system at its most fragile. If users of shareware fail to register and pay for the software that they retain and use, this method of software distribution may disappear.

Open source software is a third type of software that is usually available for free, though not always. Open source software is software that is distributed or sold to the public (as opposed to being in the public domain) with the idea that all the users of the software will collectively develop the software and share their results. Various groups have attempted to regularize the open source concept, and each has small variations on the license that creators agree to when distributing software under that group's license. GNU General Public License (Free Software Foundation, 2010), the Open Source Initiative (Open Source Initiative, n.d.), and Creative Commons (Creative Commons, 2009a) are among several groups that offer standard licensing terms for software.

As a rule, these groups require that anyone using the material covered by their licenses redistribute any derivative works under a license similar to that through which the person received the original work. So, for example, if someone used software under a GNU General Public License and created enhancements to the software, the developer would have to apply a GNU General Public License to the resulting software including the enhancements. Having an open source license does not mean that the software is free, however. The developer may, in most cases, sell his enhancements along with the base software from which he began. But if the overarching license requires the developer to provide the source code with the software, the developer must do so or forfeit his use of the original source code.

Lending software

In 1990, Congress responded to the complaints of commercial computer software producers that the lending and renting of computer software was eroding the market for their products. The Computer Software Rental Amendments Act was the result. In essence, the act granted to copyright owners (of computer software only) the right to control rental, lease, or lending of their software. However, the law did provide an exemption for nonprofit libraries (including school libraries), provided that a warning of copyright is affixed to each package. The Code of Federal Regulations specifies the exact wording of the notice:

> *Notice: Warning of copyright restrictions*
> *The copyright law of the United States (Title 17, United States Code) governs the reproduction, distribution, adaptation, public performance, and public display of copyrighted material. Under certain conditions specified in law, nonprofit libraries are authorized to lend, lease, or rent copies of computer programs to patrons on a nonprofit basis and for nonprofit purposes. Any person who makes an unauthorized copy or adaptation of the computer program, or redistributes the loan copy, or publicly performs or displays the computer program, except as permitted by Title 17 of the United States Code, may be liable for copyright infringement. This institution reserves the right to refuse to fulfill a loan request if, in its judgment, fulfillment of the request would lead to violation of the copyright law.* (37 C.F.R. 201.24)

The law further states that this notice must be "durably attached" to the package that is loaned to patrons. Some library supply houses sell stickers that feature this required statement. As a final note, remember that this exemption for lending software is allowed for libraries only. Academic departments, administrators, or computer or technology directors may not make such loans because they do not qualify for this exemption.

Single-user programs

A common act of software piracy in schools is that of purchasing a single-user copy of a program and then installing it on multiple machines. The program may be a grade book, a database manager, a word processor, or an integrated software package. The program may even be as basic as the operating system (Windows or OS) itself! Teachers and administrators rationalize the decision by saying that they aren't making any profit on the deal, and the school certainly can't afford all those single copies. Unfortunately, the end doesn't justify the means. And making more than 10 copies of a program (constituting a retail value of more than $2,500) immediately raises the penalty for infringement to up to $250,000 in fines and up to three years in prison on felony charges (18 U.S.C. § 2319(b)).

If such multiple loads currently reside on computers in a district, often software producers will sell school districts licenses (only) for software at a greatly reduced price. The license includes no disks or documentation, but it legitimizes copies currently residing on the computers.

Some DVD-ROMs require that a portion of the program be installed to the local hard disk in order to speed access to the disc. With such an installation, at the time of use, one needs only to slip the DVD-ROM into the drive, and the program will work. Unfortunately, loading even a portion of the program on multiple computers without specific exemption is technically a violation of the single-use license, and software audits will show each installation of the program "kernel" on the hard drive as an installation requiring a license. Now that most sophisticated commercial software uses the Internet to validate an installation, this issue is not as important as it once was. But when using software from smaller companies such as educational consultants and niche programs for specific states, this issue can still occur.

Networking

Network options allow multiple computers to share one copy of the software. However, networking software is not covered under fair use. All network and site licenses are contracts negotiated with the sellers—not a right under fair use. The fact that a particular piece of software *can* operate in a networked environment is immaterial. Networking a piece of computer software always requires a license. And get it in writing!

Some software permits unlimited networking within a single school, campus, or building. "Building" is not defined in the law, but if it is not defined in the license, consider a building to be an organizational campus—a group of students who have a separate administrative head. Many schools, such as a high school, will have multiple buildings composing their physical plant. There may be a central building, a field house, an annex or portable buildings, or a separate gymnasium or auditorium. As long as those buildings are part of the physical plant of that organizational unit, any computer in those buildings could qualify to access the software under the network site license. Nothing is certain without being spelled out in the license, of course, but you would have a reasonable argument for your use.

Some school-owned plots of land house two schools, however. An elementary or middle school and a high school might be on the same plot of land. They might even share network components. But for license purposes, those are probably two separate schools. If the two schools have separate names, and perhaps if they have separate administrators, the software company would be able to make an excellent case for there being two entities. It is best to be up-front with the software producer when purchasing a license in such out-of-the-ordinary circumstances.

The software police

Although the dreaded software police don't actually exist, the FBI can, and does, investigate and enforce suspected copyright violations as part of its general responsibilities. Because computer software piracy is now punishable as a felony (Marshall, 1993), prosecution is pursued much more seriously. One of the schools in a district where I worked was, in fact, visited by representatives of a software publishing firm. They asked courteously but firmly to see verification that legitimate copies of their software had been purchased. When the original packages and documentation were produced for their inspection, they thanked the librarian politely and left. They declined to say why they had selected this building for an inspection. Other districts have suffered large fines and public embarrassment for lax computer-software license enforcement (Blair, 1998).

Organizations such as the Business Software Alliance (BSA) and the Software and Information Industry Association (SIIA) advise schools and districts to conduct software audits. Essentially, this puts someone in the building and district in the position of software policeman. The SIIA even offers a training program for maintaining records of legitimate copies of software (Anti-piracy, 2010). The SIIA also recommends conducting a software audit using specialized audit software. Most work across a network and across operating systems.

In addition to locating pirated software, a software audit makes employees who put personal software on institutional machines subject to further investigation to determine whether such use is within the applicable software licenses. With few exceptions, people may not load copies of software installed at home on school machines as well (under the same license). Many school policies prohibit such installations because it is so difficult to track back licenses for software the district has not purchased. Vigorous application of a copyright compliance policy could subject employees to disciplinary procedures if they are found in violation of the copyright laws during such an audit.

Two school districts in Texas have done surprise software audits of one another. Armed with an audit program, officials from one district appear at a selected school of the other district, acting in the manner of federal marshals. They run the audit program on all computers. The program produces a printout of all the installed programs. The owner then had to produce authentication that each program was legitimate. An official of one of the districts recounted that one individual had many questionable programs on the computer's hard disk. When this employee had not accounted for programs on the computer a month later, an official letter of reprimand went into the person's file. This reciprocal checking helps keep both districts in compliance and out of court.

Checking is a good thing. The SIIA offers sizable monetary rewards (up to $1,000,000) for those who report software and content pirates, including corporate infringers (Anti-piracy, 2010). Some software producers attempt to enforce their own contract terms by selling software that can count the number of users in a network environment. For example, if the school has paid for a four-user license, the software will allow only that number of concurrent users and no more. Other makers disable or limit features of the software, such as being able to copy information to floppy disk, so that wholesale portions of the copyrighted database cannot be incorporated into someone else's work. These features or limitations should be spelled out in the license agreement and software documentation before the purchase is concluded so that both the producer and the purchaser understand the requirements and limits of the program and its data.

The Digital Millennium Copyright Act put some teeth into the law about circumventing technical protections (17 U.S.C. § 1201). In other words, if software has a password or copy protection scheme, it is now a violation to circumvent or bypass these protections. There are some complicated exceptions for libraries (17 U.S.C. § 1201(d)), but mostly, these exceptions are in place so that libraries can inspect items prior to purchasing them. In most instances, evaluation copies are available to help purchasers make sound purchase decisions, so this is less of a bonus than it might appear.

Negotiated online database licenses are just as binding as computer software licenses. The databases that are so attractive may not be legally shared with other schools or with students at home if the license states "no remote access." This contract supersedes the section 108 rights of libraries to provide information to anyone who requests it. In essence, by accepting the software license, the purchaser waives other rights under copyright, just as with regular computer software.

Copyright infringement versus plagiarism

A question arises concerning students who download or capture information from an online database, CD-ROM, or other electronic sources. As in most student situations, students may use all sorts of information for personal research. The fact that the student has used electronic means to put the information into his work rather than hand-typing is irrelevant. The problem here is not copyright infringement, but plagiarism. The student may be operating within fair use to use the copyright-protected materials, but failure to cite the sources is plagiarism. For someone attempting to prove plagiarism, having information in electronic format is actually a blessing. In pre-electronic days, the teacher had to scan printed works hoping to stumble upon the exact suspected text. Now the teacher need only do a simple text search of the source to find all instances of the wording in question.

A specific instance of plagiarism could be a copyright violation because in the absence of attribution, the student may not be covered by the fair use exemption. In dealing with ethical issues such as copyright law compliance and plagiarism, it is important for teachers and librarians to emphasize high expectations. Requirements for adherence to copyright law and rules against plagiarism should be fully detailed in student codes of conduct, with specific penalties for violations.

> *Question:* I want to use material that I have captured from the Internet and from a CD-ROM. As long as I cite the source, I can copy anything I like, right?
>
> *Answer:* Not necessarily. Just citing a source doesn't absolve you of the responsibility to get permission from the copyright owner if you don't qualify for fair use.

Software management tips

Maintain copyright and license records on all programs in the building. Keeping all the records in one place greatly facilitates response if there is any question about license status. If a site license or network copy was ordered, retain a copy of the purchase order as proof of the contract.

Make one archival copy of each program and store it off-site. Do not use or circulate the archival copy. One archival copy of software documentation is allowed as well. More than one requires permission.

Don't install non-network software on a network. Installing software on a network requires a network license.

Don't lend equipment that would facilitate copying software. Don't own programs whose sole (or primary) purpose is to "crack" software protection schemes.

Refuse to lend software to library patrons who indicate that they plan to make infringing copies. At minimum, inform them that the software is protected by copyright and that their use of the software is governed by the notice affixed to the package.

Place appropriate copyright warning stickers on all software circulated from the library. Register shareware.

Enforce multi-user limitations. Install software metering programs or use network operating system-security options to monitor licenses.

Monitor use of computer scanners and digitizers. Encourage use of public domain and royalty-free graphics.

Resources for understanding

Creative Commons encourages free distribution of software for open development. Its Web site has multiple options for licensing, and various repositories allow searches on specific Creative Commons license types. The Web address is http://www.creativecommons.org.

The Free Software Foundation supports the goal of free and open developed software. It has a searchable directory of free software. Its Web address is http://www.fsf.org/.

The Software and Information Industry Association offers an anti-piracy hotline at 1-800-388-7478. Find the SIIA online at http://siia.com. The Business Software Alliance also has an anti-piracy hotline at 1-888-NOPIRACY. Its Web address is http://www.bsa.org. Both organizations have resources for educators.

The University of Texas System has put up a handy Software and Database License Agreement Checklist that can assist you as you negotiate licenses for local and online database access as well as large-scale computer software installations. It is available here: http://www.utsystem.edu/OGC/IntellectualProperty/dbckfrm1.htm.

Works cited

Anti-piracy FAQ. (2010). Retrieved from http://www.siia.net/index.php?option=com_content&view=article&id=387:ap-faq&catid=8:anti-piracy-overview&Itemid=420.

Berman, D. (1993, May 13). Re: Questionable videotapes. Discussion on liability in the use of copyrighted videotapes. Message posted to CNI-COPYRIGHT electronic mailing list.

Blair, J. (1998, August 5). Pirated software could prove costly to L.A. district. *Education Week,* p. 3.

Creative Commons. (2009a). *About licenses.* Retrieved from http://creativecommons.org/about/licenses/.

Creative Commons. (2009b). *Identify a public domain work.* Retrieved from http://creativecommons.org/license/publicdomain-2.

Free Software Foundation, Inc. (2010). *Licenses.* Retrieved from http://www.gnu.org/licenses/licenses.html.

Goldstein, P. (2008). *Goldstein on copyright* (3d ed.). Austin: Wolters Kluwer Law & Business.

Marshall, P.G. (1993, May 21). Software piracy. *CQ researcher.*

Open Source Initiative. (n.d.). *Open Source licenses.* Retrieved from http://www.opensource.org/licenses.

Peters, M. (2009). *CC0 FAQ.* Retrieved from http://wiki.creativecommons.org/index.php?title=CC0_FAQ&oldid=21384.

ProCD, Inc. v. Zeidenberg, 86 F.3d 1447 (7th Cir. 1996).

Simpson, C. (2008). *Copyright for administrators.* Worthington, OH: Linworth.

Chapter 12

School Library Exemptions

J ust as schools have special exemptions for their nonprofit educational mission, libraries received special protections to enable them to carry out their missions as well. Although the rules were identified primarily for public libraries, these rules also apply to the various activities that go on within the school library.

School libraries have the best of all possible worlds when it comes to copyright exemptions because they get both the school and the library exemptions. The downside of this bonus is that libraries must keep track of twice as many sets of regulations. Section 108 provides an assortment of special exceptions for libraries, including copying for preservation, copying for interlibrary loan (ILL), and copying at the request of patrons for their personal use. Aside from the regulations discussed in this chapter, to qualify for the library exemptions, the library must be open to the public (or to researchers in a field). Most school libraries would meet this requirement based on the definition of "public" discussed earlier. A second requirement to qualify for the library exemptions is that all copies made must be made "without any purpose of direct or indirect commercial advantage." All copies made must contain a notice of copyright, and copying must be of single copies on "isolated and unrelated" occasions. A key phrase in the law states that "systematic reproduction or distribution of single or multiple copies" is always prohibited (17 U.S.C. § 108).

Put a dozen librarians in a room, and you will come up with two dozen plans to economize while providing exemplary library service. (All good librarians have a backup plan!) Providing outstanding service can be problematic if the library doesn't have all, or enough, of the items the patrons seek. Librarians have proposed many creative ideas to provide extra copies of materials, secure materials that libraries don't own, and get materials quickly to patrons who need information immediately. But as with all innovative solutions, new outcomes will be measured against traditional laws. Lawmakers are notoriously slow to adapt current laws to new technologies, and until they do so, one must use the old laws and attempt to extrapolate the legal requirements.

There are other exceptions for libraries. For example, if a library owns a copy of a book, and a page is damaged beyond use, it is within the library uses granted under section 108 to photocopy and tip in the missing page from another copy.[1] In fact, it is within the rights granted libraries to copy an entire book when the original is lost, damaged, or deteriorated beyond use if an unused replacement cannot be purchased at a reasonable price. The replacement exception applies only if the library owned the book originally; it may not be used to make copies of out-of-print books that the library simply wishes to acquire.

Preservation

The Digital Millennium Copyright Act added some positive permissions for libraries dealing with deteriorating, damaged, or obsolete materials. As noted in the previous section, if a work has been damaged or defaced, and an "unused replacement" cannot be purchased at a reasonable cost, the library may make the copies necessary to repair or replace the item (17 U.S.C. § 108(c)). Laura Gasaway, in a presentation to the Texas Library Association in April 2000, explained that if you own a set of encyclopedias, and someone steals or destroys a single volume, and if the publisher will not sell you a single replacement volume, you may assume that an unused replacement is not available at a reasonable price. In such an instance, she recommends making the copies necessary to repair or replace the volume.

When you are copying *unpublished* materials (diaries, family photographs, historical documents, etc.), the copying must (a) be for preservation, security, or deposit at a different library for research use (a good insurance against fire or other disaster); and (b) be of an original owned by the copying library (17 U.S.C. § 108(b)). If the copy is in digital format, the digital copy cannot be accessed from beyond the library walls. The library may make the digital copy available only on the local network (within the library, not the entire school) or on disc, but certainly not via the Internet. This rule was designed to help academic libraries and archives preserve and make available for researchers works that are too fragile to be handled. This rule will seldom come into play in school libraries.

The subsection on preservation (c) permits copies of damaged, deteriorating, lost, or stolen material if either that material cannot be replaced at a reasonable cost, or if the format in which the material is stored is obsolete. The law defines a format as obsolete "if the machine or device necessary to render perceptible a work stored in that format is no longer manufactured or is no longer reasonably available in the commercial marketplace" (17 U.S.C. § 108(c)). This section would permit a library to copy Beta-format videotapes into VHS or DVD format because the necessary equipment to play Beta-format video is no longer available on the general market. The same would hold true with filmstrips. Filmstrip projectors are no longer available for purchase in the general market. However, if the item you wish to convert is available on the market in a modern format (such as a filmstrip now available on video), you must purchase rather than convert. Phonograph records and cassette tapes are not as fortunate as Beta-formant videos because turntables and cassette players are still readily available. The same holds true with VHS format video. As long as VHS players are on the market, you may not make VHS transfers to DVD or streaming format.

When preservation copies are permitted, the copies can be in digital format *if* the copies are not made available to the public outside the library holding the original item (17 U.S.C. § 108(c)(2)). That provision can be a problem for a library wishing to circulate the preserved copy. Suppose you have a Beta-format video that you transferred to DVD (a digital format). The digital preservation copy cannot leave the premises of the library. Because the preservation exemptions are specific to the *library* and not the organization of which the library is a part, you would not be able to circulate the preserved DVD video. Students and teachers could come to the library to see it, however.

Interlibrary loan

Common sense tells us that by pooling resources, several libraries can share expensive or seldom-used materials. Interlibrary loan (ILL) has served that function for many years. As library budgets get tighter, librarians look for creative ways to make the budget dollars stretch a little further. One oft-suggested idea is to spread periodical or database subscriptions around, each cooperating library taking a portion of the lesser-used, but still important, titles. When a patron needs something from one of the titles subscribed to by one of the sharing partners, a simple interlibrary loan request will rush the information to the patron. With a fax machine or scanner, access to remote documents is almost instantaneous. Does this sound too good to be true? It is.

At this point in our plan, we run afoul of the copyright law. One of the principal tenets of the law is that copying should not affect the market for or value of the copyrighted work. Does securing a needed article or book from a remote site deprive the copyright holder of a sale? Would the patron or the library have bought the title just to have access to that particular article? Does rapid document delivery affect sales of periodical titles or database subscriptions? These are good questions and ones that the congressional committee considered when they discussed fair use in the areas of photocopying and resource sharing.

ILL copying

Items available for interlibrary loan would include books, periodicals, videos, and any other work that the library chooses to release from its premises. *Copying* for interlibrary loan, however, picks up an extensive list of restrictions. Thanks to the Digital Millennium Copyright Act, libraries may not copy for interlibrary loan a musical work; a picture, sculpture, or graphic (unless those items are included as illustrations in a textual item); or a movie or audiovisual work (17 U.S.C. § 108(i)). Libraries may copy text for interlibrary loan (subject to the CONTU guidelines, discussed later), as well as sound recordings. Libraries also may copy audiovisual works dealing with news (such as a *Dateline* program or a recording of a presidential inauguration, complete with news commentary). However, a library may not copy for ILL movies, musical sound recordings, art prints, or purchased PowerPoint presentations. Nevertheless, many items remain available for ILL copying.

The copying requirements for interlibrary loan are essentially the same as the library copying requirements listed previously. Because the 1976 law allowed libraries to participate in interlibrary loan arrangements as long as "aggregate quantities" of articles or items received did not substitute for a periodical subscription or other purchase, such as a database subscription (17 U.S.C. § 108(g)(2)), a group known as the National Commission on New Technological Uses of Copyrighted Works (aka CONTU) developed a set of guidelines that were adopted as fair and reasonable. These rules establish operational procedures that, when followed in interlibrary loan copying, assure compliance with the

> *Question:* Are there any copyright restrictions on lending an entire bound periodical volume to another school?
>
> *Answer:* If you are talking about *physically* sending the magazine to another school, there are no restrictions on that form of interlibrary loan, unless you have entered into some contract that prohibits sharing your copies. The ILL guidelines are for ILL *copying.*

Question: How many articles from each issue of a periodical can a library copy for interlibrary loan?

Answer: The providing library may make any copies requested by other organizations because it is the *requesting* library's responsibility to maintain copyright compliance according to the CONTU guidelines. However, if the providing library must use a database subscription to provide the copies, it should check its license with the database provider to determine whether providing copies to someone outside the organization subscribing to the database is a violation of the license agreement.

copyright law. The rules are not intended to apply to every situation, but Congress itself declared that they would "provide guidance in the most commonly encountered interlibrary photocopying situations" (Copyright Office, 1998, pp. 18–19).

Keep in mind that the CONTU guidelines govern interlibrary loan of periodicals and other works. *Intra*library loan is an entirely different animal. The difference? Primarily funding. The guidelines point to "common funding" as the key element in determining whether libraries are part of the same system (Ensign, 1992, p. 126). For example, all the schools in a school district would be considered part of a common system, and therefore, loans among them would be intralibrary loans. Loans between school districts would be interlibrary loans.

In dealing with intralibrary loan, sending a photocopy of an article is handled exactly the same as if the copy were being made in the patron's library by library personnel. Section 108 of the copyright law allows not-for-profit libraries to make single copies of material for patrons as long as there is no commercial advantage, the library is open to the public, and each reproduction includes a notice of copyright. *Caveat:* the law, however, has a very specific prohibition against "systematic" copying. One of the illustrations given in the guidelines as an example of systematic copying is this: "Several branches of a library system agree that one branch will subscribe to particular journals in lieu of each branch purchasing its own subscriptions, and the one subscribing branch will reproduce copies of articles from the publication for users of other branches" (Jensen, 1996, p. 67). This budget-stretching plan to share periodical subscriptions or reference books among campuses within or without a school district (or perhaps between the schools and the public library) is not in compliance with the copyright law in any case. If the articles are from a periodical database, the sharing may be a violation of the license agreement signed when the library began the subscription and could be grounds for terminating access. Check your license thoroughly for the implications of sharing digital copies or hard-copy printouts of articles from the database, and don't rely solely on the CONTU rules for distributing such copies.

The following rules outline the general rules for ILL copying:

- *Before accepting a request for an interlibrary copy, the* borrowing library *must post a "display warning of copyright" at the place the library accepts interlibrary loan orders (37 C.F.R. § 201.14(a)). Federal regulations specify the size and wording of this notice. Library supply houses sell copies. See Appendix E for exact requirements.*

- *The* lending library *may send only one copy of the requested material, and the copy must become the property of the requesting patron. This will have impact when using fax delivery. It is also significant for libraries that would like to retain the copy for their files or for local use.*

- *The* borrowing library *must abide by the "rule of five" (explanation of this rule follows).*

- *The* borrowing library *must keep records of CONTU-governed loan requests. The library must keep records for the current year and the three previous calendar years (e.g., on January 1, 2014, the records for 2010 may be discarded). A database, loose-leaf notebook, or card-based record-keeping system can track requests. See examples of forms later in this chapter.*

- *The* borrowing library *must verify copyright compliance on the ILL request. Most stock ILL forms have a section for copyright compliance, indicating CCL ("complies with copyright law," i.e., fair use) or CCG ("complies with CONTU guidelines," i.e., the rule of five).*

Figure 12.1. Sample CONTU card system

Periodical Title					
Year	Issue	Requested	Received	CCL	CCG

- *The* lending library *must mark on each copy that the "request was made in conformity with these guidelines." In general, that means the copy should be stamped with the standard notice: "This material may be protected by Copyright Law (Title 17 U.S. Code)" (see Appendix E).*

A simple 3×5 card system such as that pictured in Figure 12.1 would provide all the documentation needed for CONTU compliance. A computer database could also maintain the same type of records. Remember that the library maintains this type of record only on their own requests, not on those ILL orders they fill. Whatever record-keeping method you choose, you need to keep records of periodical requests for only four years—the current year plus the three previous years. Records of requests for materials in books should be kept for four years also, but you need consider only the current year in determining whether a particular request exceeds the rule of five.

Rule of five

The rule of five was designed to guide librarians in tracking appropriate levels of interlibrary loan copying. The rules seem complex at first, but once you grasp the five-year window, calculating the limits is very simple.

Periodicals

The CONTU guidelines pertain to periodical *titles* (as opposed to individual volumes or issues) published within five years from the date of the request. Copying older materials may be considered to be fair use on the part of the requesting library. The borrowing library may receive five photocopied articles per periodical title (not per issue) covered under the CONTU guidelines per calendar year. On the standard ILL form, these first five copies may be marked as CCG because they are permitted under the CONTU guidelines. To give a specific example, in a single year, a library that does not subscribe to *Library Media Connection* could, within these guidelines, request five single articles published within the past five years. Some exemptions apply to the numerical requirement:

A title "on order." *If you have entered an order for a periodical title, you may request unlimited copies from the title under CONTU. The rule of five does not apply.*

A title at the bindery. *If you own the title, and you have sent the issues to the bindery, you may request unlimited copies from those issues under CONTU.*

Missing issues in an owned volume. *If you already own a volume of a periodical and need to request an interlibrary photocopy to supplement a missing issue, you may make the request under CONTU. Those requests will not count in your five.*

Such exceptions need not be logged under CONTU, and CCG compliance may be claimed on the ILL form. Issues older than five years are not governed by CONTU, so CCL is the correct choice on the ILL form.

Other print materials

This category applies to materials in books, mostly. Only five copies may be requested from any single work (including collective works) per year, during the entire time a work falls under copyright protection. To illustrate this requirement, imagine that there is a book of poetry called *School Days.* Suppose that a school library has an index that lists all the poems in this book and many others. The library doesn't own *School Days,* but teachers use the index to find poems to use with their classes. The public library owns a copy of the *School Days* book, and it will supply the school library with photocopies of material from the volume. Four teachers so far this calendar year have requested copies of poems from this work. The school librarian may request one more copy of a poem from this work in this calendar year under the rule of five. After that request, the school must pay royalties on copies or purchase its own copy of the book. If the librarian places an order for the book, and the copy is not yet received, he may request other copies of poems from the book under fair use because the book has been purchased but not received. This requirement holds true even if the book is out of print. Out-of-print status is not the same as being out of copyright, and the CONTU limits will still apply. If the book were in the public domain because its term of copyright protection had expired, there would be no limits on copying material from the book.

Keeping ILL forms on file is the best method of keeping interlibrary loan records. Although one must keep the loan records for nonperiodical requests for only a calendar year, keeping a history of requests can be helpful for collection development purposes.

Examples and caveats

A library may not retain photocopies of articles ordered for patrons through interlibrary loan. Photocopies for patrons are legal only when made for specific, individual users. Including such copies in a ready reference file would not be within the guidelines for such copying. Similarly, a librarian may not request copies of articles for library purposes, no matter how relevant the article might be to the library's patrons. Such ordering would deprive the publisher of a sale of an issue or a reprint and hence does not fall within the fair use exemption (Dukelow, 1992).

For the following sample transactions, assume today's date to be June 2, 2011.

Patron requests an article from periodical XYZ, issue dated December 5, seven years ago. This is the first request for an article from this periodical this year. This request is considered fair use and need not be logged under CONTU because the periodical issue requested is more than five years old.

Patron requests an article from periodical ABC, issue dated December 5, three years ago. This is the third request for this periodical this year. This request would be filled under CONTU guidelines and should be logged as request number three on this periodical title.

Patron requests copies of six poems from a single collective work. No other items have been requested from this collection this year. Only five of the poems may be requested via ILL from this particular title. Perhaps one of the poems could be found in another collection, or the Copyright Clearance Center could be contacted for the cost to reproduce the item. Copies of the ILL request forms for the five permitted reproductions should be retained by the requesting library for one year to track requests per title.

Patron requests an article from the January 4, 2011, issue of journal PQR because the copy is missing from the library's shelves. This request may be filled under CONTU because the requesting library subscribes to the journal. The request does not fall under the rule of five, however, because the requesting library owns this title.

Patron requests an article from the September 15, 2007, issue of journal NOP. The library has already requested five articles from this journal from a single library this calendar year. Perhaps another library would be a source for five more copies? The requesting library is permitted five requests per calendar year from a single journal title. The library that supplies the requests is not considered in counting the five. All five requests may come from one library, or all five may come from different libraries. The total of five remains the same. This request would fall outside the rule of five, and royalties would have to be paid on the sixth request.

What to do when you can't meet CONTU requirements

If you have more requests for articles from a certain periodical title than you can legally request under the CONTU guidelines, what do you do? You have several options:

- *You can purchase a subscription to the periodical. Because the law and the guidelines aren't specific about how far back the subscription must go, purchasing a subscription to the current volume has been used as justification for CCG requests for back issues. This is a gray area you will have to wrestle with, assisted by legal counsel.*

- *You can borrow issues from other libraries. Sometimes you have demand only during a particular part of the school year. A public library might lend you its bound volume for a short time. Your patrons could then make their own copies without CONTU implications.*

- *Advise your patrons of other libraries in the area that either subscribe to the periodical or would make an ILL request.*

- *Request a copyright-cleared copy of the material from a document delivery service. These organizations pay royalties on each copy supplied. However, remember that a copy purchased from one of these sources is not cleared for multiple copies, except as under fair use.*

- *Write to the copyright holder for permission. (See section on permissions for sample forms.)*

- *Join the Copyright Clearance Center. This organization acts as a clearinghouse for copyright permissions, and although it doesn't supply the articles themselves, it does collect fees for copies and distributes them to copyright holders. (See chapter on permissions for more information.)*

- *Purchase back issues from the publisher, if available. Sometimes, brokers of back issues can also supply individual issues.* (Jackson, 1991, p. 87)

Interlibrary loan may not be the panacea to shrinking library budgets. The CONTU guidelines place strict limits on the number of articles a library may request from a periodical title during a calendar year. Articles more than five years old are exempt from the guidelines. A library may request only five articles from a covered title during a calendar year. The requesting library must also follow strict record-keeping requirements.

These guidelines help publishers know that they can sell adequate copies of their periodicals to stay profitable. They also assure libraries that their patrons will be able to access infrequently requested periodical titles. CONTU also governs photocopies from books in a similar manner (complies with CONTU guidelines).

Although ILL copying between library systems is always governed by CONTU, lending within a system is not. However, the law specifies that "systematic copying" is not acceptable in any circumstance, especially when such copying would take the place of the purchase of materials. The CONTU wording was intended to spell out exactly what "systematic copying" is, so the CONTU guidelines may be considered reasonable limits on ILL requests between schools in the same district.

In summary, although the CONTU guidelines initially may have been intended to deal with interlibrary loan, they do provide an ultra-conservative set of guidelines for intralibrary loans. Some clearly acceptable intralibrary loans would be denied under these rules, but the rules simplify compliance by having only one set of rules for interlibrary loan. And although some stretching of the CONTU limits might be overlooked, beware of anything that might smack of "systematic copying." For more information on copying for interlibrary loan, see this Web site: http://www.utsystem.edu/OGC/IntellectualProperty/l-108g.htm.

Facsimile

The most common technology used with ILL is telefacsimile, commonly known as the fax. Although it may simplify and speed up the ILL process, faxing creates an unforeseen copyright complication. Because most periodicals aren't loose-leaf, the sending library usually must photocopy the required pages before transmitting them via fax. This creates complications. The relevant section of the copyright law provides for interlibrary loan under the premise that one copy be made of the requested information and that the single copy become the property of the patron requesting it. In a fax situation, the sending library creates a photocopy and then faxes it to the requesting library. At that instant, two copies of the information now exist—the original photocopy and the fax copy.

Although in a literal sense there has been a technical violation of copyright, if the sending library destroys the photocopy when the transmission is complete and confirmed, the cumulative effect is the same as one copy. Libraries intending to use fax as a means for sending or receiving ILL transactions should be aware of the possible violation of copyright and have written policies and procedures to address the problem (Ensign, 1992, p. 126). One certain violation is the plan to keep the original photocopy in a ready-reference collection or vertical file. The first copy of the faxed ILL document *must* be destroyed to comply with the CONTU guidelines.

Scanning

Scanning technology is rapidly taking the place of fax delivery of interlibrary loan requests, at least in university environments. Programs such as ILLiad manage requests and deliveries and keep the necessary statistics. The same concerns apply to scanning that apply to faxing. Although the reproduction itself is not a problem, retaining a copy longer than it takes to verify receipt by the recipient could be problematic. The Library of Congress ended its Digital Interlibrary Loan project in 2008 (Library of Congress, 2008). Of course, if the library is willing to pay appropriate copyright royalty fees, scanning and direct delivery is possible with sufficient budget (see, e.g., University of Washington Libraries, 2009).

Cautions about ILL

At this point it is valuable to discuss an important limitation on interlibrary loan of physical copies of works. A regional educational consortium in New York maintained a union catalog (a combined database of the print and nonprint holdings of all the libraries making up the consortium) for its members. Members used the union catalog to locate needed materials not available on the local campus and make ILL requests for those materials. The material requested for interlibrary loan included videos. The producers of some of the videos sued the regional consortium, alleging that these loans violated the licenses attached to the videos. Unbeknownst to the schools that had purchased the videos, the video producers had changed their method of sale of their videos. The producers no longer *sold* their videos—they only licensed them.

For a library to qualify for the protections of the first sale doctrine, the library must *own* the copy of the work it is lending. In this case, the libraries only licensed the videos they were loaning through interlibrary loan. The producers claimed that the licenses restricted use of the videos to the campus that purchased the video. The case was eventually settled out of court, but research has shown that multiple video producers have switched to this new method of video distribution (Simpson, 2007). The video producers who participated in this action included Annenberg/CPB; Bullfrog Films; Chip Taylor Communications; Landmark Media; Lucerne Media/Classroom Media, Inc.; Tek Data Systems, Inc.; Advantage Source, Inc.; Film West Associated; International Television Services; Pyramid Media; and Women Make Movies (Lutzker, 2005). Use caution before loaning video through interlibrary loan, verify that you actually *own* the copies that you are lending, and be certain that you have not accepted a license limiting your distribution of the copies.

Photocopying

If a library makes copies of magazine articles or other parts of larger works for patrons to use in personal research, the library must attend to several points of operation. The copies must become the property of the user. Libraries may not make a copy for a user and then retain the copy once the user is finished. The library must not know that a copy will be used for other than personal research. The library must post the "display warning of copyright" at the point where the requests for copies are made (17 U.S.C. § 108(d)(2)). If the patron requests a copy of a *complete* work, the library may make the copies if (a) the library can determine that a copy for purchase is not available at a fair price; (b) the user will keep the complete copy to be made; (c) the library has no information that the copy will be used for anything beyond personal research; and (d) the library has an appropriate "display warning of copyright" where copying orders are placed (17 U.S.C. § 108(e)). In addition, the works copied cannot be pictures or graphics unless those are illustrations or diagrams in other works (17 U.S.C. § 108(i)).

When the library staff becomes involved in actually making copies of copyright-protected materials for patrons, additional requirements arise. Because notice of copyright can be an important factor in determining responsibility for willful infringement, the Digital Millennium Copyright Act included strict new regulations regarding removal of what the act calls "copyright management information." Such information can include the actual copyright notice affixed but also might include the names of the author and copyright holder, performers, writers, title, and so on. Removal of copyright information is especially important in cases of library photocopying. Under previous iterations of the law, a simple notice of possible copyright was sufficient to protect a library from complicity in copy infringements. Most libraries used a basic ALA-approved stamp stating, "NOTICE: This material may be protected by Copyright Law (Title 17 U.S. Code)." Under DMCA, this warning would no longer be sufficient. If a work's copyright notice can be found, the entire notice *must* be included (either photocopied or handwritten) with the copies (17 U.S.C. § 108(a)(3)). If you can find no copyright notice on the work, the former stamp would be sufficient.

Unattended copiers

Librarians want to share information with everyone. They have made photocopiers available for patrons so that they may make copies of whatever information they desire. Copyright law even says that a person may make a single copy of certain information for one's personal research and education. But what if the photocopier is located in the library, and the patron exceeds the limits of the law? Does that make the library responsible for any infringements committed there? Libraries have certain protections against being sued for copyright infringement when infringing copies are made on *unsupervised* copiers in the library (17 U.S.C. § 108(f)(1)). "Unsupervised" could be construed to mean those coin-operated or free copiers available for public use in the library. The library staff has no responsibility for the making of copies on these machines other than perhaps stocking the machine with paper and occasionally unjamming the works.

The key to the answer lies in the location of the copier. The law specifies that libraries are not held accountable for copyright infringements on "unsupervised" copiers. What is considered to be "supervised"? "Supervised" isn't defined, but there are some common-sense guidelines one can follow. If the library staff makes the copies, certainly that would mean they are supervising the making of copies, and the library would be liable for any infringements made there. A copier beside the circulation desk or reference desk could also be considered "supervised" in some instances. A self-service copier across the room from the staff, however, would be independent, even if the library staff maintains the paper and toner in the machine. Any attempt by library staff to police copies made on the machine would remove this important protection.

A prerequisite to the library exemption from liability for unsupervised copiers is an appropriate notice on the copier informing the patron that some materials may be protected by U.S. copyright law. This notice is most often placed on the lid of the copier, where the patron is sure to see it as the original is placed on the machine for copying. Many library supply houses have signs or adhesive notices just for the purpose of informing patrons of their responsibilities under the law. The statute does not specify wording in this instance, but the American Library Association suggests the following:

> *Notice: The copyright law of the United States (Title 17 U.S. Code) governs the making of photocopies or other reproductions of copyrighted material. The person using this equipment is liable for any infringement.*

This notice should be affixed to all equipment capable of making infringing copies: photocopiers, overhead projectors, opaque projectors, computers, CD/DVD duplicators, videocassette recorders, scanners, audio cassette recorders, fax machines, and any other equipment that can be used to copy video, sound, or print. Placing such a notice in a prominent position on copy-producing equipment can lessen (though never eliminate) the library's and the librarian's exposure to copyright suit if the library's equipment is used by patrons to make infringing copies. Keep in mind that this exemption in the law applies only to libraries. School-owned copiers in the office, workroom, or department do not have this exemption, so school staff must be especially vigilant about unauthorized copies on all machines.

Copying orders

If the library copier is unsupervised—that is, users make their own copies on a coin- or card- or even honor system–operated machine without intervention or supervision by the library staff—a library is not liable for copyright violations. If the school staff makes the copies, or the library staff is consulted in the making of copies, the copier is considered to be supervised, and the school will likely be held accountable for the illegal copies. The term "supervised" would also include any copies made by library staff for patrons or school staff, regardless of the location of the copier. Copies made by library staff must include the *entire* original statement of copyright as printed on the item being reproduced. This may be manually transcribed, or it may be a photocopy of the copyright statement on the item. If the item being copied has no statement of copyright, one cannot easily determine whether the item is or is not protected by copyright. In such an instance, the copies should be stamped with a notice indicating that the material copied may be covered by copyright and that appropriate use of copyrighted material is the responsibility of the patron. Although no specific wording is specified by law, many libraries use wording such as the following stamped on copies in a conspicuous color:

Notice: This material may be protected by copyright law (Title 17 U.S. Code).

It is especially important to be diligent about including the copyright statement on school- or library-made copies if one wishes to protect the building and the personnel against infringement actions. The removal or omission of the copyright statement violates the DMCA.

Copies for vertical file or item repair

Vertical files may be a foreign term to many librarians. Vertical files are also called pamphlet files or clipping files. In a vertical file the librarian stores small, easily lost materials that are valuable for student papers and reports. Typical items include brochures from foundations that support research on genetic diseases, government pamphlets, or short "how it works" sheets on specific technologies. Each topic has a file folder, and in that topical folder, the library staff collects articles and pamphlets related to that topic. The term "vertical" applies to the way file folders are stored.

Often a librarian will find an article in a magazine or newspaper that would be appropriate for inclusion in the vertical file. Perhaps the magazine title is bound, and the librarian would like to avoid mutilating the bound copy to include the article in the vertical file. Or the article is on the online encyclopedia, and having a few copies in the vertical file would mean each student doesn't have to print out a copy of the same article to free the computer for the next searcher. Such use is not within the scope of the library-permissible sections of the copyright law. However, if the library owns an item that is deteriorating or mutilated, lost, or stolen, and a replacement cannot be obtained "at a fair price," the librarian may make a replacement copy of the damaged work. The librarian may also make replacement pages for pages defaced or destroyed in materials the library already owns, but these copies are to replace the damaged sections of the magazines, not for the vertical file.

Question: Can a library include in its vertical file magazine articles or pictures cut out of magazines?

Answer: As long as the items are *cut* from the magazines, there is no problem. What is inappropriate is making copies and putting them in the vertical file, especially if this is a systematic process.

Reserves

Any library materials, or materials of faculty members, may be put on reserve at any time. Such use has no impact on copyright at all. Making *copies* for reserve, however, enters into an entirely different arena. Although there is no specific discussion of this procedure in the law, the American Library Association has written a model policy targeted to college and university libraries that takes into account various portions of the law that might impact copying for reserve. And although the policy is targeted to college and university libraries, the extension of these rational guidelines to school libraries is not unreasonable.

The document *Model Policy Concerning College and University Photocopying for Classroom, Research and Library Reserve Use* permits single copies of a book chapter, an entire periodical article, or a single poem. For multiple copies to fall within the policy, they must meet the following guidelines:

> *The amount used must be reasonable, considering the nature of the course, its subject matter and level, and the amount of material usually assigned for a single class term.*

> *The number of copies should be "less than six," unless enrollment in that course and others that will use the same material would dictate that five is insufficient to meet anticipated demand.*

> *Each copy must contain notice of copyright.*

> *The same item should not be used in subsequent semesters without permission.*

> *The effect of the copying should not diminish the market for the original. The policy strongly recommends that the library own a copy of the original.* (ALA, 1982, p. 6)

Electronic reserves

Some libraries are trying a new system of putting materials on reserve. Rather than making photocopies of materials, or putting the originals in an area behind the circulation desk, these libraries are scanning the materials and making them available to patrons via a computer network. Making copies electronically is similar to making photocopies as far as reserves are concerned, as long as you can meet the four tests of fair use. But electronic reserves touch more than just the copying provisions of the law. Each time a user pulls up the image on his screen, a display of the image takes place. If the work has video or audio accompaniment, there is a performance. Sending the image over the computer network is a transmission. There is no case law to guide us here.

The CONFU working group assigned to develop electronic reserves guidelines could not muster widespread support for the guidelines as drafted. The guidelines cover only copyrighted materials and do not include materials for which libraries have other license agreements in place, such as full-text periodical databases. The guidelines state that an article or book chapter may be scanned into an electronic retrieval system for the purpose of electronic reserve, subject to some conditions (Office of General Counsel, 2001).

- *The course instructor must request the material be placed on reserve.*

- *The school must own a lawful copy of the work.*

- *The amount of material assigned under reserve must be a relatively small part of the total assigned reading for the course.*

- *The reserve system must include on the opening screen a notice similar to that placed on copy machines, adding that further electronic distribution is prohibited.*

- *Each copy in the electronic reserve system must bear a notice of copyright in a prominent place, indicating "Copyright [date], [copyright owner]."*

- *Each copy must have appropriate attribution or citation of source.*

- *Only students and teachers enrolled in the course for which the materials are on reserve may have access to the reserve material. (The guidelines offer several suggestions to limit access.)*

- *Students may not be charged for access.*

- *After one term on reserve, permission is required for repeat use. Items may be retained in electronic form for up to three years while permission is sought. Students clearing incompletes may continue to have* brief *electronic access during this time. Because some schools allow long times to complete incomplete coursework, try to find other ways to make documents available to those few students. Because you must own the original to make an electronic reserve, consider putting the original on reserve for these few students.*

Works cited

American Library Association. (1982). *Model policy concerning college and university photocopying for classroom research and library reserve use.* Chicago: ALA.

American Library Association. (2006). *Fair use and electronic reserves.* Chicago: ALA. Retrieved from http://www.ala.org/ala/issuesadvocacy/copyright/fairuse/fairuseandelectronicreserves/index.cfm.

Copyright Office. (1998). *Circular R21: Reproduction of copyrighted works by educators and librarians.* Washington, DC: Library of Congress.

Dukelow, R. H. (1992). *The library copyright guide.* Washington, DC: Copyright Information Services, Association for Educational Communications & Technology.

Ensign, D. J. (1992, Winter). Fax—a special case: Implications of copyright law for facsimile document delivery. *The Bookmark, 50,* 125–128.

Gasaway, L. N. (2000, April 14). *Copyright law: Changes for libraries and librarians.* Concurrent session presented at the Texas Library Association Annual Conference, Houston, TX.

Jackson, M. E. (1991). Library to library: Copyright and ILL. *Wilson Library Bulletin, 66*(2), 84–87.

Jensen, M. B. (1996). *Does your project have a copyright problem? A decision-making guide for librarians.* Jefferson, NC: McFarland.

Library of Congress. (2008). *Digital interlibrary loan.* Retrieved from http://www.loc.gov/rr/loan/illscanhome.html.

Lutzker, A. (Fall, 2005). Inter-library lending and online school system union catalogs: A lesson in copyright liability. *AIME News 19*(3), 1–2.

Office of General Counsel, University of Texas System. (2001, November 12). *Fair use guidelines for electronic reserve systems.* Retrieved from http://www.utsystem.edu/OGC/IntellectualProperty/rsrvguid.htm.

Office of General Counsel, University of Texas System. (2003, January 30). *Copyright in the library: Reserve electronic copies.* Retrieved from http://www.utsystem.edu/OGC/IntellectualProperty/l-resele.htm.

Simpson, C. (2007). An ILL wind: Libraries and the interlibrary loan of audiovisuals. *SMU Science and Technology Law Review, 11*(2), 163–194.

University of Washington Libraries. (2009). *Interlibrary loan & document delivery services.* Retrieved from http://www.lib.washington.edu/ill/pilot.html.

Notes

1. "Tipping in" is a way to insert pages into a bound book. Put an extremely thin line of white glue on the interior edge of the page that will be inserted into the bound center of the book. Put two pieces of waxed paper into the space where the page should go, and then slip the glued page carefully between the waxed paper as far as possible into the binding. Press the book until dry, and then gently remove the waxed paper.

Chapter 13

Permissions

As previous chapters have shown, not all use of copyright-protected materials in schools may occur without permission or royalty payment. Once an assessment has shown that fair use does not apply, the least expensive option is to get permission for the proposed use from the copyright holder or his agent. Failing permission, the only legal option is to pay for a license or royalty through a broker or directly to the copyright owner.

Copyright versus contract

The central theme of this book is "if uncertain, ask permission." That sounds simple enough. The difficulty comes first in deciding when to ask permission and second in knowing how to ask permission.

As discussed in the chapter on fair use, for some applications, written permission is not necessary. Fair use guidelines are reasonably explicit regarding the instances for which educators need not seek permission. Some of the highly specific fair-use guidelines are, effectively, permission in advance as long as certain requirements are met. For print works, the long rules detailed in the chapter on printed materials outline instances when copies can be considered fair use. For audiovisuals, if the use meets all of the five fair use criteria, no permission is needed:

- *The performance occurs in a nonprofit educational institution.*

- *The performance is used for face-to-face teaching.*

- *The performance is presented by instructors or pupils.*

- *The performance takes place in a classroom or similar place for instruction (including the library).*

- *The performance is of a legally acquired (or legally copied) copy of the work.*

More detailed descriptions of the fair use guidelines are given in the chapters covering various types of materials.

Some materials are covered by copyright, but for a particular reason, the copyright holder has decided to withhold rights for the work. In such an instance, the copyright holder will license the work rather than sell it. This practice is quite common in the computer software area, where publishers wish licensees to have very specific, restricted rights. It is a growing practice in movies.

Copyright law allows a copyright holder to modify the blanket copyright provisions via contract. In essence, that means that you may sign away your fair use rights and not even know it if you send in a product registration card or license agreement or even fill out an order blank without reading the fine print. It is possible to modify the license or contract by simply marking out and initialing the portions of the license agreement or order form conditions that you wish to change before you send it in. The copyright owner may, or may not, agree to your modifications. If the owner refuses to accept your modifications, you may either reconsider your position or elect to purchase other materials that you may license or purchase with the rights you require.

Several years ago, some innovative software publishers and computer manufacturers tried to sneak this little-noticed feature past the buying public via so-called shrink-wrap licenses (*ProCD, Inc. v. Zeidenberg,* 1996). The main thrust of the shrink-wrap license was to bind the purchaser to a lengthy and technical set of license restrictions in a negative fashion. The purchaser was to read the provisions of the contract in super-fine print through the shrink-wrap on the package, for once the shrink-wrap was broken, the purchaser would be bound by the contract provisions. Some of the restrictions could be extreme; they included a prohibition against disposing of the software and, in the case of libraries, a prohibition against lending the software. Many licenses convey usage rights only; the software itself remained the property of the copyright holder.

Consumers were outraged. Several consumer protection agencies tackled the problem, even taking the shrink-wrap contract to several court challenges. See the chapter on computer software for more details. Because the Supreme Court has not ruled on shrink-wrap licenses as of this writing, what is legal depends on the Circuit Court of Appeals that covers your state. Check with experts in your own state to see what rights bind you in software shrink-wrap contracts.

Although shrink-wrap licenses and publishers' restrictive statements may seem discouraging, the good news is that the "home use only" stickers often found on videos are not binding on schools in any way, unless a statement agreeing to such use is part of the purchase contract. This unfortunate bit of wording serves only to explain that this particular copy of the video does not come with public performance rights. Public performance rights are not required for qualifying curricular performances, so home-use-only recordings may be used in instructional situations. Home-use-only videos *may not* be used for reward, entertainment, or time-filling situations without permission or royalty payment. Rental videos (including companies such as iTunes, RedBox, and Netflix) may be restricted to home use only if the membership agreement you signed when you got the video membership specified that there were to be no public performances of the movies rented from the video source. In such a case, a permission is required—not from the copyright holder, given that performance in a school is permissible under fair use, but from the video rental company! This is a contract problem, not a copyright issue. Few video outlets make customers sign rental agreements anymore, so this issue is mostly moot.

If your school subscribes to one of the video download or streaming services such as Blockbuster or Netflix, be sure to carefully check your contract and license to see what rights you have purchased. If your license does not specifically list public performances of the videos you will receive through the services, you do not have those rights and must rely on either the section 110(1) provisions or a licensing service such as Movie Licensing USA for your performance rights.

Schools, though nonprofit organizations, often partake in a bit of fund-raising. Video and audio are a favorite form of moneymaking. Booster clubs often sell recordings (audio or video) of athletic or band performances; drama clubs may offer a video of the class play; the journalism class may put together a video yearbook; the PTA may offer parents videos of their children in the spring field day. Any or all of these may have a bit of music to accompany the action. Unfortunately, there are some copyright liabilities that accompany the process as well. Carol Ruth Shepherd remarked on the Internet mailing list CNI-Copyright that in order to sell videos, organizations must get permission from the persons in the performance, get performance and distribution rights for any musical or dramatic works included, and get sync rights for any music used to accompany the video (Shepherd, 1996).

Permissions

After checking all the angles, you've discovered that your anticipated use of some material will not be considered fair use. You know you will need permission from the copyright holder to reproduce or use the desired material. How do you obtain this permission? What information will the copyright holder want from you? How much will it cost? How do you even find out who owns the copyright so that you can ask them? Good questions, all.

Check the back of the title page (or sometimes the introduction or acknowledgments section) for the name of the copyright holder. If the holder is a publisher, locate the address in *Books in Print, The Literary Marketplace,* or one of several directories of the publishing industry, or search for the publisher's Web site. Most publishers will not accept permission requests online—they want your request in writing, with a signature and possibly on school letterhead. If the copyright holder is an individual, the publisher may or may not be able to broker the permissions. Be especially alert to the fact that some materials appearing in copyrighted works are quoted with permission of the original copyright holder. Many books dealing with literary topics, such as literary criticism and literary collections and anthologies, will show lengthy copyright acknowledgements. Such items are usually acknowledged in a section on the same page as the copyright information or in a foreword or introduction. If any copies include this material, you will need separate permission from the copyright holders of that additional information.

Be aware that some copyright holders will attempt to abridge your rights under fair use. Their books and periodicals have a notice on the title page (or verso) that states, in some variation on these words, "This material may not be copied for any purpose." A wordier version of the statement might read, "You have infringed our copyright if a subscriber reproduces and distributes any part of the publication to anyone, within or outside of the subscriber's organization." Both of the preceding statements are not in conformance with the fair use guidelines. Even if such statements are published in the book or journal, you may still make copies if you meet the requirements of fair use *unless you have agreed otherwise.* Don't let such statements intimidate you from using such material, provided your use complies with all the fair use provisions.

Writing permission letters

In writing for permission, be sure to give a full citation of the material you wish to copy (author, title, edition); a description of the material to be copied (amount, page numbers, chapters, seconds); the number of copies to be made; how the material will be used; the method of distribution (hard copies, online behind password, online on open Web page, CD); charge (if any) for the materials; and the method of reproduction (photocopy, offset print, DVD-ROM).

Tips: There are several points to keep in mind when requesting permissions, no matter if the request is for print, music, video, or any other copyrighted material.

- *Make your request far enough in advance that the copyright owner has a reasonable chance to respond. A month in advance should be sufficient, but six weeks is better for print materials. For information from the Internet, a week's notice is usually sufficient for a first-time classroom use. For non-classroom use or repeat use, consider that the owner might be on vacation and cannot respond to your electronic request right away. Allow at least a month.*

- *Be specific in your request. Don't say, "Please grant all rights to. . . ." You'll be turned down. Try to be exact: "I would like to request archival rights to XYZ video," or "I would like to photocopy pages 4 and 5 of your book for a workshop I will be teaching." These are much more likely to receive a favorable response.*

- *Don't be surprised if there is a fee for the rights you request. Authors and producers make their living selling their products. By making copies, you are using their material without paying for a new copy. They may decide to charge a fee for the permission you request, and they are within their rights to do so. You are free to decline to pay for the permission, but in that case, you may not use the material. If you are turned down or decline to pay the requested royalty, don't decide after the fact that your use is fair. Some copyright owners anticipate that those who decide not to pay the requested royalty will go ahead and use the material without permission. They watch for such use and then jump on the users. It is much more difficult to make a cognizable claim of fair use if you first try to negotiate a license. The rationale is, if you believed the use was fair, why would you try to get a license? So the moral of the story is, do your fair use assessment first. If the use is fair, proceed under that assumption. If your use is not fair, get a license or permission, or use something else.*

- *Tracking down the copyright owner to ask permission may be the major hurdle. For works created prior to 1978, most copyrighted materials have some indication of copyright ownership, though sometimes that person or company may not be easily found. For works created after January 1, 1978, all works should be considered copyrighted unless proved otherwise. Finding out who owns these copyrights may be a frustrating procedure, especially if the initial publisher has gone out of business or has merged with a company that has again merged. Try the search options at the U.S. Copyright Office, or ask your public librarian to help you track down who owns the resources of a defunct company.*

Fortunately, the Library of Congress Copyright Office maintains records of registered copyrights. Those seeking copyright information can go to the Library and perform their own searches through the copyright records or pay the Library an hourly fee to perform searches for them. Additionally, copyright records are available through the Library of Congress online information system at http://www.copyright.gov/records/. Just remember that a work need not be registered to be copyrighted. The fact that you don't find a registration in the system does not mean the work is unprotected. It may mean you should look for a work whose copyright owner is more accessible.

When writing a letter requesting permission to reproduce or use copyrighted information, keep in mind that you may be addressing this letter to the permissions department of a large publishing house. This staff may have to deal with hundreds of titles. To speed your permission approval, help the staff as much as possible by being specific in your request. Include these items in your permission letter:

- *Author/editor/composer/performer, title, and edition of the material.*

- *Exact description of the material to be used or copied, including amount, page numbers, scenes or footage, chapters, and any other locator information. In the case of print or Web work, include a photocopy/screenshot of the material under consideration.*

- *The number of copies to be made.*

- *Purpose of the copies.*

- *How the material will be distributed or used (e.g., in class, closed circuit, modified for a mural, placed in a newsletter, used in online course behind security).*

- *Cost of the material, if any.*

- *How material will be reproduced, if copied (photocopy, ditto, photographic enlargement, archival copy, DVD-ROM, online, or other).*

In a work that includes material whose copyright is owned by many people, you may find multiple copyright dates, and you may find a long list of acknowledgments. Any material covered in the acknowledgments section of the copyright information is covered by separate copyrights. The copyright holder of the primary work cannot grant permission to reproduce material under another's copyright. You will need to apply directly to those rights holders.

Beware of the inclination to send the request for permission to the person or firm from which you purchased the material. This tendency is especially prevalent in the case of video permissions. The copyright holder may have designated its distributors as agents who can grant permissions, but this is not generally the case. There are several agencies that do nothing but broker permissions. The Motion Picture Licensing Corporation and Movie Licensing USA handle many of the feature (entertainment-type) movie permissions. ASCAP, BMI, and the Harry Fox Agency broker an assortment of music licenses. The Copyright Clearance Center (CCC) offers several types of print permission services. CCC was established after Congress suggested the industry create a mechanism to facilitate compliance with print reproduction rights, as defined by the Copyright Law of 1976. They are the "reproduction rights organization" (RRO) for the United States. Other countries have similar organizations.

Rights holders register their works with CCC and set the royalty fees that CCC collects on their behalf. Users report and pay for their copying either through a license or each time they use a registered work. CCC offers a number of services, several of which are useful for schools:

- *The Transactional Reporting Service (TRS) provides users with immediate authorization to make photocopies from over 1.75 million publications. By using CCC, educators do not have to make individual fee payments to publishers and instead pay a combined fee to CCC, which distributes it to copyright owners. This service would be useful for duplication of non-academic materials such as parenting resources, counseling information, and community education materials.*

- *The Academic Permissions Service (APS) enables a school to clear documents for academic course packs and classroom handouts. The APS provides customers with a catalog of all CCC-registered titles and royalty fees. In addition, CCC will seek permission for many titles not covered by preauthorized agreements. Permissions can be received in as little as 48 hours. This service will be useful for reproduction of documents for which fair use is not an option, such as repeated copying beyond the first term.*

- *The Electronic Course Content Service (ECCS) is similar to APS but applies to materials used in electronic format, such as online courses, electronic reserves, and electronic handouts.*

- *The Digital Permissions Service (DCS) is also similar to APS but allows users to post content via e-mail, Internet, intranet, or extranet.*

As well as offering these services, CCC has specialized services for several kinds of reproduction and distribution rights and a flat-fee annual license for volume users. For more information, contact the Copyright Clearance Center at http://www.copyright.com.

Other providers offer delivery of specialized articles. Docdel.net maintains a list of specialized document providers at http://www.docdel.net/.

If you decide to request permission directly from the copyright owner or publisher, Figures 13.1 and 13.2 will provide a simple, fill-in-the-blanks option. They are not applicable to all situations, but they will cover most requests for print permissions.

On receipt of a permissions request such as this, publishers have three options. They can approve your request as stated. In that instance, you will likely receive your letter back, stamped "approved." You might receive a letter in return, stating the terms under which the copyright holder will grant your permission. You will then be asked to sign an attached agreement and perhaps include payment of a stated fee. The last option of the rights holder is to reject your request. Remember, the item you wish to use is that individual's property. The rights holder need not offer any reason for refusal.

Figure 13.1. Request for permission

Date

Permission Department

Dear Reader:

This letter is a request for permission to duplicate/use for _____

_____ , the following:

Title: _____

Copyright: _____

Author(s): _____

Material to be duplicated: _____

_____

_____

_____

Number of copies: _____

Manner of distribution: _____

Type of reproduction: _____

Purpose of use/reproduction: _____

A self-addressed, stamped envelope is enclosed for your convenience. Please respond and notify me of fees, if any, for this permission.

Sincerely,

Name _____

School name _____

School address _____

City _____ State _____ Zip _____

Permission granted _____

Date _____

Conditions, if any _____

_____

Figure 13.2. Sample request for permission

Date **9 September 1993**

Permission Department

Company name

Street Address

City, St, ZIP

Dear Reader:

This letter is a request for permission to duplicate/use for
_____**next semester**_____ *, the following:*

Title: **Practical copyright for schools**

Copyright: **Company name, 1978, 1980, 1991**

Author(s): **J. Jones**

Material to be duplicated: **Pages 35, 36, and 37 in chapter one. See enclosed photocopies.**

Number of copies: **143 (1 per student in 5 classes)**

Manner of distribution: **There will be no charge for the materials**

Type of reproduction: **photocopy**

Purpose of use/reproduction: **Library orientation for freshman**

A self-addressed, stamped envelope is enclosed for your convenience. Please respond and notify me of fees, if any, for this permission.

Sincerely,

Name _____

School name _____

School address _____

City _____ *State* _____ *Zip* _____

Permission granted _____

Date _____

Conditions, if any _____

_____

If you receive permission to use certain material in exchange for some form of payment, and you later elect *not* to use the material, be sure to notify the agency from which you received the permission. In some instances, you will be expected to pay the fee unless you notify the rights holder that the use will not take place. These rights brokers assume the use unless they are notified.

You may never hear anything at all from your request. *No response does not equal "no objection."* There could have been any number of things that prevented the owner from responding, including never receiving your request. Remember that copyright transfers, permissions, and so on *must be in writing.* You may hear the suggestion to word your permission request like this: "If I don't hear from you by such-and-such date, I will assume I have permission to . . ." Such wording *is not* recommended. The copyright owner is not required to respond to requests, and the lack of response should not be construed as permission. Also remember that getting permission to use trademarks (such as some book characters, like Clifford the Big Red Dog) requires a similar process to getting permission to use copyrights. Because this book is limited to copyright issues, before embarking on using a trademark, check a reference work that includes ample information about licensing a trademark, such as Richard Stim's *Getting Permission: How to License & Clear Copyrighted Materials Online & Off* (Nolo, 2010).

Question: I wrote a publisher for permission to post an article on our school Web page, but it has been four weeks, and we have not heard anything. Because we have not heard any objection, can we go ahead and post the article?

Answer: Remember that a copyright owner does not have to answer your request for permission. Do you even know that the correct copyright owner received your request? When you have an educational purpose that is limited and arguably fair, you might try posting the piece briefly, while understanding that if your work is discovered and the copyright owner objects, the DMCA takedown provisions will take care of any inappropriate use. If your use is simply for general interest, you might look for a different item to substitute. Is there a way to post a link to the piece on another site rather than post it yourself? Links to online materials are generally without copyright implications if you do not obscure the source of the material.

Student and parent permissions

Publishers aren't the only ones who hold copyrights. Your students own the copyrights on their own works. Before you publish original student work, or reproduce it for a workshop or competition, or display it in a gallery, mall, Web site, or other public place, you will need permission from the student or his parents. Appendix G provides an example of the type of permission a school or teacher would require to make use of student work. Displaying work in the classroom would likely not require such permission because that use involves students and teachers in the class. Public use beyond the local classroom would require specific permission, including posting on an open Web site.

Keep in mind that if a student is a minor, he cannot grant permission himself. Parental approval is required. Make the request for permission specific, in the manner of a request to a publisher. A parent will want to know how the child will be identified with the work, to whom the work will be displayed, and for how long. Don't request or expect blanket permission to be granted for all classroom work. Although such a request is easy, it would probably be entirely too vague to be enforceable. In addition, releasing any student work that is identifiable with a specific student could be a violation of the Family Educational Rights and Privacy Act (FERPA) unless you have specific permission from the child's parent to release the work. Many districts have policies that restrict what information about students the school can post on the Web or in the newspaper. For example, the district may post only first names on student work or on student photos. Limiting acknowledgement in this way does not avoid the copyright implications of using student work. If you plan to retain student work to use as exemplars, make sure you have permission to retain the work and display it, even if you do not use the student's name when you use the work. Remember, attribution and FERPA are separate issues from copyright.

Works cited

ProCD, Inc. v. Zeidenberg, 86 F.3d 1447 (7th Cir. 1996).

Shepherd, C.R. (1996, May 24). Re: Sales of videotapes. [CNI-COPYRIGHT electronic mailing list comment]. Message posted to http://www3.wcl.american.edu/cni/9605/9323.html.

Chapter 14

Managing Copyright in Schools

Knowing the rules that govern copyright is only the tip of the copyright management iceberg when one considers the difficulty of explaining to complacent faculty and administrators that they may be at risk if they continue infringing practices. The person who brings the news that long-held beliefs in free use of all materials for educational purposes are not legally compliant may be met with anger, disbelief, or outright hostility.

Issues of managing copyright

The library media specialist is the most likely person in an individual school building to have had some training in copyright. Because the librarian is aware of the risks, and because the librarian sees all aspects of school practice, this professional is the one most apt to broach the subject of infringement. The librarian is also at some level of risk in infringement because much of the infringement-prone equipment runs through the library: computer networks, media distribution systems, overhead and opaque projectors, and more tie back to the library in many cases. If the librarian might have known that this equipment was being used to violate copyright, the librarian could be named in a copyright infringement action. In a "sue 'em all" scenario, this is a common practice.

Technology folks may also fall into this copyright-action-looking-for-a-place-to-happen scenario. They run the network that enables students to share music, download copyrighted software, or post the works of others online. But information technology staff and even educational technologists may not have the same sort of training that librarians seem to get as part of their certification programs. That's not to say a school should not rely on *all* its staff to lend a watchful eye over copyright practice in the building, but you certainly want to utilize the person with the most expertise.

Some librarians and technologists take it on themselves to be the "copyright police," perhaps thinking that they are protecting themselves from danger or protecting their schools from legal action. Although this is a noble intent, a librarian or technologist acting alone in this capacity will probably alienate the faculty with overzealous enforcement activities. Because these folks must maintain collegial relationships with virtually all the faculty and staff in order to support a school-wide information program, the librarian or technologist would be better suited as a consultant in an overall copyright management program. As the instructional and administrative leader in a building, the principal is best suited to head up the copyright enforcement efforts.

The person who is most at risk in a single school situation is the administrative leader—the principal. In virtually any copyright action against a single building, the principal is most likely to be named as a party to the case. As the instructional leader, the principal is responsible for all activities that occur under her purview, so getting this person on board a copyright management program is essential for both the building and the principal.

Managing copyright in a building really begins at the district level. When districts are cited for copyright infractions, one of the first things they are required to do in reparation is write and adopt a district copyright policy. A district policy establishes an administrative expectation of copyright compliance on the part of employees and students. Interestingly, employees seem to have more trepidation about violating district policy than they do about violating federal law. A clear, board-approved policy, with supporting staff development, can go a long way toward achieving maximum copyright compliance in a district. Chapter 16 and Appendix F provide ample examples and rationale for a strong copyright policy statement. For a building-level person to truly gain cooperation for a copyright compliance effort, a district-level policy is the best start. Understand the difference between policy and guidelines. You will need both. Policy is adopted by the school board; guidelines are established (and enforced) by the administration. Neither is helpful unless they tie together.

Beyond a policy and guidelines, there are other issues involved in managing copyright. Both things and people require some degree of modification if a copyright compliance effort is to be successful. By working to maximize both sections of the management dilemma, the administrator, librarian, technology specialist, or other copyright officer can reduce (though likely never eliminate) copyright infringements and still maintain collegial relationships.

Managing things

Managing things is a good place to begin because it is easy, and things don't complain. Having all your inanimate objects properly prepared for copyright compliance will also ease into compliance the people who must deal with the things. For those people who are new to an understanding of their obligations under copyright law, the overt and repeated notices will help remind them that each item has a copyright consideration. Although the people may not like to see the notices, they are less objectionable than a nagging voice or wagging finger; they are constant; they are visible; they don't play favorites; and they remove all doubts. In short, preparing all the things prepares you to prepare the people. Each type of thing has its own special management requirements.

> Print: *Books generally have copyright information printed on the back of the title page. Magazines will usually list copyright information on the masthead page. Making copyright control notations in the library catalog record (MARC tag 540) and/or on the protective cover for each title will facilitate inquiries. Plays are controlled under the print guidelines, but the most common abuse of the copyright of plays is performance of all or part of the play to a public audience. Keep with the scripts a record of any performance rights purchased (either in the library or in the department in which the play resides). Maintain these records as long as the scripts are held in the district. Poetry is also controlled by the print guidelines. Watch the back of the title page for copyright control information. Many collections combine copyright-protected materials from many sources. Know who is the copyright owner of the materials you use. Images are also protected under the print and/or multimedia guidelines. Individual images usually have some notice of copyright attached to the print, or listed in the credits section if published in book form. Public display of images on Web pages is a problem of which to be aware.*

Video/film: *Video requires both incoming and outgoing tracking. Know what performance rights were purchased with the recording. Public performance rights are required for non-curricular showings. Stickers on the recordings themselves make recordings with public performance rights easy to identify when staff need a video right away for rainy-day recess or when a teacher must attend a conference or leave school unexpectedly. (Purchase copyright compliance stickers from library or office supply houses or from Affordable Alternatives at http://www.alfordablealter nativesinc.com). Off-air video recordings made in-house need a prominent notice stating the expiration date of off-air rights (which may vary anywhere from the standard 10/45-day period to life-of-recording rights granted by certain producers to educational users). Any off-air recordings brought in by students or teachers should have a certification of eligibility signed before use. Prepare this form in advance and have it handy.*

Audio, including music: *Audio requirements are similar to video. Using music as background for multimedia productions will likely be the largest demand. Providing a collection of royalty-free music clips and links to royalty-free clip sites on the Internet is a way to ease the transition to compliance. Playing audio in public performances such as graduations, dances, school news broadcasts, and so on may also be problematic. Check on a municipal license from ASCAP to cover most music in non-instructional situations such as background music, passing period music, and music as a prelude to sporting events and student programs.*

Computer software: *Software checked out of libraries requires specific copyright notice. Stickers to notify borrowers of their copyright obligations are available from the suppliers listed previously. If the library staff knows that a patron plans to violate copyright, they should remind the patron of the copyright responsibilities. If the patron still indicates plans to violate copyright, refuse the loan. Home software installed on school computers should "live" at school. The box, documentation, license, and so on should be at the computer where the software is installed. The home is unlikely to be audited; the school is much more at risk. Retain license documents and purchase orders of all school-owned software, including operating systems. Retain the base license when you upgrade software because often the upgrade license doesn't qualify as a base license. This is especially true for upgraded operating systems. If you owned Windows 95 computers that were upgraded to Windows XP or Windows 7, you must have both a license for Windows 95 and a license for the XP/Windows 7 upgrade. Cases have been reported in the press of schools that were audited for software copyright infringement and challenged because they couldn't produce either the base license or old purchase orders for operating systems.*

Computer hardware: *Many common pieces of AV hardware in a school are capable of being used to violate copyright. Just as unattended copy machines must have copyright notices attached to protect the host library, placing prominent notices on other machines with infringement potential is a good plan. Consider notices for computers, scanners, interactive white boards, VCR/DVRs, document cameras, CD/DVD burners, cassette recorders, and digital audio recorders.*

Internet—*Because there are no specific guidelines for use of Internet works, interpret fair use item by item using the existing guidelines. For example, blogs are like essays. If you want to distribute an essay, what fair use factors or guidelines would you need to meet? Apply those rules to your proposed use of the blog entry. Include copyright compliance in acceptable use policies, and make information about copyright part of all Internet training. Internet is a danger spot in copyright compliance because so much material is mounted on the Web in violation of copyright. Just because something is on the Web doesn't mean it is free for use or is mounted with permission.*

Managing people

Dealing with the human factor will be the largest problem in achieving copyright compliance. Most teachers will not like a change in copyright enforcement. Some of them have been operating under the "if it's for educational use, it's okay" assumption for many years. The person who tells them that their common, convenient practice is a copyright violation is apt to be met with hostility. Help them accept the change by having materials on hand to provide simple record keeping. Offer public domain or royalty-free materials to fill in for infringing uses of protected materials. A few materials with public performance rights are always useful for those stressful times like when a teacher must leave unexpectedly, and an aide must fill in until a substitute can arrive. Public domain materials or materials with performance rights are also useful for time fillers (waiting for the bus, rainy-day recess, etc.) and reward situations (perfect attendance, achievement of academic goals, etc.). The cost of public performance rights pales in comparison to the costs of a lawsuit. Many materials come with public performance rights already. Ask vendors, or see Appendix M for a list of suppliers that offer public performance rights with their wares. Here are some tips on dealing with the human factor in copyright compliance:

Students—Students, in their short excerpts in papers and incorporation of minor images in artwork or collages, haven't been significant copyright risks for schools. Multimedia authoring software and the ability for students to publish widely on the Internet have made student use of copyright-protected materials a new area of concern.

The multimedia guidelines in the United States require that *all* multimedia presentations using copyrighted materials adhere to a set of recommendations, including opening screens that notify of copyrighted content and credit pages listing complete copyright ownership information for each item used under fair use. When students learn this procedure from an early age, documentation can simply become part of the creative process. Because wording of notices isn't specified in the guidelines, these notices can be put in terms that even second graders can understand.

Mounting student work on the Web is another concern, if the Web site belongs to the school. Double-check to make sure the student really did the work. Get permission from the child's parents to post that work online—student work is protected by copyright too. Encourage links; links seldom infringe. Remember that posting work in the classroom is fairly private. Posting work on a public Internet page is very public and difficult to restrict to educational use only.

Teachers: For many years teachers have been able to use, without challenge, whatever materials they have felt necessary or convenient. Disabusing the faculty of these notions is a monumental task. As the instructional leader of a building, the building administrator needs to take a leadership role in guiding the faculty to a new understanding of their obligations regarding copyright. This guidance can be as simple as a directive: "We will abide by all laws that affect our work." A better approach is to encourage faculty to move toward copyright compliance, with administrators taking extra pains to ensure that they model the behaviors they expect from the faculty. Don't photocopy articles from professional journals for each teacher unless the journal gives subscribers that privilege. Pay for a public performance license so that teachers can show entertainment films a few times a year. Demonstrate respect for the work of others by putting copyright notices on the things you do copy.

One technique that has worked well for many schools on the road to copyright compliance is to clear all video with the principal. This process, though painful to some, is likely to bring copyright to the forefront of discussion. One elementary school, after a vivid copyright workshop, chose to enforce appropriate use of video as their first step toward copyright compliance. All video shown in classrooms had to be preapproved by the principal to verify legitimate tie-in to the curriculum of the grade level and subject. At the end of the first school year of compliance, the librarian reported that video usage had declined by 75 percent! Incidentally, test scores also rose in the building that year, though there had been no changes in curriculum or methodology. Although no attempt was made to tie the rise in test scores to the reduction of noncompliant video, consider that if one tallied up all the entertainment and reward video shown in school and applied that time to curricular instruction, how much content might be covered?

Staff—Most staff involvement with copyrighted material will be in photocopying. With the support of the administration, training the clerical staff on copyright of print material will likely be sufficient to raise awareness of what can and should be copied. Encourage record keeping, especially for multiple copies for classroom use.

Administrators—Getting the attention of the administrator is key to copyright compliance in a school building. Bringing to his attention materials on copyright settlements in neighboring school districts, and those publicized by copyright compliance groups such as AIME and SIIA, can go a long way to opening the eyes of a reluctant administrator. Knowing that the building-level administrator is likely to be named in any copyright infringement action can also get an administrator's attention. As the instructional leader in the school, the building-level administrator is expected to be aware of all educational uses of materials within his purview. Some of the following suggestions, plus those in chapter 15, will help focus the administrator on the severity of the problem in a given building. Probably the most effective way to gain the attention of an administrator is to point out the district's copyright policy. Administrators understand board policy. They use board policy to terminate teachers who have violated board policy. Administrators know that failure to follow board policy is grounds for termination. If the district has a copyright policy, and the administrator ignores it, allows others to ignore it, or violates it herself, the administrator knows the consequences.

Important recommendations in copyright management

Here are some suggestions for getting started in a school that is less than enthusiastic about copyright compliance and that seems bent on shooting the messenger:

Suggest to the principal that you track requests in one area for a grading period. A good place to start is with video use. Prepare a report to the administration to show the extent of the problem in this area. Remind them that there are many other areas with similar or potentially worse reports. Another option for tracking is to obtain a copy of the free trial program Express Meter from Express Metrix and conduct software audits for 30 days. Seeing the results in black and white can sometimes generate significant response.

Prepare a copyright notification slip that will inform teachers and others that a particular use of a certain material is likely a copyright infringement. Make the wording helpful and informative, not accusatory. Give copies to the building administrator.

Encourage, request, and insist on a copyright policy for your building and district. Board-approved policy gives you a firm footing when trying to raise the standard of copyright compliance.

Educate, educate, educate. Consult with teachers as they plan units, help students document use of others' materials in their work, and help administrators consider copyright implications in non-curricular applications. Remember (and remind others) that plagiarism and copyright violation are totally separate and generally unrelated issues.

Chapter 15

Copyright and Administrators

Whether in charge of a building or a district, the school administrator may unexpectedly become embroiled in a legal tangle over the copy machine or the videocassette recorder. Although student performance should be the focus, the unwary administrator's attention may have to be diverted to deciphering abstruse details of copyright law. Even worse, administrators who are unprepared may find themselves and their organizations the subject of expensive litigation, costly even if the school is exonerated.

We are in an era characterized by lawsuit. One lawyer, when asked who should be named in a particularly confusing case, is said to have remarked, "Sue 'em all!" Unfortunately, this is often the mindset in copyright litigation. An administrator who is unaware of, or simply chooses to ignore, copyright violations may suddenly find a cease and desist letter on his or her desk. These letters from attorneys are written in a demanding fashion; violations are spelled out, penalties are enumerated, and few options are proposed.

Without the backing of a school board policy or building procedures supporting copyright, an administrator is likely to have little maneuvering room when the ominous letter arrives. Most school district attorneys are better prepared to deal with civil rights charges than those involving intellectual property. In fact, most details of the day-to-day operation of a building or district are much more pressing than considering the woes of authors and copyright owners. But the fact remains that an administrator who knowingly or unknowingly allows copyright infringement to occur is likely to be named among the defendants in any legal action. And although most educators have some form of immunity to most of the charges that may be leveled against them, immunity to copyright infringement unfortunately applies only to state agencies, if at all.

And the district may have to pay for the carelessness of an administrator. Penalties can be stiff. Fines begin at $750 per infringement and rise to $30,000 (17 U.S.C. § 504(c)(1)). For "innocent infringers" (those who infringe but had no reason to think they were infringing), fines are not less than $200 (17 U.S.C. § 504(c)(2)). If the infringement is considered willful, penalties can be imposed up to $150,000 per violation per day (*id.*). In the case of computer software infringements, penalties can be as high as $250,000, and the offense may be considered a felony (17 U.S.C. § 506)! The administrator need not actually participate in the infringement to be considered responsible, at least in part, for the violation.

The truth is that most copyright suits are settled out of court. Only a few well-publicized cases have made the trek through the courts to establish the precedents on which we base current practice. But even when an infringement action is settled out of court, much time is spent, considerable stress is borne, and much money is encumbered to resolve the conflict. Copyright watchdog groups use these settled claims as spoils of war to advertise their victories over infringers.

Once the cease and desist letter arrives on the administrator's desk, the die is cast. The best plan is to try to minimize losses because, like it or not, the lawyers usually have the goods; the infringements have most likely occurred, or there is enough of a smoking gun to present a good case. Your district's attorneys will do their best to make a case for fair use, but because the case will not likely see a courtroom, and pretrial matters can be very expensive in time and attorneys' fees, your district's insurance carrier is likely to insist you settle the case rather than fight it (unless you want to spend the district's money for the defense, which the board may find to be an unjustified use of school district funds). And the board generally does not look favorably on an administrator who costs the district that much money in these days of scarce resources.

So how can an administrator minimize exposure to copyright litigation? As with most endeavors, plan, plan, plan. The first and most important step is to have a comprehensive copyright policy. If the district has no policy in place, the building chief should establish a building policy. Such a policy should demand adherence to copyright law and establish a system of checks to ensure the law is followed. It also helps if the administration supports the efforts of the librarian or technologist in copyright compliance. Tracking and interpreting the many layers of copyright is no mean feat.

Faculties accustomed to free rein in plucking the fruits of authors' and artists' labors will howl that they are being hamstrung. They will moan that they can't conduct their classes without unrestricted access to the many resources they used in the past. They will most likely blame the messenger for the disturbing news.

Your building librarian may be the only person on staff who had some level of copyright training while in a preparation program. Virtually all librarians are schooled in copyright law during their training programs. Some instructional technology staff may also have had some copyright training, either during their schooling or in professional development courses afterward. Nevertheless, the librarian or technologist should not be thrust alone into the role of "copyright police." If building and district policy is to abide by the law, the librarian or technologist should not be judge and jury in the procedure.

But your copyright team must stand fast, and the administration must provide moral and procedural support. Apologies aren't necessary. As educators, we want to model responsible citizenship to our students. Among the behaviors we endorse is adherence to the laws of the city, state, and country. Copyright is federal law. We would certainly advocate paying income taxes, no matter how much we would wish they were no more. Well, copyright laws may be just as confusing, and we may wish that they allowed as many loopholes as the IRS, but we should still accept them as legal and binding until some court with authority tells us otherwise, or Congress sees fit to change them.

Once a policy is in place to endorse adherence to copyright, someone will need to be available to explain the implications to teachers who may have long ignored the requirements of the law, either because of unfamiliarity with the regulations or out of intentional oversight. The librarian or technologist must have unqualified and open support in educating students and staff on copyright issues and monitoring copyright compliance. After all, the object is to keep the entire school community out of trouble! The librarian or technologist must not be allowed to become the "bad guy" or the "fall guy" in matters of copyright.

Unequivocal policies supported vigorously by administrators and the board are essential. It is important that the administrator take a firm stance with staff regarding copyright; convey expectations to staff in no uncertain terms. Plan educational and informative sessions to inform the staff annually of their obligations under federal law and district (or building) policy.

Administrators must be ready to counter the "But we've always done this!" argument. Establish clear procedures for compliance, especially in the areas of photocopying, computer software, and use of audiovisuals. Document compliance too, so that a "paper trail" will exist in case of challenge. Establish a cooperative and collegial atmosphere. Nurture an atmosphere in which one teacher can freely say to another, "I'm not sure that use is within copyright law. Let's get an impartial opinion."

Administrative support for individual creative efforts of staff will encourage them to create, instead of borrow, intellectual property. Additional suggestions from the viewpoint of a building principal may be found in the article "Read My Lips: Copyright" by Robin Pennock in the June 1991 issue of *School Library Journal.*

If the building principal or district supervisor is in doubt about the need for administrative involvement and support, a computer software audit may be the one act that will demonstrate the need for copyright compliance. A software audit will give the administrator a list of every computer program installed on every computer in a district or building. Once equipped with the list, the school should document ownership of legal copies of every software program and operating system on the list. Why bother? Because this is exactly what will be required of the school should a representative of a computer software firm appear at the door with a search warrant and federal marshals in tow. A similar exercise could be done with videos. The results may be surprising, if not shocking.

Monitoring compliance is not something the librarian or technologist can do alone and without support. Encourage the copyright team to bring issues of copyright to the administrative office. Request that teachers document use of video with concrete tie-ins to lesson plans and district curriculum. Don't fall for ruses. Demand hard evidence. Is a showing of *The Lion King* really an appropriate curricular video for a unit on mammals? Encourage alternative rewards beyond passive television viewing.

Look on the bright side: copyright compliance can result in better, more creative teaching. Failing to monitor compliance is like leaving the keys in the ignition of a new Mustang with the doors unlocked. You shouldn't be surprised when something unpleasant happens.

Suggestions for administrators

- *Model copyright compliance. Request permission before photocopying copyrighted materials for your faculty. (There is limited fair use for copying for staff, anyway.) Mark the copies as "Reprinted with permission from. . . ."*

- *Be aware of video use in your building. How much video is used? Is it all directly related to instruction? Is it appropriate? Teachers never have enough instructional time. Can students afford to spend an hour and a half watching an entertainment video?*

- *Request that teachers document each video performance in their lesson plans. There should be a close correlation between the current lesson and district or state curriculum.*

- *Insist that teachers clear all video use through your office. Develop a form that identifies the teacher, the video, and the purpose of the showing. Teachers are less likely to use time-wasting video if they feel the administrator is aware of what is being shown.*

- *Know your curriculum. If the fourth grade studies volcanoes, why is the third-grade teacher showing a video on them?*

- *Watch extracurricular activities. The fair use exemption permits limited use of copyrighted materials in classroom situations. That exemption does not permit free use of copyrighted materials for student council dances, cheerleading posters, or video yearbooks.*

- *Look around your building. What type of decorations do you see? Are they bought from school suppliers, are they created by teachers, or are they copied from greeting cards, cartoons, movie characters, and the like?*

- *Enlist the assistance of those staff members most likely to be aware of copyright violations in the building. Teacher aides know what types of materials are being photocopied. Librarians and technologists know what video is being shown and what multimedia is being appropriated. They can assist you with record keeping, but they shouldn't be put into the role of copyright police.*

- *Help teachers find creative, non-video ways to reward students. Reward videos are public performances and require payment of royalties or written permission from the copyright holder.*

- *Keep accurate purchase records for audiovisual materials and computer software. These records should be retained as long as the materials (or their upgrades) are in use. The records may be needed if there should ever be a question of legality.*

- *Purchase a performance license for your building to show some non-instructional videos for rewards or as quick fill-ins when events get rained out or teachers are tied up in conferences.*

- *Assist staff in their efforts to stay copyright-compliant. Make sure there are enough copies of computer software (or appropriate licenses) to cover each machine that will use the software. Budget for record-keeping supplies, compliance reminder stickers for equipment, and sufficient consumables.*

- *Keep an upbeat attitude. Long-held habits die hard. Encourage efforts to stay compliant. Commiserate with those who complain that their favorite items are no longer permitted. Look on the bright side: you'll see how creative your teachers can be.*

- *Remember that a good-faith effort and an honest accounting can go a long way when someone does slip up. Everyone makes occasional mistakes. Learn from them and go on.*

Work cited

Pennock, R. (1991). Read my lips: Copyright. *School Library Journal, 37*(6), 50.

Chapter 16

Copyright Policies

Copyright policies are the skeleton that keeps your copyright compliance program together. A carefully worded, but not verbose, copyright policy states the expectation of the organization that the law be understood, obeyed, and enforced.

Why have one?

Why bother to have a copyright policy? A devil's advocate would say that there is no need for a policy. Why state the obvious? There is no policy requiring compliance with the local building code, is there? It's just common sense. One complies with the building code because it is the law. Doesn't one also comply with copyright because it is the law? Everyone obeys copyright; there's no need for a policy. Besides, who's going to catch a violator?

Well, our devil's advocate is oversimplifying. Do police departments expect all motorists to observe the speed limit because it is the law? Hardly. That's why they purchase and use radar units. Publishers and media producers are of a similar opinion. They know people will attempt to violate their rights under copyright, and they exercise various means to discover and prosecute the offenders. And although an occasional inadvertent slip might be overlooked, widespread or systematic infringement is likely to bring a hailstorm of litigation.

The purpose of a copyright policy is to state the institution's intention to abide by the law (Hoffman, 2003). The Association for Information Media and Equipment (AIME), the copyright watchdog group, boasts of its successes in redressing copyright infringement. Although most of the cases are settled out of court, AIME publishes many of the settlements in its periodic newsletters. The majority of the settlements involve the establishment of an institutional policy regarding copyright as well as comprehensive training and plans for tracking and monitoring copyright compliance. Agreements to discharge key employees or place official letters of reprimand in personnel files are sometimes included in the out-of-court settlements.

Question: Our school administration is reconsidering our copyright policy to include electronic formats and Web sites. What should we include?

Answer: If your current policy is a good one, it will not need updating. The policy shouldn't be medium-specific. It should state that employees will follow the current federal law, and it should outline the consequences for disobeying. If your policy is appropriately written, changes in the law will be covered automatically. However, you will need to train your staff on changes in the law and on the impact of copyright on new technologies.

Having an institutional copyright compliance policy is one way to beat the producers to the punch. AIME makes a good case with the following statement:

> *AIME takes the position that a copyright policy is important for an educational entity to develop. It helps to avoid confusion on the part of the staff and administrators and takes a definitive position on the importance of knowing the law and obeying it. A copyright policy also has the potential to insulate the agency or institution and administrators from liability if an infringement action were to be instituted because of activities by individuals contrary to the policy and against the law.* (Dohra, n.d.)

What should a policy contain?

Librarian and attorney Gretchen Hoffman (2003) envisions an expansive copyright policy, perhaps also incorporating copyright guidelines. She suggests including information on the following:

- *a brief review of Copyright Act scope*
- *what constitutes fair use*
- *guidelines for when permission is needed to use a work*
- *what one may do without obtaining permission*
- *how the school will address infringement claims*
- *establishing a DMCA agent*
- *information required by the DMCA*
- *information required by the TEACH Act*

Before you get quite so detailed in your policy, consider that Congress tweaks copyright law just about every year. Do you want to have to go back to the Board of Trustees to change the copyright policy every time some detail changes? Consider having the policy state aspiration, and leave the nitty-gritty details to guidelines that you can set administratively.

Appendix G is an example of a district-wide copyright policy adopted in 1993. Several points in the policy are worth noting:

1. *The policy states the institution's intention to abide by the letter and spirit of the copyright law and the associated congressional guidelines.*

2. *The policy covers all types of materials, including print, nonprint, graphics, and computer software.*

3. *The liability for noncompliance with copyright rests with the individual using the work.*

4. *The district mandates training for all personnel who might need to make copies.*

5. *The person using the materials must be able to produce, on request, copyright justification for their use.*

6. *The district appoints a copyright officer who serves as a point of contact for copyright information both within and without the district. That person will likely track licenses, serve as the registered copyright agent for the school's Web site, and oversee training of all students and teachers in copyright compliance.*

Some authorities recommend additional measures be included in a policy, such as requiring the district to develop a copyright manual for all employees, requiring notices be affixed to all copy-capable equipment, and even reprinting the entire law and guidelines (Vleck, 1987, p. 10; AIME, 1987, p. 7).

Regardless of the wording of the policy, simply having a policy that states institutional intent to obey the law will provide some small measure of protection. However, the more the faculty and staff know about copyright and the management of copyrighted materials, the better protected the organization and the employees are from threat of suit. If an infringement were to occur, the administration that has undertaken a thorough copyright education program could present a credible case that it did not condone the activity and that it had taken vigorous action to prevent infringement. The infringing employee, though, would have a poor chance of claiming "innocent infringement"—a defense for infringers who claim they had no knowledge they were infringing—because the institution would have records of staff development in correct application of copyright principles.

A further measure to protect the district from individual acts of infringement is to have employees sign a statement indicating that they have been informed of copyright laws and guidelines and that they will abide by both the institutional policy and the applicable laws (see Appendix A). This is similar to the OSHA requirement that employees be informed of hazards of chemicals in the workplace. Employees are often required to view a training video or attend a staff development session on a topic for which they are "signed off." Such record keeping indemnifies the organization from claims of negligence in informing the employees of potential hazards. Copyright infringement is certainly hazardous for both the individual employee and the organization, and having employees sign a compliance agreement or sign in at a staff development session on copyright at the beginning of the school year is not an unbearable burden when tracked at the building level.

The most efficient way to develop a copyright policy is to search out examples of copyright policies. A custom-developed copyright policy can be quickly assembled by cutting and pasting the best parts of the samples. Administrators, librarians, information technology staff, and television and media people should all have a say in the final wording. Bringing in an outside expert may be the best way to persuade doubters who believe a comprehensive policy isn't necessary. The final draft of the policy should go to the district's legal counsel for approval because collective bargaining agreements and teacher contracts may affect wording of policies. A spokesperson should be prepared to appear before the board to underscore the importance of the policy and explain the risk of leaving copyright compliance to individual employees. And a plan should be in place to train employees and monitor compliance in libraries, classrooms, and offices.

Works cited

Association for Information Media and Equipment. (1987). *A viewer's guide to copyright law: What every school, college, and public library should know.* Elkader, IA: AIME.

Dohra, A. (n.d.). *Copyright information packet.* Elkader, IA: AIME.

Hoffman, G. M. (2003). What every librarian should know about copyright, part IV: Writing a copyright policy. *Texas Library Journal, 79*(1), 12–15.

Vleck, C. W. (1987). *Copyright policy development: A resource book for educators.* Friday Harbor, WA: Copyright Information Services.

Chapter 17

Appendices

Appendix A

Copyright compliance agreement

Middletown School District

Copyright Compliance Agreement

I have been informed of the appropriate uses of instructional media, fair use guidelines, and the copyright compliance policy of the Middletown School District. I, the undersigned, acknowledge that I understand these policies and guidelines and that any uses I may make of instructional materials or audiovisual equipment in a classroom setting or online in performance of my educational responsibilities will be in accordance with both federal law and said policies and guidelines.

_____

Teacher

_____

Date

_____

Campus

Appendix B

Copyright dos and don'ts for schools

DO make sure that all audiovisual material shown to students is directly related to the curriculum. Be especially aware of movie ratings (G, PG, R).

DON'T show movies for reinforcement or reward. Encourage teachers to try games, stickers, or free time. You may rent movies for such performances, paying a minimal public performance fee, from suppliers such as Movie Licensing USA. Video rental stores cannot authorize you to give public performances.

DO ask your faculty to sign a copyright compliance agreement.

DON'T loan VCRs or DVRs with patch cords. Watch for questionable situations: why would a teacher need two recorders except to copy programs?

DO write the record date on all videos you record.

DO write the required erase date on all movies you record. This date will vary with the program. See advertisement of program or flyer from producer or calculate the fair use date.

DON'T copy commercial computer software, except to make an archival (one that isn't used) copy.

DON'T copy cartoon or TV or movie characters for decorations, bulletin boards, or handouts. Purchasing clip art, duplicator books, and bulletin board figures is acceptable, but you may not enlarge, modify, or change the medium (e.g., make slides or coloring sheets).

DO keep receipts and purchase orders for all movies and computer software. Keep the catalog (or pertinent pages) to verify purchase of public performance rights.

DO require teachers to verify recording date and source for all home-recorded movies. Fair use guidelines say that programs must be used for classroom instruction within 10 days of recording. After that date, the recording may be used only for evaluation for possible purchase. Erase after 45 days.

DO write for permission to retain recordings of useful programs. The worst a copyright holder can do is say no.

DON'T record programs off cable without investigating the recording rights first. Only programs recorded off the air (digital channels capable of being received through an antenna, if one were available) can be recorded without express permission. Look for this permission in teacher's guides that the various networks and program producers send out. These guides will also tell you the retention rights (e.g., seven days plus fair use. one year, life of tape/disc). Keep a photocopy of the permission with the recording at all times, and make sure there is a copyright notice on each copy.

DO post a copyright notice on VCRs, DVRs, scanners, computers, overhead projectors, and opaque projectors similar to the notice on your photocopy machine.

DON'T record a program because you know a teacher will ask for it later. Requests to record programs must come from a teacher in advance and in writing. Also, requests to record programs must come from the "bottom up"—that is, teachers can ask the librarian to record programs, but the principal may not.

DO remember that the person who pushes the button is also liable. So is the principal who knows copyright is being violated. We recommend you notify in writing both the principal and the teacher when you are aware of copyright infringement. Keep a copy in your own file.

DO bookmark or keep a copy of *Cable in the Classroom* to verify recording rights from the various networks.

DO encourage teachers to use the fast-forward function. Often only a portion of a movie will make as effective a point as an entire movie. Also, some producers will allow use of "excerpts" when they will not allow use of an entire program. Write for permission.

DON'T create anthologies on tape, disc, or photocopier. Copying an article, poem, or excerpt is fine, but combining them into a "new work" is usually not permitted unless there is some parody or exceptionally transformative use. Just having an easily accessible collection is likely not enough of a change. Creative mash-ups probably are transformative enough.

DON'T apologize for obeying federal law. If you would like a free copy of the law, visit the Copyright Office Web site for a copy of Circular 92.

From *Copyright for Schools: A Practical Guide, Fifth Edition* by Carol Simpson. Santa Barbara, CA: Linworth. Copyright © 2010.

Copyright for kids

When you work very hard on a project, you are very proud of yourself. You want your teacher, your classmates, and your parents to appreciate the hard work you put into your project. You don't like it when someone takes your work without your permission. It isn't fair. It isn't nice. It isn't okay. It's stealing.

When an author writes a book, or an artist paints a painting, or a photographer creates a photograph, they are also proud of their work. Not only do they want people to appreciate their work; they want to be paid for it. Writing and creating pictures are their jobs, and selling their writing or paintings or photographs is how they are paid. Authors and artists own a right to decide how their works will be used. This right is called "**copyright**," and it is part of the laws of the United States. When someone takes the work of an author, an artist, or a photographer without permission, the author, artist, or photographer doesn't get paid. It isn't fair. It isn't nice. It isn't okay. It's stealing.

Students must read the works of authors and look at paintings and photographs in books. They must often use small bits of information from books and pictures to do their schoolwork. Authors and artists understand this. An exception in the law, called "**fair use**," says that students can use these small pieces in certain ways *if* the student tells whose work it really is. If you don't tell whose work it is, you are pretending the work is your own. This pretending is called "**plagiarism**," and it is just like cheating. It's not fair. It's not nice. It isn't okay. It's stealing.

So how can students use the works of authors and artists to complete schoolwork without breaking the law? Here are some tips:

- Always say where you got the information you use. Tell the author, the book, and the page number or the Web site or the movie.

- Use as little information as you possibly can and still make the same point.

- Don't change the author's words or the artist's pictures without permission.

- Don't make copies of the schoolwork you have that uses materials from other sources.

- Don't forget that everything you write or create is yours to decide how it should be used, except for the parts you borrowed from others.

- If you make a presentation on the computer, there are very clear rules to tell you how much of someone else's work you may use.

- Ask nicely for permission to use more of someone's work. A polite request is often granted.

- Ask your librarian or instructional technology specialist for help if you don't understand how much of someone else's work you can borrow.

Appendix D

Useful sources of information

Access Copyright
1 Yonge Street, Suite 1900
Toronto, ON
M5E 1E5
800-893-5777
http://www.accesscopyright.ca/

Association for Information Media and Equipment (AIME)
P.O. Box 1173
Clarksdale, MS 38614
601-624-9355
http://www.aime.org

See also *Educational video streaming: A short primer* at http://aime.org/news.php.

American Society of Composers, Authors & Publishers (ASCAP)
One Lincoln Plaza
New York, NY 10023
212-621-6000
e-mail: info@ascap.com
http://www.ascap.com

Artists House Music
http://www.artistshousemusic.org/Legal

Association of American Publishers
71 Fifth Avenue
New York, NY 10003
212-255-0200
http://www.publishers.org/

Bound by Law (copyright graphic novel)
http://www.law.duke.edu/cspd/comics/index

Broadcast Music, Inc. (BMI)
320 W. 57th Street
New York, NY 10019
212-586-2000
http://www.bmi.com

Business Software Alliance
1150 18th Street, N.W. Suite 700
Washington, DC 20036
202-872-5500
http://www.bsa.org

Cable in the Classroom Magazine
1800 N. Beauregard Street, Suite 100
Alexandria, VA 22311
800-743-5355
http://www.ciconline.org/home

Copyright Clearance Center
222 Rosewood Drive
Danvers, MA 01923
978-750-8400
http://www.copyright.com

See also *Copyright Basics—The Video*, at http://copyright.com/viewPage.do?pageCode=pu3-n

Copyright Crash Course
http://www.utsystem.edu/ogc/intellectualproperty/cprtindx.htm

Copyright for Librarians
http://cyber.law.harvard.edu/copyrightforlibrarians/Main_Page
From the Harvard Berkman Center for Internet & Society

Cornell Copyright Information Center—Copyright Term and the Public Domain in the United States
http://www.copyright.cornell.edu/resources/publicdomain.cfm

Creative Commons
http://www.creativecommons.org

CSS Music (royalty-free music)
1948 Riverside Drive
Los Angeles, CA 90039
800-HOT-MUSIC
http://www.cssmusic.com

Digital Copyright Slider
http://librarycopyright.net/digitalslider

Discovery Channel School
P.O. Box 970
Oxon Hill, MD 20750-0970
800-321-1832
http://school.discovery.com

Docdel.net (links to document delivery services)
http://www.docdel.com/docdelnet/Full-Service_Providers.html

Electronic Frontier Foundation: Teaching Copyright Curriculum
http://www.teachingcopyright.org/

Films for the Humanities & Sciences (source of copyright-cleared sound effects)
P.O. Box 2053
Princeton, NJ
800-257-5126
http://www.films.com

Firms Out of Business (FOB)
An online database containing the names and addresses of copyright holders or contact persons for out-of-business printing and publishing firms, magazines, literary agencies, and similar organizations that have archives housed in libraries and archives in North America and the United Kingdom.
http://www.fob-file.com

Flowchart for Determining When U.S. Copyrights in Fixed Works Expire
http://www.sunsteinlaw.com/practices/copyright-portfolio-development/flowchart.htm

Freeplay Music
http://freeplaymusic.com

Fresh Music (royalty-free music)
http://www.freshmusic.com
800-545-0688

FTC Publishing Group (source of multimedia sound files)
P.O. Box 1361
Bloomington, IL 61702-1361
888-237-6740
http://www.ftcpublishing.com

Harry Fox Agency (mechanical rights for music)
711 Third Avenue
New York, NY 10017
212-370-5330
http://www.harryfox.com

Incompetech (royalty-free music)
http://incompetech.com/m/c/royalty-free/

Kit Parker Films (rental for public performance)
P.O. Box 16022
Monterey, CA 93942-6022
800-538-5838
http://www.kitparker.com

Motion Picture Association of America
15503 Ventura Boulevard
Encino, CA 91436
818-995-6600
http://www.mpaa.org/

Motion Picture Licensing Corporation
5455 Centinela Avenue
Los Angeles, CA 90066-6970
800-462-8855
http://www.mplc.org/

Movie Licensing USA
201 S. Jefferson Avenue
St. Louis, MO 63103-9954
877-321-1300
http://www.movlic.com/

Music Publishers Association of the United States
PMB 246
1562 First Avenue
New York, NY 10028
http://www.mpa.org/

National Music Publishers' Association
711 Third Avenue
New York, NY 10017
212-370-5330
http://www.nmpa.org

National Writers Union
National Office East
113 University Place, 6th floor
New York, NY 10003
212-254-0279
Fax: 212-254-0673
http://www.nwu.org/

Partners in Rhyme (royalty-free music and sound effects, some free!)
http://www.partnersinrhyme.com

PD Info (royalty-free and public domain music)
http://www.pdinfo.com/

PD Photo.org
http://www.pdphoto.org

Production Garden (royalty-free music libraries)
http://www.productiongarden.com/index.html

Purple Planet (royalty-free music)
http://www.purple-planet.com

Recording Industry Association of America
http://www.riaa.com

Showpoppers! (royalty-free video)
1948 Riverside Drive
Los Angeles, CA 90039
800-468-6874
http://www.showpoppers.com

SESAC, Inc.
421 W. 54th Street
New York, NY 10019
212-586-3450
http://www.sesac.com/

Society for Cinema and Media Studies
Statement of Best Practices for Fair Use in Teaching for Film and Media Educators
http://www.cmstudies.org/documents/SCMSBestPracticesforFairUseinTeaching-Final.pdf

Software and Information Industry Association
1730 M Street, N.W.
Washington, DC 20036
202-452-1600
http://www.siia.net
This group also provides copyright education resources.

Soundzabound Music Library
P.O. Box 492199
Atlanta, GA 30349-2199
888-834-1792
http://www.soundzabound.com

Stock Footage for Free (royalty-free video)
http://www.stockfootageforfree.com/

Swank Motion Pictures, Inc.
350 Vanderbilt Motor Parkway, Suite 203
Hauppauge, NY 11787-4305
800-876-5577
http://www.swank.com/

Taking the Mystery Out of Copyright (online video from Library of Congress)
http://www.loc.gov/teachers/copyrightmystery/#

Teaching Copyright
http://www.teachingcopyright.org/

United States Copyright Office
Library of Congress
Washington, DC 20559
202-479-0700
202-707-9100 (to order forms and circulars)

Main Web site—http://www.copyright.gov/
Circular 1, Copyright basics—http://www.copyright.gov/circs/circ1.html
Circular 21, Reproduction of copyrighted works by librarians and educators—http://www.copyright.gov/circs/circ21.pdf
Copyright law, complete text—http://www.copyright.gov/title17/

When Works Pass into the Public Domain

http://www.unc.edu/~unclng/public-d.htm

Appendix E

Copyright warning notices

All interlibrary loan (ILL) request forms must include the following notice (37 C.F.R. § 201.14). It must be printed within a prominent box on the actual order form. The notice may be on the front of the form or adjacent to the section requiring the patron's signature. The notice cannot be in type any smaller than that used throughout the form, and in no case may it be smaller than 8-point type. The notice must be clearly apparent, legible, and comprehensible to even a casual viewer of the form. Standard ALA ILL forms available from library supply houses comply with this requirement.

The same notice must be displayed at the place where ILL orders are taken. Such notice must be printed on heavy paper, in type no less than 18 points in size. It must be placed so as to be clearly visible, legible, and comprehensible near the place where ILL orders are accepted.

NOTICE WARNING CONCERNING COPYRIGHT RESTRICTIONS

The copyright law of the United States (Title 17, United States Code) governs the making of photocopies or other reproductions of copyrighted material.

Under certain conditions specified in the law, libraries and archives are authorized to furnish a photocopy or other reproduction. One of these specific conditions is that the photocopy or reproduction is not to be "used for any purpose other than private study, scholarship, or research." If a user makes a request for, or later uses, a photocopy or reproduction for purposes in excess of "fair use," that user may be liable for copyright infringement.

This institution reserves the right to refuse to accept a copying order if, in its judgment, fulfillment of the order would involve violation of copyright law.

Photocopies made by libraries, both for interlibrary loan and for patrons, should be marked with a copy of all information from the original copyright notice, or the copyright page should be copied and included with the item. If an item has no copyright notice, a notice of possible copyright restrictions must be added. Although specific wording isn't detailed in the law, many libraries use wording similar to the following:

NOTICE: This material may be protected by Copyright Law (Title 17 U.S. Code).

The multimedia guidelines specify that a notice must be on the *opening* slide (not necessarily the title slide) of a work that incorporates copyright-protected materials. The wording is not specified in the guidelines, though the content of the notice is described. Adults may use a notice similar to this:

WARNING: The following presentation uses copyright-protected materials used under the multimedia guidelines and fair use exemptions of U.S. copyright law. Further use is prohibited.

Young students must also have a compliance notice on their presentations. Following is a notice that a young student might be able to understand, yet still meeting the intent of the guidelines:

WARNING: I used other people's stuff to make my project. I followed the rules. Please don't copy it.

Software circulated by nonprofit libraries must have the following notice "durably attached" to each package:

Copy enabled equipment (photocopy machines, computers, scanners, DVRs, and so on) should have the following notice attached:

Appendix F

Sample copyright policy

It is the intent of the XYZ School District and its board of trustees, staff, and students to adhere to the provisions of current copyright laws and congressional guidelines. Employees and students are to adhere to all provisions of Title 17 of the United States Code, titled "Copyrights," and other relative federal legislation and guidelines related to the duplication, retention, and use of copyrighted materials.

Specifically:

Unlawful copies of copyrighted materials may not be produced on district-owned equipment.

Unlawful copies of copyrighted material may not be used with district-owned equipment, within district-owned facilities, or at district sponsored functions.

The legal and insurance protection of the district will not be extended to employees who intentionally and unlawfully copy and use copyrighted materials.

Employees who make copies and/or use copyrighted materials in their jobs are expected to be familiar with published provisions regarding fair use and public display and are further expected to be able to provide their supervisor, upon request, the justification under sections 107 or 110 of U.S.C. 17 for materials that have been used or copied.

Employees who use copyrighted materials in ways that do not fall within fair use or public display guidelines must be able to substantiate that the materials meet the following tests:

The materials have been purchased from an authorized vendor by the individual or the district, and a record of the purchase exists;

The materials are copies covered by a licensing agreement between the copyright owner and the district or the individual employee; or

The materials are being previewed or demonstrated by the user to reach a decision about future purchase or licensing, and a valid agreement exists that allows for such use.

The district will appoint an officer who will assist employees in fulfilling their obligations under U.S. copyright law, who will maintain records of licenses and permissions, and who will register as an agent for compliance with the Digital Millennium Copyright Act.

Appendix G

Release form

MIDDLETOWN SCHOOL DISTRICT PUBLICATION RELEASE FORM

I, the undersigned, having full authority to execute this Release on behalf of myself and on behalf of ___

_____ (child's name) of _____

(school name) hereby grant permission to MIDDLETOWN SCHOOL DISTRICT (hereinafter

called "MSD") to use the following materials provided by me or on my child's behalf to MSD, for the

purposes identified below:

My or my child's: (initial where appropriate) _____ Name _____ Voice _____ Likeness _____

Quotes _____ Papers, articles, poems, or other written material as specified: _____

_____

_____

Graphics, photographs, or other artwork as specified: _____

_____

_____

I warrant and represent that the materials submitted under this agreement are owned by and/or are

original to me or my child, and/or I have full authority from the owner of said materials to permit

MSD to use said materials in the manner described below:

_____ Newspapers, magazines, other print publications

_____ Television or radio

_____ Internet or computer network

_____ Presentation for teaching, staff development, or professional conference

_____ Retention and use as exemplars

_____ Public display or performance

I understand that MSD is and shall be the exclusive owner of any and all right, title, and interest,

including copyright, to any and all materials into which the aforementioned items are incorporated,

except as to my preexisting rights in any of the items herein released.

Date: _____

Signature: _____

Name/Relationship: _____

Address: _____

_____

Telephone: _____

Appendix H

Copyright and plagiarism guidelines for students

1. You may make a single photocopy of any material you need to do your schoolwork, or for your own personal research. You may keep the copies you make as long as you like, but you may not sell them, nor may you make copies of your copies.

2. You must respect the copyright of the materials you use. Only the creators, or the persons or companies who own the copyright, may make copies of the material, except as noted above. You may modify or change the material to fit your schoolwork, and you may you perform or display the material in conjunction with class work.

3. You may use copyrighted material to do your schoolwork, but if you use an author's ideas, you must give the author credit, either in the text or in a footnote. If you use an author's words, you must put the words in quotation marks or other indication of direct quotation. Failure to give credit to the author, artist, or photographer is plagiarism. If you use a large amount of a single work, you must obtain permission.

   - Even if you change a few words from an author, you must still put the entire material in quotation marks, with your changes in square brackets.

4. Use of copyrighted materials outside of regular class work may require written permission of the copyright holder unless you can qualify for fair use. The same rule applies to graphic material such as cartoon characters on posters or other spirit or decorative material.

   - For help in assessing if your use is fair, consult a teacher or librarian.

5. You may not copy computer software from the school computers.

   - You may not download any document through the school network that may be used to plagiarize or violate copyright.

6. Information received from the school computers may be used only for regular school-work or personal research.

   - If your teacher tells you that you may not use online sources for help for your assignment, and you use those sources anyway, you are cheating.

The source of any information used in your schoolwork should be acknowledged in the format prescribed by the teacher. Use of another's intellectual work without attribution is plagiarism, as outlined in the Student Code of Conduct.

From *Copyright for Schools: A Practical Guide, Fifth Edition* by Carol Simpson. Santa Barbara, CA: Linworth. Copyright © 2010.

Appendix I

How much material may I use in my PowerPoint presentation?

How much material may I use in my PowerPoint presentation?

Note: The following amounts apply to how much may be used by a teacher or student from one source during a semester or term.

Images:

- Up to five images from one artist/illustrator/photographer

- 15 images or 10 percent (whichever is less) from a source with images from many artists/illustrators/photographers

Music:

- Up to 30 seconds or 10 percent (whichever is less) of a musical work

  - May be combined from different sections of work
  - Includes music and lyrics
  - Includes music video
  - No prohibition on looping

- May not change fundamental melody or basic character

Video:

- Up to 3 minutes or 10 percent (whichever is less) of a video.

  - Music video is controlled by the **Music** limits

Text:

- Up to 1,000 words or 10 percent (whichever is less) of textual material from one source

  - Does not need to be continuous material

- A poem up to 250 words

  - May use it all
  - No more than three poems by one poet
  - No more than five poems from a single anthology

- A poem longer than 250 words

  - May use up to 250 words
  - Does not need to be continuous material
  - No more than three poems by one poet
  - No more than five poems from a single anthology

Source: Fair Use Guidelines for Educational Multimedia

Additional quantities may be possible if the use passes a statutory fair use assessment.

From *Copyright for Schools: A Practical Guide, Fifth Edition* by Carol Simpson. Santa Barbara, CA: Linworth. Copyright © 2010.

Appendix J

Significant copyright law section references

Rights of the copyright owner—17 United States Code, section 106

Moral rights—17 United States Code, section 106(A)

Fair use—17 United States Code, section 107

Library copying—17 United States Code, section 108

First sale doctrine—17 United States Code, section 109(a)

Circulation of computer software—17 United States Code, section 109(b)(1)(A) ff

Public display of lawful copies—17 United States Code, section 109(c)

Audio-visual face-to-face teaching exceptions—17 United States Code, section 110(1)

Distance learning performances—17 United States Code, section 110(2)

Graphics and sculpture—17 United States Code, section 113

Digital audio performances—17 United States Code, section 114(d)–(j)

Computer software requirements—17 United States Code, section 117

Architectural works—17 United States Code, section 120

Special exceptions for the blind and physically disabled—17 United States Code, section 121

Work for hire—17 United States Code, section 201(b)

Duration of copyright—17 United States Code, section 302

Certain exemptions for librarians and educators—17 United States Code, section 504 (c)

No Electronic Theft—17 United States Code, section 506

OSP liability—17 United States Code, section 512

Sound recordings and music videos—17 United States Code, section 1101

Technological protections—17 United States Code, sections 1201–1205

Appendix K

Bibliography of selected works on copyright

A&M Records, Inc. v. Napster, Inc., 239 F.3d 1004 (9th Cir. 2001).

Alfred Publishing Co. (2008). *Licensing and permission requests.* Retrieved from http://www.alfred.com/alfredWeb/front/General.aspx?pageid=296&catid=55.

American Library Association. (1982). *Model policy concerning college and university photocopying for classroom research and library reserve use.* Chicago: ALA.

American Library Association. (2002). *Video and copyright.* Retrieved from http://www.ala.org/Template.cfm?Section=libraryfactsheet&Template=/ContentManagement/ContentDisplay.cfm&ContentID=24635.

American Library Association. (2004). *Guidelines and procedures for telefacsimile and electronic delivery of interlibrary loan requests and materials.* Retrieved from http://www.ala.org/ala/rusa/rusaprotools/referenceguide/guidelinesprocedures.htm.

American Library Association. (2006). *Fair use and electronic reserves.* Chicago: ALA. Retrieved from http://www.ala.org/ala/issuesadvocacy/copyright/fairuse/fairuseandelectronicreserves/index.cfm.

Anti-piracy FAQ. (2010). Retrieved from http://www.siia.net/index.php?option=com_content&view=article&id=387:ap-faq&catid=8:anti-piracy-overview&Itemid=420.

Armatas, S.A. (2008). *Distance learning and copyright: A guide to legal issues.* Boston: American Bar Association Section of Intellectual Property Law.

ASCAP. (2008). *Common music licensing terms.* Retrieved from http://www.ascap.com/licensing/termsdefined.html.

Association of Research Libraries. (2002). *Copyright timeline.* Retrieved from http://arl.cni.org/info/frn/copy/timeline.html.

Association for Information Media and Equipment. (1987). *A viewer's guide to copyright law: What every school, college, and public library should know.* Elkader, IA: AIME.

Association for Information Media and Equipment. (1990). *Press release.* Elkader, IA: AIME.

A.V. v. iParadigms LLC, 562 F.3d 630 (4th Cir. 2009).

Bailey, J. (2008). Is "deep linking" in trouble? *The Blog Herald.* Retrieved from http://www.blogherald.com/2008/12/29/is-deep-linking-in-trouble/.

Band, J. (2001). *The Digital Millennium Copyright Act.* Washington, DC: Association of Research Libraries. Retrieved from http://www.arl.org/bm-doc/dmca_band.pdf.

Barlow, J.P. (1994). *The economy of ideas.* Retrieved from http://www.wired.com/wired/archive/2.03/economy.ideas.html.

Bender, I. (1996, Summer). The Internet—It's not free and never was. *AIME News.*

Berman, D. (1993, May 13). Re: Questionable videotapes. Discussion on liability in the use of copyrighted videos. Message posted to CNI-COPYRIGHT electronic mailing list.

Bielefield, A., & Cheeseman, L. (1997). *Technology and copyright law: A guidebook for the library, research and teaching professions.* New York: Neal-Schuman.

Bielefield, A., & Cheeseman, L. (1999). *Interpreting and negotiating licensing agreements: A guidebook for the library, research, and teaching professions.* New York: Neal-Schuman.

Blair, J. (1998, August 5). Pirated software could prove costly to L.A. district. *Education Week,* p. 3.

Blackwell Publishing Group v. Excel Research Group, LLC, No. 07-12731, 2009 WL 3287403 (E.D. Mich. Oct. 14, 2009).

Boosey v. Empire Music Co., 224 F. 646 (S.D.N.Y. 1915).

Brain, M. (2003, August 20). *How blogs work.* Retrieved from http://computer.howstuffworks.com/internet/social-networking/information/blog.htm.

Bridgeman Art Library Ltd. v. Corel Corp., 36 F. Supp. 2d 191 (S.D.N.Y. 1999).

Bridgeport Music v. Dimension Films, et al., 410 F.3d 792 (6th Cir. 2005).

Business Software Alliance. (2009, May 28). *BSA reveals top 10 industries with highest reports of software piracy.* Retrieved from http://www.bsa.org/country/News%20and%20Events/News%20Archives/en/2009/en-05282009-tenindustries.aspx.

Columbia Pictures Industries v. Redd Horne, 749 F.2d 154 (3d Cir. 1984).

Confu background. (1997, June 11). Retrieved from http://www.utsystem.edu/OGC/IntellectualProperty/confu2.htm.

Creative Commons. (2009a). *About licenses.* Retrieved from http://creativecommons.org/about/licenses/.

Creative Commons. (2009b). *Identify a public domain work.* Retrieved from http://creativecommons.org/license/publicdomain-2.

Crews, K. (1998). *Indiana University online copyright tutorial.* Bloomington: University of Indiana.

Crews, K. D. (2000). *Copyright essentials for librarians and educators.* Chicago: ALA.

Dohra, A. (n.d.). *Copyright information packet.* Elkader, IA: AIME.

Dukelow, R. H. (1992). *The library copyright guide.* Washington, DC: Copyright Information Services, Association for Educational Communications & Technology.

Eather, J. (2008, August 15). Why Jenny has taken it down [Msg #6]. Message posted to http://www.proteacher.net/discussions/showthread.php?t=102053.

eBook Mall. (2010). *Popular eBook formats.* Retrieved from http://www.ebookmall.com/choose-format/.

Education software management: A K–12 guide to legal software use. (1994). Washington, DC: Software and Information Industry Association.

Eldred v. Ashcroft, 537 U.S. 186 (2003).

Electronic Frontier Foundation. (2004). *How not to get sued by the RIAA for file-sharing.* Retrieved from http://www.eff.org/IP/P2P/howto-notgetsued.php.

Electronic Privacy Information Center. (2004). *EPIC archive—privacy.* Retrieved from http://www.epic.org/privacy/.

Ensign, D. J. (1992, Winter). Fax—a special case: Implications of copyright law for facsimile document delivery. *The Bookmark, 50,* 125–128.

Estate of Martin Luther King, Jr. v. CBS, Inc., 194 F.3d 1211 (11th Cir. 1999).

Feather, J. (1980). The book trade in politics: The making of the Copyright Act of 1710. *Publishing History, 19*(8), 39.

Fishman, S. (2000). *The copyright handbook* (5th ed.). Berkeley, CA: Nolo.

Frankel, J. (2007). *The teacher's guide to music, media, and copyright law.* New York: Hal Leonard.

Free Software Foundation, Inc. (2010). *Licenses.* Retrieved from http://www.gnu.org/licenses/licenses.html.

Gain, B. (2009, May 28). Special report: The future of file sharing. *Intellectual Property Watch.* Retrieved from http://www.ip-watch.org/Weblog/2009/05/28/the-future-of-file-sharing/.

Gasaway, L. N. (2000, April 14). *Copyright law: Changes for libraries and librarians.* Concurrent session presented at the Texas Library Association Annual Conference, Houston, TX.

Gasaway, L. N. (2002). Copyright considerations for electronic reserves. In *Managing Electronic Reserves.* Chicago: ALA. Retrieved from http://www.ala.org/ala/ourassociation/publishing/alaeditions/samplers/rosedale_er.pdf.

Gasaway, L. N. (2006). Copyright law and the practice of law in the digital age. In *The Law Library 2006: Skills, Strategies & Solutions, 125–139* (PLI Patents, Copyrights, Trademarks, and Literary Property Course Handbook Series No. 8345).

Goldstein, P. (2008). *Goldstein on copyright* (3d ed.). Austin: Wolters Kluwer Law & Business.

Harry Fox Agency. (2009). *Mechanical licensing.* Retrieved from http://www.harryfox.com/public/MechanicalLicenseslic.jsp.

Hoffman, G. M. (2001). *Copyright in cyberspace: Questions and answers for librarians.* New York: Neal-Schuman.

Hoffman, G. M. (2003). What every librarian should know about copyright, part IV: Writing a copyright policy. *Texas Library Journal, 79*(1), 12–15.

Hoffman, I. (2002). *The Visual Artists Rights Act.* Retrieved from http://www.ivanhoffman.com/vara.html.

Individuals with Disabilities Education Improvement Act of 2004, PL 108-446, December 3, 2004, 118 Stat. 2647 (2005).

Jackson, M. E. (1991). Library to library: Copyright and ILL. *Wilson Library Bulletin, 66*(2), 84–87.

Jassin, L. J., & Schechter, S. C. (1998). *The copyright permission and libel handbook.* New York: John Wiley.

Jensen, M. B. (1992, Winter). I'm not my brother's keeper: Why libraries shouldn't worry too much about what patrons do with library materials at home. *The Bookmark, 50,* 150–154.

Jensen, M. B. (1996). *Does your project have a copyright problem? A decision-making guide for librarians.* Jefferson, NC: McFarland.

JS ex rel Snyder v. Blue Mountain Sch. Dist., 593 F.3d 286 (3d Cir. 2010).

Jury awards $675K in music downloading case. (2009, August 3). *E-school News.* Retrieved from http://www.eschoolnews.com/2009/08/03/jury-awards-675k-in-music-downloading-case/.

Kelly v. Arriba Soft Corp., 280 F.3d 937 (9th Cir. 2002).

Kohn, A., & Kohn, B. (2010). *Kohn on music licensing* (4th ed.). Austin, TX: Wolters Kluwer.

Kruppenbacher, F. (1993, June 14). Re: CC and copyright. Message sent to CNI-COPYRIGHT electronic mailing list.

Kravets, D. (2009, September 17). *Linden Lab targeted in Second Life sex-code lawsuit.* Retrieved from http://www.wired.com/threatlevel/2009/09/linden/.

Layshock v. Hermitage Sch. Dist., 593 F.3d 249 (3d Cir. 2010).

Legal Information Institute. (2004). *LII: Law about . . . trademark.* Retrieved from http://www.law.cornell.edu/topics/trademark.html.

Legal issues & education technology: A school leader's guide. (1999). Alexandria, VA: National School Boards Association.

Library of Congress. (2008). *Digital interlibrary loan.* Retrieved from http://www.loc.gov/rr/loan/illscanhome.html.

Litman, J. (2001). *Digital copyright.* Amherst, NY: Prometheus.

Lutzker, A. (1999). *Memorandum.* Retrieved from http://www.arl.org/bm-doc/notice.pdf.

Lutzker, A. (Fall, 2005). Inter-library lending and online school system union catalogs: a lesson in copyright liability. *AIME News 19*(3), 1–2.

Lutzker, A. (2010). Educational video streaming: A short primer. *AIME News, 24*(1), 1–3. Retrieved from http://www.aime.org/news.php.

Marshall, P. G. (1993, May 21). Software piracy. *CQ Researcher.*

Matias, N. (2003). *What is a wiki?* Retrieved from http://articles.sitepoint.com/article/what-is-a-wiki.

MGM Studios, Inc. v. Grokster, Ltd., 380 F.3d 1154 (9th Cir. 2004).

Moser, D. J. (2006). *Moser on music licensing.* Boston, MA: Thomson.

Music Publishers Association. (2004). *Making a record: Do I have to obtain a mechanical license?* Retrieved from http://www.mpa.org/copyright/you.html#record.

Nimmer, M. B., & Nimmer, D. (2006). *Nimmer on copyright.* New York: Matthew Bender & Co.

Norah, L. (2004, May 1). *RIAA sue another 477 music sharers.* Retrieved from http://itvibe.com/news/2501/.

Office of General Counsel, University of Texas System. (2001, November 12). *Fair use guidelines for electronic reserve systems.* Retrieved from http://www.utsystem.edu/OGC/IntellectualProperty/rsrvguid.htm.

Office of General Counsel, University of Texas System. (2003, January 30). *Copyright in the library: Reserve electronic copies.* Retrieved from http://www.utsystem.edu/OGC/IntellectualProperty/l-resele.htm.

Office of General Counsel, University of Texas System. (2004, December 22). *CONFU: The conference on fair use.* Retrieved from http://www.utsystem.edu/OGC/IntellectualProperty/confu.htm.

Office of General Counsel, University of Texas System. (2007). *Fair use guidelines for educational multimedia.* Retrieved from http://www.utsystem.edu/OGC/IntellectualProperty/ccmcguid.htm.

Open Source Initiative. (n.d.). *Open source licenses.* Retrieved from http://www.opensource.org/licenses.

Peters, M. (2009). *CC0 FAQ.* Retrieved from http://wiki.creativecommons.org/index.php?title=CC0_FAQ&oldid=21384.

Peterson, G. R. (2008). Trade secret law update 2008: Including restrictive post-employment covenants. In Practising Law Institute. *14th Annual Institute on Intellectual Property Law.* New York: Practising Law Institute.

ProCD, Inc. v. Zeidenberg, 86 F.3d 1447 (7th Cir. 1996).

Recording Industry Association of America. (2002). *RIAA releases mid-year snapshot of music industry.* Retrieved from http://www.riaa.com/news/newsletter/082602.asp.

Recording Industry Association of America. (2003). *Downloading and uploading.* Retrieved from http://www.riaa.com/issues/music/downup.asp.

Recording Indus. Ass'n of Am. v. Diamond Multimedia Sys., Inc., 180 F.3d 1073 (9th Cir. 1999).

Reed, M. H. (1989). *Videotapes: Copyright and licensing considerations for schools and libraries.* Syracuse, NY: ERIC Clearinghouse on Information Resources. (ERIC Document Reproduction Service No. ED 308 855).

Roy Export Co. v. Columbia Broadcast System, Inc., 503 F. Supp. 1137 (D.C.N.Y. 1980).

Salinger v. Random House, Inc., 811 F.2d 90 (2d Cir. 1987).

San Francisco Arts & Athletics, Inc. v. U.S. Olympic Committee, 483 U.S. 522 (1987).

Schember, J. (2010, January 3). *The ABCs of e-book format conversion: Easy Calibre tips for the Kindle, Sony, and Nook.* Retrieved from http://www.teleread.org/2010/01/03/the-abcs-of-format-conversion-for-the-kindle-sony-and-nook-plus-some-calibre-tips/.

Shepard Fairey v. Assoc. Press, No. 1:2009cv01123 (S.D.N.Y.). Retrieved from http://news.justia.com/cases/featured/new-york/nysdce/1:2009cv01123/340121/.

Shepherd, C. R. (1996, May 24). Re: Sales of videotapes. [CNI-COPYRIGHT electronic mailing list comment]. Message posted to http://www3.wcl.american.edu/cni/9605/9323.html.

Simpson, C. (2007). An ILL wind: Libraries and the interlibrary loan of audiovisuals. *SMU Science and Technology Law Review, 11*(2), 163–194.

Simpson, C. (2008). *Copyright for administrators.* Worthington, OH: Linworth.

Sinofsky, E. (1993, June 14). Re: Closed-caption videotape conversion. Message sent to CNI-COPYRIGHT electronic mailing list.

Sivin, J. P., & Bialo, E. R. (1992). *Ethical use of information technologies in education: Important issues for America's schools*. Washington, DC: U.S. Department of Justice.

Software and Information Industry Association. (2005). *Educational copyright resources*. Retrieved from http://siia.com/piracy/pubs/EducationalCopyright.pdf.

Special Interest Video Sales Group. (1995). *Fair use doctrine: Excerpts from the Copyright Act*. Retrieved from http://www.sivideo.com/9fstsleb.htm.

Stanek, D. J. (1986, March). Videotapes, computer programs, and the library. *Information Technology and Libraries, 5*, 42–54.

Stim, R. (2000). *Getting permission: How to license & clear copyrighted materials online & off*. Berkeley, CA: Nolo Press.

Talab, R. S. (1999). *Commonsense copyright: A guide for educators and librarians*. Jefferson, NC: McFarland.

UCLA Online Institute for Cyberspace Law and Policy. (1998). *The "No Electronic Theft" Act*. Retrieved from http://www.gseis.ucla.edu/iclp/hr2265.html.

UCLA Online Institute for Cyberspace Law and Policy. (2001). *The Digital Millennium Copyright Act*. Retrieved from http://www.gseis.ucla.edu/iclp/dmca1.htm.

United States Copyright Office. (1999). *Fair use*. Retrieved from http://www.copyright.gov/fls/fl102.html.

United States Copyright Office. (2009). *Circular 21: Reproduction of copyrighted works by educators and librarians*. Available at http://www.copyright.gov/circs/circ21.pdf.

United States Department of Justice. (1997). *Criminal resource manual 1844 copyright law—Preemption of state law*. Retrieved from http://www.usdoj.gov/usao/eousa/foia_reading_room/usam/title9/crm01844.htm.

United States Department of Justice. (1998). *The "No Electronic Theft" Act*. Retrieved from http://www.cybercrime.gov/netsum.htm.

University of Massachusetts. (2009). *Security awareness: Laws FAQ*. Retrieved from http://www.massachusetts.edu/lawsfaq/faq.cfm#28.

University of Washington Libraries. (2009). *Interlibrary loan & document delivery services*. Retrieved from http://www.lib.washington.edu/ill/pilot.html.

Vleck, C. W. (1987). *Copyright policy development: A resource book for educators*. Friday Harbor, WA: Copyright Information Services.

Appendix L

Important Internet links for copyright information

Agreement on guidelines for classroom copying in not-for-profit educational institutions with respect to books and periodicals: http://www.washburn.edu/admin/vpaa/fachdbk/FHappen07.html

Association for Instructional Media and Equipment: http://www.aime.org/

Brad Templeton's *Ten big myths about copyright explained:* http://www.templetons.com/brad/copymyths.html

Complying with the Digital Millennium Copyright Act: http://www.utsystem.edu/OGC/Intellectual Property/dmcaisp.htm

Copyright agent designation, Library of Congress: http://www.copyright.gov/onlinesp/

Copyright and fair use, from American Library Association: http://www.ala.org/ala/mgrps/divs/alcts/mgrps/ig/meta/copyrightfair.cfm

Copyright and fair use Web site, Stanford University: http://fairuse.stanford.edu/

Copyright for music librarians: http://www.musiclibraryassoc.org/copyright/

Copyright law in cyberspace: http://www.utsystem.edu/OGC/IntellectualProperty/distance.htm

Copyright laws for theatre people: http://lecatr.people.wm.edu/copy.htm

Copyright resources for schools and libraries, from Wisconsin Dept. of Public Instruction: http://dpi.wi.gov/lbstat/copyres.html

Copyright timeline: http://www.arl.org/pp/ppcopyright/copyresources/copytimeline.shtml

Copyright Web site: http://www.benedict.com

Copyright workshop: http://www.cyberbee.com/copyrt.html

Fair use guidelines for educational multimedia: http://www.utsystem.edu/ogc/intellectualproperty/ccmcguid.htm

Guidelines for educational uses of music (for printed music): http://copyright.musiclibraryassoc.org/Resources/EducationalUseOfPrintedMusic

Guidelines for off-air recordings of broadcast programming for educational purposes (Kastenmeier guidelines): http://www.lib.berkeley.edu/MRC/Kastenmeier.html

Library and classroom use of copyrighted videotapes and computer software: http://www.ifla.org/documents/infopol/copyright/ala-1.txt

Los Angeles Unified School District copyright policy: http://www.lausd.k12.ca.us/homepage/news/update/copyright/

MARC record guidelines for copyright management information: http://www.loc.gov/marc/bibliographic/bd540.html

Online service providers, from United States Copyright Office: http://www.copyright.gov/onlinesp/

PBS Teachers: http://www.pbs.org/teachers

PDInfo—Public domain and royalty free music: http://www.pdinfo.com/

Performance rights for copyrighted videorecordings, from Wisconsin Dept. of Public Instruction: http://dpi.wi.gov/lbstat/coplicen.html

Report on copyright and digital distance education, U.S. Copyright Office: http://www.copyright.gov/disted

Software use & the law, from Software and Information Industry Association: http://www.siia.net/index.php?option=com_docman&task=doc_view&gid=212&tmpl=component&format=raw&Itemid=59

University of Texas System crash course on copyright: http://www.utsystem.edu/ogc/intellectualproperty/cprtindx.htm

Unsupervised library copying: http://copyright.columbia.edu/copyright/libraries-and-copyright/unsupervised-copying-equipment/

Use of music on a multimedia Web site: http://www.ivanhoffman.com/music.html

Using software: A guide to the ethical and legal use of software for members of the academic community: http://www.ifla.org/documents/infopol/copyright/educom.txt

A visit to Copyright Bay: http://www.stfrancis.edu/cid/copyrightbay/

World Book and Copyright Day, from UNESCO: http://www.unesco.org/culture/bookday/

Appendix M

Sources of audiovisual works with public performance rights

Source: http://www.carolsimpson.com/public_performance_rights.htm. Refer to site for latest information.

Note: Not all movies sold by these producers and distributors may have public performance rights, but all listed companies sell some materials with public performance rights. Some sell the same materials with and without such rights. Order carefully and note price differentials.

AIMS Multimedia (see Discovery Education)

Allied Video
P.O. Box 702618
Tulsa, OK 74170
800-926-5892
http://www.alliedvd.com/

Ambrose Video Publishing, Inc.
28 West 44th Street Suite 1115
New York, NY 10036
800-526-4663
http://www.ambrosevideo.com/

Note: Does not include rights to stream.

Annenberg/CPB
401 9th Street, NW
Washington, DC 20004-2036
202-879-9648
http://www.learner.org/

Note: Includes broadcast rights through dates on Web site.

Aquarius Health Care Media
18 North Main Street
Sherborn, MA 01770
888-440-2963
http://www.aquariousproductions.com

Note: No internal closed circuit allowed.

ArtMattan Productions
535 Cathedral Parkway
Suite 14B
New York, NY 10025
http://www.africanfilm.com/

Note: Titles leased, not sold, for life of recording. No first-sale rights, so interlibrary loan is doubtful. Read license.

Attainment Company

P.O. Box 930160
Verona, WI 53593-0160
800-327-4269
http://www.attainmentcompany.com/

BFA (see Phoenix Films)

BioMedia Associates

P.O. Box 1234
Beaufort, SC 29901-1234
877-661-5355
http://www.ebiomedia.com/

Note: Programs leased, not sold. No first-sale rights, so interlibrary loan is doubtful. Read license.

Bullfrog Films (all titles except those marked "home use only")

P.O. Box 149
Oley, PA 19547
800-543-3764
http://www.bullfrogfilms.com/

Note: Titles leased, not sold, for life of copy. No first-sale rights, so interlibrary loan is doubtful. Read license.

California Newsreel

149 Ninth Street
San Francisco, CA 94103
415-621-6196
http://www.newsreel.org/

Note: Titles leased, not sold, for life of recording. No first-sale rights, so interlibrary loan is doubtful. Closed circuit in house okay, but no transfer to streaming server. Read license.

Cambridge Documentary Films, Inc.

P.O. Box 390385
Cambridge, MA 02139-0004
617-484-3993
http://www.cambridgedocumentaryfilms.org/

Cambridge Educational

200 American Metro Boulevard, Suite 124
Hamilton, NJ 08619
800-257-5126
http://cambridge.films.com/

Note: Titles leased, not sold, for term contracted. No first-sale rights, so interlibrary loan is doubtful. Closed circuit in house okay, but no transfer to streaming server. Read license.

Chip Taylor Communications (discount, no-rights versions available)
2 East View Drive
Derry, NH 03038
800-876-CHIP (2447)
http://chiptaylor.com/

Note: Titles leased, not sold, for term contracted. Note extensive list of licenses. Be sure to choose the license that covers any proposed use. This vendor does sue. Read license.

Choices Video (see World Almanac Education)

Churchill Films (see Clearvue/EAV)

CinéFête
1586 Fleury East, Suite 210
H2C 156
Montreal, QC
Canada
800-858-2183
http://usa.cinefete.ca/

Note: Any duplication, streaming, format change, or centralized library circulation is prohibited without payment of additional fee. If you are in the United States, make sure you are on the U.S. side of the site because available rights vary.

The Cinema Guild (see Web site for specific limitations)
115 W. 30th Street, Suite 800
New York, NY 10001
800-723-5522
http://www.cinemaguild.com/

Note: Digitization rights reserved.

Classroom Video
4739 University Way, NE, Suite 1606
Seattle, WA 98105
800-665-4121
http://www.classroomvideo.com.au/

Contemporary Drama Service (see Meriweather Publishing, Ltd.)
http://www.contemporarydrama.com/

Coronet (see Phoenix Films)

CVLI
888-771-2854
For licensing churches for public performances of entertainment video
http://www.cvli.com/

Design Video Communications (see First Light Video)

Disney Educational Productions (see Web site for specific limitations)
3800 W. Alameda Avenue, 16th Floor
Burbank, CA 91505
818-569-5991
http://dep.disney.go.com/index.html

Note: Only when purchased from this site.

Educational Video Network, Inc.
1336 19th Street
Huntsville, TX 77340
800-762-0060
http://www.edvidnet.com/

Ergo Video (for additional fee)
P.O. Box 2037
Teaneck, NJ 07666
877-539-4748
http://www.jewishvideo.com/

Fanlight Productions (except for specific titles marked "home use")
4196 Washington Street
Boston, MA 02131
800-937-4113
http://www.fanlight.com/

Note: Streaming is specifically prohibited without purchase of digital rights.

Film Ideas, Inc.
308 North Wolf Road
Wheeling, IL 60090
800-475-3456
http://www.filmideas.com/

Note: Streaming, duplication, download, and ITV rights available for license.

Films for the Humanities and Sciences
200 American Metro Boulevard
Hamilton, NJ 08619
800-257-5126
http://ffh.films.com/

Note: Titles leased, not sold, for term contracted. No first-sale rights, so interlibrary loan is doubtful. Closed circuit in house okay, but no transfer to streaming server. Read license.

First Light Video (for non-revenue uses)
2321 Abbot Kinney Boulevard
Venice, CA 90291

800-262-8862
http://www.firstlightvideo.com/

Note: No streaming, closed circuit, or broadcast. No interlibrary loan.

Forest Glen TV Productions (for non-revenue uses in schools and colleges)
P.O. Box 101823
Fort Worth, TX 76185-1823
817-920-9662
http://texashistory.com/

GPN (Reading Rainbow and others)
1407 Fleet Street
Baltimore, MD 21231
800-228-4630
http://www.shopdei.com

Note: Sold for life of media. No interlibrary loan outside the purchasing district. Closed circuit in one building okay.

Guidance Associates
31 Pine View Road
Mount Kisco, NY 10549
800-431-1242
http://www.guidanceassociates.com

Note: No format transfer or streaming.

Home Vision (see Public Media)

Human Relations Media
41 Kensico Drive
Mount Kisco, NY 10549
800-431-2050
http://www.hrmvideo.com

Icarus Films (see First Run Features)
32 Court Street, 21st Floor
Brooklyn, NY 11201
718-488-8900
http://icarusfilms.com/

Note: Titles leased, not sold, for life of copy. No first-sale rights, so interlibrary loan is doubtful. Read license.

Insight Media (limited titles)
2162 Broadway
New York, NY 10024-0621

800-233-9910
http://www.insight-media.com

Note: No streaming or admission charge.

Instructional Video (all except those marked HUO "home use only")
2219 C Street
Lincoln, NE 68502
800.228.0164
http://www.insvideo.com/

International Historic Films, Inc. (only for additional fee)
P.O. Box 29035
Chicago, IL 60629 USA
773-927-2900
http://ihffilm.com/info.html

Keep America Beautiful
1010 Washington Boulevard
Stamford, CT 06901
203-323-8987, ext. 19
http://www.kab.org/

Note: PPR only if not edited in any way.

Kentucky Educational Television
560 Cooper Drive
Lexington, KY 40502-2200
800-354-9067
http://www.ketadultlearning.org

Note: No interlibrary loan, broadcast, streaming, or format transfer.

Knowledge Unlimited
P.O. Box 52
Madison, WI 53701
800-356-2303
http://www.thekustore.com/

Note: Performance rights for any group in school as long as no admission charged. No rights for streaming servers or closed circuit.

Landmark Media
3450 Slade Run Drive
Falls Church, VA 22042
800-342-4336
http://www.landmarkmedia.com/

Note: No transmission, copying, format transfer, or broadcast of any kind without permission.

Learning Seed

641 Lake Street
Chicago, IL 60661
800-634-4941
http://www.learningseed.com/

Note: Public performance rights only. No conversion for streaming or distance delivery without specific rights. Contact publisher.

Library Video Company (Schlessinger Media video titles only)

7 E. Wynnewood Road
Wynnewood, PA 19096
800-843-3620
http://www.libraryvideo.com/

Note: Limited public performance rights for Schlessinger titles only. Any groups in school and through closed-circuit same building. No copies to digital server. Other producers' titles receive no public performance rights.

Library Video Network

320 York Road
Towson, MD 21204
800-441-TAPE
http://www.lvn.org/

Note: Watch for titles for which no public performance rights are offered.

Live Oak Media

P.O. Box 652
Pine Plains, NY 12567
800-788-1121
http://www.liveoakmedia.com/

Live Wire Media

273 Ninth Street
San Francisco, CA 94103
800-359-5437
http://www.livewiremedia.com/

Lucerne Media

37 Ground Pine Road
Morris Plains, NJ 07950
800-341-2293
http://www.lucernemedia.com

Note: No duplication or television/cable rights available unless negotiated specifically.

Master Communications, Inc.

4480 Lake Forest Drive, Suite 302
Cincinnati, OH 45242-3726

513-563-3100
http://www.master-comm.com/

Media for the Arts (limited titles)
360 Thames Street, Suite 2N
Newport, RI 02840
800-554-6008
http://art-history.com/

Note: License to digitize analog materials available.

Meriwether Publishing, Ltd.
Box 7710
Colorado Springs, CO 80933
719-594-4422
http://www.meriwetherpublishing.com

ModuMath Multimedia Video
One Foundation Circle
Waunakee, WI 53597-8914
608-849-2424
http://www.modumath.org/

Note: Online only. Governed by license.

Motion Picture Licensing Corp.
800-462-8855
http://www.mplc.com/

Note: For licensing non-public schools, public libraries, daycare centers, YMCAs, etc. for public performance of video.

Movie Licensing USA
10795 Watson Road
St. Louis, MO 63127
877-321-1300
http://www.movlic.com

Note: For licensing public schools, public libraries, etc.

Moving Images Distribution
402 West Pender Street, Suite 606
Vancouver, BC V6B 1T6
800-684-3014
http://www.movingimages.ca/

National Film Board of Canada
350 Fifth Avenue, Suite 4820
New York, NY 10118

212-629-8890
http://www.nfbc.ca/

Note: For public performance rights, be sure to get the "Professionals" products. No networking permission given.

National Geographic Educational
School Publishing
P.O. Box 11305
Des Moines, IA 50347
800-627-5162
http://www.nationalgeographic.com/education/

Note: Only for titles bought directly from the producer. National Geographic titles bought from jobbers do not include public performance rights. No archival or transfer rights, and no editing allowed.

New Day Films
190 Route 17M
P.O. Box 1084
Harriman, NY 10926
888-367-9154
http://www.newday.com/

Note: Titles leased, not sold, for life of copy. No first-sale rights, so interlibrary loan is doubtful. Read license. No backups, digitization, or transfers allowed. Not available for distance learning. Public performance rights included in license.

New Dimension Media
307 N. Michigan Avenue, Suite 500
Chicago, IL 60601
800-288-4456
http://www.ndmquestar.com/

Noodlehead Network
10 Colbert Street
Burlington, VT 05452
800-639-5680
http://www.noodlehead.com/

Partridge Films (see Survival Anglia)

PBS Video (all lines except PBS Home Video)
1320 Braddock Place
Alexandria, VA 22314
800-424-7963
http://teacher.shop.pbs.org/

Note: Titles leased, not sold, for life of copy. No first-sale rights, so interlibrary loan is doubtful. Read license. May use on in-building closed circuit. Public performance rights (no admission charge) included in license. No editing allowed, and each program must be shown in its entirety.

Princeton Book Company

614 Route 130
Hightstown, NJ 08520
http://www.dancehorizons.com/
800-220-7149

Note: Company distributes video for several producers. Verify what rights are available for each title. Proprietary video has PPRs.

Pyramid Media, Inc.

P.O. Box 1048
Santa Monica, CA 90406
800-421-2304
http://www.pyramidmedia.com/

Note: Titles leased, not sold, for life of copy. Interlibrary loan only available if "institutional use" license is purchased and interlibrary loan is disclosed on order. Read license. Public performance rights (no admission charge) included in license.

Questar, Inc.

307 N. Michigan Avenue, Suite 500
Chicago, IL 60601
800-544-8422
http://www.questar1.com/

Note: Public performance only available for fee of $149.00. No digital rights for streaming or transfer to a digital server without purchase of additional rights. No archival rights.

Rich-Heape Films, Inc. (limited titles)

5952 Royal Lane, Suite 254
Dallas, TX 75230
888-600-2922
http://www.richheape.com/

Note: Performance rights available only for extra charge. No interlibrary loan.

Schlessinger Video (See Library Video Company)

Scholastic, Inc. (all titles except those marked "Home Use Only")

557 Broadway
New York, NY 10012-3999
800-243-5020
http://www.scholastic.com

Note: Use caution in ordering.

Shopware Films, Inc.

200 American Metro Boulevard, Suite 124

Hamilton, NJ 08619

800-257-5126

http://www.shopware-usa.com/

Note: Titles leased, not sold, for term contracted. No first-sale rights, so interlibrary loan is doubtful. Closed circuit in house okay, but no transfer to streaming server. Read license.

SISU Home Entertainment, Inc.

340 W. 39th Street, 6th floor

New York, NY 10018

212-947-7888

http://www.sisuent.com/

Note: Public performance rights only available for extra charge.

Slim Goodbody Corp.

P.O. Box 242

Lincolnville Center, ME 04850

207-763-2820

Spoken Arts

195 South White Rock Road

Holmes, NY 12531

800-326-4090

http://www.spokenartsmedia.com/

Sunburst Communications

101 Castleton Street, Suite 201

Pleasantville, NY 10570

800-338-3457, ext. 2268

http://www.sunburstvm.com/

Note: Digital delivery license needed to put media on streaming server.

SVE & Churchill Media (see Discovery)

Swank, Inc.

201 S. Jefferson Avenue

St. Louis, MO 63103-2579

800-876-5577

http://www.swank.com

Note: Licensing for individual showings of movies by a limited list of producers, including Disney. Expurgated movies (R-rated movies with objectionable material removed). For one-time showings, choose "other group showings." Also licenses films for digital distribution on a title-by-title basis; choose "K-12 digital movies."

Thinking Allowed
2560 9th Street, Suite 123
Berkeley, CA 94710
800-999-4415
http://www.thinkingallowed.com/

TMW (Tell Me Why) **Media Group** (for non-revenue uses)
2321 Abbot Kinney Boulevard
Venice, CA 90291
800-262-8862
http://www.tmwmedia.com/

Note: May not be put on streaming server.

United Learning (see Discovery Education)

VEA Inc. (Visual Education America)
10 Mitchell Place
Suite 103
White Plains, NY 10601
866-727-0840
http://www.veavideo.com

Video Aided Instruction
485-34 South Broadway
Hicksville, NY 11801-5071
800-238-1512
http://www.videoaidedinstruction.com/

The Video Project (for non-revenue uses)
200 Estates Drive
Ben Lomond, CA 95005
800-4-PLANET
http://www.videoproject.org

VisionQuest Video (see TMW Video)

Visual Learning Company
25 Union Street
Brandon, VT 05733
800-453-8481
http://www.visuallearningco.com

Note: No transfer to different format.

Weston Woods (see Scholastic)

WGBH Boston Video (see PBS Video)

Appendix N

Database of copyright actions against schools

Available at http://www.carolsimpson.com

Appendix O

Copyright questions and answers: A reproducible brochure

The following brochure is designed to be reproduced at 115 percent onto two sides of standard 8½" × 11" paper and tri-folded. Reproduction for a single-school building is permitted as long as copyright management information remains intact. For reproduction beyond a single building, please contact Linworth Publishing for fees.

Copyright For Educators

Responsibilities

copy•right \ -,rit \ *n* (1735): The exclusive right to reproduce, publish, and sell the matter and form of a literary, musical, or artistic work.

PRINT

What can I copy?

A **single copy** of a chapter from a book, a newspaper or magazine article, a short story, short essay, or short poem, or a single chart, graph, diagram, drawing, cartoon or picture from a book, periodical or newspaper may be made for personal or research use, or for use in teaching a class.

Multiple copies for classroom use?

Yes, but copy length is limited: you may copy a whole poem only if it is under 250 words (or a 250 word excerpt from a longer poem); a whole article, story or essay only if it is less than 2500 words (or an excerpt if it is less than 1000 words or 10% of a work, whichever is less); a single chart, graph, diagram, drawing, cartoon, or picture per book or magazine; and only two pages of a picture book (as long as the two pages don't contain more than 10 % of the total text of the book.).

How many copies may I make?

You may make a single copy of the items listed above if the copy is for personal use, research or to teach a class. For multiple copies for classroom use you can make only enough copies for each pupil enrolled in the course, i.e., no "extra" copies. You may not copy more than one entire item (or two excerpts) from a single author, or three articles from a single book or periodical volume during one class term (semester or year, depending on the course). You can not have more than nine instances of multiple copying per course during a class term.

May I show rented tapes in class?

Yes – if you rent a tape that applies to your instructional needs and use it in "face-to-face" instruction, and the showing occurs in a classroom or other instructional place, and only teachers and students in the class view the showing. In such a situation, the showing would fall under the AV Fair Use Guidelines.

No – if the tape is to be shown as a reward, enrichment, or entertainment, it cannot be used. Rental stores do not ordinarily purchase the public performance rights required for a reward or entertainment showing to a public group (a class constitutes a public group and therefore doesn't qualify for a Fair Use exemption without meeting the AV guideline requirements.) Many libraries purchase or receive public performance rights, but you should ask.

I wish to remove an objectionable scene from a movie I plan to show. May I edit the scene out?

You aren't required to show an entire video, but you may not edit the program. If you wish to skip the objectionable scene, you can fast forward past it.

Administrative note:

Always use discretion in showing rented videos in your classroom, making certain that you choose only those that are appropriate. Check the ratings regarding language, sex, violence, nudity and morality and if in doubt, don't show it.

This brochure was reprinted from Copyright for Schools: A Practical Guide, 5th edition, by Carol Simpson, Linworth Publishing, ©2010.

AUDIOVISUAL

How can I use a radio or television program in class?

You may record a program as it is broadcast by a local radio or television station; you may, within ten school days of recording the program, use it once with each class for instructional purposes and once again for reinforcement. From the 11th day through the 45th calendar day after the broadcast, it may be used only for evaluation purposes; after that period of time, the recording must be erased unless permission (from the copyright holder) to keep it has been obtained.

Copies of the recording may be made to meet the needs of other teachers, but all copies share the same time restrictions as the original. Unless specific permission is granted (such as with National Geographic specials and some Project Discovery programs) you may not use recordings made from cable-only television channels. See *Cable in the Classroom* Website for permissions.

I have a VHS video; it would be easier to use on DVD. Can I have it transferred?

To make a copy of an audiovisual work other than one recorded under the off-air recording guidelines (above) requires permission of the copyright holder. Works that are in an obsolete format may be transferred to other formats if that work is not available for sale in an updated format, but to be considered "obsolete" the equipment to play the medium must not be available for purchase at a reasonable price. VHS machines are still available, so you would need permission to make this transfer.

We have a video program that was very expensive to purchase and I'm worried that it might be destroyed by accident. Since it's OK to make a backup of computer software, isn't it OK to make a backup copy of a tape or DVD?

No. In order to make a backup copy of a video program, you must have purchased "archival rights" from the copyright holder or receive written permission prior to making the copy.

When and how may I use the copies?

You, the teacher, must make the decision to make the copies. (Your principal or supervisor is not allowed to tell you to make copies of copyrighted material.) You must decide to make the copies so close to the time you would need them in class that writing for permission would be unreasonable. (Two weeks would be a reasonable time.) You can only copy the item for one course (all your English I classes, for example.) Each item copied must have a notice of copyright.

This sounds hard! Why don't you just tell me what I can't copy?

You can never copy, in any form, items intended to be consumable. That includes workbook pages, standardized tests, coloring books, answer sheets, test booklets, etc. You also can't make so many different copies that you are, in effect, creating your own textbook. Copying cannot take the place of books, publisher's reprints or magazine subscriptions. You can't charge students for copying above the actual cost of the copies. And **you can't copy the same materials from semester to semester.** In other words, if you copied it last semester, you can't copy it again without getting permission from the copyright owner.

INTERNET

What can I copy?

There are no specific rules for the Web. Nevertheless, most Web applications have analogs in the print world that you can use to guide your activities.

How many copies may I make?

Consider what it is your are copying. For example, a blog entry is very much like an essay, so use the print guidelines that cover essays to guide you. An email message is very much like an unpublished letter. Letters are highly protected by copyright unless the author publishes the letter. You can probably let someone see your copy of an email, just like a letter, but you would likely not be able to forward that email or publish it in substantial part without permission.

What about Web 2.0 applications like YouTube and Twitter?

Copyright law has not caught up to these newer technologies, so you should probably apply the four tests of fair use when you wish to copy, adapt, or redistribute material from those applications. Of course, if they are similar to non-Web material, use the guidelines for those.

COMPUTER SOFTWARE

How may I use computer software?

Use of a computer program is usually governed by a license agreement, so it depends... Some licenses say you may freely make copies, other say you must pay a fee to use the software, or to install the software onto multiple machines. This is a contractual agreement and it supersedes the copyright restrictions.

You **may not** decompile a program and use program instructions in new programs. You **may not** defeat any form of copy protection built into the program. You **may not** use a single user version of software on a network. You **may not** install a program on more than one computer at a time without express, written permission from the copyright owner. This means that you cannot install the program on your computer at home and your computer at school unless you own two copies of the program or have permission to do so from the copyright owner or the software license. Depending on the program, you may also be limited in what you can do with the output of the program. Some educational licenses restrict what you can do with computer output, or mark the output as educational material. You may not defeat these copy restrictions.

What about printed materials that come with software?

Computer manuals and documentation are covered in the same manner as computer programs. You may not make multiple copies of computer documentation for classes. Copying a computer program intended for a single user onto a network is the same as making multiple copies of the program. It's a no-no. A network license if required to load a computer program onto a network, despite the fact that the program may, indeed, work in a network environment. So don't do it.

How long can I keep it?

As long as you own the program, you may keep a copy of a computer program on your hard drive and a backup copy in addition to the original diskettes or CD. If you should lose the copy on the hard drive, you may reload the program from the original or backup disks. If you sell or transfer the program to another person, you must transfer all diskettes and documentation to the new owner, and you must remove all copies of the program from your computer's hard drive and memory.

MUSIC

What can I copy?

You may make emergency copies of music for an immediate performance, provided replacement copies have been ordered.

You may copy excerpts (not to exceed 10% of a work) provided they do not constitute a performable unit, and provided you make no more than one copy per student.

You may make a single recording of a copyrighted performance by students for evaluation purposes; it may be retained, but copies of it may **not** be made.

I have an old record. May I copy it to cassette and use that instead?

For personal use, yes. For school, if the format of the record is obsolete (78 rpm, for example) and no other version is available, you may transfer the recording to a usable format. If the format is still available (33 1/3 rpm or 45 rpm) the transfer would require permission of the copyright holder. An exception would allow a teacher to make a single copy for the purpose of auditory exercises or examinations. The single copy made for such use may be retained by the teacher.

My students are preparing a presentation for class and want to use parts of popular songs. Is this permissible?

If the presentation is created with multimedia software, the students may use up to 30 seconds of a popular song. If the presentation is anything other than multimedia, such use falls into a gray area. Use by students is permitted if the students instigate the performance themselves (i.e., the students must decide on their own to use a specific song; the teacher may determine the suitability of the material, but may not tell the students to use a specific song.) The music students use should be played from legitimately purchased or borrowed recordings, or recorded off the air.

I found the parts for a musical. Can we stage the musical for the community to earn money?

Putting on a public performance of dramatic music (musicals, operettas and operas) always requires a license if the work is still protected by copyright. You could still use the music in class in the normal way for sheet music, however.

Appendix P

Copyright infringement reporting form

Copyright Infringement Reporting Form

Middletown School District

MSD has the legal responsibility to abide by copyright laws. Employees of the district shall comply with all provisions of United States Copyright Law. Board policies outline the district's copyright policy.

Name of Person(s) Allegedly Violating Copyright Laws

_____

_____

Campus _____

Date of Infringement

_____

Describe exactly what happened. Be sure to include what items were infringed, where it happened, and how many times it happened. _____

_____

_____

_____

_____

_____

_____

_____

_____

Person making report (optional) _____

Please return this form to the District Copyright Officer

Index

A

A&M Records, Inc. v. Napster, Inc., 284 F.3d 1091 (9th Cir. 2002) 101, 102, 114

A.V. v. iParadigms LLC, 562 F.3d 630 (4th Cir. 2009) 66

Abridgements 4

Acceptable use policy 135

Accumulation: definition 67
    (*see also* Anthologies, creation of)

Adaptation: audiovisual materials 75
    definition. 3
    digital materials on the Internet 134
    digital video 95
    disability accommodations 59
    expurgate (censor offensive materials) 75
    format changes 3
    graphics 63
    illustrations 56
    multimedia 116
    performance of print works 71
    poster 53
    print materials 52
    scanning graphics 66
    sheet music 107
    transferring the work to another medium 82

Admission charge: music performance 110

AIME. *See* Association for Information Media and Equipment (AIME)

Almanacs 39, 146

American Geophysical Union v. Texaco Inc., 37 F.3d 881 (2d Cir. 1994) 67

American Library Association (ALA): criticisms of multimedia guidelines 117
    library reserves (model copyright policy) 174
    notice of copyright (photocopy machines) 172
    notice of copyright (stamp obsolescence) 14, 171

American Printing House for the Blind 60

American Society of Composers, Authors & Publishers (ASCAP) 97, 111, 112, 141, 181
    performance rights 111

Answer sheets. *See* Consumable materials

Anthologies 57–59
    copyright acknowledgements 179
    creation of 67, 96
    creation of (educational use) 106
    creation of (film) 75, 82, 91
    guidelines 53
    music 106, 108
    periodical articles 58
    poetry 120
    student work 57
    substitution for 57, 63

Anti-circumvention: DMCA 15

Archival copies: audiovisual materials 92, 93, 94
    books 58
    books/recording sets 74
    computer software 92, 93, 94
    destruction 156
    format changes 92
    videos 73

ART Act (Artists' Rights and Theft Prevention Act of 2005) 17

Artwork: destruction of 7, 15
    modification of 15
    murals 50
    public display 6, 116
    reproduction 172
    student work 5, 190
    Web page display 64

ASCAP. *See* American Society of Composers, Authors & Publishers (ASCAP)

Association for Information Media and Equipment (AIME) 86, 191, 197

Attribution 122, 147, 161

Audible.com 98
Audio Home Recording Act 97–98, 117
Audio recordings. *See* Sound recordings
Audiobook 97, 148
Audiovisual materials: definition 71
   fair use assessment 77
   guidelines 59, 76
   replacement 92
   section 110 . . . . 71, 72, 73
Audit 195
   documentation 189
   reciprocal district agreements 160
   SIIA recommendations 159
Audit software 160
   Express Meter 191
AUP. *See* Acceptable use policy
Author rights: e-mail 140
   explanation for children 204
   instant message communications (chat) 141
   Web pages (source code) 142
Authorship: contractual. *See* Work for hire
Authorship: corporate 12
   difuse 12
   group 12
   pseudonymous 12
Automatic grading sheets. *See* Consumable materials
AV materials. *See* Audiovisual materials

B

Backup. *See* Archival copies
Backup copies. *See* Archival copies
Basic Books, Inc. v. Kinko's Graphics Corp.,
   758 F. Supp. 1522 (S.D.N.Y. 1991) 60, 68
Beethoven, Ludwig van 29
Berne Convention 8, 14, 137
Bible: copyright status 29
Bit Torrent 19
Blackwell Publishing Group v. Excel Research Group,
   LLC, No. 07-12731, 2009 WL 3287403
   (E.D. Mich. Oct. 14, 2009) 65, 68
Blanket licenses. *See* License, umbrella
Blind. *See* Disability accommodations
Blogger 148
Blogs 148
BMI. *See* Broadcast Music, Inc. (BMI)
Book covers 49, 51, 53
Bookmarks. *See* Web pages, bookmarks
Booktalks 144
Boosey v. Empire Music Co., 224 F. 646
   (S.D.N.Y. 1915) 101
Bounty: infringement reports 94

Brevity: definition 47, 55
   illustrations 56, 62
   periodicals and newspapers 62
   picture books 55
   poetry 55, 62
   prose 55, 62
Bridgeman Art Library Ltd. v. Corel Corp.,
   36 F. Supp. 2d 191 (S.D.N.Y. 1999) 64, 67
Bridgeport Music v. Dimension Films, et al.,
   410 F. 3d 792 (6th Cir. 2005) 101
Broadcast Music, Inc. (BMI) 111, 112, 141, 181
Broadcasting 110
BSA. *See* Business Software Alliance (BSA)
BSD license 33
Bulletin boards 48, 50, 52–53, 64, 202
Bush, George W. (President) 125
Business Software Alliance (BSA) 159, 162

C

Cable. *See* Television
Cable in the Classroom 85–86
Cable television 97
Cable television programs: recording 86
Calendars: copyright status 10
Campbell v. Acuff-Rose Music,
   510 U.S. 569 (1994) 38, 41
Cartoon characters 50, 65, 153
   Mickey Mouse 3, 16
Cartoons 51, 66
   use in multimedia 121
CCG (complies with CONTU Guidelines) 166–168
CCL (complies with Copyright Law) 166, 168
CD. *See* Compact disc
Cease and desist letters 22, 25, 146, 193, 194
Censor. *See* Expurgate
Chat. *See* Instant messenger activities (chat)
Christian Video Licensing International 81
Citation. *See* Attribution
Classroom use 53–54, 56,
                                62–63, 139, 191
Clean Flicks of Colo. v. Soderbergh,
   433 F. Supp. 2d 1236 (D. Colo. 2006) 75, 79, 102
ClearPlay 26
Clinton, William J. (President) 16
Clip art 32, 50, 115, 123, 153
Collective works 53
   (*see also* Anthologies)
   definition 67
   quantity restrictions 57, 121, 168
Coloring books 48
Columbia Law School Music Plagiarism Project 114

Columbia Pictures Industries v. Redd Horne,
   749 F.2d 154 (3d Cir. 1984) 6, 75, 102
Commentary 39
Commercial use 42, 66
Common law copyright: duration 28
   public domain materials 28
Compact disc 96, 98
Compilation copyright. 132
Compilations. 53
   (*see also* Anthologies)
   substitution for 63
Compliance agreement 199
Computer software (*see also* Digital Millennium
   Copyright Act (DMCA))
   anti-circumvention 15
   archival copies 15, 156
   audits 195
   backup copies (*see* Computer software,
   archival copies)
   borrowing, circulating, or lending 151, 153,
                                         158, 178
    circumvention of anti-copying measures 16
    copies. 156
    distribution 155
    documentation 159
    illegal Internet distribution 14
    infringement penalties. 17, 193
    licenses. 155 156, 177–178
    multiple installations. 152–153, 158, 159
    network distribution 4, 152–153, 159–161
    notice of copyright 158, 161, 189
    open source 157
    piracy 17–18, 151, 155–156, 162
    piracy (felony prosecution) 159
    public domain. 157
    records of ownership 196
    rental. 158
    requirements (Section 117). 151
    returns 156
    scenarios of use 152
    shareware 152, 155, 157
Computer Software Rental Amendments Act 158
Concordances. 4
Conference on Fair Use (CONFU) 117
Congressional guidelines 44, 47, 53, 59, 198
   (*see also* Fair use)
   multiple copies 55
   print permissions 53
Consumable materials. 53, 56–57, 61, 108, 196
   music 108
   patterns. 60

photocopying 49
types of 60
Contract law 20, 156, 178
Contracts. *See* License
Contributory infringement.
   See Infringement, contributory
CONTU Guidelines 169, 170
Copying 53–54, 56–57, 59, 61, 64, 132, 146, 164
   (*see also* Photocopying)
   digital 134
   frequency 57
   multiple. 54–60, 63–65
   preservation 98, 164
   significant amount 40
   slavish 68
   time of 64
Copyleft. 145, 152
Copyright: enforcement. 8
   England. 1
   length of protection 12
   management 187
   notice (*see* Notice of copyright)
   overview of rights 7
Copyright agent. 15, 136
   registration Web site 136
   responsibilities 198
   take down 136
Copyright Clearance Center (CCC):
   services (overview) 181
   Web site 181
Copyright free 31 32
Copyright information: library catalog records 188
Copyright infringement reporting: rewards 160
Copyright management: recommendations. 191
Copyright management information 13, 157, 171
   DMCA. 55
Copyright officer 198
Copyright ownership. *See* Author rights
   Work for hire
Copyright police 19, 45, 187, 194, 196
Copyright policy 19–20, 49, 72, 188,
                                191, 194, 197–199
   rationale 197
   requirement of TEACH Act provisions. 127
Copyright registration: research 180
Copyright responsibilities and awareness:
   administrators, ... 19, 191, 193–195
   librarians. 19
   staff. 191
   teachers 19, 190
   technicians 19

Copyright symbol 13, 28, 96, 123
Coursepacks . . . . 67–68, 181.
   See also Distance learning (course materials)
Court rulings 24
   de facto law 14
   providing legal definitions 5
Creative Commons 12, 32–33, 118, 145,
                147–148, 152, 157, 161
   licenses 32, 118, 147, 161
   public domain dedication 157
Creativity: requirement for copyright 64
Criticism 38
CTEA. *See* Sonny Bono Copyright
   Term Extension Act (CTEA)
Cumulative effect 48, 55–56, 58–59, 62
   definition 56
Current news 57, 62
   definition 67
   exemption from copy limits 63, 67
   restrictions 62
Curriculum guides 28, 81, 147, 149
Curriculum, digital 128

D

Damaged materials 52, 86
   CD-ROM 164
   library replacement copying 163, 173
   multimedia works (copies) 121
   preservation 164
   replacement copy 61, 73
Damages: actual 17, 24
   contract law 156
   monetary 18, 86
   registration requirement 8
   statutory 17–18, 24, 68
Dance: uncodified 8
Dances 98
   licensing music 112
Databases, electronic 128
Deaf. *See* Disability accommodations
Deep links. *See* Links, deep
Delicious 146
Department of Education 63
Derivative works 4, 15, 32, 65,
                  95, 118, 147, 157
Digital audio: illegal Internet files 14
   Internet 102, 114
Digital audio recordings 6, 14, 75, 92, 95,
                97, 101–102, 109
   library exemptions 135
Digital Copyright Slider 12

Digital downloads 79, 113
Digital Millennium Copyright Act (DMCA) 6, 13,
      76, 125, 135, 147, 149, 157, 160, 164–165, 171
   overview 15
   take down provisions 136, 144, 148–149
Digital Performance Right in Sound Recordings Act . . . 16
Digital rights management 128, 147
Digital sampling. *See* Sampling
Digital video servers 95
Digitization. *See* Reproduction, digital
Diig 146
Disability accommodations: adaptation rights 59
   books 56
   braille 59
   closed captioning 93
   dyslexic or slow learner 59–60
   qualification procedure 59
   technical specifications 59
Disc jockey 98
   contracts and licenses 112
   music in performance 110
   performance rights 111
Discoveries: copyright status 10
Discovery Networks Classroom Resources 85
Discussion list 140, 141
Distance education. *See* Distance learning
Distance learning 15–16, 44,
                  72, 125–126
   access restrictions 127–128
   course materials 44
   definition 126
   electronic handouts 181
   Section 110(2) 125
Distribution 163
   digital materials 14
   licensing restrictions on 82
   overview 4
   print materials 51
   right of first sale 4
   videos of school events 178
   Web pages 133
D.J. *See* Disc jockey
DMCA. *See* Digital Millennium Copyright Act
Document camera 64–65, 189
Documentation 89–90, 155, 158, 160, 189
   public domain software 157
   shrink wrap licenses 156
Dress patterns. *See* Consumable materials
DRM. *See* Digital rights management
Dyslexic learner. *See* Disability accommodations
   (dyslexic or slow learner)

E

Ebooks 16, 147–148
    fair use 148
    license 148
Educational institutions: definition 118
Educational multimedia projects: definition 118
Educational purposes: definition 118
Educators: definition 118
Egypt 8
Eldred v. Ashcroft, 537 U.S. 186, (2003) 12, 16
Eldred, Eric 12
Electronic books. *See* Ebooks
E-mail 4, 133, 140
Encyclopaedia Britannica Educational Corp. v. Crooks,
    542 F. Supp. 1156 (W.D.N.Y. 1982) 102
English language learners:
    disability accommodations 59
Ephemeral works: copyright status 7
ERIC 63
Essence of the work 40–41
    definition 40
Estate of Martin Luther King, Jr. v. CBS, Inc.,
    194 F.3d 1211 (11th Cir. 1999) 39
Ethical issues 25, 161
Exemptions 3, 16, 45, 60, 72, 76, 107, 126, 163, 167
    dramatic works 110
    library 16, 45, 163, 165
    school 16, 45, 72, 147, 163
    school library 16, 163, 175
Expurgate (censor offensive materials) 7, 75, 79, 102
Extracurricular use 54, 72, 73, 77, 81, 119, 195

F

Facebook. *See* Social networking
Face-to-face teaching 44, 74, 76–77,
          80–81, 83, 91–93, 109–110, 118, 125, 128
Facsimile 166, 170, 172
    cumulative effect 170
    interlibrary loan 165
Facts 8, 27, 39, 138, 146, 147
    charts of measures 10
    copyright status 10
    creative expression 39
    links 136
    links, individual 132
    multiplication tables 8
    recipes 10, 45
    telephone numbers 30
Fair use 35–37, 44–45, 50, 61, 110, 117, 138, 179
    audiovisuals 71, 77

brevity 47
burden of proof 36
creating sound recordings 50
cumulative effect 48
definition 36
direction to apply 54
display 76
educational exemptions 16, 36–37
exemptions 35, 45, 47, 91, 168
factors 37
HTML code 142
impact on market for (value of) a work 43
Internet 144
library exemptions 36
limits on educational use 52
(*see also* Kastenmeier report)
loss of rights 20, 32
misconceptions 35
Section 107 (overview) 47
spontaneity 48
staff development 59
statutory 36
student work 66
student-made copies 65
Fair use assessment 142
    "four tests" 35, 37–38, 44–45,
          50, 52, 54, 108, 117, 136, 138, 141, 174
    factor four 41, 54, 63, 139
    factor one 38, 138, 146
    factor three 40, 138
    factor two 39, 138
Fair Use Guidelines for Educational Multimedia 117
Fair use overview: market value, effect of use on 35
    nature of the work 35
    purpose and character of use 35
    substantiality 35
Family Educational Rights and Privacy Act 184
    application to school use of student work 66
Family Entertainment and Copyright Act 17
Family Movie Act of 2005 17
Fax. *See* Facsimile
Federal Bureau of Investigation (FBI) 19, 24, 159
Feist Publications, Inc. v. Rural Telephone Service Co.,
    Inc., 499 U.S. 340 (1991) 10, 27, 30
FERPA. *See* Family Educational Rights and Privacy Act
File sharing 109, 154
First Amendment right to free speech 36
First sale doctrine. *See* Right of first sale
Fixation 7
Flash 115
Flickr 33, 145

Ford, Gerald R. (President). 41
Forms: blank. 10
   copyright infringement reporting. 240
   ILL form notice of copyright restrictions 211
   off-air videos certification of eligibility 189
   student work release 214
   video clearance 195
Four tests of fair use. *See* Fair use
   assessment, "four tests"
Frames. *See* Web pages, frames
France. 8
Free Software Foundation 33, 161
Freeplay Music 118
Fundraising. 178

G

General cultural value 73, 81, 110
Germany 8
Gilliam v. Am. Broadcasting Cos., 538 F.2d 14
   (2d Cir. 1976) 75, 85, 102
GNU General Public License. 157
GNU public license 33, 157
Google 148
Government documents: authored by
   federal employees 27
   public domain 10, 28
Graphic novels 56
Graphics 63, 116, 161
   adaptation. 64
   infringement 65–66
   public display 64
   reproduction by libraries. 98
   school use 50
   single copies. 64
   thumbnail images 38
   use on the Internet 140
Guidelines: audiovisual materials 72, 110, 144–145
   copyright and plagarism 215
   multimedia 37, 45, 66, 111, 117–119,
                     122, 128, 188, 190
Guidelines for Educational Uses of Music. 44, 52,
                      84, 106–108

H

Handicapped. *See* Disability accommodations
Harper & Row, Publishers, Inc. v. Nation Enterprises,
   471 U.S. 539 (1985) 37, 41–43, 54
Harry Fox Agency 112–113, 181
Hearn v. Meyer, 664 F. Supp. 832 (S.D.N.Y. 1987) 3
Higher authority 48, 50, 54, 56–57, 63

Home use only. *See* License, home use only
Hotaling v. Church of Jesus Christ of Latter-Day Saints,
   118 F.3d 199 (4th Cir. 1997) 5, 68
House Judiciary Subcommittee. 44
Hyperstudio. 115

I

Ideas: copyright status 10–11
IEP (Individual Education Plan). 60, 80
ILL. *See* Interlibrary loan
Illustrations 10, 28–29, 43, 55–56, 63,165, 171
   interlibrary loan. 165
   use in multimedia 121, 124
Indexes 4
Individual Education Plan. *See* IEP
   (Individual Education Plan)
Individuals with Disabilities Education Improvement Act
   of 2004 60
Infringement 17
   action against schools 25
   affirmative defense 117
   benchmark 47
   contributory 18, 64, 151, 154
   contributory (definition) 94
   direct (definition) 153
   fines 193
   fines (felony). 17, 151, 158
   fines (Los Angeles USD settlement) 24
   fines (punitive) 18
   fines (statutory). 24, 102
   innocent 17
   systematic. 197
   willful 18
Infringement, vicarious. *See* Liability, vicarious
Ingredient lists: copyright status 10
Instant messenger applications
   (including chat). 133, 141
Intellectual property. 11, 14, 21, 133, 149
   attorneys. 24
   policy 125
Interactive white boards. 189
Interlibrary loan. 44, 163, 165–166, 170
   bindery materials 167
   copying. 165, 167
   forms 166–168
   licensed materials. 171
   materials available for loan 165
   missing issues (owned volume) 168
   notice 166–167
   notice of copyright 211
   periodicals 166

photocopies 168
records 167
restrictions 165
rule of five 166
title on order 167
Internet 131
copying 131, 139, 140, 142
copyright ownership 137
digitizing materials 141
distribution . . . 101–102, 113, 125, 134, 143–144, 190
fair use 136, 138–139, 144, 189
graphics 140, 145
illegal computer software 14, 151
illegal digital audio files 14
public display 6, 76, 137, 140–141
public performance 134–135, 140
rules (see Digital Millennium Copyright Act)
services 140
sound recordings 96, 138
streaming 143
video 84
Internet filters 16
Internet radio 7, 76, 135
Internet service provider (ISP). See Online Service
Providers (OSP)
intralibrary loan 170
definition 166
iPod 50, 73, 97, 134
iTouch 97
iTunes 73, 97–99, 144, 178
(see also Videos, public performance restrictions)
video downloads 79

K

Kastenmeier report 36–37, 48, 52, 59
(see also Congressional guidelines)
multiple copies for classroom use 54
print works 52, 59
single copies for teachers 52
Kelly v. Arriba Soft Corp., 280 F. 3d 937
(9th Cir. 2002) 38
KidPix 44, 115, 122
Kidsnet website 85
Kieselstein-Cord v. Accessories by Pearl, Inc.,
632 F.2d 989 (2nd Cir. 1980) 10
Kurzweil technology 59

L

Lawfully acquired: definition 118
Learning systems 128
Lease 2, 31, 39

Lectures 10
Lee v. A.R.T. Company, 125 F.3d 580 (7th Cir. 1997) . . . 5
Lending copyrighted material 2, 4, 82, 153,
158, 161, 165, 170–171, 178
Liability 18, 20
administrators 193, 198
DMCA requirements for OSP 136
individuals 198
library (illegal copies) 5
multimedia applications 123
music (public performances) 110
OSP 135
plagiarism 136
potential damages 42
principals 19
recent technologies 102
student work 190
teachers 19
technicians 19
vicarious 19, 72, 154
Liability, librarian. See Librarian liability
Librarian liability 64–65
photocopy equipment 19
videos 79
Library book sale 4
Library lending 4
Library of Congress 59, 180
Library of Congress Digital
Interlibrary Loan Project 170
Library of Congress Division of Blind and
Physically Handicapped 59–60
Library reserves 63, 174
ALA model copyright policy 174
electronic 174, 181
License 2–4, 11, 20, 31–33, 45, 60, 62, 81, 85,
91, 106, 110–112, 128, 136, 144–147, 157, 160–162
archival copies 92
book cover images 6
broadcast 112
building-wide (see License, umbrella)
click through 141, 156
computer software 155–157, 177
consumable materials 61
definition 20
digital download 113
exception 41
fair use limitations 147
home use only 82, 83, 178
implied 141
library-only 81
limitations on fair use 53–54

limited site 156, 159, 161
modifications 178
multiple installation 148, 151–152
municipal 112
music 42, 112–113
need to acquire 37
network 159, 161
non-commercial 147
online databases 136, 153, 160, 166, 174
open source 158
performance 2, 59, 74–75, 82, 110–113
replacement for ownership 82
reprint (lyrics or music) 113
royalty free materials. 31
share-alike 145, 147, 152
shrink wrap 21, 82, 98, 155, 178
terms. 95, 137, 144
umbrella 81, 109, 111
venue 111–112
video. 18, 73, 79, 81, 171
Links. 146
collections 132
conditions of. 136
deep 42, 43, 128, 136
Local government documents: copyright status 10

M

Maps: copyright status 10
MARC records: copyright control information. 188
Marcus v. Rowley, 695 F.2d 1171 (9th Cir. 1983) 41
Market value 43
Mashups. 138
Media distribution systems. . . . 4, 75, 89, 92, 94–95, 187
definition. 94
MGM Studios, Inc. v. Grokster, Ltd.,
380 F.3d 1154 (9th Cir. 2004). 101
Mickey Mouse: copyright extension 16
Microblogs. 149
Mirage Editions, Inc. v. Albuquerque A.R.T. Co.,
856 F.2d 1341 (9th Cir. 1988) 5
Monty Python 102
Moral rights 7, 75
Motion Picture Licensing Corporation 81, 181
Movie Licensing USA 72, 81, 83, 178, 181
Movies. *See* Videos
MP3 files. *See* Digital audio recordings
Multimedia guidelines. *See* Guidelines, multimedia
Multimedia projects 32, 115
attribution 118, 122
background music 97, 115, 120, 189
copying. 121

definition. 118
network access 119, 120
notice of copyright 122, 211
notice of copyright (children) 211
notice of copyright (sample) 122
quantity limits. 120
retention 119, 120
students 115
teachers 115
use at workshops 119
Murals. 65
Museums: claim of copyright
in public domain work 64
Music: arrangement 97
background. 98, 107, 111–112
dramatic 112
emergency copies 108
lyrics 120
public domain. 97, 109
public performance 106, 110
recording performances 107
royalty-free 123
sheet 29, 52, 105
sheet, performance exemption 110
sheet, reproduction 48, 105, 108
Music Library Association: copyright guide 114
Music Publishers Association. 108, 112
Music Publishers Association Copyright
Resource Center 114
Music video 120
Musicals. 98, 106–107, 110, 112, 128
broadcasting. 111
MySpace. *See* Social networking

N

National Association for Music Education. 108
National Commission on New Technological
Uses of Copyrighted Works (CONTU). . . . 37, 165, 166
interlibrary loan. 170
National Instructional Materials Access Center 60
NET ("No Electronic Theft") Act. 14, 96, 151
criminal penalties 102
Netflix 178
(*see also* Videos, public performance restrictions)
News feeds 141
News reporting 39
Newsgroups 137, 140–141
Newsletters 4, 49, 52, 197
Newspaper: school 39
Nixon, Richard (President) 41
Nonprofit educational 138

Notice of copyright 139, 163
   audiovisual materials 128
   computer software. 158, 161, 189
   copy-capable equipment: 198
   definition. 67
   DMCA requirements 14, 172
   multimedia equipment 65, 189
   music 96, 108
   networked multimedia. 119
   off-air videos. 89, 189
   photocopies 173
   photocopy machines. 172
   print copies. 54, 55
   print materials. 188
   removal. 171
   stickers 189
   student work (age appropriate wording) 190

O

Obsolete materials. 4, 82, 93, 96, 164
   Beta format videotapes 15
   definition. 15, 164
Off-air recording. *See* Television,
   off-air recording
Online Service Providers (OSP) 15, 135, 148–149
Opaque projector. 64, 172, 187
Open Source: license 158
Open Source Initiative. 33, 157
Operas. 110, 112, 128
Operettas. 110
Out-of-print: dealers 168
   music 112–113
   works 2, 13, 40, 51, 54, 60, 112, 163, 168
Overhead projector 53, 64–65, 172, 187

P

Painting. *See* Artwork
Pantograph 65
Parody. 41, 138
Patterns. *See* Consumable materials
Peer-to-peer file sharing. *See* File sharing
Penalties. 19
   (*see also* Infringement, fines)
   criminal. 102
Performance: definition 5
Performance license, music: municipal. 110
Performing rights organization 110–111
Performing rights societies. *See* the names
   of the various societies
Periodical volume: definition. 67
Periodicals: interlibrary loan. 167

Permission . . . . 2–3, 11, 147.
   See also License
Permissions 177, 179, 176–185
   fees. 180
   music materials. 111, 114
   request procedures 179
   retention rights information. 85
   time frame. 179
   verbal agreements. 11
Permissions requests 56, 62
   lack of response 60, 184
publisher response 181, 184
Phonograms. *See* Phonorecords
Phonorecords 3, 50–51, 96–97, 135, 143
Photocopy machines. 48
   unsupervised 172
Photocopying 49, 59
   "bottom up," 48, 50, 89
   charging recipients for 57, 58
   classroom use. 48, 53
   classroom use (multiple) 54
   consumable materials. 53
   copyright notice 13, 211
   damaged materials 52
   directed by higher authority 53
   for profit 18
   frequency 53, 60
   interlibrary loan. 168
   library 171
   materials on order. 49, 57
periodicals 61
   replacing purchased materials 52–53
   single copies for teachers 52
   versus manual copying. 3
   vertical file 173
Photocopying in anticipation of need 48
Photographs: use in multimedia 121
Photoshop. 146
Physically handicapped.
   See Disability accommodations
Picassa 145
Picture book 40, 43, 56, 65
   brevity. 56, 58
   characters 3
play performance. 3
Piracy. *See* Computer software, piracy or Videos, piracy
Plagiarism. 161
   copyright infringement, comparison 161, 191
   explanation for children 204
   student code of conduct 161
Plates 4

Playaway 95
Plays 188
Podcasts 143–144
   terms of service 144
Poetry 188
   educational use 55
Policy: development 198
   Board of Education 127
   questionable materials 79
   sample district copyright policy 213
Postermaking machines 53
Posters 63
Preservation of Orphan Works Act 17
Princeton Univ. Press v. Michigan Document Svcs., Inc.,
   99 F.3d 1381 (6th Cir. 1996) 67
Print guidelines. *See* Kastenmeier report
Privacy statues 21
ProCD, Inc. v. Zeidenberg, 86 F.3d 1447
   (7th Cir. 1996) 156, 178
Pub Domain 29
Public, defined 75
Public display 134
   artwork 6, 65, 116
   photograph 6
print materials 52
   Web page images and graphics 188
Public domain 7, 12–13, 16, 27–29, 31–33, 63
   Creative Commons 32
   example materials 29
   literature 29
   locating materials 29
   movies 117
   photographs 29
   research 29
   restrictions 29
Public performance 2, 6, 75
   audiovisual materials 72
   definition 5
   digital audio 96
   Interenet (*see* Internet, public performance)
   movies (classroom use) 81, 92
   music 110
   rights 18, 77, 83, 90–92, 178, 190
   video 81
Publication 39, 141
Purpose and character of use: definition 38

Q

Questionable materials: documentation policy 94
   policy statement 80
Questionnaries. *See* Consumable materials

R

Rainforest Maths 139
Recipes. *See* Facts—recipes
Recording Indus. Ass'n of Am. v. Diamond Multimedia
   Sys., Inc., 180 F.3d 1073 (9th Cir. 1999) 99
Recording Industry Association of
   America (RIAA) 101–102, 109
RedBox 178
Register of Copyrights 125
Registration of copyright 7–8
   fees 8
   prior to 1978 13
   procedures 8
   requirements Web site 13
   types of materials 13
Reporting: school television 39
Reproducible magazines 4
Reproduction 1, 3–4, 14, 18, 36, 43, 63,
                         66, 74–75, 105
   cartoons 65
   coloring books 65
   digital 51, 116
   (*see also* Scanning)
   overview 3
   posters 65
   print materials 51
Reproduction rights organization (RRO) 181
RIAA. *See* Recording Industry Association of
   America (RIAA)
Right of first sale 4–5, 82
   definition 4
   used CDs 5
Rights: owned by copyright owner 2
Roy Export Co. v. Columbia Broadcast System, Inc.,
   503 F. Supp. 1137 (D.C.N.Y 1980) 40
Royalties 2
   royalty free versus copyright free 31
Royalty free materials 31–32
   sources 33
Royalty-free music. *See* Music, royalty-free
Royalty-free video. *See* Videos, royalty-free
Rule of five: definition 168
   interlibrary loan 166

S

Salinger v. Random House, Inc., 811 F.2d 90
   (2d Cir. 1987) 40
Sampling 99–101
   quantity limits 101
San Francisco Arts & Athletics, Inc. v. U.S. Olympic
   Committee, 483 U.S. 522 (1987) 43

Satellite television programs: recording 86
Scanning. 3, 49, 51, 64, 66, 127, 170, 174
    book covers 6
    graphics 65
    illustrations. 56
    maps. 51
    multimedia 51
    photos. 51
Scantron sheets. *See* Consumable materials
Scope of employment 11
Sculpture. *See* Artwork
SESAC, Inc., ... 97
Shareware. *See* Computer software, shareware
Sheet music. *See* Music, sheet
Shepard Fairey v. Assoc. Press, No. 1 2009cv01123,
    (S.D.N.Y. 2009). 66
Shrink wrap license. *See* License, shrink wrap
Significant amount: definition 40
SIIA. *See* Software and Information
    Industry Association (SIIA)
Single copies for teachers. 53
Snapfish 145
Social bookmarking 146
Social networking pages 142–143
Software and Information Industry
    Association (SIIA) 159–160, 162, 191
Sonny Bono Copyright Term
    Extension Act (CTEA) 12, 16
Sony Corp. of Am. v. Universal City Studios,
    464 U.S. 417 (1984). 84
Sound recordings 10, 50, 74, 96, 143
    archival copies 95, 98
    copies 106
    copyright. 109
    digital transmissions. 7
    foreign language education. 99
    Internet distribution. 102
    library copies 98
    license 99
    public performance. 97, 135
Spoken word recordings 95
Spontaneity. 48, 62
    assessment questions. 48
    definition. 56
Staff development 59, 111, 188
Standardized tests. *See* Consumable materials
State government documents: copyright status. 10
State jurisdiction: contract law 20
    privacy statutes. 21
    sound recordings 20
    videos. 20

Statute of Anne 1
Streaming servers. *See* Digital video servers
Streaming video. *See* Videos, streaming
Student work: copyright ownership 8, 65, 97, 184
    Internet liability. 190
    moral rights 7
    multimedia restrictions 119
    notice of copyright 190
    permission 184
    public display 8, 52, 184
    Web publishing. 4
Stuffed animals 65
Sync rights 113, 178
Systematic reproduction 24, 163, 166, 170, 197

T

Talent shows 112
TEACH Act 15–16, 44, 74, 76, 118,
                    125–126, 131, 143–144, 147, 149
    application 129
    distance learning policy 127
    restrictions 128
Teacher Tube. 144
Teachers: documentation (audiovisual materials) 94
Technological protections 160
Technology, Education And Copyright Harmonization Act.
    See TEACH Act
Technorati. 146
Television 72
    broadcast channels. 84
    broadcast, cable, and satellite. 84
    cable programming. 85
    educators' guides 85
    home recording. 88
    off-air recording 84, 94
    off-air recording copies. 89
    off-air recording of rebroadcasts. 85
    off-air recording retention 86
    recording in anticipation of need. 85, 89
    satellite programming 85
Television transmissions: broadcast,
    cable, and satellite 74
Templates. *See* Consumable materials
Ten percent rule (myth) 40
Term: definition 67
Terms of service 33, 98, 136–137,
                       144–145, 147–149
Test booklets. 49
Ticketmaster v. Microsoft, U. S. District
    Court for the Central Dist. of Calif.,
    Civil Action Number 97-3055DPP 42

Title 17, United States Code, Public Law 94-553,
　　90 Stat. 2541 . . . . 1, 35
　　Circular 92 (free copy of the law) 203
Titles: copyright status 10
Trade secret law 21–22
Trademarks 21, 42, 51
Training: copyright education program 199
　　mandated 197
　　requirements 127
　　staff 191, 199
Transformativeness 38, 41, 51, 54,
　　　　　　　　　　　　　　　　101–102, 139, 143, 146
Translations . . . . 3–4, 43, 52.
　　See also Derivative works
Transparency 49, 51, 56, 138
Turnitin.com 66
Twitter 149
TypePad 148

U

Umbrella licenses. *See* License, umbrella
United States Copyright Office 180
United States Department of Justice 19
United States Patent and Trademark Office 21
Unpublished materials 13, 28, 40–41, 164
Useful articles: copyright status 10

V

Vertical file. *See* Photocopying, vertical file
Vicarious infringement. *See* Liability, vicarious
Video distribution systems. *See* Media distribution
　　systems
Video software:anti-circumvention 15
Videos 98, 189,
　　(*includes* films, filmstrips, movies, cartoons)
　　digital downloads 79
　　digital format (cartoon) 4
　　home use only 82–83
　　off-air recording 79
　　piracy 18, 20
　　public performance restrictions 81, 83, 91–92
　　public performance rights 74
　　recording logs 86
　　rental 178

reward or entertainment showing 80, 92
　　royalty-free 123
　　streaming 75, 85
VHS format 164
Visual Artists Rights Act 14

W

Walt Disney Productions, Inc. 51
Warez (illegal software) 154
Washington, George (President) 1
Watermark 64
Web 2.0. *See* names of specific applications
　　such as Twitter or Facebook, or technologies
　　such as wikis or microblogs
Web pages 42, 141
　　bookmarks 132
　　copying 42
　　distribution 141
　　educational use of materials 140
　　frames 136, 141, 146
　　links 136
　　published work 40
　　scanning 6
　　source code 142
　　volunteers for school Web site 12
Web-based material. *See* Internet
Wiki 32, 126, 146–147
Wikipedia 146–147
WordPress 148
Work for hire 10–12, 145, 149
Workbooks . . . . 2, 48, 56, 108, 143.
　　See also Consumable materials
Worksheets. *See* Consumable materials
World Wide Web: copyright status 28
　　(*see also* Web pages)

Y

Yearbooks 42, 51–52
　　video 178, 195
YouTube . . . . 144.
　　See also Music, performance
　　Videos, public performance rights